ATLAS OF AFRICAN-AMERICAN HISTORY

Revised Edition

James Ciment

☑ Checkmark Books®
An imprint of Infobase Publishing

Atlas of African-American History, Revised Edition

Copyright © 2007 by Media Projects Inc.

Media Projects Inc. Staff
Project Editor: Carter Smith
Principal Writer: James Ciment
Production Editor: Laura Smyth
Indexer: Diane Brenner

Checkmark Books
An imprint of Infobase Publishing
132 West 31st Street
New York NY 10001

Library of Congress Cataloging-in-Publication Data
Ciment, James.
  Atlas of African-American history / [principal writer, James Ciment]. — Rev. ed.
    p. cm.
  Includes bibliographical references and index.
  ISBN 978-0-8160-6713-8 (hardcover : alk. paper) — ISBN 978-0-8160-6714-5 (pbk. : alk. paper)
  1. African Americans—History. 2. African Americans—History—Maps. 3. African Americans—History—Pictorial works. I. Title.
  E185.C55 2007
  973'.0496073—dc22   2007015796

Checkmark books are available at special discounts when purchased in bulk quantities for businesses, associations, institutions, or sales promotions. Please call our Special Sales Department in New York at (212) 967-8800 or (800) 322-8755.

You can find Facts On File on the World Wide Web at http://www.factsonfile.com.

Text design by Laura Smyth
Cover design by Takeshi Takahashi
Maps and graphics by Dale Williams

Printed in China.

TOPPAN 10 9 8 7 6 5 4 3 2 1
    (pbk) 10 9 8 7 6 5 4 3 2 1

CONTENTS

ACKNOWLEDGMENTS

The authors and editors wish to thank the many people who have contributed greatly to both the first edition of the book as well as this revised and expanded second edition. Many thanks to Facts On File's Eleanora von Dehsen, Nicole Bowen, Terence Maikels and Gene Springs for their work on the first edition. Special thanks goes to Dorothy Cummings, editor of this revised and expanded edition. Throughout this project, Dorothy has exhibited not only an unerring editorial sense of what the project demands, but also perseverance, patience, and expertise. It was a pleasure working with her.

Thanks also to Facts On File's master cartographer Dale Williams for producing such richly detailed and informative maps and graphs.

On the editorial side, an enormous amount of research went into this project, and we are grateful for all the hard work on that front performed by Melissa Hale, Karen Covington, Kenneth West, and Kimberly Horstman.

NOTE ON PHOTOS

Some of the illustrations and photographs used in this book are old, historical images. The quality of the prints is not always up to modern standards, as in many cases the originals are from old negatives or the originals are damaged. The content of the illustrations, however, made their inclusion important despite problems in reproduction.

INTRODUCTION

"We hold these truths to be self-evident...That all men are created equal." So wrote Thomas Jefferson in the Declaration of Independence, in 1776. This founding principle outlined what was at the time a quite radical idea, but that idea has remained one of the cornerstones upon which the United States has been built.

Of course, when the U.S. Constitution was ratified 13 years later, the exceptions to that principle were made clear. Voting rights, one of the preeminent badges of individual equality, were denied to women outright. What is more, while the Declaration of Independence pronounced the equality of "all men," only landowning white men were deemed fit to vote by the drafters of the Constitution. Enslaved Africans, in fact, were not even acknowledged as fully human. In deciding how to allot state-by-state representation in the U.S. Congress, each slave was declared equal to three-fifths of a man.

This conflict between the lofty promise of Jefferson's Declaration of Independence and the U.S. Constitution's limitations on that promise are at the heart of what may well be the central dilemma of U.S. history. Jefferson himself was a slaveowner, who unlike other founding fathers never freed the majority of his slaves, even upon his death.

In many ways, this book depicts the struggle that the United States has undergone to live up to the promise spelled out by the Declaration of Independence. While it is expressly concerned with the African-American experience, the history of African Americans cannot be separated from the story of all Americans, any more than the story of the nation's presidents or military conflicts can.

In addition to the national struggle to fulfill the promise of "life, liberty and the pursuit of happiness" for all Americans, readers will find other themes running throughout this story.

One such theme has been the conflict between the goal of integration into the larger American community on the one hand and separation from that community on the other. Whether the figures or organizations involved are the African Colonization Society in the early 19th century, Marcus Garvey's United Negro Improvement Association in the early 20th century, or Louis Farrakhan's Nation of Islam in the late 20th century, the impulse toward separatism has been a consistent response to the scourge of racism.

By the same token, those calling for an equitable integration have held their position with an equal fervor, and that struggle is well documented in these pages, from the quiet nobility of Benjamin Banneker, who lobbied Jefferson to recognize that achievement was less a matter of race than of opportunity, to the commanding stature of former general Colin Powell, who proved through his actions and character that he was fit for any office in the land, if he chose to pursue it.

The struggle for African-American equality, then, should not be defined by a series of government laws passed over time granting increased rights to black citizens. Instead, it is the story of African Americans and their allies forcing these changes through concerted action. It is the story of well-known heroes such as Harriet Tubman and Frederick Douglass, of Booker T. Washington and W. E. B. DuBois, and of Martin Luther King Jr. and Malcolm X. However, it is equally the story of those unknown, everyday heroes who face the enormous obstacles of personalized and institutionalized racism, have not only maintained their dignity and strength but have moved mountains in the process.

In many ways, movement itself is yet another crucial theme of this book. In one sense, the struggle for civil rights is referred to as a movement. On a more basic level, the migration of people from place to place is another form of movement. This form of movement, as much as any other theme stated above, is at the heart of the African-American experience. Beginning with the epoch of the African enslavement and diaspora, movement has defined African-American history. As enslaved Africans from diverse regions of Africa arrived in first in the Caribbean and Latin America, and then in the North American colonies, they carried old traditions—and formed new ones—that reshaped their new world. With emancipation came new eras of movement, as freedpersons traded shackles for life in the North, in the West, and elsewhere, once again transforming their new homes. It is for this reason that the form of this book—an atlas—is especially appropriate. It is our hope that the maps included in these pages will help give concrete life to the story of how geographic as well as cultural and political borders have been crossed over the centuries. Likewise, we hope readers come away with an understanding of the consequences of these crossings, and the barriers that remain in the road to fulfilling the promise of Thomas Jefferson's revolutionary vision of equality for all.

THE AFRICAN HERITAGE
A Short History of a Continent

Mother Africa, the land has been called, for it is in East Africa's Rift valley that scientists believe that humans first evolved. These human ancestors emerged as a distinctive genus, or grouping of species, within the primate order (apes, monkeys, lemurs, etc.) of mammals approximately 5 million years ago. There is little resemblance, of course, between these ancient hominids, roughly defined as primates who walked on two legs, and people today. It would take millions of years of evolution to transform these small-statured and -brained primates into modern human beings. Nonetheless, archeologists say that fossil evidence confirms that humanity first emerged in East Africa.

The African heritage, then, is the heritage of humankind.

THE BIRTHPLACE OF HUMANKIND

Evidence of the very first hominids is scant: an arm bone at Kanapoi, part of a jaw at Lothagam, a molar at Lukeino—all archaeological digs in the modern-day nation of Kenya. The earliest substantial fossil find was made at a place called Laetoli, in neighboring Ethiopia, in 1974. It was so complete a skeleton that the archaeologists who discovered it gave it a name—Lucy. About 3.5 million years old, Lucy was an *Australopithecine*, part of a genus of the hominid family about four to five feet tall and with a brain about one-third the size of the modern human brain. More precisely, she was labeled an *Australopithecus afarensis*. (Archaeologists are always careful to note that the precise line of descent from Lucy to modern humans is not always direct. This fact should be kept in mind in the following discussion. Some of the different species listed below lived side by side, and some died out rather than evolving into more modern human form.)

For the next 1.5 million years—or about 75,000 generations—*A. afarensis*

evolved through a series of *Australopithecus* species, including *A. africanus* and *A. robustus*, each somewhat larger and bigger-brained than its predecessors. Then, about 2 million years ago, humanity's first direct ancestors arrived on the scene, the genus *Homos*.

It was the great archaeologist Richard Leakey who discovered the first of the *Homo* species, *habilis*, at Olduvai Gorge in Kenya in the early 1960s. The name *Homo habilis* means "handy man," and it comes from the fact that *H. habilis* is the first human ancestor whose remains have been found accompanied by evidence of tool-making. About half a million years later came *H. ergaster*, "upright man," which lived beside *A. robustus*.

Homo sapiens, or "thinking man," appears in the East African fossil record about 500,000 years ago. Here was a human ancestor with our physical size, a brain almost equal to our own, and the ability to make tools and harness fire. *H. sapiens*, like some of the earlier *Homo* species, made its way out to southern Africa and out of the continent to Asia and Europe.

Finally, about 100,000 years ago, however, *Homo sapiens sapiens* or "wise thinking man"—a being biologically identical to ourselves—appeared in East Africa. *H. sapiens sapiens* would migrate even farther than earlier *Australopithecus* and *Homo* species, settling not just in Asia and Europe, but in Australia (about 40,000 years ago) and the Americas (about 15,000 years ago) as well. And wherever it went it displaced—through competition or mating—more primitive forms of human beings. Halfway between the emergence of *H. sapiens sapiens* and today comes evidence of multipiece weapons, tools, and even jewelry. And, again, it shows up in eastern and southern Africa first.

For the next 40,000 years or so—until the end of the last ice age 10,000 years ago—human beings in Africa and elsewhere largely lived as bands of hunters and gatherers. Groups remained small—probably no more than 150 or so persons—and ranged widely, requiring up to 300 square

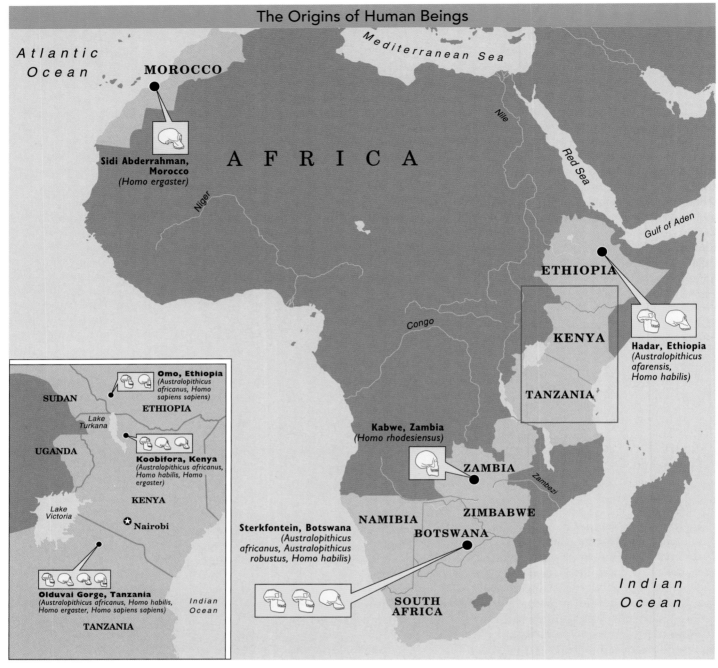

The Origins of Human Beings

Atlantic Ocean

MOROCCO

Mediterranean Sea

A F R I C A

Nile

Red Sea

Niger

Sidi Abderrahman, Morocco
(Homo ergaster)

Gulf of Aden

ETHIOPIA

Congo

KENYA

Hadar, Ethiopia
(Australopithicus afarensis, Homo habilis)

TANZANIA

Kabwe, Zambia
(Homo rhodesiensus)

ZAMBIA

Zambezi

ZIMBABWE

NAMIBIA

BOTSWANA

Sterkfontein, Botswana
(Australopithicus africanus, Australopithicus robustus, Homo habilis)

SOUTH AFRICA

Indian Ocean

Omo, Ethiopia
(Australopithicus africanus, Homo sapiens sapiens)

SUDAN

Lake Turkana

ETHIOPIA

UGANDA

Koobifora, Kenya
(Australopithicus africanus, Homo habilis, Homo ergaster)

KENYA

Lake Victoria

✪ Nairobi

Olduvai Gorge, Tanzania
(Australopithicus africanus, Homo habilis, Homo ergaster, Homo sapiens sapiens)

Indian Ocean

TANZANIA

miles to support each group. The entire continent of Africa supported perhaps a million people.

A MASTERY OF NATURE

Drawings on rocks and cave walls reveal a fascinating story. Etchings from 12,000 years ago depict the wild beasts—giraffes, elephants, and rhinoceroses—hunted by these Paleolithic, or Old Stone Age, people. In art from approximately 7,000 years ago, both the subject and the style begin to change. Etchings are replaced by paintings made from oxidized minerals and clay, mixed perhaps with blood, animal fat, or urine to make the colors bind to the rock. These paintings also depict people hunting and herding. Archaeologists theorize that this new emphasis on human beings in control of the animal world reflects a new mastery of nature, as the people of Africa had begun to domesticate animals such as cattle, sheep, and goats.

But even during its wetter and greener eras of long ago, the Saharan climate—punctuated by long periods of drought—made life difficult and uncertain for its inhabitants. As historian John Reader has written, "the Sahara acted as a pump, drawing people from surrounding regions into its watered environments during the good times, and driving them out again as conditions deteriorated (though not necessarily returning them to their point of origin)." Among the places of refuge in dry times was a green and narrow valley near the eastern end of the desert, watered by a meandering river that would come to be called the Nile.

Modern human beings probably lived in the Nile valley for tens of thousands of years, but the best picture of what their life was like comes from 19,000-year-old remains at an archaeological dig at Wadi Kubbaniya, in modern-day Egypt. Hunting was rarer in the valley than in the surrounding territories. There were just too many people in too small an area. Fishing, however, was critical, as was the gathering of seeds, fruit, and root crops such as nut-grass tubers. The lives of the people followed the rhythms of the river. Indeed, the vegetable and fish stocks gathered after the river crested in late summer and early fall were stored away against the lean times. The incredible richness of the valley and the need to protect agricultural surpluses led to settlement in villages of 500 persons or more by about 7000 B.C., 4,000 years before the first pyramids were built.

The development of agriculture marked the great leap between the Paleolithic times, or Old Stone Age, and the Neolithic times, or New Stone Age. Most archaeologists agree that it first occurred in the Fertile Crescent of the Middle East, a particularly fertile region stretching from modern-day Iraq to Israel. But the legumes and grains first domesticated there soon found a home in the Nile valley, along with a locally domesticated grain from North Africa called sorghum. The seeds of a future civilization, both literally and figuratively, had now been planted.

ANCIENT CIVILIZATIONS

The Nile valley of Egypt—along with Mesopotamia, China, the Indus valley, and Meso-America—is often referred to as one of the "cradles of civilization." The civilization that arose along the lower reaches of the Nile—between the cataracts at Aswan in the south and the Mediterranean Sea in the north—was a

unified state with a common culture. It was ruled by a king, or pharaoh, and administered by an army of literate bureaucrats. It developed an indigenous form of writing, art, and religion and built massive monuments and engineering projects, many of which have weathered the millennia and are visited today by millions of tourists.

ANCIENT EGYPT

It is no accident that civilization first arose in the Nile valley. Archaeologists and historians have long noted that most of the early civilizations on Earth arose in river valleys. River valleys, such as the Nile, have rich soils and access to stable supplies of water. Thus, they can support larger numbers of people and agricultural surpluses. These surpluses relieve some members of society from raising food,

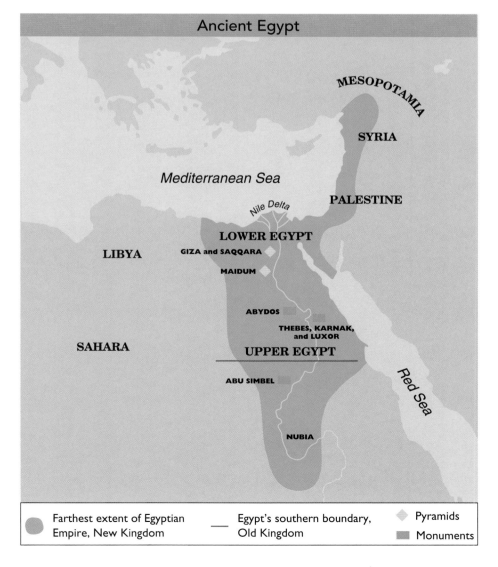

Ancient Egypt

MESOPOTAMIA

SYRIA

Mediterranean Sea

PALESTINE

Nile Delta

LOWER EGYPT

LIBYA

GIZA and SAQQARA

MAIDUM

ABYDOS

THEBES, KARNAK, and LUXOR

SAHARA

UPPER EGYPT

ABU SIMBEL

Red Sea

NUBIA

● Farthest extent of Egyptian Empire, New Kingdom

— Egypt's southern boundary, Old Kingdom

◆ Pyramids

■ Monuments

The Great Pyramids and the Sphinx in a late-19th-century photograph (Library of Congress)

leaving them free to devote themselves to art, crafts, engineering, writing, religion, war-making, and governing. River valleys also create connectedness, unity, and ease of transportation, allowing for the spread of ideas, inventions, culture, and law. The process eventually becomes self-sustaining. Surpluses support greater numbers of officials and soldiers who can command greater numbers of people. Large numbers of laborers could be conscripted to work on—or taxed to pay for—large irrigation and other engineering projects. These, in turn, would create greater surpluses, which would result in larger populations and larger bases for taxation and labor, and so on.

While all of this explains why and how civilization arose in ancient Egypt, it doesn't explain why that civilization took the form that it did. Two other features of the Nile are necessary for that. First, unlike the rivers of nearby Mesopotamia, the Nile is stable, flooding in predictable amounts at a predictable time of year. This produced a remarkable continuity in Egyptian civilization over time. Moreover, the continuity of the river helped instill the idea of the continuity of life. Egyptians saw life and death as a continuum and built great monuments to ensure that their pharaohs would live on forever to protect Egypt and ensure the continuity of the Nile and its life-giving floods. The second unique feature of the Nile valley is its location. Surrounded by great deserts, it was relatively isolated. Over the course of its first 2,500 years, Ancient Egypt was conquered only once by foreign invaders. This security added to the sense of continuity inherent in Egyptian history and culture.

EGYPT'S AFRICAN ROOTS

As a glance at a map shows, the Nile valley is located in the northeastern corner of Africa but connected to the Middle East and the Mediterranean world as well. Although Egypt is on the African continent, scholars continue to debate the degree to which Ancient Egypt was of Africa. In other words, how African was Egyptian culture and how Egyptian is African culture? The first of these questions is the easier one to answer. Even though a significant minority did come from what is now the Middle East and the

Mediterranean parts of Europe, Egypt was largely settled by peoples from all over Africa. In that sense, Egypt is most certainly African.

Regarding the question of Egypt's influence on the rest of the African continent, there can be little doubt that Egyptian culture heavily influenced the Nubian civilizations that bordered it immediately to the south, a region the ancient Egyptians referred to as Punt. As early as 2450 B.C., the pharaoh Sahure sent an expedition to the region, in what is today the nation of Sudan. Its mission was not a friendly one. Upon their arrival in Punt, the invading Egyptian military plundered or demanded in tribute a king's ransom of timber, precious metals, and incense. Later expeditions from Egypt would bring back grain, ivory, cattle, slaves, even an "exotic" Mbuti (or pygmy, as they have been commonly called). The enormous value that Egyptians placed on African commodities can be measured by the extremes the Egyptian pharaohs went to acquire such treasures. In 1472 B.C., for example, Egyptian Queen Hatshepsut had an armada of ships carried across the desert from the Red Sea to the upper reaches of the Nile. Gradually, Egypt established control over the region, turning Nubia, or Kush, as the Egyptians referred to it, into a vassal state.

THE KINGDOM OF KUSH

The Egyptians, however, offered as much as they took. The merchants of Kush soon grew rich on trade and adopted Egyptian art, culture, and religion. Indeed, Kush grew so rich and powerful that it was able to conquer and rule Egypt itself for about a 60-year period in the 8th and 7th centuries B.C. By the time the Romans conquered Egypt in the 1st century B.C., Meroë, the capital of Kush, was among the wealthiest cities in the world. But what made Kush and Meroë great also unmade them. Unlike Egypt— where softer bronze tools and weapons predominated—Kush was built on iron. More heavily wooded than its neighbor to the north, it had the timber resources necessary to fuel its forges. Gradually these forests were depleted, leading to heavy erosion and a collapse of the critical agricultural base. By the 2nd century A.D., Meroë had fallen.

For a long time, historians believed that the people of Meroë fled their dying civilization for West and Central Africa, bringing their iron-making technology with them. Indeed, there is some evidence that both Meröe and Egypt had a linguistic influence across the breadth of the continent. For example, numerous words in the language spoken by the Wolof people of modern-day Senegal, at Africa's most-western extreme, bear a strong resemblance to Egyptian. Where the Wolof say *gimmi* for "eyes," the Egyptian used *gmk* for "look"; Wolofs say *seety* for "prove" where Egyptians used *sity* for "proof." More recently, however, historians have become skeptical of this earlier theory, since no material evidence of such a technology transfer exists.

Some scholars—pointing to distinct kinds of iron-smelting furnaces found in different parts of the continent—argue that iron-making technologies were entirely indigenous to Africa. But most historians and archaeologists believe that iron-making emerged from the Middle East, where iron was first forged 4,500 years ago in Anatolia, a region in modern-day Turkey. From there, they say, it spread throughout the Middle East, was brought to North Africa by the seafaring Phoenicians, and then traded across the Sahara by Berbers, the indigenous people of North Africa. Early forges, dating back to about 600 B.C.—as old as those in Meroë—have been found in what is now Nigeria.

The importance of iron cannot be overestimated. It is stronger and more versatile than copper or bronze—the earliest metals to be forged—and its ores are far more widespread, though making it requires much hotter furnaces. A culture that possesses iron-making technology has a distinct advantage over one that does not. And while there is evidence of the effects of this technological edge in many parts of the world, nowhere is it more obvious than in sub-Saharan Africa. It is not a coincidence, say historians, that the earliest sub-Saharan cultures to adopt iron-making—those of the Bantu-speaking people in modern-day Nigeria and Cameroon—were the ones that came to dominate Africa below the Sahara Desert.

The iron-making technologies also served as an engine that propelled social and economic change in sub-Saharan

COMPARING LANGUAGES

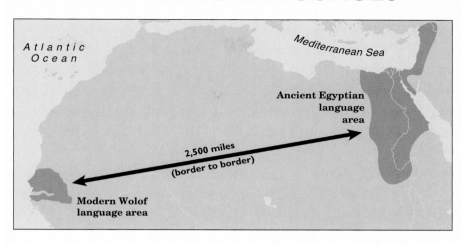

Egyptian word	Meaning	Wolof word	Meaning
nb	basket	ndab	calabash
ro	mouth	roh	to swallow
tpn	example	top	to follow
gmk	look	gimmi	eyes
sity	proof	seety	to prove
kite	ring	khet	ring
r db	in exchange	dab	to shake hands
ta tenem	first land made by the gods	ten	clay God used to make the first humans
aar	paradise	aar	divine protection
tefnut	the god that created the sun by spitting it out	tefnit	to spit
geb	dirt	gab	to dig
kau	above	kaou	heaven
auset	Isis, wife of Osiris	set	wife
tiou	five	diou-rom	five
etbo	floating sun at the beginning of time	temb	to float

Africa. Large-scale iron-making required specialized craftspeople who ate the agricultural surpluses of farmers who, in turn, became more productive through the iron tools they used. Regions where iron was forged became food importers, creating a lasting network of trade and exchange. At the same time, the use of iron had its consequences. High-temperature iron furnaces (2,200°F/1,200°C) have an insatiable appetite for wood charcoal. Some archaeologists theorize that the ecological deterioration caused by deforestation delayed the rise of large centralized states in some parts of sub-Saharan Africa. Still, by A.D. 1000 empires and federations of trading cities stretched across Africa from modern-day Ethiopia in the east to Senegal in the west.

THE BANTU MIGRATION

The sheer scale of the Bantu conquest and its impact on Africa makes it one of the most important developments in human history, and one of the most remarkable. Beginning about 2,000 years ago, many Bantu-speaking peoples begin migrating to central Africa. By at least 1,000 years ago, they had reached east to modern Tanzania, south to Mozambique and southwest to Angola. In West Africa, they mixed with Sudanic peoples from modern Chad and Sudan.

Again, the reasons for the success of this massive migration can be found in the unique properties of iron and the special requirements of iron-making. The strength of the metal makes it ideal for tools. According to archeologists and historians who have found few weapons in sites dating back to the migration epoch of 2,000 to 2,500 years ago, the Bantu-speaking peoples achieved most of their success wielding the hoe and not the sword. Iron hoes allowed the Bantu-speakers to produce more food on more land, allowing for greater population growth and spread. Local hunters and gatherers, such as the Mbuti (often referred to as pygmies) of central Africa and the Khoisan (sometimes called bushmen) of southern Africa were pushed into marginal lands, such as the deep rain forests of the Congo River basin and the Kalahari Desert of southern Africa. Indeed, there is no geographically larger region of the world with such a wide array of closely related languages as in sub-Saharan Africa. Bantu languages are spoken today in countries as far afield as South Africa, Senegal in West Africa, and Kenya in East Africa. Even American English has been affected. Such everyday American words as banjo, jiffy, and bozo have their roots in Bantu.

The Bantu Migration

AFRICAN KINGDOMS

The Bantu peoples enter written history—as opposed to the history recreated through archaeological finds and oral traditions—around 1,000 years ago, when there arose in West Africa a series of kingdoms and empires. Based on trade, they mixed elements of the indigenous cultures of the region with the Islamic civilization of North Africa and the Middle East.

The wealth of these kingdoms—and most especially of Mali—is revealed in the spending of their rulers. In the 13th century A.D., one ruler named Kankan Mansa Musa led a caravan of 25,000 camels to Mecca, as part of the pilgrimage all good Muslims are expected to take at least once in their lifetime. Mansa Musa ordered the construction of a new mosque—or Islamic temple—every Friday, to honor the weekly Muslim sabbath. Moreover, the cara-

Trade Routes in Northern Africa, A.D. 1000

Atlantic
Ocean

Bougie · Tunis

Fez

Marraksh

Sijilmasa

Tripoli   Mediterranean Sea

Ghadames   Cairo

Sokna

EGYPT

Teggazza
SALT

Zawila

Ghat

Red Sea

In Salah

Tademekka
SALT

In Ekker

SALT

Bilma

Walata

Gao

Timbuktu

Takedda

**KINGDOM OF
KANEM-BORNU**

Jenne

Kano   SLAVES

Niani

SLAVES   SLAVES
IVORY

Salaga

——	Trade routes
•	Trade cities
SLAVES	Objects of trade
EGYPT	Neighboring kingdoms

van contained so much gold that it brought down the price of the precious metal wherever it went.

As with much of African history, the origins of Mali lie in a complex interplay of indigenous developments and outside influences. Around 1000 B.C., the Mande-speaking people of what is now western Sudan and Chad shifted their economy from hunting and gathering to agriculture, domesticating native plants like sorghum and millet. Farming can support far greater numbers of people than hunting. Among the Mande it produced a population explosion that led them to settle across a vast territory stretching to the Atlantic Ocean by A.D. 400. As population densities increased, federations of villages under a single king spread across the Sahel, the semi-dry grassland region south of the Sahara. But what turned these small federations into great empires—of which Mali was just one—was only partly the doing of the Mande. In fact, the foundations of Mali and the other great Sahelian empires rested on the back of the camel.

TRADE ROUTES
OF NORTH AFRICA

While camels are difficult to handle, they are ideally suited for desert travel and commerce—able to carry 500 pounds 25 miles a day without a sip of water for a week at a time. Not surprisingly, the camel—originally from Asia—spread rapidly through North Africa after its introduction around A.D. 200. It opened up an immensely lucrative trans-Saharan trade network between the Mediterranean and sub-Saharan Africa, a network that put the Mande in the middle. Great cities arose at the southern edge of the Sahara, where the main caravan routes emerged from the desert: Walata (in present-day Mauritania); Tekedda and Agades (Niger); and, most famously, Gao and Timbuktu (Mali). There, Arab, Berber, and Mande merchants—all Muslim peoples from North and West Africa—exchanged silk cloth, cotton cloth, mirrors, dates, and salt for ivory, gum, kola nut (a stimulant), and gold. By the 11th century, the mines of West Africa had become the Western world's greatest source of gold, turning out nine tons of the precious metal annually.

Also making its way across the Sahara was a new faith. Islam was born in the Arabian cities of Mecca and Medina in the early 7th century. A crusading religion that preached the power of Allah and the equality of all men, Islam—under the Prophet Muhammad and his successors—quickly spread throughout the Middle East and North Africa. By A.D. 1100, the Maghreb—Arabic for "land of the setting sun," that is, modern-day Morocco, Algeria, and Tunisia—boasted major Berber and Arabic Islamic empires. South of the Sahara, a major kingdom built on the wealth of the trans-Saharan trade was emerging in what is now Mauritania and Mali. While its subjects—a Mande-speaking people known as the Soninke—called it Aoukar, outsiders referred to it as Ghana, after the title taken by its warrior-kings, and the name stuck.

GHANA, MALI, AND SONGHAI

By any name, Ghana was a remarkable place, so well-administered that scholars throughout the Western world praised it as a model for other kingdoms. To assure the royal lineage, for example, the kingdom was inherited not by the king's son—in an age before genetic testing, paternity could never be determined with one hun-

dred percent accuracy—but by his nephew, that is, his sister's son. And while the king and his people retained their ancestral religion—commissioning exquisite altars and statues to worship ancestors and guardian saint-like spirits—much of the merchant class and the government bureaucracy were Arabic-speaking Muslims. It was a potent combination of ideas, wealth, and military strength. By the end of the first millennium, Ghana had conquered almost all of the trading cities of the western Sahel, covering a territory roughly the size of Texas, where it exacted tribute, or taxes, from trans-Saharan merchants, subordinate kings, and local chiefs.

Despite its good governance, Ghana collapsed around 1100 and divided into small kingdoms, which warred on each other for more than a century until a new dynasty of warrior-kings, founded by the great Sundiata, united the region from their capital at Niani (present-day Mali). Even more extensive than Ghana, the kingdom of Mali and its successor—the Songhai Empire—dominated much of West Africa from the 13th to 16th centuries. Even more than Ghana, these were thoroughly Islamic empires, where many of the rulers, such as Mansa Musa, were driven as much by faith as power. And as medieval Islam valued literacy and learning above all other earthly pursuits, the kingdoms of Mali and the Songhai were renowned for their scholarship. By the late 15th century, Timbuktu was home to the largest university in Africa, outside of Egypt, funded by the wealth derived from trans-Saharan trade.

But while that wealth went to build mosques, universities, and great cities, it came at an immense cost. Along with the gold, salt, and cloth transported by trans-Saharan caravans, there was human cargo—slaves.

While never reaching the scale of the transatlantic slave trade of the 16th through 19th centuries, the trans-Saharan trade was still immense. It is estimated that up to 10,000 slaves were annually carried northward across the Sahara (along with a small trickle southward) at the height of the trade in the 10th and 11th centuries. In all, historians estimate over 4 million men, women, and children were transported from West Africa to the Islamic realms of the Mediterranean and Middle East between the years 650

Islamic Expansion in Africa

(Southern Iberian Peninsula under Muslim control, 711–1490s)

SPAIN

Lisbon (711)
Gibraltar (711)
Tunis
Qairawan (670)
Tripoli (644)
Mediterranean Sea
Alexandria (642)
Cairo (641)
Arabia
Nile
Medina
Mecca
Red Sea

A F R I C A

Timbuktu (1076)

Atlantic Ocean

Indian Ocean

Islamic Expansion, A.D. 622–1076		
622–634	634–656	661–715

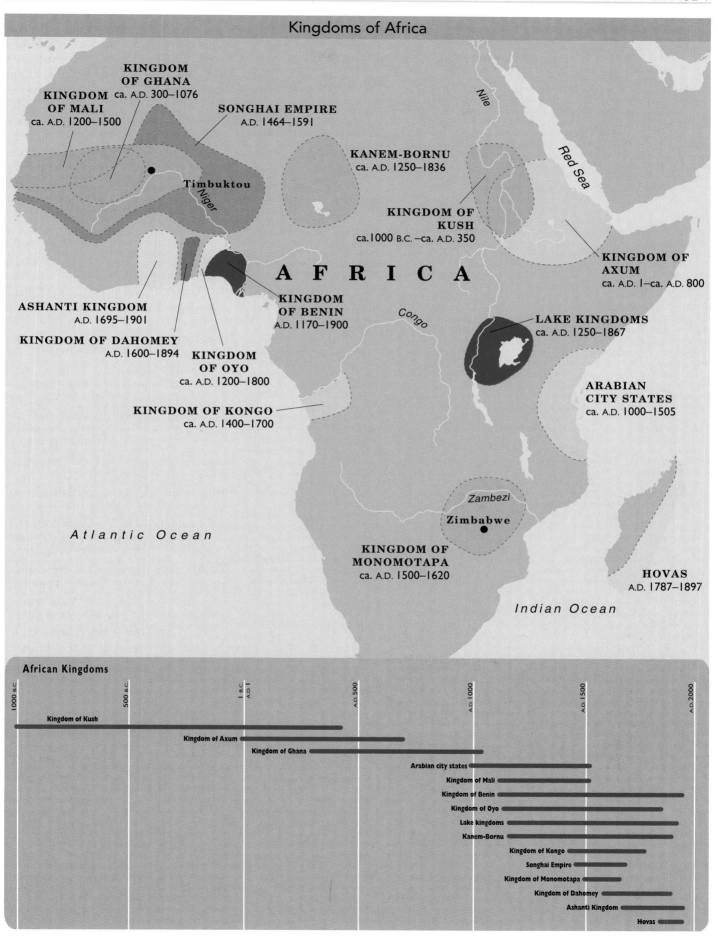

Kingdoms of Africa

KINGDOM OF GHANA
ca. A.D. 300–1076

KINGDOM OF MALI
ca. A.D. 1200–1500

SONGHAI EMPIRE
A.D. 1464–1591

KANEM-BORNU
ca. A.D. 1250–1836

KINGDOM OF KUSH
ca. 1000 B.C. –ca. A.D. 350

KINGDOM OF AXUM
ca. A.D. 1–ca. A.D. 800

Timbuktou

Niger

Nile

Red Sea

A F R I C A

ASHANTI KINGDOM
A.D. 1695–1901

KINGDOM OF DAHOMEY
A.D. 1600–1894

KINGDOM OF OYO
ca. A.D. 1200–1800

KINGDOM OF BENIN
A.D. 1170–1900

Congo

LAKE KINGDOMS
ca. A.D. 1250–1867

ARABIAN CITY STATES
ca. A.D. 1000–1505

KINGDOM OF KONGO
ca. A.D. 1400–1700

Atlantic Ocean

Zambezi

Zimbabwe

KINGDOM OF MONOMOTAPA
ca. A.D. 1500–1620

HOVAS
A.D. 1787–1897

Indian Ocean

African Kingdoms

1000 B.C.	500 B.C.	1 B.C. A.D. 1	A.D. 500	A.D. 1000	A.D. 1500	A.D. 2000

Kingdom of Kush

Kingdom of Axum

Kingdom of Ghana

Arabian city states

Kingdom of Mali

Kingdom of Benin

Kingdom of Oyo

Lake kingdoms

Kanem-Bornu

Kingdom of Kongo

Songhai Empire

Kingdom of Monomotapa

Kingdom of Dahomey

Ashanti Kingdom

Hovas

and 1500. As in the Americas, the black slaves of the Arab world were largely put to work as laborers—in mines, plantations, workshops, and households.

Still, there were significant differences between Islamic and transatlantic slavery. For one thing, many of the Islamic slaves became soldiers, where they could often earn their freedom through military valor. And because race and color had little to do with status—the Arab world also imported slaves from Europe and western Asia—there was far more social intermingling of free people and slaves, including extensive intermarriage. Indeed, it was in this multi-cultural Mediterranean setting that African slaves first came to the attention of European Christians, including the Spanish and Portuguese. And when these Europeans looked for people to work the plantations of their transatlantic empires after 1500, they increasingly turned to Africa.

The Grande Mosque, in Djenne, Mali, is the world's largest mud brick structure. It was originally built in the 13th century by Koy Konboro, Djenne's first Muslim ruler. (Corbis)

THE SLAVE TRADE

"Sir," began the letter that the king of Kongo, Nzinga Mbemba, wrote in 1526 to King João III of Portugal. "Your Highness should know how our Kingdom is being lost in so many ways . . . by the excessive freedom given by your agents and officials to the men and merchants who are allowed to come to this Kingdom to set up shops with goods and many things which have been prohibited by us, and which they spread throughout our Kingdoms and Domains in such abundance that many of our vassals [subjects], whom we had in obedience, do not comply because they have the things in greater abundance than we ourselves; and it was with these things that we had them content and subjected under our vassalage and jurisdiction. . . . "

Mbemba, the son of the first central African king to encounter Europeans, was probably not the first African ruler, and certainly not the last, to learn that the trade goods that Europeans brought with them in their ships came with a steep price tag. In 1506, Mbemba had invited Portuguese merchants, administrators, and government officials to live in his central African kingdom and introduce European ideas, faith, and commodities to his subjects. But as the 1526 letter between Mbemba and King João III makes clear, the European presence proved to be destructive. Portugal's representatives freely sold Mbemba's subjects alcohol, firearms, and other goods, thereby undermining the Kongo government. And, of course, the goods were only part of the trade. In exchange, the Portuguese demanded the kingdom's most valuable asset. "We cannot reckon on how great the damage is," Mbemba's letter goes on to say, "since the mentioned merchants are taking every day our natives . . . and get them to be sold; and so great, Sir, is the corruption of licentiousness [sin] that our country is being completely depopulated." The king of Portugal's response to the African leader was less than encouraging; Kongo, he argued, had nothing else of value to Europeans. If Mbemba wanted to continue to receive the European goods that his kingdom now depended on, he would have to let Portuguese slave traders conduct their business without interference from his government. Although Mbemba's successors would attempt to prevent Portugal from dominating the kingdom's affairs by fostering trade with the Dutch as well, by the late 17th century, Kongo had splintered apart. Two centuries later, French and Belgian colonies, known as French Congo and Congo Free State (later renamed Belgian Congo) would complete Kongo's transformation from independence to colonial subjugation.

SLAVERY IN PRE-COLONIAL AFRICA

As in many regions of Earth in ancient times—including Asia, Europe, and the Americas—slaves and slavery were part of everyday life in Africa. As the biblical book of Exodus recounts, the Egyptians enslaved thousands of Hebrews—and Nubians—putting them to work constructing some of the greatest monuments of the ancient world. The Phoenician trading empire of Carthage—in modern-day Tunisia—exported African slaves throughout the Mediterranean world several centuries before Christ. And, as in everything they did, the Romans took the trade to another level, enslaving tens of thousands of Africans (including a small number of black Africans), slaves, and others to work the plantations and crew the sea-going galleys of the empire. The fall of Rome in the 5th century did not end slavery, although it did temporarily curb the trafficking in human beings in the Western world. Still, the barbarian successors to Rome in North Africa maintained slavery, and the coming of the Arab armies in the 7th and 8th centuries expanded the trade, although the religion they brought with them established some of the first moral codes on the treatment of slaves.

As noted earlier, human beings were among the most common and valuable commodities of the trans-Saharan trade, with Arab merchants working hand in hand with local officials and traders to secure the cargo. While evidence of slavery in all great medieval kingdoms of Africa is relatively scarce, a pattern seems to emerge: the more trade-oriented the kingdom, the more common was slavery. Thus, in the relatively self-contained and long-lived Christian kingdom of Axum—which existed in what is now modern-day Ethiopia from the 3rd to 11th centuries—

slavery appears to have been somewhat rare. But in the great West Africa trading empires of Mali and Songhai, forced labor played a much greater role in economic life, with slaves doing much of the back-breaking labor in salt mines and on plantations, as well as serving as a lucrative export.

Evidence of a significant trade in human beings—as well as the widespread use of slaves for agriculture and mining—exists for the early kingdoms of Oyo and Benin (in the modern-day countries of Benin and Nigeria) from the 15th century onward and in the kingdom of Great Zimbabwe in southern Africa from 1200 to 1500. The slave trade was also an essential component of the economies of the Islamic city-states established by Arab merchants along the Indian coast of Africa from modern-day Eritrea to Mozambique. Finally, many smaller African societies kept slaves, although the institution there was very different from what it was in the great empires and trading states of West Africa and the East African coast.

Amongst the villages and tribal confederations of sub-Saharan Africa, slavery was a more intimate affair. In terms of numbers, it was much smaller in scale and slaves lived with, worked among, and often married into the families who owned them. Before the arrival of European slavers and outside the orbit of the great Islamic and African empires, slaves were not simply commodities in a vast trading system. While slaves in such societies were not always treated benignly—wherever one person holds power over another there is the potential for abuse—they were still treated as human beings. A person became a slave because of misfortune—losing a war and becoming a prisoner or losing a crop and being a debtor—or because of individual misdeeds, as in the case of criminals. Thus, slavery was rarely an inherited status and slaves were not necessarily viewed as an inferior form of humanity.

THE TRANSATLANTIC SLAVE TRADE

While the transatlantic slave trade organized first by the Portuguese and later by other Europeans is more properly the subject of chapter 2, a few comments

MAJOR THEMES IN AFRICAN ART

Traditionally, African art exhibits several features: 1. It always serves a purpose or conveys a message; 2. It is usually produced to be used by the community of the artist who made it; 3. It often has a spiritual element to it. The art below, though created by 20th century artists, maintains these traditions.

Fertility/Fortune
This piece was produced by an artist of the Bena Lulua ethnic group of contemporary Congo. The stomach and navel symbolize female fertility. Note the baby clinging to the mother's side.

Death
This coffin from modern-day Ghana is an example of how African art adjusts to changes in the cultural environment. The coffin shown here was built for an airplane pilot by a member of a community of woodcarvers working outside of the Ghanian capital.

Protection of the Living
This *ejiri*, or altar, was created by an artist from the Ijo ethnic group of Nigeria. It depicts a man riding a trunkless elephant. The man is the head of a family, two members of which are represented by faces on elephant's legs. Together, man and elephant represent a spirit of family protection. The altar is meant to be kept in the home.

Ancestor Adoration
This piece is a *bieri*, produced by a member of the Fang ethnic group of Gabon. It was meant to be fitted into a container and carried in spiritual processions.

Transatlantic Slave Trade

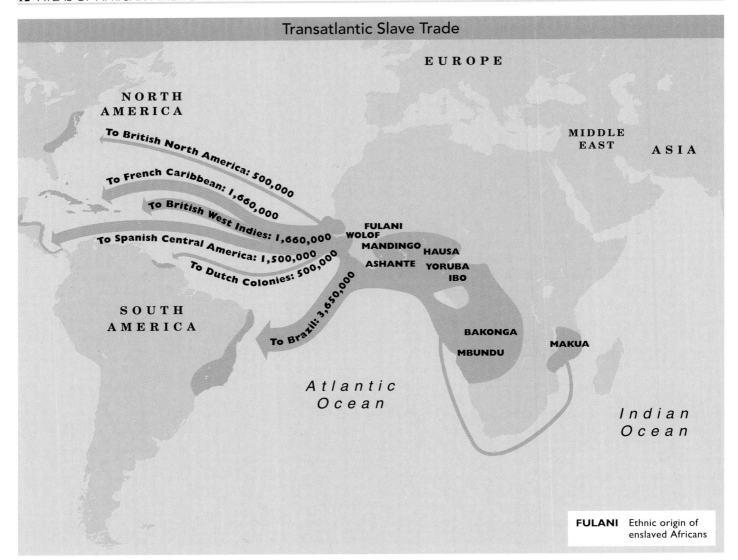

Between 1505 and 1870, over 9 million Africans were forcibly transported to the Americas as slaves. It is estimated that approximately one in six enslaved Africans died en route to their destinations. All told, 3.6 million Africans were sent to Brazil, with most of the rest heading for European colonies in the Caribbean. The map above outlines the main points of origination and destination in the transatlantic slave trade and the number of Africans involved.

about its impact on Africa are appropriate here. First, the Europeans expanded the slave trade beyond any scale ever dreamt of by the most ambitious trans-Saharan merchant. The development of New World plantation agriculture and the decimation of Native American populations by disease and war after 1500 led to an insatiable demand for labor, and the African slave trade was expanded exponentially to meet that demand. Over the course of the 16th century, the trade gained momentum slowly, with the Portuguese dominating. By 1600, the transatlantic trade drew, even with the trans-Saharan network, about 5,000 slaves being transported every year along each of these routes. With the arrival of the more

efficient Dutch, British, and French traders in the 17th and 18th centuries, the transatlantic trade easily outdistanced the trans-Saharan trade. By 1800, nearly 80,000 Africans were being forcibly transported to the New World. During the course of the 19th century, the numbers leveled off and then declined, as first Great Britain, then the United States, and finally other European countries banned first the trade in slaves and then the practice of slavery itself.

All of these numbers represent controversial estimates. But one fact should always be kept in mind: the numbers of slaves actually taken to the New World represents only a fraction—probably less than half—of the total numbers of

Africans enslaved. For example, historian Patrick Manning has estimated that approximately 9 million persons were brought to the Caribbean, Brazil, and the United States as slaves at the height of the trade between 1700 and 1850. But, he adds, some 12 million died within a year of their capture and another 7 million were enslaved for domestic use within Africa. Altogether, for the length of the transatlantic slave trade—from about 1500 to the late 1800s—it is estimated that as many as 18 million persons were forcibly taken from tropical Africa: 11 million from West Africa across the Atlantic; 5 million more from the Sahel across the Sahara and Red Sea; and yet another 2 million from central and southern Africa to the Middle East and the sugar islands of the Indian Ocean. The demographic effect of this trade was even greater than these numbers indicate. Scholars estimate the population of sub-Saharan Africa at about 50 million in 1850; absent the slave trade, however, it would have been closer to 100 million.

SLAVERY'S IMPACT ON AFRICA

While the cultural impact of the slave trade on those transported to the New World was profound beyond measure, the political and economic impact of the business on the lands they were taken from is more difficult to gauge. Indeed, there are two mutually exclusive schools of thought on the subject. One argues that slavery—horrendous as it was—had little impact because it was spread so thinly over so vast a territory. As one historian points out, an African's chance of being enslaved at the height of the trade was no worse than that of a modern American being killed in a car crash. It is also pointed out that new food crops brought eastward across the Atlantic from the Americas—like cassava and corn—made African agriculture significantly more productive, counterbalancing the demographic impact of the westward trade in slaves.

Other historians disagree and use a number of convincing arguments to bolster their cases. First, they point to the dramatic demographic impact that the population drain caused by the slave system produced. Despite the fact that most of the territory south of the Sahara is adequately watered and fertile enough for agriculture, the African continent remains significantly underpopulated, despite the population explosion of the late 20th century. While China and India together have only 60 percent of the amount of territory of Africa, they contain roughly three times as many people. This underpopulation, say scholars, has hampered the development of agriculture, trade, manufacturing, and nation-building. Furthermore, slave traders preyed upon the youngest, healthiest, and most productive members of African society.

Slave trading also created great insecurity and fear wherever it existed. Most slaves were captured in raids, either conducted on a major scale by armies or on a smaller scale by professional kidnappers. Precious resources in societies living on the very edge of subsistence had to be devoted to defense, and fear of capture kept villagers close to home, limiting their ability to trade or farm far afield. Olaudah Equiano—who wrote his autobiography years after being captured as a slave in what is now Nigeria—explained the anxieties engendered by the slave trade. "Generally, when the grown people in the neighborhood were gone far in the fields to labour, the children assembled together . . . to play; and commonly some of us used to get up a tree to look out for any assailant, or kidnapper, that might come upon us; for they sometimes took these opportunities of our parents' absence to attack and carry off as many as they could seize." Indeed, Equiano and his sister were taken from their own frontyard.

Politically, the slave trade encouraged the growth of predator states. The Dahomey and Oyo kingdoms of modern-day Benin and Nigeria grew rich and powerful in a vicious cycle of trading slaves for firearms, with the latter being used to capture more slaves. But as these kingdoms drained whole territories of people, they too collapsed as the European traders moved elsewhere in their search for cheap and plentiful human beings. The trade in slaves also stunted local industry, as Africans traded slaves for cheap European cloth and metal goods, thereby undermining local producers, as was the case in Mbemba's Kongo of the 16th century. At the same time, alcohol became more plentiful, while the problems associated with it spread throughout slave-trading territories.

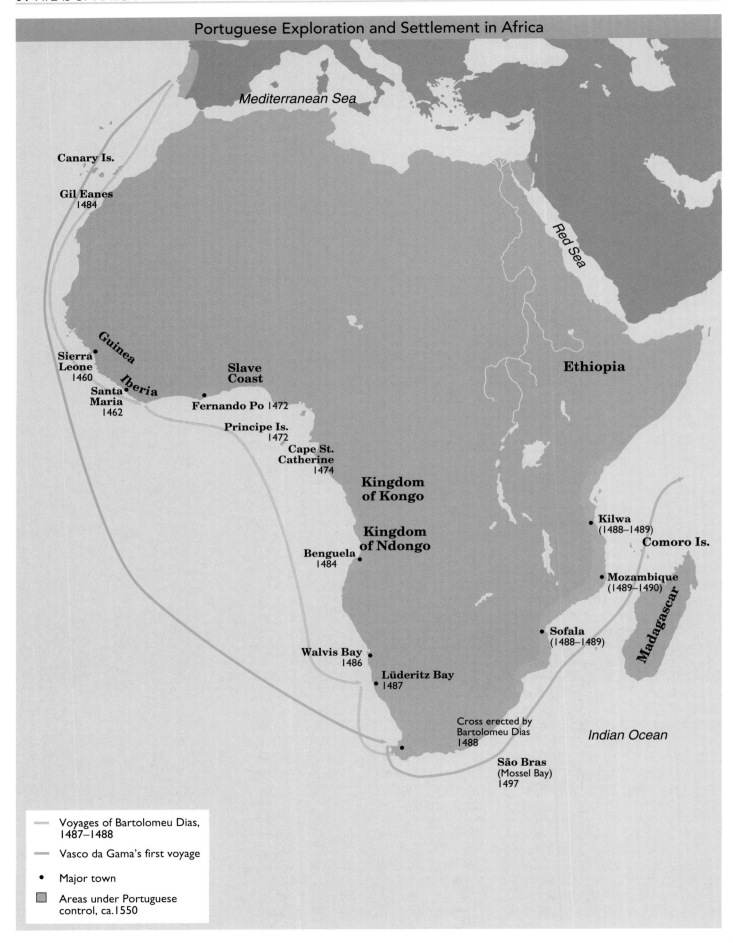

Portuguese Exploration and Settlement in Africa

Mediterranean Sea

Canary Is.

Gil Eanes
1484

Red Sea

Sierra
Leone
1460

Guinea

Iberia

Santa
Maria
1462

Slave
Coast

Fernando Po 1472

Principe Is.
1472

Cape St.
Catherine
1474

Ethiopia

**Kingdom
of Kongo**

**Kingdom
of Ndongo**

Benguela
1484

Kilwa
(1488–1489)

Comoro Is.

Mozambique
(1489–1490)

Madagascar

Sofala
(1488–1489)

Walvis Bay
1486

Lüderitz Bay
1487

Cross erected by
Bartolomeu Dias
1488

Indian Ocean

São Bras
(Mossel Bay)
1497

— Voyages of Bartolomeu Dias,
1487–1488

— Vasco da Gama's first voyage

• Major town

▨ Areas under Portuguese
control, ca.1550

Perhaps worst of all, the transatlantic and Indian Ocean slave trades expanded the use of slaves within Africa itself, spreading violence, destroying legitimate trade, disrupting the social order, and undermining the freedom of millions who never even had to see the inside of a slave ship before becoming enslaved. Historian Joseph Miller likens the effect of slave-trading in Africa to a tidal wave. "It tossed people caught in its turbulence about in its wildly swirling currents of political and economic change. Like an ocean swell crashing on a beach, it dragged some of its victims out to sea in the undertow of slave exports that flowed from it, but it set most of the people over whom it washed down again in Africa, human flotsam and jetsam exposed to slavers combing the sands of the African mercantile realms left by the receding waters." Ultimately, the slave trade would render Africa far more vulnerable to European colonization and would place the African people in a politically and economically subservient role—a role from which they have yet to fully emerge.

EUROPEAN COLONIZATION

If, by some magic, all European settlers had disappeared from sub-Saharan Africa in 1800, they would have left behind scant evidence of their presence: some British, and French slave forts along the coasts of western and southwestern Africa, a few Portuguese trading posts along the southern and east African coast and, most notably, a scattering of Dutch towns and farms at the Cape of Good Hope (modern South Africa), where the Mediterranean climate was more conducive to European settlement. Until the 19th century, European settlers and colonists kept their distance from Africa, and for good reasons. First, the tropical parts of the continent were full of diseases deadly to outsiders, with malaria in particular felling most of those who tried to settle there. Even the freed slaves from North America who settled in Liberia—all distant descendants of the African motherland—often succumbed to disease. Not for nothing had tropical Africa earned the terrifying name "white man's grave."

Topography also played a role in keeping the Europeans at bay. Much of interior Africa is made up of high plateaus, which drop off steeply near the coast. Turbulent rapids and falls mark the lower reaches of most of the great African rivers, making them all but impassable to navigation. Finally, there was the human factor. For European governments and merchants of the 17th and 18th centuries, there was no need and little chance to penetrate more than a few miles from the coast. Africa's most valuable and coveted export—slaves—was largely controlled by powerful, militaristic African states. Until the advent of more sophisticated and deadly weaponry in the late 19th century—such as the Maxim gun—no European force could effectively challenge the African middlemen of the slave trade, armed as they were by those same Europeans.

EUROPEAN SETTLEMENTS

As with exploration and the slave trade, the Portuguese were the first to settle in sub-Saharan Africa. For much of the 15th century, the Portuguese monarchs—most notably Prince Henry the Navigator—sent ships southward, looking for an all-sea route to the Indies. Two years after Christopher Columbus's 1492 "discovery" of America, Pope Alexander VI helped

Goree Island, one of the most notorious slave forts in Africa, is located in what is now the nation of Senegal. (Corbis)

European Trading Posts on the West African Coast, 15th to 19th Centuries

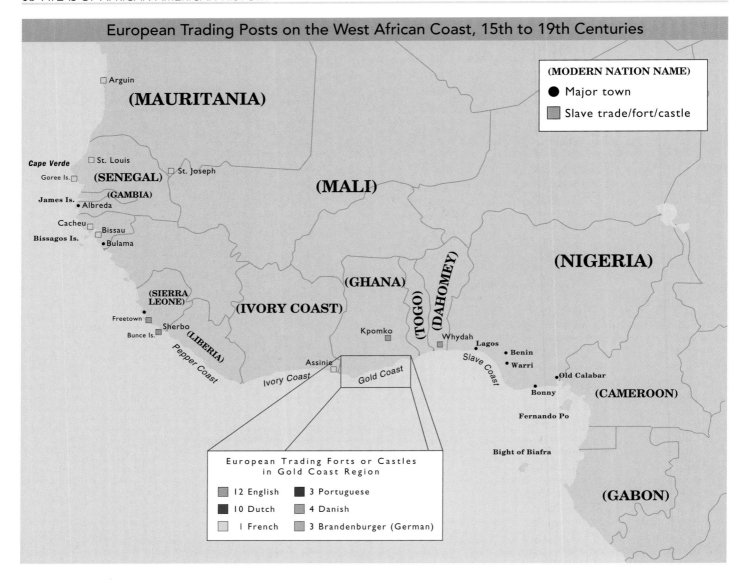

(MODERN NATION NAME)
● Major town
▪ Slave trade/fort/castle

□ Arguin

(MAURITANIA)

Cape Verde
Goree Is. □ St. Louis
(SENEGAL) □ St. Joseph
James Is. □ (GAMBIA)
● Albreda
Cacheu □
Bissagos Is. □ Bissau
● Bulama

(MALI)

(NIGERIA)

(SIERRA LEONE)
(GHANA)
(IVORY COAST)
(TOGO) (DAHOMEY)

Freetown ▪
Sherbo ▪ (LIBERIA)
Bunce Is. ▪
Pepper Coast
Ivory Coast

Kpomko ▪
Assinie □
Gold Coast
Whydah ▪
Slave Coast
Lagos
● Benin
● Warri
● Old Calabar
● Bonny
(CAMEROON)
Fernando Po
Bight of Biafra

(GABON)

European Trading Forts or Castles in Gold Coast Region

▪ 12 English ▪ 3 Portuguese
▪ 10 Dutch ▪ 4 Danish
□ 1 French ▪ 3 Brandenburger (German)

arrange the Treaty of Tordesillas, dividing the non-European world into Spanish and Portuguese spheres: most of the Americas and the Pacific for Spain; Asia, Brazil, and Africa for Portugal. In 1497, Portuguese explorer Vasco da Gama finally rounded the Cape of Good Hope at the southern tip of Africa, sailed on to India, and returned to Portugal. Although his expedition was less than successful financially—his European trinkets were of little interest to local African merchants—it did prove three things: the voyage was possible; the Portuguese had bigger guns than the locals (and could force them to sell); and the spice price differential between India and Europe (the source of profits) was enormous.

Over the next several decades, the Portuguese would establish trading posts and factories at Elmina (modern-day Ghana) and Luanda (Angola), while forcibly taking the Arab trading cities of Sofala, Moçambique, Pemba, Zanzibar, and Mombasa on the Indian Ocean coast. In 1652, the Dutch East India Company established a colony of farmers and traders in the region around the modern-day city of Cape Town, to serve as a provisioning station for ships bound to and from the East Indies. At the same time, and on through the 18th century, British, Dutch, French, Spanish, and even Danish merchants built slave factories, or fortified trans-shipment centers, along the West African coast from Senegal to Nigeria, many of which thrived well into the 19th century.

But while the early years of the 19th century saw the peaking of the transatlantic slave trade, subsequent decades would see its decline, outlawing, and disappearance. In 1807, the British—then the most powerful maritime power in the

EUROPEAN COLONIZATION OF AFRICA

1415: The Portuguese capture the North African city of Ceuta.

1441: Antonio Gonsalvez of Portugal, at the request of Prince Henry the Navigator, travels down the west coast of Africa and kidnaps 12 Africans, taking them back to Lisbon.

1453: The Ottoman Turks capture Constantinople, blocking Europe's overland routes to East Asia.

1469–1475: Portuguese navigator Gernao Gomes explores the African coast from Sierra Leone to Gabon.

1487–1488: The Portuguese explorer Bartolomeu Dias rounds the Cape of Good Hope.

1494: Pope Alexander VI divides the world into Spanish and Portuguese spheres; Africa is given to the latter.

early 1500s: The Portuguese destroy Islamic forts along the east coast of Africa.

1505: The first African slaves are transported to the Western Hemisphere; by 1870 an estimated 12 million Africans are forcefully removed to the Americas.

1517–1574: The Ottoman Turks conquer Egypt and North Africa.

1571: The Portuguese establish the colony of Angola.

1600s: British, Dutch, and French displace Portuguese from West Africa and establish their own slaving forts.

1652: The Dutch East India Company founds a settlement at Cape of Good Hope when Jan van Riebeeck and a small group drop anchor in Table Bay.

1698: Fort Jesus, a Portuguese fortification in Mombassa, in East Africa, falls to the Imam of Oman, signaling the waning power of Portugal's African empire.

1717: The Dutch East India Company announces that the use of African slave labor would be favored over the use of free labor in the Cape of Good Hope settlement.

1787: The British establish the colony of Sierra Leone for freed slaves from the Americas.

1806: The British take Cape Colony from Holland. The Dutch settlers, or Boers, decide to escape northward. In doing so they will come into increasing conflict with the Zulu.

1807: The British ban the international slave trade and establish patrols in the Atlantic.

1816: Shaka, king of the Zulus, begins to turn his army into the most powerful, well-trained military force in black Africa.

1822: Freed slaves from the United States found Liberian settlements.

1830: France invades Algeria.

1833: The British outlaw slavery in their empire.

1835: The Boers begin what is known as "The Great Trek," in which 12,000 men, women, and children head northward from their former Cape Colony. Despite fierce resistance from the Zulu people, the Boers found new republics, which they call Natal and the Orange Free State.

1847: Liberia declares itself the first independent black republic in Africa.

1848: The French outlaw slavery in their empire.

1854–1856: Scotsman David Livingstone explores central Africa from east to west and promotes the commercialization of Africa by Europeans.

1856: Britain takes control of Zanzibar.

1860: The French expand into West Africa from Senegal.

1866: Diamonds are discovered in southern Africa.

1869: The Suez Canal opens in Egypt.

1874: The British attack the Ashanti in West Africa.

1879: The Zulu Nation routs the British at Islandhlwana only to later be destroyed by a heavily armed British force.

1881–1885: Sir Charles George Gordon, military governor of the Anglo-Egyptian territory of Sudan, angers Muslim leaders by waging a campaign against slavery. Muslim rebels besiege Gordon and an Egyptian garrison for ten months. Despite a British rescue mission, Gordon is killed.

1882: The British take control of Egypt.

1884: Germany takes control of the West African territories of Togoland and Cameroon.

1884–1885: At the Berlin Conference, Africa is divided between English, French, German, Spanish, and Portuguese colonizers.

1885: Leopold II of Belgium sets up the colony of the Belgian Congo, not in the name of his country but in the name of a private company, which he heads.

1886: Gold is discovered in South Africa. Industrialist Cecil Rhodes begins to envision British rule extending from Egypt to the Cape Colony.

1890: Cecil Rhodes becomes prime minister of Cape Colony. That same year, he takes control of mines in Rhodesia (named after him in 1895 and since renamed Zimbabwe).

1896: The forces of King Menelik I of Ethiopia defeat the Italian army when it attempts to conquer that nation.

1899–1902: Dutch Boers fight British troops in South Africa's Boer War.

1904–1907: Germany pushes Herero men, women, and children into the Omaheke Desert of present-day Namibia. After poisoning water holes, the Germans surround the desert and bayonet all who try to crawl out. Survivors are sent to forced labor camps. By 1911, over 80 percent of the Herero are dead.

1911: Italy conquers Libya.

1914–1915: During World War I, the British and French seize German colonies.

1935: Italy invades Ethiopia.

1942: The Allies defeat Nazi armies at El Alamein, Egypt, beginning the drive of Germans from North Africa.

1948: The apartheid system is established in South Africa.

1952: The Mau Mau rebellion begins in Kenya.

1954–1962: Algerians wage a war of independence.

1957: Ghana becomes the first European colony in sub-Saharan Africa to win its independence.

1960: The Year of African Independence. Dozens of countries earn freedom from European colonizers.

1965: Whites of Rhodesia declare independence from Britain.

1975: Angola, Mozambique, and other Portuguese colonies gain their freedom.

1975–1994: Civil wars, with rebels armed by both the United States and South Africa, occur in Angola and Mozambique.

1989–1990: Namibia gains independence from South Africa.

1994: Nelson Mandela becomes the first majority-elected president of South Africa.

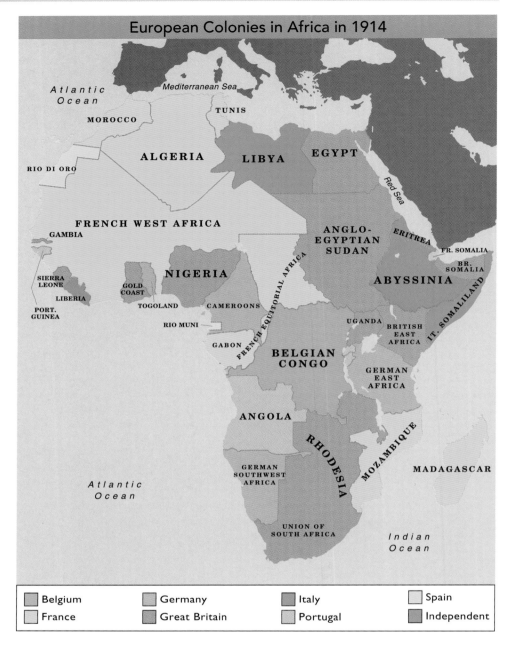

European Colonies in Africa in 1914

Atlantic Ocean

Mediterranean Sea

MOROCCO

TUNIS

ALGERIA

LIBYA

EGYPT

RIO DI ORO

Red Sea

FRENCH WEST AFRICA

ANGLO-EGYPTIAN SUDAN

ERITREA

GAMBIA

FR. SOMALIA

BR. SOMALIA

NIGERIA

ABYSSINIA

SIERRA LEONE

GOLD COAST

LIBERIA

TOGOLAND

CAMEROONS

UGANDA

IT. SOMALILAND

PORT. GUINEA

RIO MUNI

BRITISH EAST AFRICA

GABON

FRENCH EQUITORIAL AFRICA

BELGIAN CONGO

GERMAN EAST AFRICA

ANGOLA

RHODESIA

MOZAMBIQUE

MADAGASCAR

Atlantic Ocean

GERMAN SOUTHWEST AFRICA

UNION OF SOUTH AFRICA

Indian Ocean

	Belgium		Germany		Italy		Spain
	France		Great Britain		Portugal		Independent

world—banned the trade in slaves, followed by the Americans a year later. Naval patrols scoured the Atlantic in an effort to prevent the illegal trade. But the struggle was a long and frustrating one. As the quantity of slaves diminished, prices went up, encouraging even more ruthless and greedy traffickers in human flesh. Eventually, as first the British (1833), then the French (1848), the Americans (1865), and the Spanish and Portuguese (1880s) outlawed slavery in territories under their control, the transatlantic slave trade died out. (The trans-Saharan trade continued well into the 20th century; while internal African slavery survives in pockets—such as Sudan—today.)

THE SCRAMBLE FOR AFRICA

Yet even as they halted their slave trading, Europeans were expanding their holdings on the African continent. During the first 75 years of the 19th century, the French invaded Algeria and pushed into Senegal, the British established a protectorate over the Gold Coast (modern-day Ghana) and took possession of the Cape Colony from the Dutch, forcing the latter to trek northward into the interior, and the Portuguese expanded their settlements into the Zambezi River valley of Mozambique. The goals were generally the same in each; establish direct control over a small but growing trade in gold, palm oil, dyewoods, and other tropical products. Still, as late as 1875—decades after the colonization of India and centuries after the conquest of the Americas—the vast interior of Africa remained under the control of indigenous African empires, kingdoms, and chiefdoms. Several related events, however, would bring this era to an abrupt close and usher in, in less than a quarter of a century, the direct colonization of African territories nearly six times the collective size of the colonizing countries themselves—Belgium, Britain, France, Germany, Italy, Portugal, and Spain.

First came the explorers. As late as 1800, much of the African interior was unknown to outsiders and unmapped. Over the next 75 years, however, numerous European expeditions had crossed Africa from north to south and east to west, discovering interior highlands conducive to European settlement in the Eastern and Southern Africa and two vast, navigable river networks—the Congo and its tributaries and the Niger—in the center and west of the continent respectively. Next came the miners. In the 1870s and 1880s, the world's richest deposits of gold and diamonds were discovered in South Africa, spurring a rush of miners that would bring much of southern Africa under the sway of the British Empire. Finally came the imperialist governments in a grab for territories that would see the entire continent—except for Ethiopia and Liberia—divided among seven European powers in little more than 20 years.

If one man could be said to be responsible for the "great scramble," it was the king of Belgium, Leopold II. Frustrated by his relative weakness as titular ruler of one of Europe's smallest countries, Leopold had great ambitions to carve out a personal empire in the heart of Africa by using his vast fortune. Beginning in the late 1870s, the Belgian monarch laid a personal claim to the vast Congo River basin of Central Africa, establishing a colony called the Congo Free State that he ruled not in the name of Belgium, but as a personal kingdom, with the primary aim of extracting as much of the Congo's natural resources—particularly rubber—as possible, regardless of the human cost to Congo's population, who were treated as his personal slave labor force. Leopold's actions set off alarm bells in other European capitals, though not for any moral reasons. Leopold's European competitors were concerned that if they did not act quickly, the opportunity to exploit Africa's resources would be lost to them. Soon Britain, France, and Germany were scrambling for control over territories from one end of the continent to the other, while Portugal attempted to maintain its hold on Angola and Mozambique.

THE IMPACT OF COLONIALISM

To prevent a conflict that might spill over to Europe itself, the great powers met in the winter of 1884–1885 to resolve their conflicting territorial claims in Africa. At the Berlin conference, the politicians and diplomats considered a host of items: African resources, colonial borders, existing European settlements—everything but the African people themselves, none of whom were invited to attend. By the time they were through, the governments of Europe had created a web of internal boundaries that paid little heed to existing African patterns of ethnicity, language, or trade. In some places, ethnic groups were divided by the new borders; in others, antagonistic peoples were lumped together in the same colony.

But the European colonizers had just begun the process of stamping their will on the African continent. First came the struggle for colonial political control, as expeditionary forces—officered by Europeans, soldiered by African mercenaries, and armed with the latest rapid-fire guns—broke the power of African kingdoms throughout the continent. In Southwest Africa (now Namibia), German colonizers launched the 20th century's first genocide, virtually exterminating the region's Herero people after they rose up against European land grabs and forced labor demands. Colonial administrators were then sent in to collect taxes and forcibly recruit laborers. In Leopold's misnamed Congo Free State (which he ruled as his own personal colony), tens of thousands of Africans were slaughtered as Leopold's representatives sought to exploit the rich rubber resources of the territory, setting off the first international human rights crusade, which eventually forced Leopold to turn his personal colony over to the Belgian government.

Independence in Africa

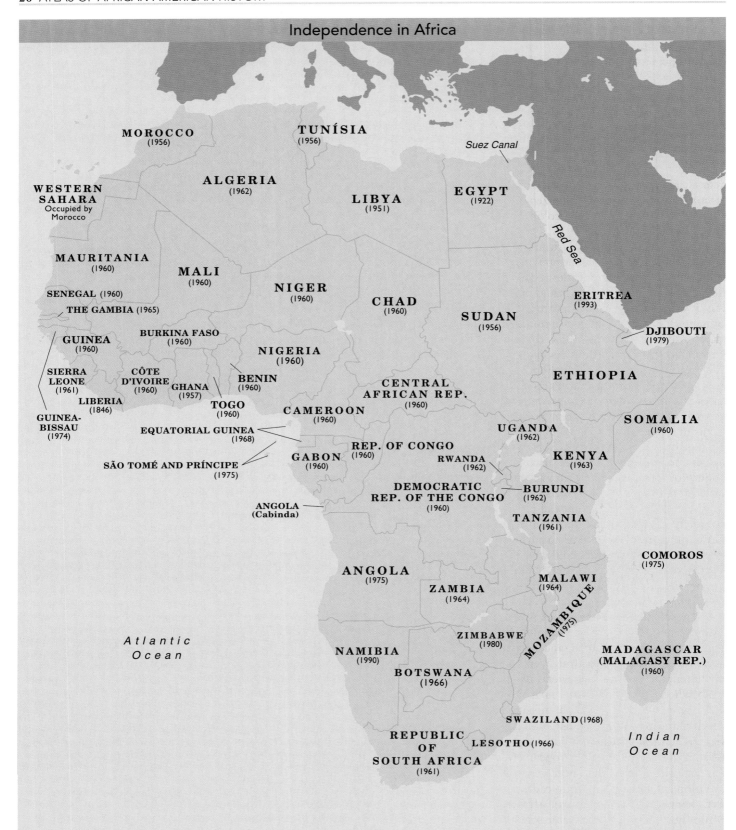

MOROCCO (1956)

TUNÍSIA (1956)

Suez Canal

WESTERN SAHARA
Occupied by Morocco

ALGERIA (1962)

LIBYA (1951)

EGYPT (1922)

Red Sea

MAURITANIA (1960)

MALI (1960)

NIGER (1960)

CHAD (1960)

SUDAN (1956)

ERITREA (1993)

SENEGAL (1960)

THE GAMBIA (1965)

GUINEA (1960)

BURKINA FASO (1960)

NIGERIA (1960)

DJIBOUTI (1979)

SIERRA LEONE (1961)

CÔTE D'IVOIRE (1960)

GHANA (1957)

BENIN (1960)

CENTRAL AFRICAN REP. (1960)

ETHIOPIA

LIBERIA (1846)

TOGO (1960)

CAMEROON (1960)

SOMALIA (1960)

GUINEA-BISSAU (1974)

EQUATORIAL GUINEA (1968)

UGANDA (1962)

SÃO TOMÉ AND PRÍNCIPE (1975)

GABON (1960)

REP. OF CONGO (1960)

RWANDA (1962)

KENYA (1963)

DEMOCRATIC REP. OF THE CONGO (1960)

BURUNDI (1962)

ANGOLA (Cabinda)

TANZANIA (1961)

COMOROS (1975)

ANGOLA (1975)

ZAMBIA (1964)

MALAWI (1964)

MOZAMBIQUE (1975)

Atlantic Ocean

NAMIBIA (1990)

ZIMBABWE (1980)

MADAGASCAR (MALAGASY REP.) (1960)

BOTSWANA (1966)

Indian Ocean

SWAZILAND (1968)

REPUBLIC OF SOUTH AFRICA (1961)

LESOTHO (1966)

Note: Republic of Cape Verde (not shown), located off the western tip of Africa, gained independence from Portugal in 1975. The Republic of Seychelles, made up of 90 widely scattered islands located roughly 1,000 miles east of Kenya and Tanzania in the Indian Ocean, gained independence from Great Britain in 1976.

"UNDERDEVELOPING" AFRICA

The Europeans masked their greed with righteousness. The French called their African campaigns a *mission civilatrice*, a civilizing mission, bringing legitimate (nonslave) commerce, European technology and ideas, and religion to the "dark continent." But much of this so-called development offered little for the Africans themselves. Indeed, much of the infrastructure developed by the colonizers was designed to better exploit the colonized. Mines and plantations—using cheap African labor and exploiting African lands and resources—generated enormous profits for foreign investors, while railroads and highways linked the mines and plantations to ports, leaving Africa with a disconnected transportation system that largely served the interests of the European colonizers. Even to this day, it is far easier to fly or make a telephone call from Abidjan (Ivory Coast) to Paris (capital of the former colonizing power)—a distance of 3,000 miles—than it is to Accra (in neighboring Ghana), less than one-tenth the distance. It was for these reasons that famed African historian Walter Rodney titled his best-known book *How Europe Underdeveloped Africa*.

Even as Europeans were exploiting the wealth of Africa, they were trying to establish control over the minds of Africans. Christianity took hold wherever missionaries were present. While many of the missionaries spent their time railing against what they called "African superstition," some—like France's Albert Schweitzer—offered more practical help, establishing clinics, schools, and hospitals, as well as churches. But even the most beneficent facilities were often established for ulterior motives. Essentially, the schools and missions served three purposes: to instill obedience to European rule, to inculcate a belief in the superiority of European civilization and, during the latter years of the colonial enterprise, to train cadres of civil servants to run local affairs. Ironically, it would be these same schools and missions that bred the nationalist leadership that would overthrow colonialism in the mid-20th century.

The process by which a pro-European curriculum turned into an African nationalism is a fascinating one. While the colonizers tried to keep schools focused on technical training and loyalty to empire, bigger and more dangerous ideas tended to creep in. French teachers, for example, in recounting their nation's history, could hardly avoid the great revolutionary ideas that shaped it: "liberty, equality, and brotherhood." African students could not help but notice how little their colonial masters practiced the ideals they preached. The European missions and schools, by bringing together different ethnic groups from around each colony, also helped undo some of the destructive divisiveness European governments had fostered.

To step back a moment, most European colonizers practiced a simple method of control—"divide and rule"—which pitted one African ethnic group against another. The tiny central African nations of Rwanda and Burundi provide examples with the most horrific consequences. For centuries, the Tutsis—just 10 percent of the population—and the majority Hutus had together created feudal kingdoms in which elite Tutsis ruled over Hutu farmers and non-elite Tutsi cattle-herders. Hutus and poor Tutsis paid tribute to their rulers and, in turn, were protected by them. Although tensions occasionally broke into violence, the two ethnic groups lived amongst each other and frequently intermarried.

Like other European colonialists, the Germans and Belgians (the latter taking over the colonies from the former during and immediately after World War I) created misconceived racial myths about the peoples they conquered in Africa. In the case of Burundi and Rwanda, they imagined the taller and less Negro-looking Tutsis to be a superior, more intelligent ruling race (some even said, ridiculously, that they were actually distant relations of the Europeans) and the Hutus a race of subservient, less intelligent farmers. Tutsis were given special rights, education, and police powers over the Hutus. This bred contempt among the Tutsis and resentment among the Hutus. When the Belgians left in 1962, they turned power over to the Tutsis in both countries. In Rwanda, the Hutu majority quickly overthrew the Tutsis; in Burundi, the Tutsis clung to power. Both countries would then be plunged into decades of bloodshed, with Tutsi killing Hutu in Burundi and Hutu killing Tutsi in Rwanda, a trend

Nelson Mandela (Photo courtesy of African National Congress)

that culminated, in the latter country, in the genocide of 1994, in which 800,000 Tutsis and their Hutu sympathizers were slaughtered in a few months.

INDEPENDENCE

Indeed, independence—which came to most of sub-Saharan Africa in the 1950s and 1960s—began with great hopes that were quickly disappointed. The problems inherited by the first national leaders of Africa were many. The European colonialists had done very little to prepare their colonies for independence. In most new African nations, there were a handful of trained civil servants and but a few university-educated people. The economies—geared to meet the needs of the European colonizers—were oriented toward the export of raw materials. During the boom years of international capitalism in the 1960s, some African nations prospered. But with the oil crisis and worldwide recession of the 1970s and 1980s, prices for natural resources—except oil, for a time—collapsed. Declining revenues and rising foreign debt produced internal tensions that resulted in coup after coup across Africa. Making things worse were the ethnic rivalries fostered by Europeans and the internal ethnic divisions created by European-imposed borders. In 1967, Nigeria—the most populous nation in Africa—was plunged into a brutal, ethnic civil war. By the 1980s and 1990s, such conflicts had spread to Algeria, Angola, Congo, Ethiopia, Liberia, Mozambique, Sierra Leone, and a host of other countries—in some cases fueled by cold war tensions between the United States and the Soviet Union.

APARTHEID

While hardly spared the conflict that engulfed much of the rest of the continent, southern Africa experienced a different kind of struggle, a result of its special geography and history. Like Rhodesia (today's Zimbabwe)—its smaller neighbor to the north—South Africa possesses a mild climate conducive to white settlement. That climate and the fabulous mineral wealth of the region created a different kind of African colony—a settler colony of minority whites ruling over a majority African population. Over the course of much of the 20th century, the white farmers, businessmen and skilled workers of South Africa and Rhodesia enjoyed great economic and political privileges, while blacks were forced to farm marginal lands or work the mines, often separated from their families for months on end. In South Africa especially, a system of apartheid, or racial separation by law, was instituted. Virtually everything that was fine and good in the country—the best schools, jobs, lands, restaurants, hotels, parks, and beaches—were reserved for whites only.

The black majority hardly took this injustice lying down. In 1960, they protested in the black township of Sharpeville and were gunned down. In the early 1970s, guerrilla movements rose up to challenge white rule in Rhodesia, eventually forcing the minority to cede power to the majority in 1980 elections. Meanwhile, new protests erupted in Soweto and other black townships around Johannesburg in the mid-1970s, leading to a nationwide struggle that lasted through the 1980s. For a time, the white government cracked down on the protesters with unprecedented brutality. By the decade's end, however, some of those in power recognized that the apartheid system was doomed. Adding to its troubles was a growing international movement to end investment and trade with the minority-ruled regime. In 1990, President F. W. de Klerk freed Nelson Mandela, the leader of the anti-apartheid African National Congress (ANC), after Mandela had spent more than a quarter of a century in prison, and legalized his organization. Four years later—in what many considered a political miracle—Mandela was elected the first president of majority-ruled South Africa and the ANC became the country's dominant political party. While serious problems like crime, health issues and black economic underdevelopment inherited from the apartheid regime continue to plague the country, South Africa, by far the wealthiest nation on the continent, has the potential to lead Africa into a more prosperous and peaceful 21st century.

SLAVERY IN EARLY AMERICA

In 1441, a Portuguese sea captain named Antam Gonçalvez led nine of his crewmen ashore in a place they called Rio d'Ouro, or River of Gold. It lay along the northwest African coast, in what is now the territory of Western Sahara. Known locally as Baldaya, Rio d'Ouro had been renamed five years earlier by the first Portuguese explorers to encounter it. At first, those earlier adventurers thought it was a waterway that led deep into the legendary gold fields of West Africa. But a quick look at the area revealed otherwise. Rio d'Ouro had no river and no gold, being merely a bay on a parched stretch of coastline where the Sahara Desert met the sea.

Gonçalvez knew that. But he was after another prize. As darkness fell along the African coast, Gonçalvez and his crew—augmented by men from another Portuguese ship—descended on some tiny villages. The ship's chronicler related what happened next: "And when our men had come nigh to them [the African villagers], they attacked them very lustily, shouting at the top of their voices . . . the fright of which so abashed [surprised] the enemy, that it threw them all into disorder. And so, all in confusion, they began to fly without any order or carefulness."

No Portuguese were hurt in the encounter, but four Africans were killed. More significantly, ten were taken prisoner and brought back to Portugal. And Gonçalvez—knighted for his efforts by the Portuguese king—found a place in the history books as the first European since ancient times to enslave Africans.

Not that Africans were unknown in Europe before 1441. Indeed, blacks were so highly prized in the palaces of Renaissance Europe that they fetched many times the price of white servants, and Africans were widely sought after as actors, musicians, and dancers. But as Portuguese ships sailing the West African coast brought an increasing number of Africans, a new and more ominous role for blacks in Europe emerged—as slaves. In 1444, the first sizable shipment arrived in Lisbon.

By the late 1400s, thriving slave markets emerged in the ports of Portugal, Spain, France, and Italy, with a thousand Africans arriving annually in the Portuguese capital of Lisbon alone. A century later, black Africans represented roughly 10 percent of Lisbon's population. Even distant Great Britain had a population of some 15,000 Africans by 1600, around the time William Shakespeare created one of the most memorable African characters in English literature, *Othello*.

Ultimately, black slavery did not take root in Europe for a variety of reasons—religious, political, economic, even climatic. Traditionally, slavery was justified in medieval and Renaissance Europe on religious grounds. Enslaving Muslims and "heathens" was not only acceptable, it was considered a righteous crusade, according to a papal bull of 1452. The problem was that if a slave converted to Christianity, as many slaves did, he or she often gained freedom. Nor did slavery make economic sense in Europe. Slavery worked best on plantations in tropical lands where the workforce labored throughout the year. Most of Europe had neither the open space nor the warm climate for such a plantation regime.

In the end, however, slavery was doomed in Europe because it ran against political and historical trends. By the 1400s, slavery and similar forms of labor—such as serfdom—were fast disappearing across the face of western Europe. Peasants were gaining their freedom and a new economic and political system was emerging. An attempt to revive an archaic form of labor like slavery was economically counterproductive and politically explosive. And so it was never seriously tried.

Even as slavery was dying out in Europe, it was gaining a new and far more vigorous lease on life in those parts of the world coming under European hegemony—first the Atlantic Islands, and then the Americas. Madeira, an island 600 miles southwest of Portugal, and the Canary islands, 300 miles south of that,

Bartolomé de Las Casas
(Library of Congress)

were "discovered" by Portugal and Spain respectively in the 14th century, although both had probably been known to the Romans more than a millenium before. Their settlement in the following century set a pattern that would hold true for the conquest of the Americas as well. The Atlantic islands proved an ideal laboratory in which to establish what would become the trans-Atlantic slave trade.

SLAVERY IN THE SPANISH COLONIES

With rich soil and subtropical climates, Madeira and the Canary Islands were well suited for the growing of sugarcane, a crop originally from Southeast Asia and introduced to Europeans by the Arabs in the Middle Ages. By the early 1500s, the Spaniards had wiped out the indigenous people of the Canaries, the Guanche. They imported thousands of slaves from West Africa to work the sugarcane plantations. The Portuguese did the same in Madeira, except there were no indigenous people to exterminate. Both Madeira and the Canary Islands also served as important provisioning stops for exploratory voyages down the African coast and, after 1492, to the Americas. But significant as the islands were as a template for conquest and plantation agriculture, their output of sugar—and their plantations' needs for African slaves—soon paled beside that of the Caribbean islands and tropical Latin America.

Christopher Columbus's 1492 voyage to America introduced Europeans to a whole "new world" across the Atlantic.

In the century after Columbus, much of the Americas—including the Caribbean, Mexico, Central America, and large parts of South America—was utterly transformed by Europeans.

Between 1492 and the late 1700s, European explorers—who often traveled with multiethnic crews that included Africans—visited and charted every major landmass in the world, with the exception of Antarctica. Within the first 100 or so years after Columbus's voyage, Spanish and Portuguese explorers led expeditions to virtually all of the islands of the Caribbean, as well as the Central, South, and North American mainlands. Exploration of the Caribbean and the American mainland was followed by conquest and, for the original inhabitants of the Caribbean, death. Within 50 years after Columbus's first major landfall, the native Taino and Carib population on the island of Hispaniola (modern Dominican Republic and Haiti) had fallen to 200, from a precontact level of 250,000 to 500,000. In the rest of the Caribbean, the story was much the same. Some native peoples were killed by Spanish swords, muskets, and dogs; the vast majority, however, were felled by diseases such as smallpox and measles. On the American mainland, the numbers were even more appalling, with millions dying. Again, most succumbed to disease, though a significant minority were worked to death in mines or starved when their lands were taken to raise Spanish cattle. Horrified by the carnage he was witnessing, Spanish priest Bartolomé de Las Casas pleaded for mercy for his Indian charges. "For God's sake and man's faith in Him, is this the way to impose the yoke of Christ on Christian men?" he asked King Charles I. "They are our brothers."

Ultimately, the king agreed with Las Casas. But if not American Indians, then colonizers would need others to work the mines that fed the Spanish treasury and the ranches and farms that fed the miners. Las Casas suggested Africans, though he would later regret the idea and condemn African slavery as well. There was both precedence and practicality behind his suggestion. By the early 1500s, there were thousands of African slaves living in Spain and the Canary Islands. Moreover, Africans—living in roughly the same disease environment as

Azores, Madeira, and the Canary Islands

PORTUGAL

Azores

SPAIN

Madeira

Atlantic Ocean

Canary Islands

AFRICA

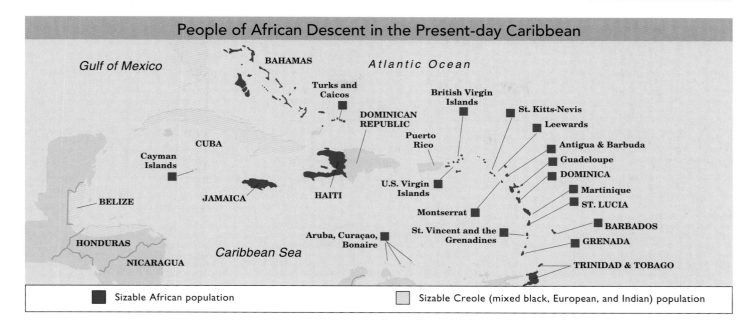

People of African Descent in the Present-day Caribbean

Gulf of Mexico

BAHAMAS

Atlantic Ocean

Turks and Caicos

British Virgin Islands

St. Kitts-Nevis

DOMINICAN REPUBLIC

Leewards

CUBA

Puerto Rico

Antigua & Barbuda

Cayman Islands

Guadeloupe

DOMINICA

HAITI

U.S. Virgin Islands

Martinique

BELIZE

JAMAICA

ST. LUCIA

Montserrat

BARBADOS

Aruba, Curaçao, Bonaire

St. Vincent and the Grenadines

GRENADA

HONDURAS

Caribbean Sea

NICARAGUA

TRINIDAD & TOBAGO

■ Sizable African population   □ Sizable Creole (mixed black, European, and Indian) population

Europeans—did not succumb as easily to pathogens carried by the Spaniards. Africans could and did convert to Christianity, especially after they arrived in the Americas. But the Europeans—desperate for slave labor—changed the rules, eliminating baptism or conversion as a justification for emancipation.

SLAVERY IN THE CARIBBEAN

Still, African slavery took root only on the periphery of the Spanish empire in the Americas. Despite the decimation of Native Americans, millions survived in Central and South America. (Because Spanish settlement in North America did not begin until the very end of the 16th century—and remained relatively sparse even as late as the the early 18th century—the scope of the threat from Spanish settlement was not as great for Native Americans in North America as it was for their counterparts in other parts of New Spain.) And while formal Indian slavery was banned after 1542, other forms of coerced labor—such as the encomienda system—assured a steady supply of Indian muscle for Spanish mines and ranches during the 16th and 17th centuries. Equally important, the Spanish—more interested in plundering American gold and silver than settling there—were slow to make the kinds of investments that would assure new sources of wealth, like plantation agricul-

ture. It would take the more enterprising and emigration-oriented countries of northern Europe to realize that wealth and economic development could be realized through new products, new markets, and new sources of labor. During the 1500s and 1600s, the Dutch, the English, and the French came to supplant the Spanish in much of the Caribbean and the southern part of the North American mainland, turning these tropical and subtropical lands into vast areas of plantations worked largely by African slaves growing crops for a mass European market.

The profits from plantation economy could be quite substantial, as the ledger of one Jamaican sugar grower makes clear. Investing some £41,480 in land, buildings, and stock—including 250 African slaves at an average £70 each—Bryan Edwards was able to realize an annual net profit of £2,990 (or roughly $750,000 in current U.S. dollars), for a profit percentage of more than 7 percent. While some planters complained that this profit margin was far too low, some sources suggest that many planters did far better than Edwards—often netting as much as a 21 percent profit. Moreover, unlike Spanish wealth in gold and silver, plantation profits were self-sustaining, although subject to world price fluctuations. In addition, slavery offered profits in two ways—the trade in products realized by slave labor and the profits realized in the slave trade itself.

THE BUSINESS OF SLAVERY:
A CARIBBEAN PLANTER'S LEDGER

Caribbean planters often complained about what they considered the high costs and thin profit margins of the slave economy. In 1793, Bryan Edwards, an English planter on Jamaica, published this ledger sheet, showing a profit of 7 percent on an initial investment of over 41 thousand pounds in English currency. Whether that rate of return gave Edwards cause for complaint is a subjective question. However, it should be noted that other sources have put typical profits at a rate three times that level. According to one source, Jamaican planters reaped a 21 percent annual profit between 1687 and 1787. At any rate, the human cost of this equation was left out entirely. Note the manner in which "250 Negroes" were listed no differently than mules or steers.

Ledger Sheet
INITIAL INVESTMENT

Lands		£ 14,100
Buildings		£ 7,000
Stock		
250 Negroes @ £70 ea	£ 17,500	
80 steers @ £15	£ 1,200	
60 mules @ £28	£ 1,680	
Total in Stock		£ 20,380
TOTAL INITIAL INVESTMENT		£ 41,480
		(Jamaican currency)

INCOME FROM CROPS

200 Hogshead of sugar, @ £15 sterling	£ 3,000	(sterling per hogshead)
130 Puncheons of rum @ £10 sterling	£ 1,300	(sterling)
GROSS RETURN FROM CROPS	£ 4,300	(sterling)
GROSS RETURN FROM CROPS	£ 6,020	(Jamaican currency)

PLANTATION EXPENSES

ANNUAL SUPPLIES (Imported from Great Britain and Ireland)
(Estimates not available for each item)
Negro Clothing
1,500 yards of Osnaburgh cloth or German linen
650 yards of blue bays, or pennistones, for a warm frock for each negro
350 yards of striped linseys for the women
250 yards of coarse check for shirts for the boilers, tradesmen, domestics, and the children
3 dozen coarse blankets for lying-in women and sick negroes
18 dozen coarse hats

Tools
For the carpenters and coopers, to the amount of £ 25 sterling, including 2 or three dozen falling axes.

Miscellaneous

COST OF IMPORTED SUPPLIES	£ 850	(sterling)
COST OF IMPORTED SUPPLIES	£ 1,190	(Jamaican currency)

ANNUAL EXPENSES (Not imported)
(Jamaican currency)

Overseer's or manager's salary	£ 200
Distiller's salary	£ 70
Two other white servants, £60 each	£ 120
A white carpenter's wages	£ 100
Maintenance of 5 white servants, £40 each exclusive of their allowance of salted provisions	£ 200
Medical care of the negroes (at 6 s per annum for each negro and extra cases, paid for separately)	£ 100
Millright's, coppersmith's, plumber's, and smith's bills, annually	£ 250
Colonial taxes, public and parochial	£ 200
Annual supply of mules and steers	£ 300
Wharfage and storeage of goods land and shipped	£ 100
American staves and heading, for hogsheads and puncheons	£ 150
A supply of small occasional supplies of different kinds, supposed	£ 50
COST OF NON-IMPORTED SUPPLIES (Jamaican currency)	£ 1,840
GRAND TOTAL OF ANNUAL EXPENSES (Jamaican currency)	£ 3,030
GROSS RETURN FROM CROPS (Jamaican currency)	£ 6,020
GRAND TOTAL OF ANNUAL EXPENSES (Jamaican currency)	£ 3,030
PROFIT (Jamaican currency)	£ 2,990
PROFIT PERCENTAGE	7.2 %

Source: History, Civil and Commercial of the British Colonies in the West Indies

THE TRAVELS OF ESTÉBAN DORANTES

Estéban Dorantes, second from left in this modern depiction of the journey of Cabeza de Vaca, who is seen in the foreground, to the right of Estéban. (National Park Service)

Among the most remarkable stories of early European exploration took place in what is now the American Southwest. It was led by a Spanish-speaking African slave named Estéban Dorantes. Born in Morocco, Estéban Dorantes had first come to the Americas in 1527 as a member of an expedition led by Pánfilo de Narváez, the newly commissioned Spanish governor of Florida. Landing near what is now Sarasota, Florida, the 500-man expedition wandered through what is now the southeastern United States and northern Mexico. Poorly managed and struck down by disease, the crew was eventually reduced to four men, who survived by convincing local people that they were healers and shamans. According to Álvar Núñez Cabeza de Vaca, the surviving leader, Estéban "was our go-between; he informed himself about the ways we wished to take, what towns there were, and the matters we desired to know." Eight years after setting out, Estéban and his three companions reached a Spanish outpost in Mexico.

Three years later, Estéban became the logical choice for guide of an expedition to the American Southwest launched in search of Cibola, or El Dorado, the legendary "seven cities of gold." To mark his progress, Estéban was told to send back crosses to the Mexican governor. For a time, they arrived, each larger than the last, along with stories of hundreds of Indian followers showering Estéban in jewels and gold. Then the crosses stopped coming; Estéban had disappeared, fate unknown. Some say Estéban lived on, shedding his slave status for that of American Indian shaman. But a legend among the Zuni—a people living in the region Estéban explored—say the "black Mexican" was killed by one of their own in about 1539.

THE TRIANGLE AND RECTANGLE TRADES

The transatlantic triangle slave trade began with the Portuguese and Spanish in the 1400s, and was greatly expanded by Dutch, English, and French slavers in the 1600s and 1700s. North American—and, after 1776, U.S.—slavers were also active, particularly toward the end of the 18th century. In the early 19th century, first England, then the United States, France, and other powers outlawed the trade. But with slavery legal in the British Empire (until 1833), French overseas holdings (until 1848), the United States (until 1865), Brazil (until 1888), and the Spanish Caribbean islands (Cuba and Puerto Rico, until the 1880s), the smuggling of Africans remained big business through much of the 19th century.

A great debate has emerged about the number of Africans transported across the Atlantic as slaves. Most scholars estimate the figure at roughly 9 to 12 million, with about 50,000 coming in the 15th century, 300,000 in the 16th, 1.5 million in the 17th, 5.8 million in the 18th, and 2.4 million in the 19th (despite international sanctions against the slave trade). About 40 percent during the entire period came from the coasts of West Central Africa (modern-day Angola, Congo, Gabon), another 35 percent from the Bights of Benin and Biafra (Cameroon and Nigeria), 10 percent from the Gold Coast (Ghana), 5 percent from the Windward Coast (Ivory Coast, Liberia, Sierra Leone), 5 percent from Senegambia (Gambia, Guinea, Senegal) and 5 percent from southeastern Africa (Mozambique, Tanzania).

Over the centuries, the source of slaves changed. During the early years of the trade—through 1600—90 percent came from the West Central African coast. That declined to 55 percent in the 1600s and 37 percent in the 1700s, only to climb back to 48 percent in the 19th century. Meanwhile, the percentage coming from the Bights of Benin and Biafra stayed at roughly 35 percent from 1600 to 1800, dropping off in the 19th century to just about 25 percent. Southeast Africa saw its proportion rise from 1 percent in the 1600s to roughly 15 percent by the 1800s, although many of the slaves taken

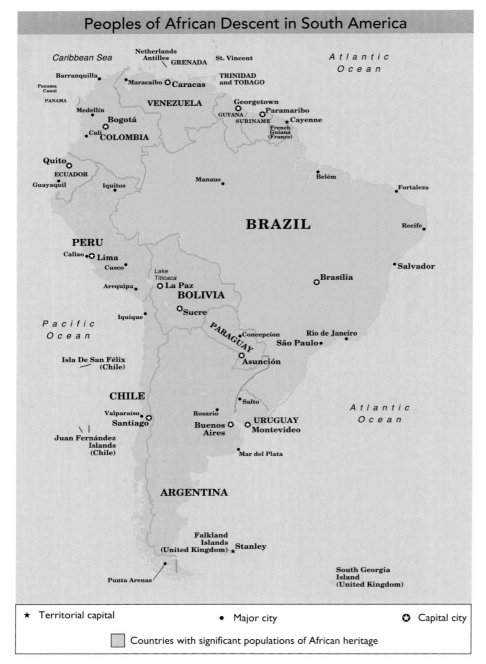

Peoples of African Descent in South America

Caribbean Sea
Netherlands Antilles
GRENADA
St. Vincent
Atlantic Ocean
Barranquilla
Maracaibo
Caracas
TRINIDAD and TOBAGO
Panama Canal
PANAMA
VENEZUELA
Georgetown
Medellín
GUYANA
Paramaribo
Bogotá
SURINAME
Cayenne
Cali
COLOMBIA
French Guiana (France)
Quito
ECUADOR
Guayaquil
Iquitos
Manaus
Belém
Fortaleza
BRAZIL
Recife
PERU
Callao
Lima
Cusco
Salvador
Lake Titicaca
La Paz
Brasília
Arequipa
BOLIVIA
Sucre
Iquique
PARAGUAY
Concepción
Rio de Janeiro
São Paulo
Pacific Ocean
Asunción
Isla De San Félix (Chile)
CHILE
Salto
Atlantic Ocean
Valparaíso
Rosario
Santiago
Buenos Aires
URUGUAY
Montevideo
Juan Fernández Islands (Chile)
Mar del Plata
ARGENTINA
Falkland Islands (United Kingdom)
Stanley
South Georgia Island (United Kingdom)
Punta Arenas

★ Territorial capital   ● Major city   ✪ Capital city

Countries with significant populations of African heritage

The map above, illustrating which present-day South American nations have the highest concentrations of peoples of African descent, documents the ethnographic impact of the African slave trade on South America.

from this region ended up on the French sugar islands of the Indian Ocean rather than in the Americas.

Africans were settled across the length and breadth of North, Central, and South America and the Caribbean. Overall, about 40 percent (or 4 million) of all enslaved Africans were sent to the Portuguese colony of Brazil. The next most common destinations were the British holdings in the Caribbean, with about 20 percent of all slaves (or 2 mil-

lion). Spanish American colonies on the mainland and in the Caribbean took about 17.5 percent (or 1,750,000), French holdings in the Caribbean (mostly Saint-Domingue, modern Haiti) took in 13.5 percent (or 1,350,000), and the tiny Dutch and Danish Caribbean islands received about 2.5 percent (or 250,000). Finally, British North America and (after independence) the United States, took in 650,000 slaves, or 6.5 percent of the total.

SLAVERY IN SOUTH AMERICA

As with the source of slaves, the destinations changed over time, depending on economic and political developments in the Americas. For example, in the early years of the slave trade, fully 75 percent of all enslaved Africans ended up in the Spanish colonies, a figure that declined to 35 percent in the 1600s, and 20 percent in the 1700s, only to climb to 30 percent with the growth of the sugar industry in Cuba and Puerto Rico in the 19th century. Maintaining its slave system well into the late 1800s meant that Brazil's percentage of slave arrivals reached some 65 percent of the total in that century. As for the British mainland colonies and the United States, they never reached 10 percent of the total in any century, peaking at some 9 percent in the 1700s.

THE MIDDLE PASSAGE

In the context of the transatlantic trading system, the shipment of slaves from Africa to the Americas represented what was known as the Middle Passage, one leg of a triangular trade that saw European manufactures transported to Africa, where they were exchanged for slaves, and American plantation crops carried to Europe. (In reality, the system was far more complex, with ships traveling to and from many different ports in many different lands and with all kinds of goods.) At the height of the trade in the 1700s, an adult male slave could be purchased at a slave-trading post on the African coast such as Goree Island off French Senegal; Bonny, off British Nigeria; or Benguela, off Portuguese Angola, where hundreds or even thousands of captured Africans were kept in holding pens called barracoons. While a

The Triangle and Rectangle Trades

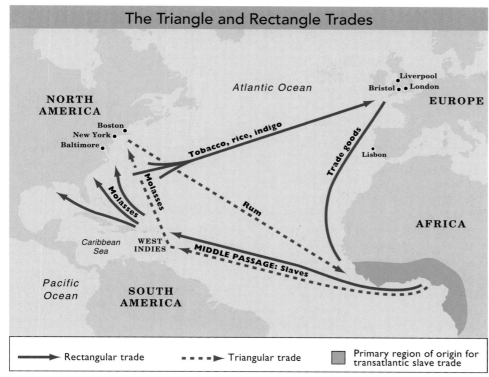

The term triangle trade *has often been used to describe the trade routes used during the years of the transatlantic slave trade. African slaves would be traded in the Caribbean for molasses, which would then be sent to North America, where it would be used to produce rum, which in turn would then be traded in Africa for more slaves. Historians have also begun referring to the* rectangle trade, *in which North American agricultural products such as tobacco, rice, and indigo were sent to Great Britain, which in turn would send trade goods to Africa in exchange for slaves, thus adding another leg to the trade cycle.*

slave ship merchant might pay about 12 ounces in gold for a slave in Africa, Africans sold for several times that amount in an American port. Therefore, with ships carrying anywhere from a few dozen to more than 100 slaves, the human cargo on a larger ship could equal more than a million dollars in today's money.

Slave ships ranged in size from small sloops to ships weighing several hundred tons, the latter with extensive crews that included doctors, carpenters, and other skilled workers, as well as sailors. Upon arriving on the African coast, ship captains would have to pay a variety of fees to local rulers, merchants, and pilots, the latter to guide them over the numerous sandbars. While some crewmen gathered provisions, the captain and his guards went ashore to purchase slaves, kept in densely crowded cells in coastal barracoons.

The enslaved Africans there, meanwhile, had already undergone a terrible ordeal, for the process of enslavement was both capricious and brutal. Some were captured in raids by neighboring tribes;

others were kidnapped by slave-hunting bandits; some were sold into slavery by their own chiefs. Captured, they were roped or shackled together and marched to the coast, sometimes across hundreds of miles of scorching tropical grassland and dank and muddy rain forest. Poorly fed and barely clothed, many grew weak and sick. But the pace remained relentless, as the raiders were eager to deliver their human cargo to the Europeans on the coast. If a prisoner faltered, he or she was beaten and forced to move on. If captives proved physically unable to continue, they were left by the side of the trail to die.

At the oceanside slave fort, the misery continued. In the hot and humid climate of the West African coast—a climate unfamiliar and uncomfortable to the many Africans coming from the drier interior—the slaves remained in their barracoons even after they were purchased. This was because the slave ships that would take them across the Atlantic often lay at anchor for weeks and months waiting for a full cargo.

Olaudah Equiano (Library of Congress)

Conditions aboard ranged from the awful to the horrendous, depending on the attitude of the captain, the company he worked for, the quality of the ship, and the length of the voyage. Some slavers believed in tight-packing, cramming as many slaves into the hot and unsanitary holds as possible, while others were loose packers. The former, of course, meant more cargo, but also more loss of lives and potential profits. Death rates for slaves in the Middle Passage therefore ranged greatly between voyages, but they averaged about 15 to 20 percent in the first couple of centuries of the trade, dropping off to about 5 to 10 percent in the latter years. (Nor was the crew much better off, suffering similar mortality rates on the voyage from diseases picked up on shore or from the slaves themselves.)

While these numbers explain deadliness of the business, it requires the words of participants to convey the true horrors of the Middle Passage. "I was soon put down under the decks, and there I received such a salutation in my nostrils as I had never experienced in my life: so that with the loathsomeness of the stench and crying together, I became so sick and low that I was not able to eat," wrote Olaudah Equiano, an African enslaved near the Bight of Benin in the 1750s. He continued, "I now wished for death to

relieve me." Not surprisingly, during this loading period—as during the transatlantic trip itself—the crew had to remain ever vigilant. Escapes, rebellions, and suicides were common occurrences throughout the process, but particularly so in the first few weeks. Indeed, crews let the slaves out of the holds for only a few brief moments while the ship was still in sight of land, and sometimes confined them to the hold for the entire voyage.

To keep their human cargo alive on the voyage, the crews sometimes forced food on them. The provisions—usually little more than a mealy porridge and perhaps some fish heads for protein—were unfamiliar to the Africans. Moreover, in the tropical climate, it often became rotten and bug-infested, leading to stomach illness, diarrhea, and vomiting, which further polluted the crowded holds in which they were kept. Alexander Falconbridge, a doctor who served aboard British slave ships in the 1770s and 1780s, described conditions thus:

> *Upon the Negroes refusing to take sustenance, I have seen coals of fire, glowing hot, put [on] a shovel, and placed so near their lips, as to scorch and burn them. Exercise being deemed necessary . . . they are sometimes*

Slave traders inspect captured Africans. (Library of Congress)

obliged to dance. . . . If they go about it reluctantly, or do not move with agility, they are flogged. . . . The poor wretches are frequently compelled to sing also; but when they do so, their songs are generally, as may naturally be expected, melancholy lamentations of their exile from their native country.

After a voyage that could take several weeks or many months, the vessel arrived in port, usually on one of the Caribbean islands or in Brazil. Slaves were then prepared for sale by being given plentiful fresh water and local produce and meats, so as to make them appear healthier and hence more valuable. Depending on the facilities available, the slaves would either be herded ashore or local slave traders would come on board to examine the merchandise. The first to go were the youngest and strongest, with the sick and the old being sold to the poorest colonists. It was, recounts Equiano, yet another terrifying episode in a saga of fear and suffering. "Without scruple," he later wrote, "are relations and friends separated, most of them never to see each other again."

THE CARIBBEAN PLANTATION SYSTEM

Africans came to be the labor of choice for the grueling work on the sugar plantations of the Caribbean, particularly after the Dutch, English, and French secured Hispaniola (Saint-Domingue, later Haiti),

Jamaica, and most of the Lesser Antilles in the 1600s. (The Dominican Republic on the eastern two thirds of Hispaniola was politically and economically linked to Saint-Domingue or Haiti almost continuously through 1844.)

Barbados, the first Caribbean island extensively settled by the British, offered a model for African life and labor in much of the English-speaking Caribbean. Conquered by the Spanish—who killed or drove away the entire native population of Carib in the 16th century—Barbados was first encountered by the English in 1625. Two years later, a ship carrying 80 British colonists and 10 African slaves arrived. Laboring on small tobacco and cotton farms, much of the population consisted of white indentured servants until the 1640s, when sugar cultivation was introduced from Brazil by Dutch traders.

Involving grueling work and large-scale capital investment for refining equipment, sugar cultivation soon displaced cotton and tobacco, even as plantations took over farms and African slave labor replaced independent white farmers and servants. In 1645, Barbados counted just under 6,000 slaves; by 1685, there were ten times that number; and by the end of the century, some 135,000. In the process, the vast majority of whites—some 30,000—fled to other Caribbean islands, England, or the British colonies in North America, particularly South Carolina. Thus, like much of the Caribbean but unlike mainland North American colonies, Barbados became predominantly black. More than 90 percent of its population was of African descent by the end of the 1700s.

Captured Africans in the hold of a slave ship (Library of Congress)

SOCIAL CONDITIONS IN THE CARIBBEAN

Another factor differentiated Barbados and other Caribbean islands from the mainland of North America—a constant influx of new African slaves, until the outlawing of the slave trade in the early 1800s. While it might seem pointless to discuss the relative merits of slavery in one place or another, it was less fatal on the North American mainland. This was mostly due to two interrelated reasons. First, North American slaves ate better. For example, while mainland slaves enjoyed diets with ample vitamins and minerals, it is estimated that Caribbean slaves received only 90 percent of their vitamin A needs, less than 50 percent of their calcium needs, and only a third of the vitamin C they required. Second, the more poorly fed Caribbean slaves were more likely to succumb to disease. Nearly 40 percent of Jamaican slaves were listed as dying from fevers, compared to just 11 percent of Virginia slaves. At the same time, twice as many slaves in Virginia—albeit a still miniscule 7.3 percent—died of old age.

This difference was due more to economic calculation than the relative kindness of the mainland master class. On tiny Caribbean islands, most of the land was devoted to sugar, forcing planters to resort to costly imported foodstuffs, which they rationed out parsimoniously. Plentiful land in North America allowed planters and farmers to raise both commercial and food crops. Moreover, mainland planters soon came to the realization that healthy slaves worked harder, had more babies, and did not need to be replaced. Thus, by the early 1700s, the North American slave population had reached a point where it could sustain growth without further imports while the English-speaking Caribbean islands required slave imports right up until abolition in 1833 to sustain their populations. (It should be noted that sugar cultivation in a tropical climate is far more grueling than tobacco or cotton farming in a temperate climate.)

Quality of life issues go beyond nutrition, disease, and work. Because of the high proportion of Africans in the population and the constant influx of new Africans, Caribbean blacks were able to retain more of their culture, especially in terms of language, religion, and social customs. Even today, Caribbean blacks are more likely than their North American counterparts to practice a faith that blends Christianity with traditional African religions, and their English is laced with more Africanisms. Moreover, their demographic dominance also gave birth to a fuller history of rebellion and resistance, especially on the largest of the English-speaking Caribbean islands, Jamaica.

Encountered by Columbus on his second voyage to the Americas in 1494, Jamaica saw virtually its entire indigenous population of Taino wiped out by infection, overwork, and murder within a few decades. First settled in 1506, Jamaica developed slowly under the Spanish, with only about 1,000 white and black inhabitants in 1655 when it was conquered by the British, who quickly took advantage of its tropical climate and, for the Caribbean, abundant land. Soon, more than 100,000 African slaves—along with 10,000 European masters, overseers, and skilled workers—were working in gangs producing the largest sugar crop in the English Caribbean.

The European colonies in the Caribbean were usually the first stop for enslaved Africans that eventually came to North America. Jamaica and Saint-Domingue in particular had large slave populations. Slaves would often be "seasoned" in the Caribbean sugar fields before being resold to North American planters. (Corbis)

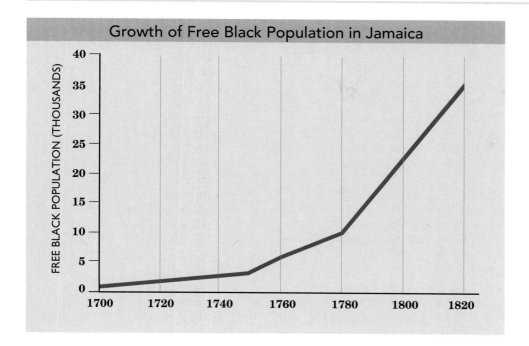

Growth of Free Black Population in Jamaica

FREE BLACK POPULATION (THOUSANDS)

THE MAROONS

While Jamaica's abundant land produced abundant sugar, it also offered opportunity for runaway and rebellious slaves. From the late 1600s onward, Jamaican runaway slaves established numerous independent settlements in the mountainous interior, where they effectively fought off British soldiers and Mosquito Indian troops, recruited by the English from Central America. Known as maroons (from the Spanish *cimarrones*, or runaway cattle), they numbered nearly 40,000 by the time slavery was prohibited in 1833.

The first maroons, known as *libertos* (Spanish for liberated ones), emerged in 1655 when their Spanish masters freed them as the English captured the island. British forces tried to recapture them but the maroons' growing familiarity with the nearly impenetrable interior frustrated their efforts. In the 1680s, a guerrilla war broke out between the maroons and the British. Led by such legendary fighters as Accompong, Quao, and Nanny, the maroons held out for some 50 years.

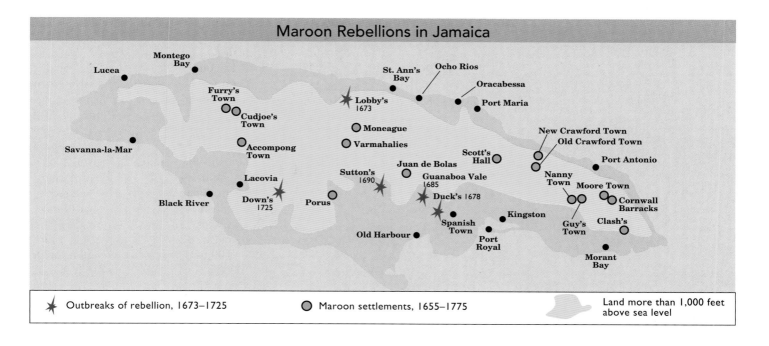

Maroon Rebellions in Jamaica

Lucea · Montego Bay · St. Ann's Bay · Ocho Rios · Oracabessa · Furry's Town · Lobby's 1673 · Port Maria · Cudjoe's Town · Moneague · New Crawford Town · Old Crawford Town · Savanna-la-Mar · Accompong Town · Varmahalies · Scott's Hall · Port Antonio · Lacovia · Sutton's 1690 · Juan de Bolas · Guanaboa Vale 1685 · Nanny Town · Moore Town · Black River · Down's 1725 · Porus · Duck's 1678 · Cornwall Barracks · Old Harbour · Spanish Town · Kingston · Guy's Town · Clash's · Port Royal · Morant Bay

✴ Outbreaks of rebellion, 1673–1725   ⬤ Maroon settlements, 1655–1775   Land more than 1,000 feet above sea level

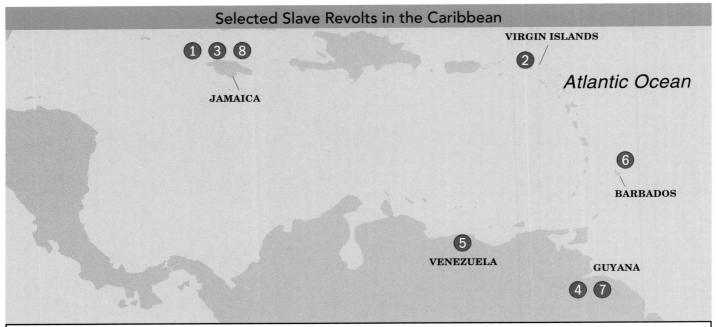

Selected Slave Revolts in the Caribbean

1 **1663** The first serious slave revolt in Jamaica takes place. It involves 400 slaves.

2 **1733** At least 150 slaves are implicated in a slave revolt on St. John in the Danish West Indies.

3 **1760** On Jamaica, an uprising known as Tacky's rebellion involves about 1,000 slaves.

4 **ca. 1763** Two thousand slaves revolt in Berbice, Guyana, and kill 200 of the settlement's 350 whites.

5 **1795** Three hundred slaves rise up at Coro, Venezeuela.

6 **1816** On Easter Sunday, slaves on approximately 60 plantations rise up on Barbados.

7 **1823** Between 10,000 and 20,000 slaves on 50 plantations revolt in Demerara, Guyana.

8 **1831** The Christmas Uprising of 1831, a revolt by 20,000 slaves, takes place in Jamaica. The revolt leads to the end of slavery in the British Caribbean.

In 1739, however, maroon leaders signed a controversial treaty with the British. While granted their freedom, the maroons agreed to stop raiding European plantations, stop protecting runaways, and assist the British in quelling slave insurrections. The treaty preserved the maroon communities, but at the cost of dividing them from the much larger slave population. Still, after the 1833 declaration of emancipation in the British Empire, many former slaves migrated to the maroon communities, rather than work as wage laborers on the European-owned sugar plantations of the lowlands.

The Haitian Rebellion

Impressive as the Jamaican maroon experience was, it did not end European rule or the plantation system. As is discussed later in this chapter, the United States would become the first nation in the Americas to free itself from European colonialism when it won independence from Britain in

the Revolutionary War of 1775–1783. That victory, however, did not end the plantation system. That would not be achieved anywhere in the Americas until the start of the 19th century—not in the United States, but on a Caribbean island 120 miles to Jamaica's east.

Unlike Jamaica, Hispaniola was heavily settled by the Spanish, who established their first city in the Americas at Santo Domingo. Indeed, through Santo Domingo came the first African slaves to the New World. With virtually the entire native population wiped out in the first 50 years of Spanish conquest, Hispaniola supported a population of 6,000 Europeans and 30,000 Africans by the 1540s. The vast majority lived on the eastern two thirds of the island (modern-day Dominican Republic), leaving the western third (Haiti) largely uninhabited. In 1697, France began settling in Haiti. Over the next century, France turned Saint-Domingue, as they called it, into the "pearl of the Antilles," producing fully 60 percent of the world's coffee and 40 per-

The Haitian Rebellion

Campaigns

Battles

Present-day boundaries

Cap Français

Le Cap
1791

Bois Caiman
1791

1791

Ennery
1792

Gonaives
1804

SAINT-DOMINGUE (HAITI)

Ravines à Couleuves
1802

Fort Bedurete
1802

Crete-à-Pierrot
1802

Croix des Bouques
1791

Port-au-Prince
1791

SANTO DOMINGO

Les Cayes

cent of its sugar. At the same time, the colony also developed a unique racial system, where some 25,000 mixed-race mulattos, or *gens de couleur*, lived amongst 30,000 Europeans and 450,000 African slaves. The vast majority of the mulattos were free and, to the dismay of local whites, a growing number were becoming wealthy, slave-holding planters themselves.

By the 1780s, the Europeans had passed a series of laws banning these free people of color from possessing firearms and holding political office. In 1789, the growing resentment at these restrictions by the free people of color was fanned by the startling news from Paris: revolution had overthrown the ancien régime. Calls for freedom and citizenship by the free people of color were soon taken up by the African majority, leading to a slave insurrection in the north of the country in August 1791. Under the leadership of an ex-slave named François Dominique Toussaint Louverture, an army of freedpersons (ex-slaves) and free people of color had driven the French—and the

institution of slavery—from Saint-Domingue, now called Haiti (adapted from Ayti, the native Arawak word for the island). French efforts under Napoleon to retake the island—including the dispatch of thousands of troops—failed in the face of black resistance and tropical disease. Under Jean-Jacques Dessalines, an ex-slave who replaced Toussaint Louverture, after the latter's surrender to and imprisonment in France, Haiti became the second independent nation in the Americas, after the United States, and the world's first black republic.

As will be seen in chapter 3, the black revolution in Haiti spread fear through the corridors of power in Washington and Paris. In 1793, Congress passed the first fugitive slave law, allowing owners to reclaim escaped slaves who had crossed state lines. A decade later, a humbled Napoleon decided to sell France's largest American possession—popularly called the Louisiana Purchase—to the United States. For Haiti itself, the revolution proved a mixed blessing. Dessalines was

François Dominique Toussaint Louverture (Library of Congress)

Blacks in Haiti (formerly the French colony of Saint-Domingue) take their revenge on captured French officers during the Haitian Revolution. Illustrations such as this one, which first appeared in the 1805 publication "An Historical Account of the Black Empire of Hayti," struck fear among white plantation owners in the American South. (Library of Congress)

assassinated just two years after independence and was replaced by Henry Christophe, a paranoid dictator who nearly bankrupted the country by building huge forts and castles for protection against French forces that never came. The tensions between the free people of color and pure Africans intensified over the years, leading to numerous coups, U.S. military invasions, political repression, and economic stagnation, which have continued to this day.

Far to Haiti's south was Brazil, a country now home to the largest black population in the world outside of Africa. Claimed and settled by the Portuguese in the 1500s, Brazil became a major sugar producer and, as noted earlier, the largest recipient of slaves from 1600 through the end of the transatlantic trade in the late 1800s, 3.75 million Africans in all. Unlike its Spanish colonial neighbors, Brazil achieved independence peacefully, in 1821. At the same time, slavery lin-

gered on far longer in Brazil than anywhere else in South America, and was finally prohibited in 1888.

Many scholars have compared Brazilian to North American slavery favorably, pointing out the tradition of social intermingling and even intermarriage between slaves and masters and the protections offered slaves by the powerful Catholic Church, which sanctified slave marriages, making it illegal for masters to separate husband and wife. Moreover, the continuous arrival of large numbers of Africans assured a cultural continuity to the old country that can be seen in Brazilian music, religion, and such traditions as *capoeira*, a martial art and dance with African roots. (Originally, *capoeira* was a form of self-defense and combat that employed swift and subtle physical movement to compensate for the slaveowners' edge in weaponry.) Still, the reason so many Africans were imported into Brazil was that so many died from overwork, poor diet, and disease. Slaves in North America experienced fertility rates—a good measure of overall health—twice those of slaves in Brazil. And as for the claim that Brazil's milder forms of slavery led to a more racially tolerant country, the record is mixed. Brazilian blacks never suffered from the kinds of degrading segregation that North American blacks had to endure. At the same time, by virtually every measure of health, wealth, and education, Brazilians of African descent still lag significantly behind whites, who continue to control both the country's economy and government.

SLAVERY COMES TO NORTH AMERICA

In 1619, slaves—if not slavery itself—came to Jamestown, Virginia, Britain's first permanent colony on the North American mainland. As would become the pattern in British North America, the 20 or so slaves aboard the Dutch ship probably came from the Caribbean, and not directly from Africa. While they were quickly sold off to local tobacco farmers, it is not clear if Virginia's first Africans were slaves or servants. Nor is it clear that they inherited a status that condemned them and their offspring to perpetual servitude.

Jamestown was founded in 1607 by the Virginia Company, a business enterprise chartered by Britain's King James I to settle the Chesapeake Bay region, "propagate the Christian religion" among the "savages," and reap profits for the company's investors. The plan sounded good on paper, but it proved disastrous in execution. Expecting to find large Indian populations eager to be "civilized" and work for the English—or, at least, trade with them—the early settlers were entirely unprepared to do the hard work of carving farms out of forests. But the Indians had little gold or wealth to exchange, and absolutely no intention of serving these invading white men. When the malaria-ridden and starving English tried to raid Indian food stores, the latter fought back or moved away. Of the first 120 settlers who arrived, less than a third survived.

Still, the colony limped on, saved by a local Indian ruler named Powhatan who saw in the English a useful ally against his Native enemies. The great breakthrough, however, occurred in 1612 when Jamestown leader John Rolfe imported tobacco seeds from the West Indies. Smoked for centuries among the local tribes—and increasingly popular in England and Europe—tobacco grew extremely well in Virginia. By the end of the decade, plantations were being established up and down the rivers and estuaries around the Chesapeake, sparking conflicts with the Indians that culminated in major wars in 1622 and 1644. Because the Indians refused to be part of the British scheme, the planters needed to look elsewhere for labor. They first turned to their homeland, importing thousands of indentured servants who agreed to seven years' labor in exchange for their passage, some land, and the supplies needed to set up on their own at the end of their indenture. It was in this context that the first Africans arrived in a colony that had yet to draw up slave codes.

For the first 50 or so years, however, the African population in Virginia remained small. By 1670, they represented just 5 percent of the estimated 40,000 settlers in the colony. Slavery also came equally slowly to the colony, even though slave laws began to appear on the books by the 1640s. A simple calculation explains the reluctance. With most people dying within a few years of their arrival—often in their first year, the so-called sea-soning period—it made no sense to pay the higher initial cost of a slave. Two things, however, altered the calculation. First, as the colony became more firmly established, more settlers survived the "seasoning" and became independent farmers, or yeomen. Second, these yeomen—both white and black—were becoming increasingly discontented with their lot. Because the best land along the tidewater was already owned by planters, yeomen were forced to work for planters or stake out tobacco farms on the frontier, where they fought incessantly with Indians outraged at the Englishmen's greed for their land. Meanwhile, the colony's government—the House of Burgesses—was largely a tool of the planters and had little sympathy for the yeomen's demands of fairer taxes and more protection.

THE CODIFICATION OF SLAVERY

In 1676, the yeomen's anger boiled over. In an uprising known as Bacon's Rebellion after its ringleader, Nathaniel Bacon, a former aristocrat who sided with the poor farmers, the yeomen turned on the Indians first. But when the Natives proved elusive, the rebels turned on the planters and would have driven the latter into the sea but for the fortuitous arrival of an English warship and the death of Bacon himself. Among the last to surrender was a mixed regiment of black and white yeomen.

Victorious, the planters and burgesses were also wiser for the near-death experience. Indentured servants became yeomen and yeomen insisted on their rights as Englishmen, even if some of them were African. Slaves could make no such claims. But—for both cultural and legal reasons—it was not possible to enslave Englishmen. Borrowing a page from the English colony of Barbados, the Virginia planters turned to Africans. But instead of going to Africa for their laborers, the tobacco farmers went to the Caribbean, importing slaves who had already been "seasoned" to plantation agriculture. By 1700, the population of Africans in Virginia—the vast majority enslaved—had multiplied tenfold to 20,000. Over the course of the next 50 years, no less than 100,000 slaves would be imported into the Chesapeake region.

The first Africans in North America, at Jamestown, in 1619 (Library of Congress)

Changes in labor reflected—and drove—changes in the law. In the 1660s and 1670s, a series of new statutes discriminated on the basis of race and turned informal slavery into an institution. For example, white servants who ran away were punished with added years tacked onto their indentureship, while black runaways received a life sentence. In the wake of Bacon's Rebellion, whites were placed in jail; blacks received corporal punishment—the thinking being that only physical pain would teach them a lesson. Most crucial were a series of laws passed between 1667 and 1671 that said baptism and Christianity did not qualify African servants for eventual freedom. In 1692, marriage and sexual relations between whites and blacks were outlawed. Finally, in 1705, the burgesses ended all half measures by passing a law that read: "All servants imported or brought into this country by sea or land who were not Christians in their native country shall be accounted and be slaves."

There was both economic and racial reasoning behind these decisions. Not only did the laws assure a secure and docile labor force—and one that could be easily identified by skin color—it also made race, rather than class, the dividing line of Virginia politics. Even the poorest and most disenfranchised whites now had a stake in the existing order of things. They owned property—their white skin—and this fact would help ally them to their social and financial betters among the ruling planter class, even if their economic interests differed. The pattern set in Virginia would soon be adopted in all of the English colonies of North America. And with it, "black" and "African" became synonymous with "slave" and "inferior" in the eyes of white America for generations to come.

SLAVERY IN GEORGIA AND THE CAROLINAS

Aside from the Chesapeake region—which included parts of both Virginia and Maryland, a colony established in the 1630s for persecuted English Catholics—slavery's deepest roots developed in British North America along a stretch of coastline several hundred miles to the south in what is now the Carolinas and Georgia. Of these the colony of Carolina (which was located mostly in modern-day South Carolina) was the earliest to be founded and the most important. It was supposed to be different from the Chesapeake, based not on narrow commercial gain but political and social idealism—its first constitution was written by philosopher John Locke—where small land-holding farmers would govern themselves, enjoy a host of freedoms, and trade harmoniously with the Indians. To that end, land-hungry white settlers—already "seasoned" to life in the colonies—would be recruited from the British West Indies. At first, the plan seemed to work. Small farmers—generally older than settlers in the Chesapeake and with families in tow—poured in, mostly from Barbados. Lacking a commercial crop, most lived on small farms

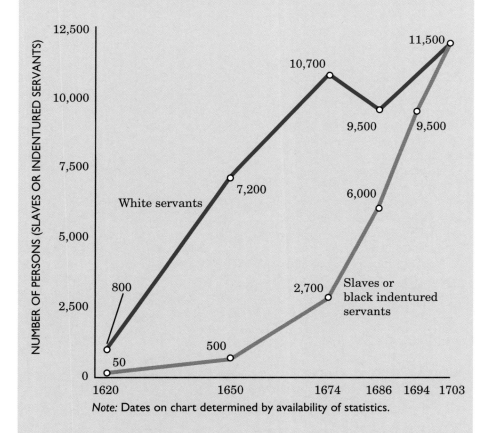

Slave Region of the Atlantic Coast

The number of African slaves in the Virginia colony during the 17th century rose rapidly, while the number of indentured servants declined before rising again at a slower rate, particularly after armed white servants and small farmers began a series of revolts, which culminated in Bacon's Rebellion in 1676.

Note: Dates on chart determined by availability of statistics.

Source: American Slavery, American Freedom: The Ordeal of Colonial Virginia near the coast, growing food for their own consumption.

Soon, however, things began to change. The younger sons of wealthy West Indian planters—short on land, but rich in slaves—settled the Carolina low country, taking control of millions of the best acres. They raised cattle and engaged in trade with the Indians (including enslaving Indians and selling them to the Caribbean), both only nominally profitable businesses. To escape the worst effects of the subtropical climate and diseases, many of the wealthier landowners settled in Charleston, which became the largest seaport south of the Chesapeake. Combined with the fact that cattle-raising on lands that were unfenced required slaves to roam far and wide, this urban-rural split produced a very different pattern of slave-master relations in Carolina, with slaves living and working separately from their owners and enjoying an unusual degree of cultural autonomy. This arrangement become even more entrenched once Carolina discovered a lucrative commercial crop.

Rice is not an easy crop to grow or process, even under ideal conditions like those in the wet and fertile lowlands of Carolina. Hydraulic systems had to be created to periodically flood the fields; large numbers of workers were necessary to separate the tough outer husk from the edible grain within. The English knew nothing of rice farming because the plant cannot be grown in such a cool climate. And white settlers' first efforts to grow rice in Carolina failed dismally. But West Africans were accomplished rice farmers—particularly those from the Windward Coast (modern-day Sierra Leone and Liberia), where a bag of rice remains an alternate unit of currency. They brought the rice-growing skills and technology to the Carolina coast, which led to enormous wealth for the planter class that exploited their knowledge and labor. Beginning in the 1680s, rice exports rose from almost none to 17 million pounds in 1730 and 75 million pounds by the American Revolution, not including millions more that were consumed locally.

The slave population of the colony grew in stride from a few thousand at the beginning of the 18th century to nearly 40,000 seventy years later. By the eve of the American Revolution, there were two blacks for every white in South Carolina.

Because whites dreaded the malarial rice-growing districts and avoided it much of the year, the African population was left pretty much to its own devices. Slaves—under sporadic white supervision—were organized into teams who were required to produce a certain quantity of the grain each year. As with earlier cattle herding—but on a far vaster scale—rice planting produced a more autonomous black culture than that in the Chesapeake. This development was most notable for the rise of the Gullah community and its language, a hybrid of English and various African dialects unique to the region. (The Gullah language is fast disappearing as the Carolina coast and Sea Islands have shifted to an economy based on the tourism and retirement industries.)

The work environment and the climate put enormous strain on the African slaves, however. The hot and humid climate was often brutal in the growing season. Malaria and other diseases were rampant in the swamps. Slaves saw little of the wealth that their labor generated and enjoyed even fewer material comforts than their counterparts in the Chesapeake.

Moreover, the fact that South Carolina remained a majority black and slave colony (and later, state) made whites particularly edgy. The laws they enacted, such as this 1712 slave code, reflected a virulent kind of racism:

Whereas, the plantations and estates of this province cannot be well and sufficiently managed

SLAVERY IN EARLY VIRGINIA

1607 Jamestown is founded.

1617 Tobacco is planted for the first time.

1619 First shipment of Africans arrives in the colony.

1623 William Tucker, born in Jamestown, becomes the first black child born in the English colonies.

1639 The Virginia legislature enacts a law that provides arms and ammunition to all colonists except blacks.

1642 Virginia passes a fugitive slave law to penalize those who help slaves escape.

1649 The Virginia colony's black population reaches 300.

1657 A Virginia law establishes a colonial militia to track down runaway servants.

1658 To encourage slave trade, Virginia lowers import duties for merchants who carry slaves into the colony.

1661 The Virginia legislature legally recognizes slavery.

THE LEGAL FOUNDATIONS OF SLAVERY

While slavery did not officially begin in the Chesapeake Valley until the latter half of the 17th century, the region's courts distinguished between white and black indentured servants from the beginning. This chart of court cases illustrates the different punishments held for whites and blacks.

YEAR	CRIME COMMITTED	OFFENDER	PUNISHMENT
1630	Sleeping with a black maidservant	White servant	Whipped for "defiling his body by lying with a Negro"
1640	Conspiracy to escape	Four white servants and one black servant	White servants are sentenced to extra service; black servant is whipped, branded, and required to wear shackles for a year
1641	Running away	Two white servants, and John Punch, a black servant	An extra year of service for the whites, lifetime servitude for Punch
1661	Running away in the company of slaves	White servant	2 years of extra service
1660s	Maidservant becomes pregnant	White servant	2 years of extra service
1660s	Stealing a hog	White servant	1,000 pounds of tobacco or a year's extra service
1660s	22 days absent	White servant	3 months of extra service and the loss of one year's crop
1669	Disobeying the master	Black slave	Toes cut off
1707	Killing a slave	White master	No penalty

and brought into use, without the labor and service of negroes and other slaves; and forasmuch as the said negroes and other slaves brought into the people of this Province for that purpose, are of barbarous, wild, savage natures, and such as renders them wholly unqualified to be governed by the laws, customs, and practices of this Province; but that it is absolutely necessary, that such other constitutions, laws, and orders, should in this Province be made and enacted, for the good regulating and ordering of them, as may restrain the disorders, rapines and inhumanity, to which they are naturally prone and inclined, and may also tend to the safety and security of the people of this Province and their estates; to which purpose, be it therefore enacted . . . that all negroes, mulattoes, mestizoes [mixed white and Indian], or Indians, which at any time heretofore have been sold, or now are held or taken to be, or hereafter shall be bought and sold for slaves, are hereby declared slaves; and they, and their children, are hereby made and declared slaves, to all intents and purposes. . . .

The citizens of South Carolina—and their Georgian neighbors to the south—had good reason to worry about the docility of the slave population. Situated near the edge of British North America, they represented the first line of defense against a hostile Spanish regime in Florida that offered freedom and land to any black who fled the colony.

In 1738, that defense was tested when some 69 slaves made their way to St. Augustine, leading to rumors of an even bigger "conspiracy... formed by Negroes in Carolina to rise and make their way out of the province." When war broke out between England and Spain the following year, rumor became reality as some 75 slaves killed several whites, seized weapons, and headed for Florida "with Colours displayed and two Drums beating." Most of the Stono rebels—named after the river where they plotted their uprising—were quickly hunted down and killed before they could make it to Florida or spark a general uprising. Still, the Stono Rebellion put enough fear into the hearts of southern planters that imports of African slaves declined for a time, for fear that the slave to citizen ratio had become dangerously high.

Slave Community and Culture

In addition to outright rebellion, enslaved Africans asserted themselves in the face of their condition in other ways. While the slave system actively worked to destroy any tangible links to the African past, enslaved Africans in the New World retained critical elements of their culture, particularly in those areas—like the South Carolina and Georgia Sea Islands—where slaves represented the vast majority of the population. Not surprisingly, it was those cultural elements most easily transported that survived: music, dance, names, and faith. African rhythms and instruments—like the banjo and drums—remained popular throughout the Americas. Traditional faiths—often fused with the Christianity of the European enslavers—lived on. Even in areas like the inland American South—where Africans represented a minority—cultural traits persisted. Historian Herbert Gutman notes that North American slaves continued to follow West African customs when naming their children, who often refused to answer to the names given to them by their masters.

By 1750, a distinctive slave system had emerged in the British North American colonies from the Chesapeake south that would remain relatively unchanged until its destruction in the Civil War more than a century later. It was a system based on harsh laws, rigorous policing, and unspeakable brutality, made more horrifying by its very ordinariness. Thomas Jefferson—one of history's most eloquent spokespeople for freedom and a large slaveholder himself—spoke of generations of whites "nursed, educated, and daily exercised in tyranny." The relationship between slave and master, he wrote, "is a perpetual exercise of the most unremitting despotism on the one part, and degrading submission on the other. Our children see this and learn to imitate it."

With cruelty came want. The material poverty of the slaves' lives was acute, especially when set against the lavish lifestyle of many of their owners. A European traveler visiting the slave quarters on a mid-18th century plantation described them as

. . . more miserable than the most miserable of the cottages of our peasants. The husband and wife sleep on a mean pallet, the children on the ground; a very bad fireplace, some utensils for cooking. . . . They work all week, not having a single day for themselves except for holidays. . . . The condition of our peasants is infinitely happier.

Yet despite the squalid living conditions, the exhausting work regimen, and the brutality of the master class, the African-American population of the southern colonies thrived, at least demographically. While less than 250,000 slaves were imported into British North America between 1619 and the beginning

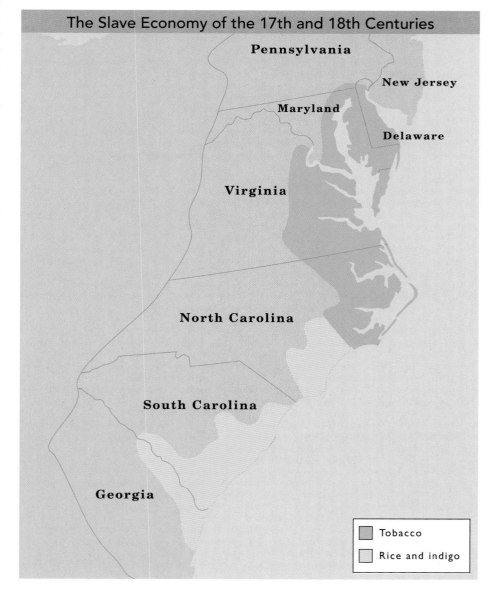

The Slave Economy of the 17th and 18th Centuries

Pennsylvania

New Jersey

Maryland

Delaware

Virginia

North Carolina

South Carolina

Georgia

Tobacco

Rice and indigo

THE PRESERVATION OF CULTURE: GRIOTS, TALKING DRUMS, AND CALL AND RESPONSE SINGING

Although slavery did much to disconnect slaves from their African heritage, many African traditions not only survived but adapted and shaped American culture as well. Music is one such tradition. As Africans were taken from Senegambia, from the Slave Coast stretching from Sierra Leone to Cameroon, and finally from Congo-Angola, the musical traditions of each of these regions traveled with them.

THE GRIOTS: In Senegambia, singers and musicians belong to a social class known as griots. Griots often sing songs of praise about the rich and powerful in return for payment. Because those songs turn to insults if the griots are not paid, griots are both respected and feared. Griots also serve as musical historians by singing songs that tell the stories of their people. Some griots play in groups to provide accompaniment to farmers and other workers. Griots have often been compared to the songsters and blues musicians who traveled the Mississippi Delta in the first decades of the 20th century.

THE BANJO: Partly because there are few forests from which large drums can be made, Senegambian music emphasizes stringed instruments. Music historians trace the roots of the modern banjo to this region.

THE TALKING DRUM: The complex music of the Slave Coast region relies heavily on drums, rattles, bells, and other percussion instruments. Western jazz drumming has much in common with this sound. Among the most famous drums of West Africa is the "talking drum" used by Nigeria's Yoruba people. The talking drum has strings that when squeezed vary the tension on the drumhead, thus altering the sound the drum produces. Drummers also use a curved drumstick and, by changing pitch and rhythm, can make the instrument "talk" in "language" based on spoken language.

The people of the Congo-Angola river basin are best known for complex singing, often containing whoops, shouts, and hollers. Some music historians have compared this style to that of Western artists such as James Brown.

CALL AND RESPONSE: Music has always been at the center of West African life. Religious rites, farming, building houses, and other activities all have their own songs, often performed by entire villages in a musical pattern known as "call and response." A lead vocalist sings a line, then everyone else sings a response. Call and response singing has influenced American popular music, from gospel to rhythm and blues to hip-hop.

VOCAL MASKING: In village rituals, celebrants often wear masks to represent various gods or other figures. These masked figures would also "mask" their singing voices by drastically changing the pitch and tone of songs, using growls, shrieks, and other unusual effects. Some masks have layers of material in their mouthpieces, which change the singer's voice even more. In America, vocal masking can be heard in many African-American church sermons, as well as in a wide range of popular music.

AFRICA

SENEGAMBIA

SLAVE COAST

CONGO-ANGOLA

of the Civil War, the African-American population in the colonies stood at more than 500,000 in 1770. Indeed, the share of the population of the southern colonies—and, after 1776, the southern states—that was of African descent remained consistently between one third and two fifths during the 1700s. With free white immigration into the region roughly balancing slave imports, this meant that the reproductive rates of black slaves equaled those of free whites, a rather remarkable fact when compared to the Caribbean and Brazil, where only through the massive import of new slaves was the black population sustained. The fact that the slave population in North America reproduced in such significant numbers would have profound effects on African-American culture.

A population that grows through natural increase is going to be quite different than one that grows through importation. For instance, slave traders preferred males. They could not control the male-female balance in natural birth rates, however. For this reason, the enslaved African population in North America was far more balanced between males and females and also featured more offspring than that of the Caribbean. The higher birth rate in North American slave communities was also partly due to the fact that North American slaves were generally better fed and clothed than their Caribbean and Brazilian counterparts. In short, family life took hold more firmly among Africans in the British North American mainland. Of course, because slaves were merely property under English (and pre–Civil War American) law, slaveowners had the right to do with them as they wished, including breaking up married couples and families for sale. This was a relatively regular occurrence in colonial times when slaveowners—like everyone else—died young and their estates were split up among heirs or sold off to pay debts. This was the fate of Jefferson's Monticello plantation, for instance.

Despite such obstacles, African Americans began to create families, kinship networks, and communities as their numbers increased. Indeed, one half of African Americans in the 18th century lived on plantations with at least 20 slaves. And even those who lived on smaller farms experienced a sense of community in more densely settled areas. Recalling West African custom, African Americans created elaborate kinship networks of aunts, uncles, and cousins—both biological and fictive—which were reinforced by traditional naming patterns. These patterns and networks assured that each child belonged to a family and would have a guardian in the event of sale or death of a parent.

Slave families and community also allowed for development of a distinct African-American culture—some of it inherited from the old country, some of it borrowed from the European-American community, much of it a hybrid of the two. The development of this culture—thwarted by the fact that slaves came from so many different societies in Africa and spoke so many different languages—came into full flowering once the majority of slaves had been born and raised in America. It was a culture created out of a life of pain and poverty. It included art forms—like music, dance, and oral storytelling—that required little in the way of material wealth, though wood carvings, daily utensils, and even housing fashioned by slaves bore a remarkable resemblance to African forms and styles. Increasingly anchored in a deep and ecstatic Christianity that promised release from suffering and an ultimate judgement against the sin of slaveholding, the culture of African-American slaves in the southern colonies extolled resistance and rebellion as the spiritual duty of believers.

AFRICAN AMERICANS IN THE NORTHERN COLONIES

Not all 18th-century African Americans were slaves and not all lived in the southern colonies. Small communities of free blacks survived, in southern ports like Charleston, in older rural regions like the Chesapeake, and in the growing cities of the northern colonies. Although commonly associated with the South, slavery was also legal and practiced in all of the British North American colonies, including New England. In the middle colonies—and especially New York—slavery thrived, though in a very different and far more truncated form than the South. According to the first national census in 1790, 7.6 percent, or 25,875 persons, of the population of New York State was African American; in Pennsylvania, the figure was 2.4 percent, or 10,238 persons, and in Massachusetts just 1.4 percent, or 5,369.

In rural areas of the North, African Americans—either slave or free—were indeed rare. Slavery did not take hold in the northern colonies for one simple reason: climate. Colder weather and a shorter growing season made it impossible to farm labor-intensive crops like tobacco, sugar, and rice, which required nearly year-round maintenance. Those

A slave auction house in New York Harbor (Library of Congress)

commercial crops that did thrive in the North—largely grains—had highly seasonal labor demands. Lots of hands were only needed at planting and harvest time. Thus, it made little economic sense to buy and maintain slaves who only worked part of the year. It was better to hire labor as it was needed. But while African Americans were rare in rural areas of the North, they were common in the tiny colonial cities. Approximately 10 percent of Boston and fully 20 percent of New York—both with total populations under 20,000—were black. Whether slave, indentured, or free, African Americans were often among the most impoverished urban residents, consigned to the poorest-paying professions like day laborers, cartmen, or merchant seamen.

The harsh conditions bred discontent and, on some occasions, rebellion. Not surprisingly, given the multicultural nature of the city, African Americans often found allies among other the members of oppressed groups. In 1712, about 25 Indian and black slaves set fire to an outhouse, then lay in ambush, killing nine men and wounding seven others who came to put the fire out. The punishment meted out was even more horrific than the crime. More than 20

slaves—including a pregnant woman—were hanged; another three were burned to death; one was broken on the wheel. Moreover, slave codes were toughened—slaves found meeting in groups larger than three were subject to a punishment of 40 lashes—and arson was made punishable by death for anyone in the colony.

Harsh codes, however, did little to assuage the fear of wealthy white New Yorkers living in a city increasingly dominated by the poor and nonwhite. A series of suspicious fires in 1741—just two years after the Stono Rebellion in South Carolina—led to rumors of a slave and indentured servant insurrection. Although no conclusive evidence of a conspiracy could be found, authorities rounded up poor African Americans and whites. Some of them were tortured; others were offered a reward for turning in other slaves and servants. In all 30 blacks and four whites were executed for their supposed roles in the alleged conspiracy. Although not as dependent on slaves for their wealth as southern planters, northern merchants nevertheless feared those whom they had enslaved—the black people who served them daily and helped keep the city running.

THE AMERICAN REVOLUTION

The American Revolution represented the first great colonial rebellion in modern times, and it also contributed ideas of freedom and citizenship that served as an inspiration to revolutionaries in France and Latin America in the late 1700s and early 1800s, and later to peoples all around the world. Indeed, many anticolonial leaders in Africa of the 20th century found in those revolutionary ideals inspiration for their own struggles against British, French, and Portuguese imperialists. At the same time, the Revolution was a deeply flawed affair that left African Americans—fully 20 percent of the population of the country in 1776—mired in bondage or forced to live on the margins of freedom.

By the mid-18th century, Britain had established a string of 13 colonies stretching from New Hampshire in the north to Georgia in the south, with a population of about 2 million, including almost half a million people of African descent. Under the principle of mercantilism, the colonies were supposed to serve imperial interests, providing raw materials for the home country as well as a market for finished goods from Britain. Moreover, all trade was supposed to be kept within the empire and under Britain's control. The slave-based economies of the southern colonies largely fulfilled that role, producing tobacco, rice, and cotton for the home market. But the northern colonies, with their growing manufacturing base and merchant fleets, increasingly competed with British economic interests. In response, Britain instituted a series of laws designed to enforce the mercantilist system. But with the colonies continuing to enrich Britain, these were enforced lackadaisically.

All that changed after 1763 when Britain emerged triumphant, although financially strained, from a seven-year war with France. To help pay its wartime debt, the British government issued a series of especially unpopular taxes, duties, and mercantilist laws. Parliament's thinking was simple: the colonists benefited from the war and the elimination of the French enemy in North America. Therefore, they should pay their fair share. Moreover, as Parliament represented all the peoples of the empire—what political thinkers of the time called "virtual" representation—it was perfectly

The Boston Massacre (Library of Congress)

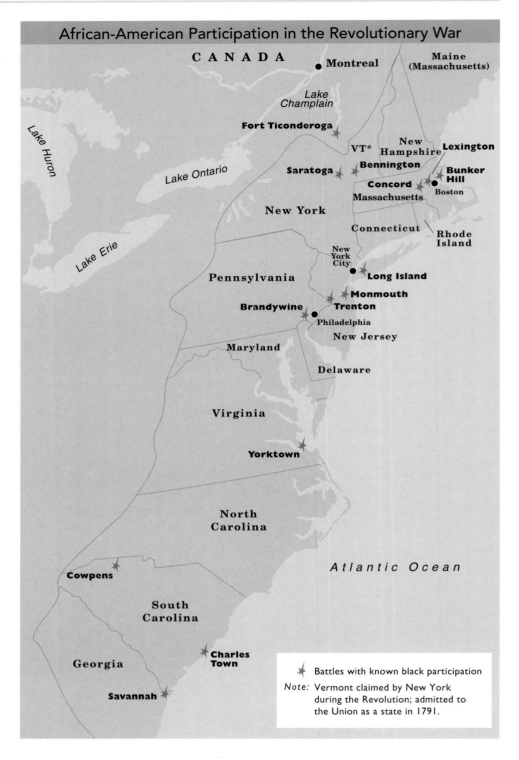

African-American Participation in the Revolutionary War

✳ Battles with known black participation

Note: Vermont claimed by New York during the Revolution; admitted to the Union as a state in 1791.

within its rights to impose such taxes. But the Americans had other ideas. For over a century, they had been largely left to their own devices, permitted to govern themselves. During that period, the colonists had developed a very different idea of governance—local representation. By their thinking, taxation imposed by this distant parliament was "taxation without representation."

BLACK PATRIOTS

In 1765 Parliament imposed the Stamp Act—placing a tax on dozens of items of everyday use. Colonists up and down the Atlantic seaboard refused to pay, forcing London to back down. Parliament was determined to prevail and followed with the Townshend duties on imported goods two years later. The colonists responded with a boycott of British products, as urban crowds attacked customs officers and their houses. On March 5, 1770, a crowd confronted British redcoats in Boston, provoking a fusillade that felled five of the protesters. One of the leaders of the demonstrators—and the first to die in America's struggle with Britain—was a half-Indian, half-black dockworker named Crispus Attucks. A freed slave, Attucks had grown up in a highly stratified colonial society where lowly workmen—white or black—deferred to their social superiors on political matters. Participation in acts of rebellion—and, later, the American Revolution—would change all that.

In short, colonial elites who wanted to free themselves from British rule needed the support of the masses of poor and working colonists to win independence. On January 13—less than six months before the Declaration of Independence was proclaimed in Philadelphia—a petition was presented to the legislature. Signed by dozens of enslaved blacks in Massachusetts, it read:

> *[We] have in common with all other men a natural and inalienable right to that freedom which the Great Parent of the heavens has bestowed equally on all mankind and which [we] have never forfeited by any compact or agreement whatever. . . . Every principle from which America has acted in the course of their unhappy difficulties with Great Britain pleads stronger than a thousand arguments in favor of your petitioners . . . [that] they may be restored to the enjoyments of that which is the natural right of all men—and their children who were born in this land of liberty—not to be held as slaves.*

When war between the colonists and Britain finally began in April 1775, African Americans—at least, the small proportion not enslaved—were faced with a dilemma: fight alongside their fellow colonists who denied them full membership in society or side with the British. In fact, black colonists had a long tradition of military service by 1775, having served as militia men in various colonial wars fought between Britain and its European rivals, France, Holland, and Spain, as well as in numberless skirmishes with Native Americans. Even slaves fought, occasionally winning their freedom in the bargain. At the same time, free blacks and runaway slaves signed up for naval duty, usually aboard independent privateers. Unlike the militia—where they were generally relegated to support positions—the privateers offered black sailors near equality of pay, while the camaraderie of close-quarter shipboard life eliminated segregation and undermined white racist attitudes.

The tradition of black military service continued with the Revolution, with African-American militia men fighting alongside whites at the battles of Lexington and Concord and Bunker Hill in 1775 and at numerous other major engagements. Still, racial prejudice remained deeply entrenched. George Washington, commander of the Continental Army, did not open the ranks to free blacks until 1777, and only then because he was suffering manpower shortages. Soon thereafter, colonies in the North and upper South—where slavery was becoming less important to the agricultural economy—passed laws permitting the manumission (or freeing) of

In this 19th-century print by Currier and Ives, George Washington (second from right), is shown with his slaves at his Virginia home. (Library of Congress)

any slaves who joined up to fight against the British. Ultimately, about 5,000 African Americans—both slave and free—joined the Continental Army between 1777 and the end of the war in 1781. Others joined the various colonial militias—including an all-black Massachusetts company nicknamed the "Bucks"—as well as the Continental navy.

BLACK SOLDIERS ON THE BRITISH SIDE

As with white colonists, North American blacks were divided in their loyalties, especially after the British began to promise emancipation in exchange for military service. In late 1775, for example, more than a thousand blacks answered the plea of Lord Dunmore ("Liberty to slaves!"), royal governor of Virginia, to form the all-black Ethiopian Regiment. In the end, however, it was not so much black soldiers—who remained small in number on both sides—but African-American slaves that nearly changed the outcome of the war.

The decision by France and Spain's to back the colonists, along with Patriot victories in the North, forced the British to launch a new attack plan in 1778: an invasion of the southern colonies. The decision made sense both strategically and tactically. First, the British valued the commercial agricultural colonies of the South far more than they did those of the North, where a growing manufacturing base competed with British imports. Second, British commanders understood

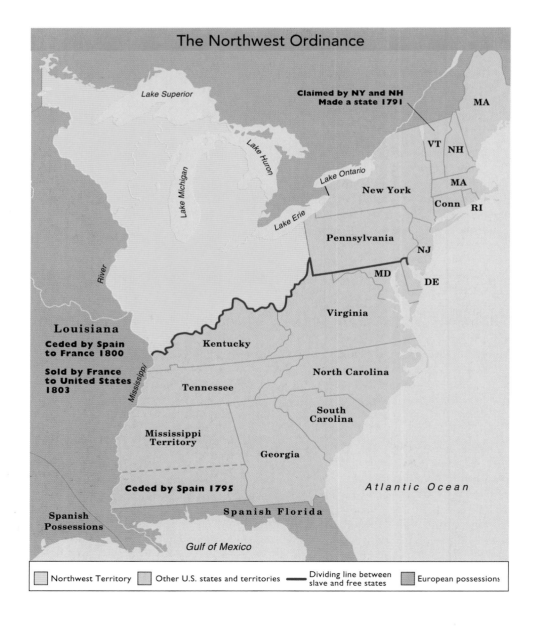

The Northwest Ordinance

that the slavery system burdened southern colonists with an extra handicap. Planters did not dare to arm their slaves—who outnumbered whites in many areas and who were also critical to the economy of the region—nor did they risk leaving the plantations themselves to enlist in the American cause, which would have left their slaves free to escape. But escape they did. As British forces marched from victory to victory through Georgia and the Carolinas, tens of thousands of escaping slaves flocked to their ranks. In exchange for their freedom, they were put to work carting supplies, constructing earthworks, and doing all the other hard labor required of an army in the field. Indeed, Britain's "southern strategy" almost worked, right up to Yorktown, the decisive October 1781 defeat in southeastern Virginia that forced the main British armies in North America—surrounded by Washington's troops on land and the French fleet at sea—to surrender.

AFRICAN AMERICANS IN THE FEDERAL PERIOD

The American Revolution offered an ambivalent legacy for African Americans. For black Loyalists—free blacks who joined the British cause—defeat brought exile. Like their white counterparts, they were forced to flee. Most were first transported by the British to Nova Scotia. But the cold climate, poor lands, and lingering prejudice caused many to emigrate once again, this time to Sierra Leone, a British colony for freed slaves established on the coast of West Africa. As for slaves, the British largely honored their promise of freedom—shipping thousands to the Bahamas and elsewhere—though some runaways were returned to their masters.

Slavery and the Constitution

On the American side, emancipation became—for a brief moment—the order of the day, particularly in the states of the upper South and North. The impetus came from both idealism and economics. For many whites, the contradictions of the independence struggle were too much to

bear. "It always appeared a most iniquitous Scheme to me," Abigail Adams wrote to her husband, patriot leader John Adams, "to fight ourselves for what we are daily robbing and plundering from those who have as good a right to freedom as we have." By 1784, four northern states—including Adams's Massachusetts—had abolished slavery. Within the next 15 years, every state north of Delaware would do the same, though some did so far more gradually than others. A 1799 law in New York, for example, offered emancipation to the children of slaves only, and then only when they reached 25 years of age. Thus, as late as 1810, nearly one fourth of the black population in the North remained in bondage.

In the upper South, slavery was retained, but laws were passed making manumission easier. Within a decade, Virginia's planters had freed upward of 10,000 slaves. Indeed, many of the great Virginian leaders of the Revolution had decidedly mixed feelings about free blacks. Washington, Jefferson, and Constitution author James Madison all expressed support for abolition, but only Washington was willing to free his slaves in his will, though only upon the death of his wife, Martha, and only then, say critics, because he had no other heirs to will them to. In fact, the motives of many emancipation-minded Virginia planters were not always purely idealistic. As the colony's economy shifted from one based on a labor-intensive tobacco plantation system to one based on grain-based farming, large slave forces were less economically critical.

To Virginia's south, however, two factors led to a hardening, rather than easing, of slavery. First, the labor-intensive plantation agriculture in the region—notably, rice, indigo, and long-staple cotton crops—required an inexpensive labor force that could be forced to work in disease-ridden swamps. Only slaves would suit the purpose. Second, the maintenance of a large slave population led to fears of uprising among planters and other whites. And those fears bred harsher slave codes and policing. The Revolution's powerful rhetoric of freedom was clearly meant, as far as the Deep South was concerned, for white ears only.

When it came time to forge a new system of government for the fledgling country, southerners were determined to

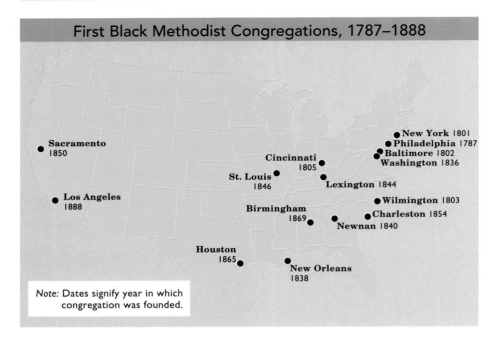

First Black Methodist Congregations, 1787–1888

Sacramento 1850

Los Angeles 1888

St. Louis 1846

Cincinnati 1805

Lexington 1844

Birmingham 1869

Newnan 1840

Houston 1865

New Orleans 1838

New York 1801
Philadelphia 1787
Baltimore 1802
Washington 1836

Wilmington 1803
Charleston 1854

Note: Dates signify year in which congregation was founded.

Richard Allen, founder of the African Methodist Episcopal Church (Library of Congress)

ensure that nothing threatened their "peculiar institution." Concerned about the passage of the Northwest Ordinance in 1787—which outlawed slavery in the territories between the Ohio River and the Great Lakes—southern delegates to the 1787 Constitutional Convention in Philadelphia wrung a compromise from northerners on the slavery question. For the purposes of apportioning representation, slaves would be counted as three-fifths of a person, giving southern states controlling power in the Congress and the ability to squash any abolitionist legislation. The southerners were also able to postpone the abolition of the international slave trade for 20 years.

THE AFRICAN METHODIST EPISCOPAL CHURCH

Still, for many African Americans, the effects of the American Revolution were both powerful and lasting. For one thing, there were more free blacks. From a few thousand strong in 1776, the free black population of the North and upper South grew to 200,000 in less than 50 years. For the first time, there was the critical mass necessary to create independent black communities and institutions, including voluntary mutual aid associations like the African Union Society of Rhode Island and the Free African Society of Philadelphia. Perhaps the most important development, however, was the rise of

free black congregations. Among these, the African Methodist Episcopal (AME) Church was the most significant.

Richard Allen, its founder, was arguably the most influential black American of his day. Born a slave in 1760, Allen experienced a religious awakening in his late teens, purchased his freedom at 20, and became an itinerant preacher in his early twenties. In 1786, the Methodists of Philadelphia asked him to preach to free blacks in the congregation. Although liberal for its time on racial issues, the white Methodists of Philadelphia were too controlling for Allen's taste and, in 1816, he founded the AME Church, the first independent black religious organization in the United States. To win their independence from the existing white Methodist church, Allen and his congregation successfully sued in the Pennsylvania Supreme Court.

While the AME retained the baptism and communion practices of the Methodist church, it made them distinctly African American. The hymn-singing that predominated in both the white and black churches became more spontaneous in the AME church and services were marked by shouting and praying out loud. It was also more openly political, engaging in social activism and promoting the idea of black nationalism, or a separate culture for African Americans within the United States. Evangelical like the white Methodist church, the AME targeted black communities in the American South, the Caribbean, and Africa for religious outreach. Today, the AME has branches in 20 countries on three continents. In the 20th century, the church provided much needed social services and a religious community for the millions of rural blacks migrating to northern cities. And the AME church played a very active role in the civil rights movement, including the filing of lawsuits against segregation in public education.

THE COTTON GIN

For all of the strides made by African Americans in the wake of the Revolution, the gains were dwarfed by the obstacles that remained. Slavery was still entrenched in half the nation; 90 percent of blacks remained in bondage; and, even in the so-called free states, legal restrictions

BENJAMIN BANNEKER

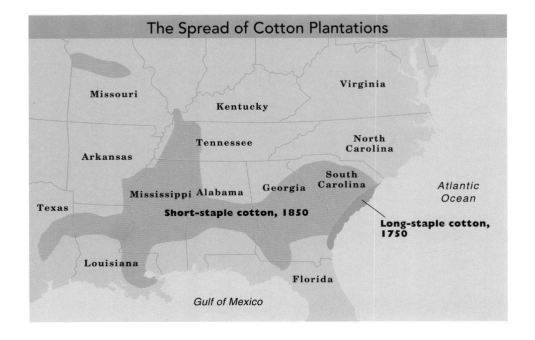

(Library of Congress)

Along with the expanded numbers, the growth of free African-American communities, and the development of independent black institutions came a newfound confidence. No individual better personified the new free black identity of the early American republic better than Benjamin Banneker. Born to free black parents in 1731, Banneker grew up and lived on the Maryland tobacco farm he inherited from his father. From an early age, Banneker showed an aptitude for science and mathematics, building one of the first mechanical clocks in the colonies at age 21. In the late 1780s, he developed an interest in astronomy and, borrowing books and instruments from a neighboring white planter, Banneker published his first astronomical almanac in 1791. After reading Jefferson's *Notes on the State of Virginia*—and taking exception to the author's remarks about black mental inferiority—Banneker sent the Declaration of Independence author a copy. The two began an exchange of letters on the subject of African-American intelligence and ability. While recognizing Banneker's extraordinary achievement—Jefferson helped get him appointed surveyor for the new capital city of Washington—the Virginia planter nevertheless ignored the astronomer's arguments against slavery and privately remained skeptical that Banneker had produced the almanac on his own.

and racial prejudice made a mockery of the democratic ideals so recently fought for by Americans of all colors. Moreover, a dark shadow loomed over the future of African Americans and the union itself. In 1793, Eli Whitney—a New England teacher working as a tutor on a Georgia plantation—came up with a solution to the age-old problem of cotton processing. For years, American planters were confined to growing only long-staple cotton, a seedless variety that can only be grown in a subtropical environment, such as the Sea Islands of Georgia and South Carolina. With its numerous seeds that

had to be picked from the boll by hand, the far hardier short-staple cotton remained economically impractical. Whitney's gin—which did the work of 50 persons—changed all that.

The implications were enormous. Overnight, much of the southern United States—including a vast area in the southwestern territories—was rendered ideal and economically viable cotton-growing land. Fueled by the growing demand of textile mills in Great Britain and, later, the northern states, cotton farming spread rapidly and, with it, the institution of slavery. Thus, a slave population of roughly

The Spread of Cotton Plantations

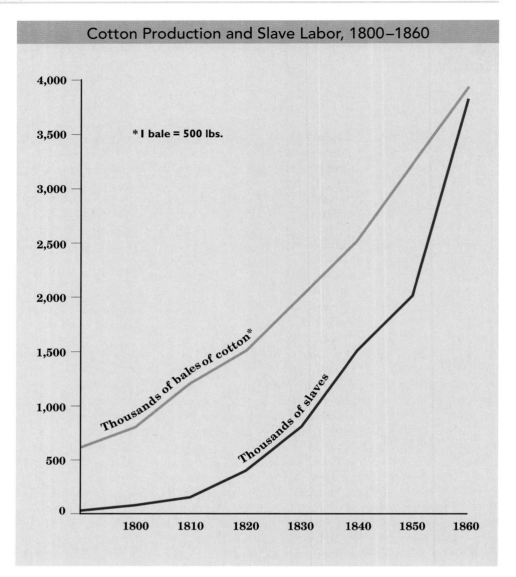

Cotton Production and Slave Labor, 1800–1860

*I bale = 500 lbs.

Thousands of bales of cotton*

Thousands of slaves

200,000 in 1790 had grown to nearly 4 million by 1860. By the end of that period, the southern states were producing two thirds of the world's cotton. The white stuff had become far and away America's number one export, drawing in foreign capital that helped finance canal, railroad, and factory construction. Northern merchants and bankers—as well as southern planters—grew rich off the trade. It was a rare politician that dared to challenge the institution.

In 1790, many people in both the North and South were convinced that slavery was on the road to gradual and peaceful extinction. Fifty years later few subscribed to that view. As the fiery abolitionist John Brown—on trial for launching a failed slave uprising in 1859—presciently told the nation: "I...am quite certain that the crimes of this guilty land...will never be purged away; but with Blood."

"Cruel, unjust, exploitative, oppressive, slavery bound two peoples together in bitter antagonism while creating... [a] relationship so complex and ambivalent that neither could express the simplest human feelings without reference to the other." So wrote the historian of American slavery Eugene Genovese.

Indeed, American slavery was complex. On the one hand, masters and slaves were part of a modern and dynamic economic system that yoked together one of civilization's oldest forms of labor—slavery—with modern, global free markets. Planters were businessmen (and occasionally women), willing to use any means necessary to realize the maximum return from their investments in human flesh. And their slaves were hyper-exploited workers who saw virtually all of their surplus labor value—that is, the value of what they produced minus the cost of keeping them alive—taken from them, literally by force.

At the same time, slavery was more than just a labor relationship. Slavery—as encoded in the laws and customs of the 19th century South—gave to one class of people absolute control over the lives of another. For slaves, marriage, family, friendship, home, labor, leisure—all depended upon the whims of the master.

Thus, slaves were more than workers and masters were more than employers. The two shaped each others lives and identities in ways that went far beyond a simple economic relationship. Together, the descendants of Africa and the descendents of Europe created a unique southern American culture and civilization that, despite the destruction of slavery, exists to this day.

THE EXPANSION OF SLAVERY

As noted in the previous chapter, slavery appeared to be on the road to extinction in the years immediately following the American Revolution. Revolutionary ideals about "all men [being] created equal" prompted some planters to manumit, or legally free, their slaves. More important, grain farming was on the rise in the North and the upper South. Grains—like wheat and corn—required heavy labor at sowing and harvest times only. It made more economic sense to hire labor when it was needed than to make a heavy investment in slaves who would only be used part of the year. Thus, in 1790, the institution of slavery thrived largely along a narrow, coastal corridor of rice and long-staple cotton plantations in South Carolina and Georgia. While hugely profitable, the agricultural economy of this region was not replicable in the territories of the West for climatic reasons. Eli Whitney's simple invention of the cotton gin changed all that. By making short-staple cotton—which could be grown across much of the lower South—profitable, the gin revived slavery as an institution.

Between 1800 and 1860, cotton production doubled every 10 years. By the latter year, the American South was producing two thirds of the world's supply. At the same time, cotton exports were worth double the amount of all other goods and crops exported by the United States. Although of paramount importance, cotton was not the only commercial crop grown in the slave South. Rivaling the spectacular growth of cotton—although on a much smaller geographic scale—was sugar. Primarily grown in Louisiana, sugar production multiplied by a factor of five between 1800 and 1860. Meanwhile tobacco remained important, with exports doubling between 1790 and 1860, even though its percentage within the total exports of the country fell from 15 to 6 percent. In short, slavery—and the agricultural commodities it produced—was a very big business in antebellum America.

Production of the commercial crops of the South—sugar, tobacco, rice, and above all cotton—required three critical ingredients: land, capital, and labor. Land was the foundation. In 1790, the farms

A slave at work (Library of Congress)

Tecumseh (Library of Congress)

Tenskwatawa, the Shawnee Prophet
(Library of Congress)

and plantations of the South—from Maryland to Georgia—were largely confined to a strip of land between the Atlantic coast and the Appalachian Mountains, although pioneers had begun to settle the future states of Tennessee and Kentucky. Divided into low-lying tidewater and upland piedmont areas (areas by the base of the mountain), the settled territories of the eastern seaboard ranged between 50 and 200 miles in width.

RESETTLEMENT OF NATIVE AMERICANS

West of the Appalachian crest was Indian country, primarily occupied by the so-called Five Civilized Tribes: the Cherokee and Creek of the western Carolinas and eastern Alabama and Tennessee; the Choctaw and Chickasaw of western Alabama and Mississippi; and the Seminole of Florida. These Indian nations were designated "civilized" for a simple reason: their societies most resembled that of whites. They were settled and agrarian. Some even produced commercial crops for sale and owned black slaves, although on a smaller scale and with a far more relaxed attitude about interracial mixing.

Yet despite their "civilized" ways, the Native Americans of the trans-Appalachian South saw virtually all of their lands seized by whites between 1800 and 1840. At first, these seizures occurred on a case by case basis, as the federal and various state governments insisted that traditional communal lands be divided into individual property holdings, a form of land tenure unfamiliar to most Indians. Lent money by local merchants, many Native American landholders saw their lands seized when they could not pay the interest on their debts, the concept of interest also being completely alien to them. This led to clashes between whites and Native Americans, including an uprising of a confederacy of Indian groups organized by two Shawnee brothers—Tecumseh and Tenskwatawa—between 1809 and 1814. Their defeat at the Battle of Horseshoe Bend in Alabama ended much of the armed resistance.

By the time the federal government decided to remove all of the remaining Native Americans east of the Mississippi River to Oklahoma in the 1830s, it encountered little armed resistance, although the forced midwinter marches—known as the Trail of Tears, for the thousands who died from malnutrition, cold, and disease—remains one of the most brutal episodes in American history. At the same time, the settlement of these new lands in the Old Southwest (Alabama, Arkansas, Mississippi, Lousiana, Tennessee, and the western parts of Georgia and North Carolina) was accelerated by developments in transportation technology, most notably the steamboat. This linked the South and West into an integrated economic region based on the Mississippi River and its tributaries. This early economic integration had important political repercussions, creating a South-West alliance in Congress dedicated to the protection of slavery, at least in the South and Old Southwest. (The Old Northwest Territory was declared free under the Northwest Ordinance of 1787, with most new states there banning both slavery and the in-migration of free blacks.)

NATIVE AMERICAN SLAVEHOLDERS

Ironically, the removal of Native Americans from east of the Mississippi led to the expansion of slavery west of it. While enslaving war prisoners had long been common, Native Americans did not use slaves on a large scale. By the 1820s, however, a small number of Indians of mixed white and Cherokee, Choctaw, or Chickasaw descent began owning black slaves.

As legions of whites moved onto traditional Native lands during the early 19th century, some Native Americans of mixed heritage argued that if they assimilated with whites, they would be peacefully accepted. Tribal leaders wore European clothing, lived in brick houses, practiced large-scale farming—and used black slaves to work the land. Historians estimate that by 1824, the Cherokee owned 1,277 slaves. By 1860, the and Chickasaw owned as many as 5,000 slaves. The tribes also created laws limiting slave rights. In 1827, for example, the Cherokee banned slaves from owning property, made it illegal to buy goods from slaves, and prohibited marriage between black slaves and Indians or whites.

Despite arguing in favor of leaving their traditional lands, slave-owning Indians found that Oklahoma was fit for neither traditional hunting and gathering nor plantation agriculture. Still, as selling slaves become more profitable, slavery among the Cherokee, Choctaw, and Chickasaw increased. Tribal leaders actively enforced the Fugitive Slave Act when it was passed in 1850.

At the start of the Civil War, the Civilized Tribes renounced treaties with the United States and allied with the pro-slavery South. Stand Waitie, a Cherokee, served as a Confederate general. When he surrendered in June 1865, he was the last Confederate general to do so. After the war, the Civilized Tribes signed new treaties with the U.S. government. Each tribe freed its slaves and all but the Choctaw granted them full citizenship.

FINANCING THE SLAVE SYSTEM

Meanwhile, former tribal lands in the Old South began to fill up with white farmers and planters determined to expand the cotton empire. And to the hundreds of thousands of square miles of ideal short-staple cotton-growing land now available, they now added the two other crucial ingredients mentioned earlier—capital and labor. The former came largely from Britain and the northern states.

Like all commercial farmers, the cotton growers of the Old South were perpetually in debt, borrowing to meet this year's living and operation expenses against next year's crop. To meet this need, there arose a financing system stretching as far as New York City and London and linking northern and British money and textile interests with southern farmers and planters. Much of the business was handled by commission merchants or "factors" who lived in the South and offered a variety of services to planters, including loans, warehousing, and shipping. In addition, these factors helped finance western settlement, providing large loans to cover the first four or five costly years of plantation development. But these services came at a high price. Factors typically skimmed off a fifth to a quarter of the crop in payment. By the 1850s, more than $100 million in cotton profits was annually siphoned off

to northern banks, giving major financial centers in the North a direct stake in preserving the slave-based cotton system of the South.

This outside financing was also heavily responsible for supplying the final ingredient in the spread of slavery to the territories of the Old Southwest: labor. New plantations needed new labor forces, and factors helped finance the huge growth in the domestic slave trade between 1820 and 1860. Like many aspects of slavery, the domestic trade and slave prices were market-driven phenomena. With the growth of slavery increasing demand and the abolition of the international slave trade in 1807–1808 reducing supply, the price of slaves began to climb. Indeed, areas of early slave population concentrations along the eastern seaboard began to see rising profits from the sale of slaves, even as their depleted land (both cotton and tobacco drain nutriments from the earth) resulted in decreased productivity. By the 1850s, slave-owners were shipping more than 25,000 slaves from east to west, in the process breaking up African-American families and communities.

Slave sales represented some of the most cruel and frightening moments in an African American's life. Often purchased by slave traders—notorious even among whites for their barbarity—slaves would be shackled and forcibly marched up to hundreds of miles to auction houses, where they were warehoused for days, weeks, and months on end. Paraded in front of potential buyers—who poked and prodded them like cattle, often peering into their mouths to check their teeth—slaves were auctioned off to the highest bidder, often with little regard to family and marriage ties. (Some planters—both as buyers and sellers—made a point of keeping families together for fear that breaking them up would produce an unhappy and, hence, unproductive or recalcitrant slave force.)

LIFE ON THE PLANTATION

The slave-owning population increased alongside the geographic expansion of cotton farming. Between 1820 and 1860, it rose from just under 200,000 to around 400,000, many of them coming from the ranks of poor and middling farmers.

John Ross, a Cherokee leader, owned over 100 slaves. He agreed to move his people from their traditional homelands in the Southeast to Indian Territory west of the Mississippi River. (Library of Congress)

Eli Whitney (Library of Congress)

The cotton gin (Library of Congress)

Indeed, at that time the goal of becoming a slaveowner was the southern white version of the American dream.

SLAVE OWNERS

Slave ownership was, however, confined to an ever-smaller percentage of southern whites. This was because the overall population of the white South was expanding even more rapidly than was the number of slave owners. Between 1830 and 1860, the percentage of southern whites who owned slaves fell from 36 to 26, a drop of more than 25 percent. Despite the diminishing rate of slave ownership, the institution itself was strongly defended by virtually the entire white population of the South.

Nonslaveholding whites stood by the system for two reasons. First, the existence of a class of people whose very skin color assigned them the lowest rung on the societal ladder elevated the social standing of poor whites. As Frederick Douglass, an abolitionist born into slavery, argued, the poorest white could always lord it over any black he/she encountered, thereby enhancing his or her own self-esteem and allying him/her politically with planters. Second, poor southern whites—like all Americans—believed strongly in social mobility, the opportunity to rise out of their social station through native ability and hard work. In the South, that meant buying and working slaves, most likely on western lands. Indeed, the very system of slavery relied on the cooperation of poor whites. More numerous than planters, they could be called upon to act as a police force, questioning, detaining, and returning any slave found off the plantation.

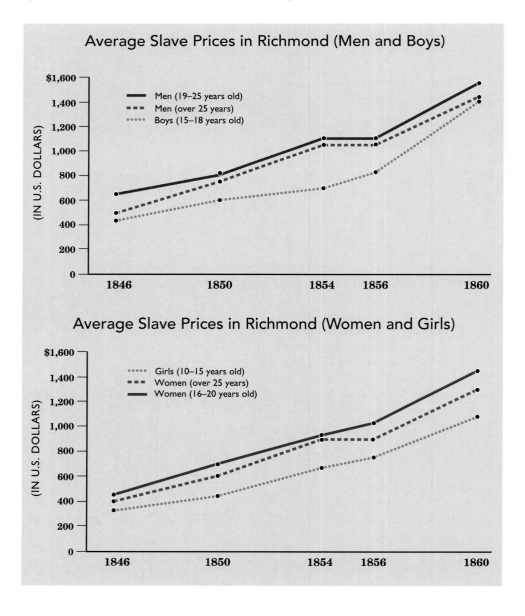

**Percentage of Sales Involving the
Breakup of Marriages and/or Families, 1850**

Children Sold Without Either Parent as Percentage of All Trades		Married Adults Sold Without Spouse	
AGE IN YEARS	PERCENT	GENDER/AGE	PERCENT
0–7	2	Women (15–19)	12
8–11	8	Women (20 and over)	7
12–14	15	Men (20–24)	11
		Men (25 and over)	8

There were also great economic disparities within the slaveholding class. Most owned just a few slaves and perhaps $3,000 in land, making them economically far better off than nonslaveholders but poor in comparison with the middling planters who might own 10 to 50 slaves, and large planters, with 50 to several hundred. Indeed, most small slave owners—as well as poorer nonslaveholders who might rent their slaves at critical periods in the growing season—were highly dependent on the large planters, turning to them to help process, store, and market their crops. This created a system in which a small number of planters controlled the governments of the South, with poorer white elements deferring to them on political matters. The skewed distribution of slaves also created a demographic paradox. Simply put, the vast majority of slave owners owned few slaves, but well over 50 percent of southern African Americans lived on plantations with 20 or more slaves. These numbers—combined with the fact that most plantations lay in so-called black belts (named for the richness of the soil and not the color of the laborers' skin)—meant that the majority of slaves lived in places where African-American communities could develop. This fact would have enormous consequences for the development of a distinct black culture in the antebellum South.

WHITE PATERNALISM

Most male slave owners—and the vast majority were men—fancied themselves aristocrats and modeled their lives after English country squires. They tried to cultivate an aristocratic way of life, which placed an emphasis on culture, elegance, refined manners, and leisure, as opposed to the hectic pace and moneyed pursuits among their northern counterparts in finance and manufacturing. Most lived on isolated plantations where, like the lords of the manor celebrated in the novels of Walter Scott, the Old South's favorite writer, they controlled all aspects of the lives of their subordinates. Out of this mentality grew a self-styled system of control known as paternalism. That is to say, planters imagined themselves as father figures—strict but essentially caring—of a vast family of slaves. According to the planters, theirs was a system superior to that of the North, where laborers were hired and fired as needed, with little concern for their well-being and livelihood.

The whole notion of paternalism was deeply flawed, though, for several reasons. First, it was based on an extremely racist conception of African-American capabilities. A slave, wrote Virginia

A slave auction (Library of Congress)

A slave wearing shackles around his neck (Library of Congress)

A Louisiana sugar plantation

planter George Fitzhugh, "is but a grown-up child, and must be governed as a child [while] the master occupies toward him the place of parent or guardian." Over the years, slave masters elaborated an ideology in defense of slavery. In the early 19th century, the planters of the South and their intellectual defenders in the press and academia argued that because blacks and whites were inherently different, the two could not live on an equal social and economic footing. Forced to survive amidst a superior white population, the argument went, blacks would sink into poverty, crime, and violence. Slavery, then, was necessary to keep southern society and the economy that underpinned it functioning.

Gradually, the "necessary evil" argument metamorphosed into one that insisted slavery was a "positive good." As James Hammond, a South Carolina planter and senator, put it, every society had to have a "mud-sill class" of people who did the hard and dirty work of heavy labor and domestic servitude. In societies where these tasks were performed by free laborers, such as the North, dangerous rifts in the social and political order could result. But the South, he said, had found a perfect solution to this dilemma in assigning those tasks to an "inferior" race perfectly suited and willing to per-

forming them, albeit under close white supervision. The absurdity of this racist proposition would be put to the test in the immediate post–Civil War era, when former slaves proved neither particularly vengeful nor helpless.

Another flaw in white paternalism was its tendency to gloss over the essential brutality of the slave system, in which the threat or practice of corporal punishment—oftentimes slipping over the line into outright torture—was ever-present. In the antebellum South—as in every society—practice varied from individual to individual. Some masters could be quite harsh in their treatment of slaves; others more benevolent. However, the system and the racist ideology it perpetuated rested on inherent brutality for two reasons.

First, slaves were legally considered as chattel, that is, living property, not unlike livestock. For both social and psychological reasons, reducing someone to less than human status—that is, making someone the property of another—invites cruelty and abuse, as abolitionists were wont to argue when the slave masters suggested that their system was inherently more benevolent than the northern wage labor system.

Second, slaves were not just property but workers who had virtually all of the wealth produced by their labor taken from them by force. Without the positive incentives of wages, few slaves were willing to perform the backbreaking labor of plantation agriculture without the threat or application of force. To get labor out of their slaves, then, planters employed a host of punishments that included beating, branding, shackling, and the selling off of recalcitrant slaves or their loved ones. (Some planters also offered a few meager incentives like an extra day or two off at Christmas, a larger tobacco ration, or the right for their slaves to earn a few dollars raising crops on their own plots or from selling their labor.)

Next to physical punishment, the most important method for labor control was maintaining ignorance. Masters—and southern state law—prohibited teaching slaves reading and writing. This had immediate and practical reasons, as well as more subtle, long-term ones. When masters sent slaves off the plantation on errands, they supplied them with written passes to explain their presence. A slave who could write was also a slave who

Cane Fields

Sugar House

Slave Quarters

Stable

Kitchen

Office

Garconnière

Main House

Garconnière

Note: On Louisiana sugar plantations, garconnières were the homes of the planter's sons.

could counterfeit a pass. But more profoundly, masters did not want their slaves learning of the outside world. They did not want them to know that there was any world other than that of the plantation and any authority other than that of the planter. Thus, planter regimes in the South made it a point to ban all abolitionist literature, for fear it might fall into the hands of the few free blacks or slaves who could read and would pass the ideas on to the majority who could not.

Ultimately, the idea of the plantation as family was undermined by the contradiction inherent in a system where slavery and capitalism were intimately linked. That is to say, planters had to make a profit, or they would fail. In a competitive world market, where planters and farmers had little control over the prices their crops fetched—that meant lowering the costs of production. This could be done by finding more and better land—hence the move westward—or by lowering labor costs. Since slaves were not paid a wage, lowering labor costs meant scrimping on necessities, driving the labor force harder, or both when prices for crops dropped. These imperatives usually overrode any paternalistic pretensions toward benevolence. Planters who truly tried to live up to some fictional aristocratic ideal were likely to find themselves in financial trouble, forced to sell off their human property—a slave's greatest fear as it meant separation from family and friends—to meet debt payments.

While a few of the wealthier planters tried to make showcases of their plantations, most slaves were housed in windowless, dirt-floored cabins. Furnishing usually amounted to little more than a rough-hewn table and chairs, a few utensils, and itchy straw-tick mattresses. Clothing was skimpy and of the cheapest grades of cloth, often reduced to rags because they were rarely replaced. And while food was often plentiful, it was usually of the poorest and most basic quality. A weekly ration typically included a few pounds of salt pork and 16 pounds of cornmeal—a diet lacking in essential vitamins and minerals. (To supplement this unhealthful and monotonous diet, many slaves fished, trapped, or worked small vegetable gardens of their own, though this meant laboring on their one day of rest a week.) Thus, slaves worked far harder and with far less return, if any,

than even the most exploited farm laborer or factory worker in the North.

SLAVES

Because southern plantations were often self-contained economic units—with all but the luxuries gracing the planters' lives grown or manufactured on the premises—African Americans found themselves asked to perform a host of tasks. Thus, some slaves were skilled workers—blacksmiths, carpenters, coopers (barrel-makers), or other craftspersons. A few slaves were promoted to overseer status, which put them in the delicate position of having to drive or discipline their fellow slaves—although this position was often reserved for poor whites. But the most significant division in the labor force was that between house slaves and field slaves. The former were usually lighter-skinned and sometimes, as in Thomas Jefferson's household, were offspring of the planter. Although under the close supervision of whites who could call on them day and night, house slaves often had an easier workload and a higher standard of living.

A whipping victim (Library of Congress)

In the Currier & Ives lithograph shown here, two carefree slaves dance while a third rests idly on a log, even as a steamboat waits to be loaded with a supply of cotton. Depictions of enslaved African Americans as childlike and lazy were common in the 19th century and helped to enforce the concept of white superiority. (Library of Congress)

This could produce tensions in the slave community as the house slaves sometimes saw themselves as superior, while field slaves saw the house slaves as allies of the planters.

The vast majority of slaves worked in the fields. But even here the types of labor varied depending on the crop produced. There were essentially two kinds of field labor. Most typical was gang labor, the kind usually employed on cotton plantations. Here, slaves worked in gangs under the close supervision of overseers, with the pace of planting or picking set by the fastest-working slave. The other form of labor was called the task system and was usually employed on rice or tobacco plantations, which required more skilled and delicate work than cotton farming. Here, groups of slaves were given specific tasks for the day, week, or season. Involving greater autonomy, the task system allowed slaves less white supervision and even time off for themselves once the task was completed. Finally, many slaves were rented out by their masters to work for others. Often, the hirers of slaves had little incentive to properly care for them since the slaves' long-term health was of little concern to them.

In any case—gang, task, or rental—the slave system allowed for little gender difference. While 19th-century white America believed in a strict differentiation of women's work from men's—or, in the case of upper class families, exempted women from labor altogether—slave owners demanded that all hands—female or male—work in the fields. Children,

SLAVERY'S IMPACT ON AFRICAN-AMERICAN CUISINE

Peppers: According to an old Yoruba proverb, "The man who eats no pepper is weak, for pepper is the staff of life." Hot and sweet ground red pepper and red pepper oil were commonly used to season meals in Africa. In slave cooks' efforts to enliven their food, they used generous amounts of red pepper, which they brought with them, or green peppercorns and cayenne pepper. A typical dish using pepper was okra soup infused with fresh mashed green peppers, which became a plantation staple in antebellum days.

Corn: Corn was a common staple food for enslaved Africans. Weekly rations typically included about a peck (16 pounds) of cornmeal, which when mixed with salt and water made cornbread, or as it was also variously called pone, johnny cake, corn dodger, or hoecake. On some large plantations, owners used a ritual called the shucking party to squeeze extra work out of slaves. Husking parties occurred at night, with the slaves singing as they worked. When work was done, the slaves took the corn directly into the plantation kitchen where they received a special meal—commonly thick soup and small amounts of whiskey—in return. The meal was often followed by a dance.

Peanuts: Africans used peanuts in their cuisine in different ways. For example, they often served fresh peanuts as a vegetable or ground them up as a soup base. This tradition continued especially in the South, and many typical southern dishes used peanuts in versatile ways. Peanuts were often prepared in a cream sauce, or for more exotic tastes, were mashed with yams and eggs, sprinkled with crumbs and seasoning, and formed into cakes and fried.

Deep Frying: African cooks used animal fat or palm oil to deep-fry their foods. Using big pots of oil, they fried a variety of foods, such as yams, okra, plantains, and bananas. Slaves continued this cooking style on the plantations, using the lard available from their pork rations. Fish such as catfish, butterfish, haddock, and trout were often prepared this way.

too, were put to work as soon as they could, while infants and toddlers were left in the care of slaves too old to work.

Family Life

Amidst the grueling work, grinding poverty, and abject cruelty of the plantation—and the constant specter of sale and separation—African Americans in bondage forged a uniquely powerful and sustaining social order, based primarily on family and religion. The preservation of a coherent and nurturing family life in spite of the cruelty of the slave regime of the antebellum South is one of the most remarkable achievements of African-American history.

The obstacles against maintaining such a structure were significant. One obstacle was the law. Unlike in Catholic slave countries of Latin America, slave marriages did not have legal standing. The North Carolina Supreme Court offered a typical interpretation of the matter in an 1853 ruling: "Our law requires no solemnity or form in regard to the marriage of slaves, and whether they 'take up' with each other by express permission of their owners, or from a mere impulse of nature, in obedience to the [biblical] command 'multiply and replenish the earth' cannot, in the contemplation of the law, make any sort of difference."

Another obstacle was the auction block. While some slaves might live out their lives on a single plantation, most would be transferred to another owner at least once in their lives, even if it was just to the plantation of their first owner's heir. Similarly, while most slaves were sold locally, leaving the possibility of visiting spouses and children on Sundays, many were not, especially after the 1820s, as the long-distance domestic slave trade

THE PRESERVATION OF CULTURE: SLAVE CRAFTS

Blacksmithing: Many enslaved Africans possessed sophisticated metalworking skills closely rooted in traditional African techniques. These slaves often helped build the lavish antebellum plantations of the American South, forging practical and ornamental objects such as wrought-iron balconies, grilles, doors, tools, and kitchenware. The wrought-iron gates shown here illustrate the high-quality detail present in African artisans' work.

Pottery: A number of pottery "face vessels" have been attributed to 19th-century slaves. Ranging in height from one inch to one foot, they are typically glazed in dark colors such as green, brown, or black. Certain characteristics, such as large inlaid eyes and wide mouths, displaying prominent teeth, also appear in ancient sculptures found in what is now the Democratic Republic of Congo. Although the function of these vessels is debated, they appear to have been of personal value, as many of them were found near Underground Railroad homes.

Basket Weaving: Basket weaving has a long African heritage, and the tradition was preserved by African slave communities in the antebellum South. Sweetgrass baskets, still commonly found in South Carolina, are similar to those found in West Africa. These baskets have distinct geometric patterns. Craftspeople weave tan-colored sweetgrass with darker strips of pine needles, binding them together with palmetto leaves. They still prefer to use traditional tools, such as nails, the flat ends of teaspoons, and even sharpened oyster shells.

Wood Carving: Many slaves of the American South were also familiar with West African wood carving techniques. The tradition of carving wooden canes and walking sticks with reptilian imagery (symbolic of spiritual strength) continued in bondage. The cane shown here is attributed to Henry Gudgell, who lived and worked on a 19th-century Missouri plantation. The motifs—the lizard, the tortoise, and the serpent wrapped around the base—are all of African derivation.

A slave family (Library of Congress)

between the eastern seaboard and the Old Southwest increased. Despite their profession of deep Christian faith, slave owners routinely ignored this bedrock of the faith as far as slaves were concerned. Again, racist ideas offered a rationalization that overrode reality. African Americans, it was argued, could not understand the meaning of holy matrimony and, being childlike, did not share the emotional sophistication necessary for romantic love—this, despite the common scenes of heartbreaking grief of spouses and parents suddenly separated on the auction block from their loved ones.

But if racism offered a justification for ignoring Christian tradition, the fundamental reason for ignoring slave marriage was economic. Slaves were property pure and simple. If a master needed to break up a slave marriage or family for economic necessity, then the state—controlled by that same master class—was not going to get in the way with laws in defense of slave marriages. In registering newly freed slaves after the Civil War, Union army officials in Mississippi found that fully one quarter of all male slaves had been torn from their wives at least once by sales.

Highlighted in much of the antislavery literature of the day, though couched in delicate language, was another, deeply shameful obstacle placed in the path of

African-American family life on the plantation. It was not uncommon for slave owners, their sons, and the white overseers they hired to take mistresses from among the slave quarters. Some did it by coercion—even rape; others used incentives to gain the company of slave women. Whatever the method, the taking of mistresses by white masters cast a dark shadow over the security and sanctity of families and marriages within the slave quarters.

Despite all of these obstacles the African-American family survived, largely by retaining African customs and adapting them to the painful and disruptive daily life under the slave regime. Although slave marriages carried no legal weight, African Americans married in ceremonies—such as jumping over the broom to symbolize domestic wedlock—that resonated with African tradition. Unless broken up by sale, these marriages often lasted a lifetime and were the core of strong nuclear families. Beyond that, African Americans retained the extended family networks familiar back in the homeland. To establish heritage in a world where families could be broken up at any moment at the will of the master or the market, children were named in ways that created links with the past—such as being named after the day of the week on which they were born, a customary practice in

West Africa. Or they might be named after an aunt, grandparent, or cousin who had been sold off or died.

Extended families might also include fictive kin, or close friends who were not actually related by blood or by marriage but who nonetheless considered themselves part of an extended family through unofficial adoption. Like extended families, this practice hailed back to the West African homeland and was adapted to slave society in the Americas. By these methods of naming and adoption, enslaved African-American parents could be fairly certain that their children would be taken care of should they themselves die or be sold off.

RELIGION

Religion was the other mainstay of African-American life on the plantation. In certain isolated areas like the Louisiana Delta or the Sea Islands off South Carolina and Georgia—where blacks vastly outnumbered whites and imports from Africa and the Caribbean continued up to the international slave trade ban in 1807–1808—this religion might include strong African elements, as was the case with voodoo practices in New Orleans. But for the most part, slave religion was Christian, usually Baptist or Methodist, but occasionally Episcopalian.

Planters could hardly deny religion to their slaves. One of the pillars of the slaveholder ideology was that slavery was a halfway house on the path from savagery to civilization. Civilization in 19th-century America was synonymous with Christianity. Thus, masters often encouraged religious practice on their plantations as they hoped it might inculcate the values they wanted in their slaves—loyalty, obedience, submission to a God-given order where blacks were subservient to whites, and the reward of everlasting freedom in the afterlife. But slave congregations were taught and absorbed a very different Christian message. In secret meetings, self-taught slave or itinerant free black preachers emphasized liberation in this world and not just the next, with an emphasis on the Book of Exodus and its story of Moses leading the Hebrews out of their Egyptian bondage.

As all faith is intended to do, the Christian religion of the slaves attempted to fuse daily practice with a larger meaning and purpose to life. Slavery, black preachers sermonized, was a wicked and sinful institution created and maintained by the devil. As good Christians, slaves were bound by their faith to fight sin and wickedness—hence, to fight slavery. Every act of resistance, every attempt to subvert the will of the master, then, was infused with a higher purpose, fulfilling God's will.

RESISTANCE AND ESCAPE

The record of African-American resistance to slavery is a long and proud one. Some aspects of it—particularly the Underground Railroad and the great slave rebellions, like the one led by Nat Turner in 1831—are well chronicled in most history books. But most went on quietly, in everyday life. For example, slaves stole from their masters. George Washington once complained that his slaves were drinking more of his wine than he was. To many whites, thievery by slaves only confirmed the racist belief that it was in the very nature of the black man to steal.

At the most basic level, the main cause of stealing by slaves was that they were all too often underfed. But, to slaves, stealing also had a moral element—for to them, stealing was really an act of taking back what properly belonged to them, the fruits of their labor confiscated by their masters.

SUBVERSION AND RESISTANCE

Taking a master's property was only one form of everyday subversion. Slaves also found effective ways to withhold their labor power. Slaves sometimes feigned illness to get out of work. Many African-American communities had developed a whole host of herbal concoctions that were not just used to cure the sick but to make someone appear to be so. Slaves also sabotaged equipment. By breaking a hoe, a slave in the fields would have to make the long walk back to the toolshed to get a replacement or have their broken one fixed. This provided both a much-needed break from their backbreaking labor and the satisfaction of knowing they

VOODOO

During the first half of the 19th century, New Orleans, Lousiana, was an important center for free blacks. Many had come to New Orleans from Haiti during that country's revolution. They brought with them many of the spiritual traditions of the Yoruba religion to their new home. These rites were known as voudun, or voodoo, meaning "spirit" or "deity" in the West African Ewe language. Adherants of voodoo believe that life can be improved or destroyed by any of the over 400 spirit forces, or loas, in the voodoo pantheon. Worshippers pray for good fortune and protection from evil using amulets, dolls, spells, and rituals.

Voodoo thrived in New Orleans's black community despite laws dating back to 1724 requiring all Africans to be baptized into the Roman Catholic Church. Voodoo thus coexisted and even mingled with Catholicism, creating a system of syncretic imagery and belief that exists to this day.

During the 19th century, Marie Laveau (1796–1879) reigned as Queen of Voodoo in New Orleans. Born a free Catholic, her reputation as a voodoo priestess solidified soon after she became a member of the religion in 1826. In her house near Congo Square, she practiced her religious magic, making and selling charms, or *gris-gris*. Mesmerized by her beauty and spiritual powers, both Africans and whites consulted her on matters such as love, wealth, death, and happiness. Laveau sometimes invited whites suspicious of voodoo to rituals, thus helping dispel mistaken beliefs that these events were barbaric and rife with human sacrifice. To this day, voodoo worshippers pay homage to Laveau, visiting her grave and making offerings.

THE ORAL TRADITION

The African-American oral tradition was a direct response to the powerlessness that enslaved blacks felt. Numerous stories were passed from generation to generation in a subtle expression of subversion. The most famous of these stories were the Br'er (Brother) Rabbit tales, featuring a cunning protaganist based on West African trickster figures. Below are other examples, collected by the early 20th century writers Langston Hughes and Arna Bontemps in their seminal 1958 work, *The Book of Negro Folklore*, followed by explanations:

Story: *They say that in the beginning, God was getting the races together and He told the people, He say, "now, yawl git to the right." But He couldn't hear so good, so he make them all "white." Then He say, "yawl standin' aroun', stand aroun', git aroun'!" They all got brown.*

Explanation: Many black folktales tried to make sense of the race question. In this story, the reasons for racial differences are made to look silly—that God simply made a mistake.

Story: *Dese two old black slaves and their massa were waiting in line at St. Peter's gate to be let into hebbin [heaven]. Ol' St. Peter, he say, to the two blacks, you two go on over there to those little cabins by the creek. Then he say to their massa, you there, you got that big white house on the hill. The first slave, he say, dis ain't fair. That bad ol' master gettin' the fine house in hebbin and we gettin' the same ol' cabins like back on de earth. How come? And ol' St. Peter, he say, you two dumb as wood. We got plenty o' black men up here, but dat one be the first white man we ever got.*

Explanation: In most slave stories, the white man is usually punished in the afterlife. But in this one, he is rewarded. The twist of the story, of course, is that white men generally are made to look bad.

had put one over on the master. Out of this tradition of quietly subverting the will of the master came an oral tradition, some of which was eventually written down after the Civil War as the tales of Br'er (short for Brother) Rabbit and Br'er Fox. Based on the West African figure of the trickster, Br'er Rabbit—though physically weak and helpless—was always outsmarting Br'er Fox.

Ultimately, these small acts of rebellion by slaves were intended—consciously or unconsciously—to maintain a sense of power and control over one's life in a world where slaves had little or none. But they also signified that deep down slaves occupied a critical place in the southern order of things. Planters were after profits; profits came from crops; crops were raised by slaves. If a slave could deny his or her labor, he or she could exert power. Of course, this had to be done very carefully, since planters had a host of punishment available to them all the way up to exile (that is, sale) and even execution (masters were never

prosecuted for killing slaves, though few did so since it meant loss of a major investment).

Unlike free laborers, of course, slaves could not go on strike, at least not overtly. And yet, there was a way to strike out against the master, and that way was to escape. Slaves escaped frequently or, at least, temporarily absented themselves from the plantation. Most slaves who ran away did so locally, to the nearby woods, and for short periods of time, not permanently (the odds against long-distance escape were enormous, as discussed in the next section). The reasons were many: to visit a loved one on another plantation, to supplement a meager diet by hunting or fishing, or to escape punishment. This could be a form of negotiation, particularly at critical points in the growing season when all hands were needed. Desperate to recover the lost slave, a master might send another slave to talk the runaway into coming back (often, other slaves secretly brought food to a runaway and knew his or her whereabouts). All of this did not mean that planters and slaves negotiated as equals on questions of punishment and other matters, but simply that slaves did exert some power in their own way. They were not the completely helpless victims of the master's will.

THE UNDERGROUND RAILROAD

While most slaves made their escapes temporary, thousands of African Americans did manage to break free of slavery and the South altogether, usually by escaping to the North and Canada. A few in the Deep South made it to the swamps of Florida, where they joined the Seminole Nation or stowed away on boats bound for the Caribbean, while some Texan slaves made their escape to Mexico, which had banned slavery upon independence from Spain in 1821. But the odds against escaping the South were long. The distances were enormous. White patrols, supplemented with bloodhounds, constantly patrolled the roads. Any black person off the plantation was presumed to be a runaway, and if stopped by a white—who was usually armed—would be forced to produce a pass. Thus, the odds were best for those who lived near the free states. Still, it is estimated that approximately 1,000 slaves annually made it to freedom during the 1840s and 1850s. Many were aided in their escape by a network of black and white abolitionists—that is, those who opposed slavery on moral grounds—that came to be called the Underground Railroad.

Because of the intense secrecy that shrouded its operations, much about the Underground Railroad has been lost to history. As slaves were property, freeing them was a form of theft under state and federal law. Penalties for those who participated were severe, especially for blacks. While whites risked arrest, prison, and fines, black "conductors" and "station masters"—as guides and owners of safe houses (places where runaway slaves could hide) were respectively called—risked being sent back into slavery. Even free blacks in the North could be re-enslaved if caught aiding runaways. For instance, abolitionist Frederick Douglass, born a slave on the Eastern Shore of Maryland, made his way north by borrowing the papers of a free black sailor. Had Douglass been caught, it is highly likely that the sailor would have been punished by enslavement.

While some slaves, like Douglass, made their way north by boat, most traveled by land routes. In general, a slave's best chance of escape came if he or she was escorted northward by a "conductor," a free black or former slave living in the North who traveled South to serve as a guide. The most famous of these was Harriet Tubman. Like Douglass, Tubman was born a slave on Maryland's Eastern Shore, not far from the free state of Pennsylvania. As a teen, she was severely injured when her owner threw a two-pound weight at a runaway slave Tubman was shielding. The weight hit Tubman in the head, leaving a deep scar and a propensity for headaches and dizzy spells the rest of her life. After marrying a free black in 1844, Tubman searched for ways to escape bondage. She first tried the law and, when that failed, she escaped to the North in 1849. (Her husband refused to go along so she went alone.)

Working as a maid and cook in Philadelphia, Tubman saved her earnings and plotted a trip to Baltimore to free her sister and her sister's two children in 1850. Between that year and the outbreak of the Civil War, Tubman—despite

a bounty on her head, dead or alive—made more than 15 trips into the South, liberating some 200 slaves, including her entire family. Unlike conductors in the early years of the Railroad—when most runaways were settled in the free black communities of the North—Tubman had to deal with the Fugitive Slave Act, which required northern authorities return all runaways or face federal criminal prosecution. To cope, she linked with a network of safe houses and guides who could lead escaped slaves to Canada.

For those slaves living in the Deep South, escape to Mexico and Florida were alternatives to the North. Before the Civil War, hundreds of Texan slaves made their way to freedom in Mexico. In the mid-1850s, noted landscape architect

Harriet Tubman (Library of Congress)

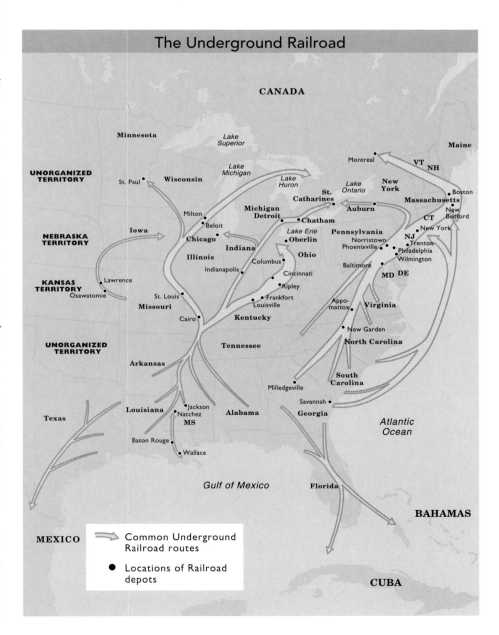

Fredrick Law Olmstead reported meeting an escaped slave in Mexico:

> *He very civilly informed me . . . that he was born in Virginia, and had been brought South by a trader and sold to a gentleman who had brought him to Texas, from whom he had run away four or five years ago. He would like . . . to see old Virginia again, that he would— if he could be free. He was a mechanic, and could earn a dollar very easily, by his trade, every day. He could speak Spanish fluently, and had traveled extensively in Mexico, sometimes on his own business, and sometimes as a servant or muleteer. . . . He had joined the Catholic Church, he said, and he was very well satisfied with the country. Runaways were constantly arriving here; two had got over, as I had previously been informed, the night before. He could not guess how many came in a year, but he could count forty, that he had known of, in the last three months. . . .*

THE SEMINOLE WARS

Far more runaways found their way to Florida, a then sparsely settled territory of marshes, subtropiocal forests, and scrubland. Ensconced in these wilds were runaway blacks and a nation of Indians, known as the Seminole, who continued to resist southern planters and even the U.S. Army right up to the verge of the Civil War. The Seminole—named from a Creek version of the Spanish word for "runaway" or "wild"—had been one of the "Five Civilized Tribes" of the Southeast, displaced by white settlers and the government in the late 1700s and early 1800s. Rather than being moved to Oklahoma, however, most of the Seminole escaped to Florida, which as a Spanish colony, lay outside the jurisdiction of the United States.

There, the two communities—Native American and African American— developed a symbiotic relationship whereby the latter did much of the agricultural work while the former offered land and protection against invading whites. Technically, the blacks were slaves of the Native Americans but that was chiefly for legal cover. In fact, the two lived largely as equals, with blacks assuming many positions of leadership within the tribe. For blacks, the existence of an independent mixed race society on slavery's southern border was a ready inducement for escape. For British and later American planters, the existence of this independent black and Indian community was a major irritant. During colonial times, the Spanish encouraged these runaways, going so far as to arm them as a defense against British incursions. In the early years of the American republic, planters and militiamen from Georgia launched periodic raids to recapture runaways.

Beginning in 1816, U.S. Army troops got into the fight. In that year, General Andrew Jackson led a major expedition against the Seminole and their stronghold on Apalachicola Bay, a place known as Fort Negro. Surrounded by cannon fire from land and sea, 300 Seminole men, women, and children held out until a well-placed shot from a U.S. warship struck the fort's ammunition dump, causing an explosion that killed most of the defenders. Hundreds of other Seminole living in the Pensacola region continued to resist. By 1818, the year before Florida itself was purchased from the Spanish and incorporated as a U.S. territory, most Seminole had been pushed farther south. With this U.S. victory, what is known as the First Seminole War had ended, although scattered skirmishes continued over the next several years.

Then U.S. policy was to promise land to the Native Americans, in exchange for the return of runaway slaves. While Seminole leaders generally refused to turn over runaway slaves, fear of such a deal caused many black Seminole to set up separate communities within the wilds of Florida. But many blacks continued to live among and marry Native Americans. In the 1830s, the U.S. government again began pressuring Seminole to join the other "civilized tribes" in emigrating to Oklahoma and other lands west of the Mississippi River. In 1835, some of the Seminole chiefs were tricked into signing a misleading treaty that appeared to promise them the right to remain in Florida but actually called for their removal. When the truth about the treaty was revealed, an army of black and Native American Seminole launched attacks on white plantations and U.S. Army outposts, sparking the Second Seminole War.

For several years, the U.S. Army and the Seminole clashed throughout northern and central Florida. Under the leadership of chiefs Osceola, King Philip, and Wild Cat, Seminole warriors pursued a guerrilla strategy of hitting the U.S. Army when they least expected it, and then disappearing into the swamps they knew so well. With Seminole facing extradition to Oklahoma and blacks re-enslavement, the fighting became bitter. General Thomas Sidney Jesup, commander of U.S. forces in the Second Seminole War, recognized the importance of the black Seminoles in the resistance. "This, you may be assured," he told his superiors in Washington, "is a negro and not an Indian war.... Throughout my operations I found the negroes the most active and determined warriors; and during my conferences with the Indian chief [Osceola] I ascertained that they exercised an almost controlling interest over [him]."

However, using trickery and overwhelming force, Jesup and the U.S. Army were eventually able to capture Osceola and wear down much of the Seminole's resistance. By 1842, most of the Seminole had surrendered, with hundreds sent west to Arkansas and Oklahoma and many blacks forced back into slavery. A reporter for *Harper's Weekly* noted in that year, "The negro slaves are, in fact, the masters of their own red owners.... The negroes were the master spirits, as well as the immediate occasion, of the Florida wars. They openly refused to follow their masters if they removed to Arkansas; it was not until they capitulated that the Seminoles ever thought of emigrating."

Still, a small band of African Americans and Seminole continued to hold out in the Everglade swamps of southern Florida. A series of sporadic skirmishes, sometimes called the Third Seminole War, continued until 1858. These last survivors won a major concession from the federal government, which allowed them to stay on in southern Florida, where they live to this day. Today's mixed-race Florida Seminole are

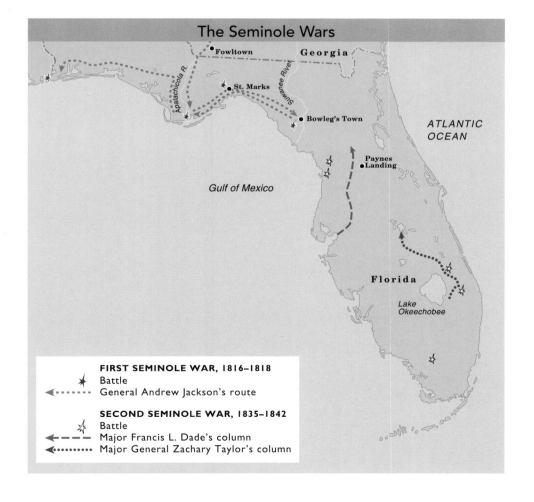

The Seminole Wars

Fowltown

Georgia

Apalachicola R.

Suwannee River

St. Marks

Bowleg's Town

ATLANTIC OCEAN

Paynes Landing

Gulf of Mexico

Florida

Lake Okeechobee

FIRST SEMINOLE WAR, 1816–1818
✳ Battle
◄······· General Andrew Jackson's route

SECOND SEMINOLE WAR, 1835–1842
✳ Battle
◄‒ ‒ ‒ Major Francis L. Dade's column
◄········· Major General Zachary Taylor's column

proud to say that they fought the longest war in American history against the U.S. government and that they never signed a treaty ending the war.

SLAVE REBELLIONS

The mixed-race Seminole represent the most long-lived armed resistance to the slave regime in American history and the best example of a runaway slave community surviving within U.S. territory. But armed resistance to the slave regime of the South was hardly confined to Florida and the Seminole. The first major slave uprising in American history occurred in South Carolina on September 9, 1739, when hundreds of slaves gathered along the Stono River and then marched from plantation to plantation killing masters and freeing slaves. The rebellion, which lasted but a single day, resulted in the deaths of some 60 people including 35 slaves and was put down by colonial militias. The Stono Rebellion resulted in a series of harsh edicts that restricted freedom of movement and assembly and revoked the right of slaves to earn money or learn to read. In addition, the colonial assembly outlawed the "speaking drum," an African instrument that was used at Stono to call slaves to rebellion. While numerous acts of violent resistance continued throughout the colonial period, most were small-scale and many have been lost to history. It would take more than 60 years for African Americans of the South to attempt another major uprising against the slave regime, this time in the Virginia area.

The 1790s and 1800s were a tense time in the upper South; the wave of manumissions following the Revolution had largely come to an end. As discussed in the previous chapter, however, planters

SLAVE UPRISINGS IN NORTH AMERICA, 1663–1831

1 **1663** African slaves join white indentured servants in Gloucester County, Virginia, to plan a revolt. When the plan is discovered, the black leaders are beheaded and their heads publically displayed in the village square.

2 **1712** Twenty-one slaves are executed in New York City for their part in an uprising.

3 **1739** Fifty to 100 slaves at Stono, South Carolina, flee the South with stolen arms, killing all whites who attempt to stop them. They are later captured.

4 **1741** Although the evidence is scant, 31 slaves are charged with burning down several properties in New York and executed.

5 **1741** In Boston, slaves are caught trying to escape to Florida in a stolen boat.

6 **1800** Gabriel Prosser, a Virginia slave, plans an attack on Richmond, Virginia. Most of the 40,000 slaves living in the region were thought to know the plan. Before the revolt is set to take place, the plan is discovered and Richmond placed under martial law. Then torrential rains on the evening that the uprising is set to begin disrupt the plan completely. Prosser is captured and hanged a month later.

7 **1822** Denmark Vesey, a free black carpenter, plans a revolt to conquer Charleston, South Carolina. When his plan is discovered, he and 47 others are executed.

8 **1831** Nat Turner, a slave whose father had escaped to freedom, leads a group of slaves through Southampton County, Virginia, after swearing to kill all whites in surrounding plantations. Just over 24 hours later, he and his men have killed more than 60 white men, women, and children. In retaliation, whites throughout the South kill more than 100 blacks, regardless of their involvement in the revolt.

- - - - Western frontier

* Vermont claimed by New York during the Revolution; admitted to the Union as a state in 1791.

proud to say that they fought the longest war in American history against the U.S. government and that they never signed a treaty ending the war.

SLAVE REBELLIONS

The mixed-race Seminole represent the most long-lived armed resistance to the slave regime in American history and the best example of a runaway slave community surviving within U.S. territory. But armed resistance to the slave regime of the South was hardly confined to Florida and the Seminole. The first major slave uprising in American history occurred in South Carolina on September 9, 1739, when hundreds of slaves gathered along the Stono River and then marched from plantation to plantation killing masters and freeing slaves. The rebellion, which lasted but a single day, resulted in the deaths of some 60 people including 35 slaves and was put down by colonial militias. The Stono Rebellion resulted in a series of harsh edicts that restricted freedom of movement and assembly and revoked the right of slaves to earn money or learn to read. In addition, the colonial assembly outlawed the "speaking drum," an African instrument that was used at Stono to call slaves to rebellion. While numerous acts of violent resistance continued throughout the colonial period, most were small-scale and many have been lost to history. It would take more than 60 years for African Americans of the South to attempt another major uprising against the slave regime, this time in the Virginia area.

The 1790s and 1800s were a tense time in the upper South; the wave of manumissions following the Revolution had largely come to an end. As discussed in the previous chapter, however, planters

SLAVE UPRISINGS IN NORTH AMERICA, 1663–1831

1 **1663** African slaves join white indentured servants in Gloucester County, Virginia, to plan a revolt. When the plan is discovered, the black leaders are beheaded and their heads publically displayed in the village square.

2 **1712** Twenty-one slaves are executed in New York City for their part in an uprising.

3 **1739** Fifty to 100 slaves at Stono, South Carolina, flee the South with stolen arms, killing all whites who attempt to stop them. They are later captured.

4 **1741** Although the evidence is scant, 31 slaves are charged with burning down several properties in New York and executed.

5 **1741** In Boston, slaves are caught trying to escape to Florida in a stolen boat.

6 **1800** Gabriel Prosser, a Virginia slave, plans an attack on Richmond, Virginia. Most of the 40,000 slaves living in the region were thought to know the plan. Before the revolt is set to take place, the plan is discovered and Richmond placed under martial law. Then torrential rains on the evening that the uprising is set to begin disrupt the plan completely. Prosser is captured and hanged a month later.

7 **1822** Denmark Vesey, a free black carpenter, plans a revolt to conquer Charleston, South Carolina. When his plan is discovered, he and 47 others are executed.

8 **1831** Nat Turner, a slave whose father had escaped to freedom, leads a group of slaves through Southampton County, Virginia, after swearing to kill all whites in surrounding plantations. Just over 24 hours later, he and his men have killed more than 60 white men, women, and children. In retaliation, whites throughout the South kill more than 100 blacks, regardless of their involvement in the revolt.

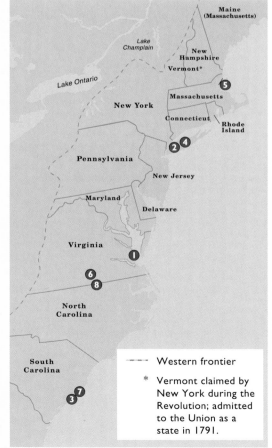

Western frontier

* Vermont claimed by New York during the Revolution; admitted to the Union as a state in 1791.

about the treaty was revealed, an army of black and Native American Seminole launched attacks on white plantations and U.S. Army outposts, sparking the Second Seminole War.

For several years, the U.S. Army and the Seminole clashed throughout northern and central Florida. Under the leadership of chiefs Osceola, King Philip, and Wild Cat, Seminole warriors pursued a guerrilla strategy of hitting the U.S. Army when they least expected it, and then disappearing into the swamps they knew so well. With Seminole facing extradition to Oklahoma and blacks re-enslavement, the fighting became bitter. General Thomas Sidney Jesup, commander of U.S. forces in the Second Seminole War, recognized the importance of the black Seminoles in the resistance. "This, you may be assured," he told his superiors in Washington, "is a negro and not an Indian war.... Throughout my operations I found the negroes the most active and determined warriors; and during my conferences with the Indian chief [Osceola] I ascertained that they exercised an almost controlling interest over [him]."

However, using trickery and overwhelming force, Jesup and the U.S. Army were eventually able to capture Osceola and wear down much of the Seminole's resistance. By 1842, most of the Seminole had surrendered, with hundreds sent west to Arkansas and Oklahoma and many blacks forced back into slavery. A reporter for *Harper's Weekly* noted in that year, "The negro slaves are, in fact, the masters of their own red owners.... The negroes were the master spirits, as well as the immediate occasion, of the Florida wars. They openly refused to follow their masters if they removed to Arkansas; it was not until they capitulated that the Seminoles ever thought of emigrating."

Still, a small band of African Americans and Seminole continued to hold out in the Everglade swamps of southern Florida. A series of sporadic skirmishes, sometimes called the Third Seminole War, continued until 1858. These last survivors won a major concession from the federal government, which allowed them to stay on in southern Florida, where they live to this day. Today's mixed-race Florida Seminole are

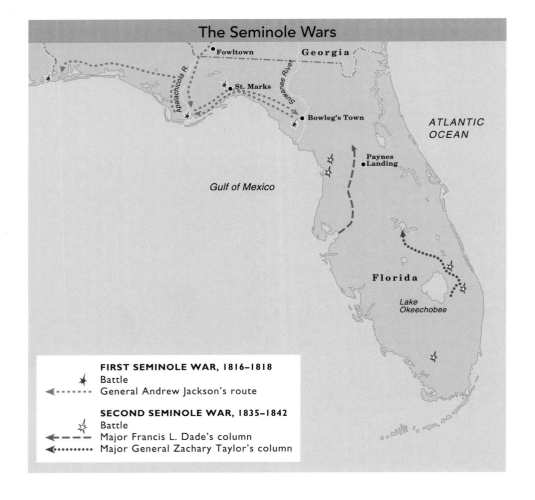

The Seminole Wars

Fowltown

Georgia

Apalachicola R.

St. Marks

Suwannee River

Bowleg's Town

ATLANTIC OCEAN

Paynes Landing

Gulf of Mexico

Florida

Lake Okeechobee

FIRST SEMINOLE WAR, 1816–1818
✳ Battle
◄····· General Andrew Jackson's route

SECOND SEMINOLE WAR, 1835–1842
✩ Battle
◄ — — Major Francis L. Dade's column
◄····· Major General Zachary Taylor's column

in the United States had closely followed the violence in Haiti that began in 1791 and ended with the overthrow of the white regime in 1804. Two years after the Haitian rebellion started, the U.S. Congress passed the first fugitive slave law, allowing owners to reclaim escaped slaves who had crossed state lines. In 1800, a self-educated blacksmith in the Richmond area named Gabriel Prosser organized a rebellion that may have involved up to 600 slaves. Angry at the fact that his master kept most of his earnings as an itinerant craftsman—and believing that the nation was facing an imminent political crisis during an election year that saw Democrats take over the government from Federalists—Prosser selected the night of August 30 for the uprising. But a major thunderstorm forced him to postpone the rebellion for 24 hours, during which time several slaves betrayed the plot to whites. Though hundreds of African Americans were arrested, Prosser escaped on a schooner to Norfolk. Unfortunately for him, another slave—enticed by a $300 reward—revealed his whereabouts. Prosser, along with 26 other slaves, were tried and executed. In response, Virginia strengthened its laws against slave assemblies and literacy, as well as bolstering its militia.

Betrayal also doomed the new republic's second major rebellion, this one in Charleston, South Carolina, in 1822. Fear of slave uprisings was particularly acute in the state as the population of blacks had outnumbered that of whites for nearly a century. Moreover, Charleston was one of the few cities of the Deep South with a significant number of free blacks. Among these was Denmark Vesey, a former slave who had purchased his freedom after winning a state lottery in 1799. A successful carpenter, Vesey had amassed $8,000 in savings by 1822, a fortune for a free black man of the South in those years. Despite his personal prosperity, Vesey dedicated his life to destroying the institution of slavery, speaking at gatherings in black churches and workshops. By 1822, he had gathered a small cadre of like-minded blacks—both enslaved and free—willing to launch an uprising against the white population. Planned for late July, the conspiracy was betrayed by several slaves in May. Cash awards were offered to those who turned in conspirators and, on July 2, Vesey was

The broadside above depicts Nat Turner's Rebellion as follows: 1. A woman pleads for the life of her children; 2. Mr. Travis is murdered by his own slaves; 3. Mr. Barrow defends himself so his wife can escape; 4. Mounted dragoons in pursuit of slaves. (Library of Congress)

arrested. Refusing to confess, Vesey and 34 other African Americans were executed. Once again, harsh laws were passed in response, including a law that required all free black sailors be jailed while their ships were in port.

Despite such measures, rebellions large and small continued across the South, reaching a culmination in the bloodiest slave uprising in American history: the Nat Turner revolt of 1831. Turner was born a slave in Virginia's Southampton County on October 2, 1800, just five days before the execution of Gabriel Prosser. His father had run away when Turner was a boy, where it is believed he lived out his life as a runaway slave in the Great Dismal Swamp along the North Carolina border. Turner's mother was just seven years removed from Africa when she gave birth to Nat and constantly told her son that he was destined for great things. Deeply spiritual and a self-educated biblical scholar, Turner claimed to receive visions all of his life. In 1821, his master, Benjamin Turner, hired a particularly violent overseer and Nat escaped for a month, during which time he claimed God told him to lead a slave rebellion. Over the next decade, Turner became an itinerant preacher, traveling from plantation to plantation giving sermons on the necessity of violent liberation. An eclipse of the sun in February 1831 was, in Turner's mind, a signal that the time for revolt was ripe. He soon began recruiting a small band of followers with the symbolic date of July 4 as their day to launch the rebellion. When Turner got sick, the date was pushed back six weeks.

On August 22, Turner and his followers began their attack, striking first on the plantation of Joseph Travis, where Turner then lived. The strategy was simple and brutal; they would move from plantation to plantation slaughtering masters and their families until they had intimidated the local white community and raised an army of rebel slaves. At that point, the killing would cease and the

slave army would head for Jerusalem, Virginia, the site of a major arsenal. Armed, they would make their way to the Great Dismal Swamp where they would establish an armed free black community impervious to white counterattack. Over the next couple of days, the rebels—now some 60 or 70 in all—murdered 57 whites, though it is believed that Turner himself killed no one. But as the element of surprise faded, local white militias counterattacked, killing some 100 blacks and ending the uprising. Turner, however, escaped and was not apprehended until October 30. Following a brief trial, he was executed on November 11, 1831.

Like the Prosser and Vesey rebellions before it, the Nat Turner uprising led to harsh new disciplinary edicts and practices. Beyond that, the Turner rebellion marked a pivotal moment in the history of American slavery and in the

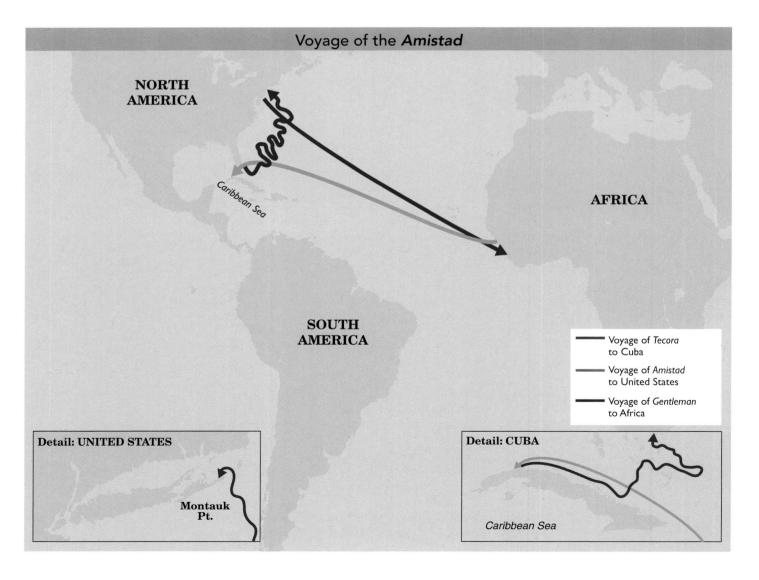

Voyage of the *Amistad*

NORTH AMERICA

Caribbean Sea

AFRICA

SOUTH AMERICA

— Voyage of *Tecora*
   to Cuba

— Voyage of *Amistad*
   to United States

— Voyage of *Gentleman*
   to Africa

Detail: UNITED STATES

Montauk Pt.

Detail: CUBA

Caribbean Sea

Death of Capt. Ferrer, the Captain of the Amistad, July, 1839.

Don Jose Ruiz and Don Pedro Montez, of the Island of Cuba, having purchased fifty-three slaves at Havana, recently imported from Africa, put them on board the Amistad, Capt. Ferrer, in order to transport them to Principe, another port on the Island of Cuba. After being out from Havana about four days, the African captives on board, in order to obtain their freedom, and return to Africa, armed themselves with cane knives, and rose upon the Captain and crew of the vessel. Capt. Ferrer and the cook of the vessel were killed; two of the crew escaped; Ruiz and Montez were made prisoners

development of the antislavery movement. The uprising ended any lingering thoughts that slavery might fade away peacefully in the upper South. It also dispelled the belief that slaves were largely contented with their lot.

The *Amistad*

In April 1839, slave traders in Lomboko (modern-day Sierra Leone) loaded captured Africans aboard the slaver *Tecora* and set off for Havana, Cuba. Once there, the 53 Africans were purchased by Spaniards Jose Ruiz and Pedro Montes and placed on board their ship, the *Amistad*. On July 1, an African named Joseph Cinque, who was the son of a Mende chief, led his companions in rebellion against the ship's crew. The Africans killed the captain, cook, and two sailors but spared Ruiz and Montes, who promised them passage back to Africa. For almost two months, the ship zig-zagged up the Atlantic coast as the slave owners sailed the ship toward Africa by day, then back toward the Americas at night.

In late August, the *Amistad* came ashore at Culloden Point, Long Island, and was seized by Lieutenant Thomas Gedney of the U.S. Coast Guard. Cinque and his companions were accused of murder, mutiny, and piracy. Roger Baldwin, a Connecticut lawyer, took up their defense, aided by a committee of abolitionists. The case riveted the attention of abolitionist and proslavery Americans alike, as well as President Martin Van Buren, who feared a diplomatic rift with Spain.

Beginning in September 1839, Baldwin and his team argued the case of *Gedney v. l'Amistad* in front of the U.S. District Court of Connecticut. The complex case involved three separate but intertwined legal issues.

The first concerned the legal status on three African girls, who had been on board the ship but had not participated in the revolt. Baldwin asked Judge Smith Thompson to set the girls free. In making his case, however, Baldwin chose not to focus on the girls themselves. Instead, he laid the groundwork for an argument that would set free all the Africans. He contended that the Africans had committed no acts that violated U.S. law, but that laws may have been broken by either Lieutenant Gedney for bringing the Africans into the United States or Montes and Ruiz for slave-trading. He also pointed out that the United States had no treaty with Spain obligating it to turn over the slaves. Justice Thompson accepted Baldwin's arguments but ruled that the girls should be held as witnesses until all questions involving the status of their fellow Africans could be settled.

The second legal issue was whether the Africans should be charged with murder. Thompson ruled that because the revolt took place on a Spanish ship in international waters U.S. courts had no

Sierra Leone and Liberia

CAPE VERDE IS.
MAURITANIA
MALI
NIGER
SENEGAL
THE GAMBIA
GUINEA-BISSAU
GUINEA
BURKINA FASO
GHANA
NIGERIA
CÔTE D'IVOIRE
SIERRA LEONE
LIBERIA
CAMEROON
TOGO
BENIN
EQUATORIAL GUINEA
SÃO TOMÉ E PRÍNCIPE
GABON
CONGO

Freetown, the present-day capital of Sierra Leone, was founded in 1787 by the British Sierra Leone Company as a haven for former slaves from Great Britain, North America, and the Caribbean. In 1820, the American Colonization Society (ACS) sent the first group of freedpersons from the United States to Sierra Leone. Two years later, that group moved south to present-day Liberia, where they founded the city that would later become Monrovia. Liberia became the first independent republic in 1847.

Paul Cuffe (Library of Congress)

jurisdiction and the Africans could not be held as criminals. However, because their legal status had not yet been determined, he ruled that the Africans be held in jail until the matter was resolved. They remained in jail for two years.

The third and most complex issue involved the right of various parties to claim the Africans as property. With backing from the Spanish government, Ruiz and Montes made a legal claim. The U.S. government, for its part, demanded the return of the Africans to Montes and Ruiz and also (in contradiction) their consignment to President Van Buren so that he might return them to Africa. In January 1840, U.S. District Judge Andrew Judson ruled that since slavery did not exist in Connecticut, neither Ruiz and Mendes nor Lieutenant Gedney had any right to the Africans as property and that they should therefore be returned to Africa. He also ruled that because the Africans were no longer being held on criminal charges, they should be housed someplace besides jail. Judson offered to set them free on bail equivalent to the Africans' "appraised value" in the Cuban slave market. Baldwin turned down the offer on principle, and the Africans remained in jail.

At the request of Spain, the United States appealed Judson's ruling in February 1841 to the Supreme Court. Baldwin was joined by former president John Quincy Adams, who condemned Spain for demanding the return of the *Amistad* and its cargo. He also criticized

President Van Buren for giving in to Spanish pressure. His argument was made mostly on moral, not legal grounds, but his eloquence and stature as a former president lent weight to the Africans' case. In restating his case, Baldwin concentrated on Spanish law and existing treaties between the United States and Spain, as well as on New York and Connecticut laws, to argue that the Africans were not slaves, that the United States had no obligation to turn them over, and that the United States had no legitimate interest as a party to the case in the first place. Ultimately, the Court decided in favor of the Africans, and in November 1841 the 35 who were still living set sail for Sierra Leone aboard the *Gentleman*.

ANTISLAVERY MOVEMENT

Many of the founding fathers believed that the African and Caucasian races—given the history of black subjugation and the supposedly different abilities of the two races—could not live in peace in the same land. As a Virginia legislator, Thomas Jefferson had advocated sending freed blacks to "a far away place selected as the circumstances of the time should render most proper." As hopes that the American Revolution might lead to a more equal society for African Americans faded in the late 18th century and early 19th century, the idea of "colonization"—as the return to Africa proposal was called—caught on among leading whites and a few free blacks.

AFRICAN COLONIZATION

Among the free blacks who supported re-Africanization was Paul Cuffe, a wealthy black shipowner from New Bedford, Massachusetts. Cuffe believed he had a duty to help his fellow Africans, both in America and Africa. Sending blacks back to Africa offered a way to do both. For African Americans, it would mean an opportunity to escape white racism and build a community of their own, proving to the world that blacks were capable of self-government. These settlers would also bring civilization and Christianity to their long-lost brothers in Africa. In 1811,

William Lloyd Garrison's *The Liberator* (Library of Congress)

Cuffe visited Sierra Leone, a British colony established as a haven for former slaves from Britain, North America, and the Caribbean. Four years later, he sent the first shipload of settlers to Sierra Leone at his own expense. But his death two years later ended the project.

Meanwhile, a group of influential whites—including Kentucky senator Henry Clay, future president Andrew Jackson, "Star Spangled Banner" author Francis Scott Key, and Bushrod Washington, nephew of George—established the American Colonization Society (ACS) in Washington in 1816. The goals of the society were decidedly mixed. "Can there be a nobler cause," Clay, a wealthy planter and slaveowner, asked his fellow colonizationists, "than that which, while it proposes to rid our own country of a useless and pernicious, if not dangerous, portion of the population, contemplates the spreading of the arts of civilized life, and the possible redemption from ignorance of a benighted portion of the globe?" Indeed, from the beginning, colonization was tainted by its association with slaveholders and denounced by free blacks and, later, abolitionists as a way to force free African Americans—many of whom traced their ancestry in America back for generations—out of the country, while preserving slave status for the vast majority of blacks. "We have no wish to separate from our present homes for any purpose whatsoever," declared a statement issued by 3,000 African Americans meeting at Philadelphia's Bethel Church in 1817. "We only want the use of those opportunities...which the Constitution and the laws allow to us all."

Still, the ACS achieved some success. In 1820, it sponsored its first shipment of 86 blacks to the British colony of Sierra Leone. After a sojourn ridden with disease, colonists moved southward to found the colony of Liberia. Over the next four decades, more than 10,000 African Americans settled in Liberia. In 1847, the colonists—a mix of free blacks from the North, freed slaves from the South, and Africans recaptured from slavers on the high seas—declared their independence from the ACS, making Liberia Africa's first republic. For roughly 150 years, Liberia was ruled by the descendents of African Americans—the so-called Americo-Liberians—until their regime was overthrown in a 1980 coup.

ABOLITIONISM

Although somewhat successful, the colonization idea was displaced in the 1830s by a new and more radical movement—abolitionism. While colonizationists spoke of a gradual end to slavery through emigration—an impossible proposal given the millions of blacks living in America—abolitionists called for the institution's immediate demise. They dismissed the colonizationists as co-conspirators of planters, seeking to rid the country of its unwanted free black population.

Meanwhile, throughout the North, free black communities in the 1820s were endorsing ever more radical measures to end slavery, even if they involved violence. In 1829 came the most incendiary statement yet. The pamphlet *An Appeal...to the Colored Citizens of the World* declared to whites: "We must and shall be free...in spite of you....And woe, woe, will be it to you if we have to

William Lloyd Garrison (Library of Congress)

THE LIFE OF FREDERICK DOUGLASS

". . . If there is no struggle there is no progress. Those who profess to favor freedom and depreciate agitation are men who want crops without plowing up the ground, they want rain without thunder and lightning, they want the ocean without the awful roar of its mighty waters."

—Frederick Douglass

Of figures from the 19th century, Frederick Douglass is among the most revered. Following his escape from slavery in 1838 at the age of 21, he became an international figure, speaking out against the "peculiar institution" of slavery throughout the North and in England. Although the abolition of slavery was his primary concern, he increasingly spoke out on a wide range of human rights causes, from prison reform and public education to international peace. His speeches often pointed out the hypocrisy of the fact that the same patriotic Americans who fought for liberty and freedom could enslave an entire people. His ties were particularly strong with the women's suffrage movement until he broke with movement leaders in 1866 over whether black men should be granted voting rights before women. Through his alliances with other abolitionists such as William Lloyd Garrison, the publisher of *The Liberator*, he was able to further the cause of emancipation for the enslaved.

1817 or 1818: Frederick Augustus Washington Bailey is born in Tuckahoe, Maryland.

1826: At age nine, he is sent to Baltimore, Maryland, to work as a houseboy. While there, his master's wife teaches Bailey to read and write, although educating slaves was illegal.

1833: He is returned to his plantation home as a field hand.

1836: He attempts an escape but fails; soon thereafter, he is sent back to Baltimore to work as an apprentice to a ship's caulker. Soon after arriving there, he meets Anna Murray, a free black woman and his future wife.

1838: After Anna Murray gives him money for an escape attempt, Bailey borrows a sailor suit and some official looking papers and escapes by sea. He makes his way to New York City, where he is joined by Anna Murray. The two then move to the Quaker fishing center (an abolitionist stronghold) of New Bedford, Massachusetts, where the newlyweds adopt the last name Douglass.

1841: Without the benefit of written notes, Douglass gives an impassioned address to the Massachusetts Anti-Slavery Society in Nantucket and is immediately employed as one of their agents. For the next four years, he travels on speaking engagements throughout the North.

1843: On speaking tours of New England and the Midwest, Douglass is joined on the podium by a former slave named Isabella Baumfree, who states that she has been called by God to rename herself Sojourner Truth. Although illiterate, she matches Douglass in her powerful oratory skill.

1845: Douglass publishes his autobiography *Narrative of the Life of Frederick Douglass, An American Slave* in order to refute those who claim that because of his powerful speaking ability he could not actually have been a slave. Following the publication of the book, he moves to England to avoid recapture. While there, he continues to speak out publicly against slavery. He also broadens the scope of his efforts by speaking in favor of Irish home rule, on behalf of landless European peasantry, and on such issues as prison reform, free public education, and women's suffrage.

obtain our freedom by fighting." Written by David Walker, a used clothing salesman and pamphleteer living in Boston, Walker's Appeal also refuted white claims to racial superiority. "I do declare that one good black man can put to death six white men," wrote Walker, who soon gained an enthusiastic black audience. The pamphlet went through three printings and even showed up among free black communities in the South.

Sentiment was shifting among white opponents of slavery as well. The wave of evangelical Christianity that swept much of the upper Midwest, upstate New York, and New England in the 1820s inspired a new condemnation of slavery. The religious message of the Great Awakening—as the movement was called—emphasized the individual moral agency of all human beings. Being a good Christian meant choosing to follow God's plan. By keeping African Americans in bondage, slave owners were keeping them in darkness, unable to make the moral choice God had given all human beings. The implications of this argument were clear: slavery was a sin and slaveholders were contravening God's will. To many evangelicals, there could be no compromise with slavery, no gradualist approach to its extinction. Nat Turner's 1831 uprising seemed like a sign to many that God's patience with America and its compromise with the forces of evil—that is, with slavery—was running thin.

That same year, William Lloyd Garrison, a Boston-based printer and evangelical Christian, launched a weekly abolitionist newspaper, *The Liberator*. In its first issue, the editor made his intentions clear: "I will be harsh as truth and as uncompromising as justice. . . . I am in earnest—I will not equivocate—I will not

1847: As Douglass prepares to return from England, a group of British female abolitionists pay $711.96 to buy him his freedom. They also supply him with a printing press. Rejoining his family, Douglass moves to Rochester, New York, and begins to publish his antislavery newspaper *The North Star.* Douglass is also elected president of the New England Anti-Slavery Society.

1848: Douglass becomes president of the Colored Convention Movement, which advocates racial solidarity and economic improvement. He is a featured speaker at the Seneca Falls, New York, convention, organized by Elizabeth Cady Stanton and Lucretia Mott, that launches the women's suffrage movement.

1849: The Women's Association of Philadelphia forms to help Douglass raise money for *The North Star.* By this time, the Douglass's household has become an Underground Railroad "station." Although Frederick Douglass is often away from home, Anna Murray Douglass sees that runaways are always welcome.

1851: Douglass publicly splits with William Lloyd Garrison over the issue of moral pressure versus political participation as a means towards abolition of slavery. Douglass joins the abolitionist Liberty Party and is named its candidate for vice president.

1855: He publishes a revision of his autobiography entitled *My Bondage and My Freedom (Part I: Life as a Slave, Part II: Life as a Freedman).* The Liberty Party nominates him for the post of New York secretary of state, making him the first African American nominated for statewide office.

1859: Douglass is invited by John Brown to participate in his raid on Harper's Ferry, Virginia. Douglass denounces the plan as suicide. Nonetheless, following the attack, he is accused of supporting it and is forced to flee to Canada and then London.

1860: Douglass returns from England after learning of the death of Annie, his youngest child, at age 11. He campaigns for the repeal of a New York law that requires black men to own $250 in order to vote.

1861: Douglass campaigns for blacks to be allowed to serve in the Union army.

1863: Douglass helps recruit African Americans in Massachusetts, New York, and Pennsylvania to serve in the all-black Fifty-fourth Massachusetts Regiment and visits President Abraham Lincoln to protest discrimination against black troops.

1864: Douglass appeals for black male suffrage.

1866: Douglass attends an Equal Rights Association convention and breaks with women's rights leaders over whether African-American men should receive the vote before the same right is given to all women as well.

1872: After the Douglass home in Rochester is destroyed by fire, the family moves to Washington, D.C.

1874: Douglass becomes president of the financially troubled Freedmen's Bank. To encourage investment, Douglass deposits his own money and appeals to the U.S. Senate for aid. Nonetheless, confidence in the bank continues to fall, and the bank collapses.

1877–1881: Douglass serves as marshal of the District of Columbia.

1881–1884: Douglass serves as recorder of deeds for the District of Columbia.

1889–1891: Douglass serves as minister to Haiti.

1895: Douglass dies in Anacostia Heights, D.C. Congressman George Washington Murray (R-SC) attempts to have his body lie in state in the Capitol rotunda, but House Speaker Charles Crisp (D-GA) refuses to permit it.

---

excuse—I will not retreat a single inch—AND I WILL BE HEARD." In later issues, Garrison would go on to denounce the U.S. Constitution—with its unwritten acceptance of slavery—as "a covenant with death, an agreement with Hell." Garrison's fiery language and uncompromising convictions attracted other like-minded opponents of slavery. In 1833, Garrison joined with Theodore Weld—an upstate New York preacher—and Arthur and Lewis Tappan—wealthy merchant brothers from New York City—to form the American Anti-Slavery Society.

The society's members took two approaches to their crusade. The first was aimed at the public. Borrowing techniques from the revivalist churches, they held public meetings where eloquent and passionate speakers offered the equivalent of sermons on the theme of abolitionism. Many evangelical women became caught up in the crusade, going so far as to speak to mixed-sex audiences on the subject, unprecedented events that shocked the gender sensibilities of the day. (Indeed, the antislavery movement proved to be one of the seedbeds of the women's movement, which grew to fruition in the same abolitionist strongholds and culminated in the first women's rights convention in American history, held at Seneca Falls, New York, in 1848.)

And, of course, the abolitionist movement drew on black speakers as well. In 1841, a white abolitionist in New Bedford, Massachusetts invited a young escaped slave named Frederick Douglass to speak at a meeting on Nantucket Island. The power and conviction of Douglass's testimony won him a role as abolitionism's most famous and effective spokesperson. In addition, abolitionists published hundreds of thousands of pamphlets, flooding the North and the South with antislavery propaganda. The purpose of this apdeproach, known as "moral suasion," was to create a moral climate in which slave owners would recognize the error of their ways and move to end slavery. While the campaign did little to change the moral stance of most slave owners, it did increase the public pressure on them. In response, southern officials began routinely raiding post offices to seize and destroy the literature.

The abolitionists also published—and sometimes ghost-authored—slave narratives. Usually written in the melodramatic style of 19th century literature, these narratives told of the unspeakable barbarities of the slave regime—beatings, torture, rape, and the anguished cries of mothers torn from their children at slave auctions. To modern readers, the most powerful narratives were those written in the clear and unadorned prose of the former slaves themselves. Among the most famous of these tracts are Frederick Douglass's *Narrative of the Life of Frederick Douglass, an American Slave*, Solomon Northrup's *Twelve Years a Slave*, and Harriet Jacobs's *Incidents in the Life of a Slave Girl*.

A second strategy of the abolitionists was aimed at politicians. In order to convince Congress of the depth of antislavery sentiment in the North, the Anti-Slavery Society encouraged local chapters to inundate Congress with petitions calling for laws that were in its purview to pass, including the abolition of slavery in Washington, D.C.; a ban on the interstate slave trade; the removal of the "three-fifths compromise" in the Constitution, which enhanced southern legislative representation; and a ban on the admission of new slave states. (As slaves were considered legal property, slavery was protected by the Constitution; banning slavery required a constitutional amendment.) So many petitions flooded Washington that, in 1836, southern congressmen and their northern sympathizers pushed through the "gag rule," whereby all petitions against slavery were automatically tabled so that they could not become the subject of debate. The law—a clear denial of the 1st Amendment—would remain in effect for eight years.

Eventually, the efforts of the political wing of the abolitionist movement led to the establishment of the Liberty Party in 1840, the first political party in American history expressly devoted to ending slavery. Winning less than 3 percent of the northern vote in the 1844 presidential elections, the Liberty Party eventually gave way to the Free Soil Party in the late 1840s, a much larger party with a more popular—less radical—mandate of preventing the spread of slavery to the West. The Free Soil Party—with ex-president Martin Van Buren as its nominee—won more than 10 percent of the vote in 1848 and paved the way for the antislavery Republican Party of the 1850s.

Despite this success, the political strategy helped split the abolitionist movement. Radical white abolitionists—led by Garrison—believed that working with politicians compromised the idea of abolitionism as a moral crusade against evil. At the same time, more moderate white abolitionists and the majority of black abolitionists—coalescing around Douglass— took a more pragmatic approach, hoping that political and legislative action would gradually put slavery on the road to extinction. Ultimately—with proslavery power increasing in the 1850s—Douglass and anti-Garrisonian radicals like John Brown would come to the conclusion that neither the political nor the moral suasion route offered a solution to the slavery problem. Instead, direct action was necessary, though when Brown and a number of radical white abolitionists suggested an invasion of the South in 1859, Douglass dismissed the idea as folly.

The abolitionists' place in history is a complicated one. On one hand, most of their efforts—either radical or pragmatic—failed. Few slave owners were ever convinced of the error of their ways and Congress failed to pass any of the legislation abolitionists desired, at least until the Civil War. Indeed, the rhetoric and action of the abolitionists stirred up a hornets' nest of protest in the North, where many whites feared a flood of unwanted black migrants should slavery be ended in the South. Abolitionist speakers like Douglass and Garrison were often attacked verbally and even physically by antiabolitionists. In 1837, the movement got its first martyr in Elijah Lovejoy, an abolitionist editor murdered by a white mob in Alton, Illinois.

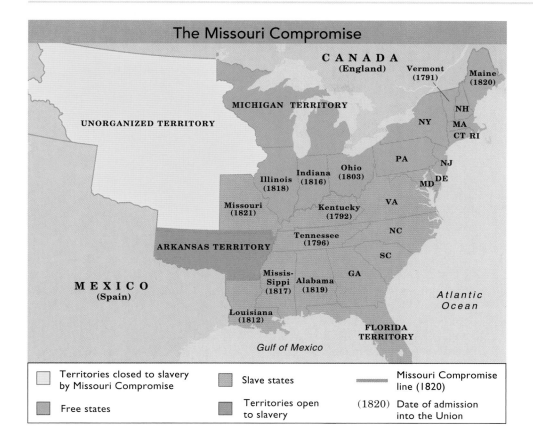

The Missouri Compromise

CANADA
(England)

Vermont
(1791)

Maine
(1820)

MICHIGAN TERRITORY

NH

UNORGANIZED TERRITORY

NY

MA
CT RI

PA

NJ

Ohio
(1803)

Indiana
(1816)

MD DE

Illinois
(1818)

VA

Missouri
(1821)

Kentucky
(1792)

NC

Tennessee
(1796)

SC

ARKANSAS TERRITORY

MEXICO
(Spain)

Missis-
sippi
(1817)

Alabama
(1819)

GA

Atlantic
Ocean

Louisiana
(1812)

FLORIDA
TERRITORY

Gulf of Mexico

- ☐ Territories closed to slavery by Missouri Compromise
- ▣ Free states
- ▣ Slave states
- ▣ Territories open to slavery
- ── Missouri Compromise line (1820)
- (1820) Date of admission into the Union

And yet through this very controversy, abolitionists achieved success of a kind. Until the crisis decade of the 1850s, most Americans accepted slavery as a fact of national life. For southerners, it was a way of life; for northerners, it was a distant and abstract issue. For almost all Americans, it didn't seem worth fighting over. And politicians did their best to keep things that way. Slavery was a no-win issue: support it too strongly and one offended northerners; oppose it, and one alienated the South. It was best to just ignore it. But abolitionists, with their speeches, pamphlets, and petitions, made it increasingly hard to ignore slavery as a political and moral issue. Moreover, as proslavery politicians and white mobs attacked abolitionists, they turned them into martyrs, not so much to the cause of black freedom but to the causes of freedom of speech, assembly, and press. Most northerners were both racist and against slavery. They wanted to keep blacks—enslaved or free—out of the North and West. As southern politicians and their northern allies passed proslavery legislation, northerners felt that their political will was being ignored or subverted. Abolitionists, then, were critical in raising the national political tempera-ture high enough to spark the Civil War, which ultimately destroyed slavery.

THE MARCH TOWARD WAR

Slavery as a political issue went back all the way back to the Constitution. In creating a document that would appeal to southerners, northern statesmen—who wanted a constitution that created a strong, pro-trade central government—agreed to a compromise whereby slaves would count as three-fifths persons for the purposes of apportioning representation. As the South was then the largest region of country, it was expected that it would have the largest population and the most representatives. In short, northerners got the kind of government they wanted but at the price of allowing southerners to run it. This compromise rested, however, on a premise that ultimately proved to be false. Because of the presence of a slave labor force, few immigrant laborers moved to the South and the North soon surpassed it in population.

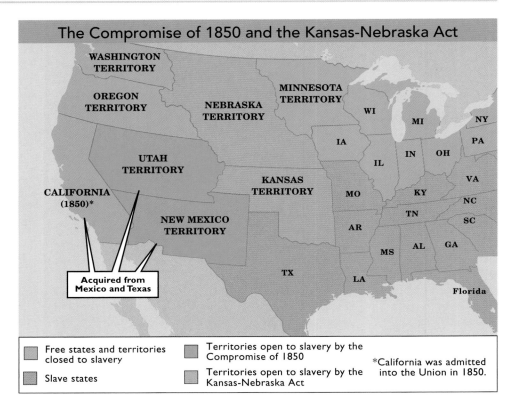

The Compromise of 1850 and the Kansas-Nebraska Act

- Free states and territories closed to slavery
- Slave states
- Territories open to slavery by the Compromise of 1850
- Territories open to slavery by the Kansas-Nebraska Act

*California was admitted into the Union in 1850.

MISSOURI COMPROMISE

In 1819, a challenge to the three-fifths compromise emerged. After accepting the admission of several slave states in the 1810s, northern politicians finally put their foot down when Missouri asked to join the Union as yet another. For two years, Congress divided bitterly over the issue, until a compromise was hammered together by House Speaker Henry Clay of Kentucky. Under the Missouri Compromise, that state would join the Union alongside the free state of Maine. Thus was inaugurated a new sectional balancing act, whereby states would enter in pairs—one free state for every slave state. And so while the House of Representatives—which was based on population—came to be dominated by northerners, the Senate—which guaranteed each state two members—would maintain a balance of power between the two regions. Moreover, to satisfy lingering northern suspicions of slavery dominating the West, a line was drawn from Missouri's southern border—at 36° 30' latitude—to the Pacific Ocean, even though most of this territory belonged to the newly independent country of Mexico. To many Americans—including an aging Thomas Jefferson—the Missouri Compromise portended dangerous divisions within the republic. "This momentous question, like a firebell in the night," wrote the retired president, "awakened and filled me with terror."

THE MEXICAN WAR AND THE COMPROMISE OF 1850

Jefferson's fears were not idle ones. In the mid-1830s, Texas won its independence from Mexico—partly to escape the latter's edicts against slavery—and sought to enter the American Union as a slave state, a move blocked by antislavery forces in the North. Angry southerners then began pressuring the national government to acquire western lands open to slavery below the Missouri Compromise line, a plan that was bound to lead to hostilities with Mexico. In 1845, southerners won the admission of Texas into the Union as a slave state. A year later, President James Polk, a slave owner from Tennessee and a determined expansionist, provoked a war with Mexico by sending American troops into disputed territory along the Rio Grande. When Mexican soldiers fired on the Americans, Polk and southerners in Congress declared war. David Wilmot, a Free Soil congressman from Pennsylvania, tried to undermine the southerners' plans by introducing a proviso making all territories acquired from Mexico free, but his efforts were brushed aside by proslavery forces in Congress.

From the beginning, the war was an unequal one. Mexico proved to be no match for the United States and, after two years of hostilities, was forced to cede the northern third of its territory to the United States for a nominal payment of $15 million. Suddenly, southerners had what they wanted—vast new American territories for the expansion of slavery. Although mollified by the acquisition of the Oregon territory from Britain in 1846, northerners cried foul, arguing that the war was part of a southern conspiracy to spread slavery and dominate the Union. The sense of crisis was stoked by the discovery of gold in newly acquired California in 1848. With hundreds of thousands of settlers—largely from the North—pouring in, the Pacific Coast territory asked to join the Union as a free state in 1850.

But with no equivalent slave territory ready to enter the Union, California's request provoked the most serious sectional crisis since Missouri. After some of the bitterest debate in congressional history, an elaborate new compromise was reached. Although involving a series of delicately balanced elements, the Compromise of 1850 boiled down to two controversial provisions. First, California would be admitted into the Union as a free state, giving the North a 16 to 15 state advantage in the Senate. Second, as a concession to southerners, Congress passed the infamous Fugitive Slave Act. For the first time, the federal government became a seriously active participant in enforcing the law against runaway slaves. Under the act, fugitive slaves and even free blacks anywhere in the Union were subject to potential enslavement or re-enslavement. Finally, the Fugitive Slave Act made it a crime for any northerner to interfere in the apprehension of an alleged escapee. Northerners were outraged, and not just because law-abiding blacks were subject to arrest. Suddenly, it seemed to them as if the entire federal government had been hijacked a "slave power conspiracy."

"POPULAR SOVEREIGNTY" AND THE DRED SCOTT DECISION

The events of the 1850s only seemed to confirm northern fears. With pioneers beginning to settle the lands to the immediate west and northwest of Missouri, a proposal was floated by the powerful Illinois senator Stephen Douglas to establish two organized territories—Kansas and Nebraska. To gain southern

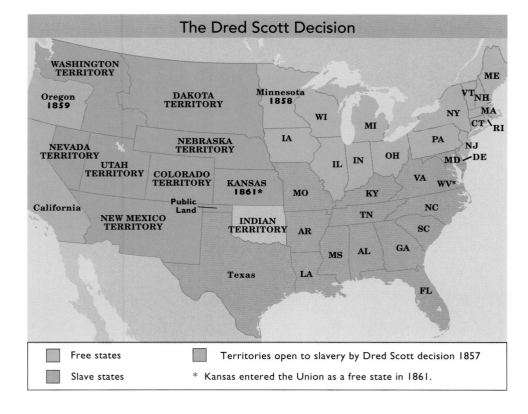

The Dred Scott Decision

Free states
Slave states
Territories open to slavery by Dred Scott decision 1857
* Kansas entered the Union as a free state in 1861.

Dred Scott and his wife (Library of Congress)

THE POTTAWATOMIE CREEK MASSACRES, MAY 24, 1856

① John Brown and his gang drag James Doyle and his sons, William and Drury, from their home and hack them to death with swords. They spare the lives of Mrs. Doyle, a daughter, and 14-year-old John.

② Brown and his men move to the home of Allen Wilkinson and take him prisoner. They also steal two saddles and a rifle.

③ The group moves on to the home of James Harris, where Harris, his wife, young child, and three other men, including William Sherman, are sleeping. Sherman is executed. Brown makes off with more weapons, a saddle, and a horse.

RAID ON HARPER'S FERRY, OCTOBER 16, 1859

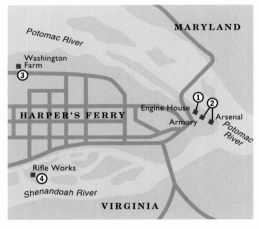

① **The Engine House:** Brown and his men use the engine house as a base of operations.

② **The Federal Armory and Arsenal:** After capturing these installations, Brown distributes weapons to all his troops and then steals enough weapons to arm a force of 1,500.

③ **Washington Farm:** Brown and his men kidnap Colonel L. W. Washington and a number of his slaves. At the height of Brown's assault, he and his men hold 40 captives in the engine house.

④ **Rifle Works:** Brown's men also hold the rifle works until they are killed or captured by local townspeople.

was determined to enforce its will on the entire country.

In fact, as some contemporaries pointed out, the debate was misguided. The cold, dry plains of Kansas and Nebraska—as well as the deserts of the southwestern territories taken from Mexico—were hardly places to support cotton and other slave-based plantation crops. But in the heated political climate of the 1850s, few people were able to think in such terms. For both southerners and northerners, the West represented the future, a land of opportunity for poor but aspiring white settlers. Yet northerners feared the competition of slave labor in the West, while southerners worried that the presence of antislavery northerners in the territories would make the institution of slavery untenable there.

Meanwhile crisis followed crisis as the decade unfolded. In 1856, violence erupted in Kansas as pro- and antislavery forces clashed, leading to murders, skirmishes, and massacres. In the summer, more than 700 proslavery men attacked the free town of Lawrence, burning it to the ground. In response, abolitionist John Brown and a small gang of followers descended on a settlement at Pottawatomie Creek, where they murdered five proslavery settlers in their homes. The violence over the slavery issue even penetrated Capitol Hill. Following a fiery speech on the floor of Congress—in which he denounced South Carolina senator Andrew Butler for taking up with "the harlot slavery"—Massachusetts senator Charles Sumner was beaten unconscious by Butler's nephew, Representative Preston Brooks.

With Kansas in flames and Congress bitterly divided, the Supreme Court moved into the breach, seeking to resolve the issue through a broad judicial ruling. The case that came to them involved a slave named Dred Scott who, with the help of abolitionist lawyers, was suing for his freedom. Scott's master, an army surgeon, had taken his slave with him when assigned to serve in the free state of Illinois and the free territory of Wisconsin. When his master died, Scott—citing his habitation on free soil—claimed his freedom. His late master's heirs insisted he belonged to them. In a highly controversial decision, the Supreme Court ruled against Scott in March 1857, saying that he was a slave no matter where he lived. To northerners, the implications were dire. Legally, a slave-owner could now bring his slaves with

support for the measure, Douglas insisted that the settlers decide their status as slave or free. Because the territories lay north of the Missouri Compromise line, antislavery northerners cried foul, arguing that the lands were supposed to be free. Despite their protestations, the "popular sovereignty" elements of the Kansas-Nebraska bill passed, providing yet more evidence to suspicious northerners that the "slave power conspiracy" impunity to any northern state, rendering the entire Union slave territory. Once again, it seemed to many in the North that the "slave power conspiracy" was winning the day.

JOHN BROWN'S RAID AND THE ELECTION OF 1860

Southerners, meanwhile, had their own fears. Outnumbered and outpaced by a rapidly growing and industrializing North, they felt hemmed in on all sides. Britain had outlawed slavery in its empire in 1833, followed by France in 1848. The bestselling novel of the day—popularized in countless theatrical productions across the North—was Harriet Beecher Stowe's *Uncle Tom's Cabin*, a powerful melodrama on the evils of slavery. A new and popular antislavery party—the Republicans—was fast becoming the majority in the northern states. Then, in 1859, came the final blow. In October, John Brown—the abolitionist fighter from Kansas—led an armed gang on a raid of the federal armory at Harper's Ferry, Virginia (now West Virginia), hoping to launch a general slave insurrection. Brown's plan was as crazy as it was audacious. There were few African Americans in the mountainous region around Harper's Ferry and Brown's small force was quickly killed or dispersed by a Virginia militia headed by Robert E. Lee, future commander of Confederate forces in the Civil War. Brown himself was captured alive.

At first, northerners and southerners were largely in agreement on Brown; he was seen as a dangerous and misguided fanatic who threatened the peace and welfare of the country. But during his trial, Brown spoke with such great eloquence on the evils of the slavery system and on the necessity of destroying it that he won over the majority of public opinion in the North. Following his conviction and execution by hanging, Brown's body was shipped north to a burial site in New York's Adirondack Mountains, where he had lived much of his life. In Philadelphia, his body was taken from its original coffin—which had been built by slaves—and placed in one made by free blacks. Along the train's route, large crowds came out to pay their respects to the man they now viewed as a national hero. To proslavery

southerners, this was further proof that all northerners were secret abolitionists. This was a mistaken assumption, of course. Most northerners did not want to ban slavery in the South, just to prevent it from spreading to the West. But, in politics, opinion often counts for more than fact, a rule that would be proven—with disastrous results—in the presidential election year of 1860.

By the end of the 1850s, many of the institutions that had previously bound the nation together had divided into mutually hostile northern and southern wings. Fraternal organizations, churches, and the Whig Party had all broken over the question of slavery. During the election campaign of 1860, the only remaining national party—the Democrats—would come apart as well. At their national convention in Charleston, South Carolina, southern and northern delegates debated the question of popular sovereignty and the expansion of slavery in the western territories. When the northerners—who only weakly supported both—won out, the southerners walked out on the convention. Ultimately, the Democratic Party ran two candidates for president— Stephen Douglas and Kentucky senator John Breckinridge. Along with a third party candidate, former Tennessee senator John Bell of the Constitutional Union Party, the Democrats split the southern and border states of Delaware, Kentucky, Maryland, and Missouri between them. Meanwhile the Republicans, united behind Lincoln, swept the northern states and took the election with a plurality of just 40 percent of the national popular vote.

As far as southerners were concerned, the election results were the final straw. In their opinion, Lincoln was a closet abolitionist, despite his protestations that he did not intend to ban slavery where it already existed. Lincoln had also made clear his belief that the Union would "become all one thing, or all the other."

The capture of John Brown, by Currier & Ives (Library of Congress)

CIVIL WAR

On December 20, 1860, a convention to consider secession from the Union was held in Charleston. The meeting was dominated by so-called fire-eaters, who argued several points. First, they insisted the Union was a voluntary compact of states, making secession legitimate, even though the Constitution offered no clear language on the subject. They also argued that the original Constitutional Compromise—in which the North got the strong central government it wanted as long as the South dominated it—had been violated by the election of an anti-southern president. Finally, pointing out that Lincoln had received almost no votes south of the Mason-Dixon Line, southerners argued they no longer had a government to represent them. Thus, like the Patriots of 1776, the secessionists of 1860–1861 believed they had a perfect right—in the words of the Declaration of Independence—"to throw off such Government, and to provide new guards for their future security."

SECESSION AND FORT SUMTER

In the end, the fire-eaters won the day. Over the next six weeks, six more states—Alabama, Florida, Georgia, Louisiana, Mississippi, and Texas—joined South Carolina. In February, commissioners from the seven seceded states met in Montgomery, Alabama, to form a new nation, the Confederate States of America. Meanwhile, in Washington, Kentucky senator John Crittenden offered a compromise—renewing the Missouri Compromise line and adding a constitutional amendment defending slavery forever. But President-elect Lincoln and congressional Republicans rejected the compromise.

More worrisome for the Union were military developments. Throughout the South, pro-secession forces had all seized federal forts except Fort Sumter, situated on an island in Charleston harbor; that was being blockaded. Upon his inauguration, President Lincoln was facing the worst crisis in the history of the Republic. His inaugural speech offered familiar concessions to the South—no punishment for secession and assurance that slavery would remain undisturbed there—and tough measures if the seceding states did not return to the Union. It was a difficult balancing act, threatening the Deep South with punishment while easing fears in the

critical states of the upper South, most especially Virginia.

Fort Sumter presented Lincoln with his first strategic decision. To abandon it would be to destroy the Union's credibility. To break the blockade by armed force risked making the North the aggressor and thereby causing the states of the upper South to join their Deep South sisters in secession. Lincoln chose the middle ground. The fort's defenders were running out of food and fresh water, so Lincoln dispatched a relief expedition. With the new supplies, southern leaders realized, Fort Sumter could hold out for months. A federal fort situated in the symbolic capital of the South was intolerable to Confederate leaders, who began an artillery barrage against the fort on April 12. Though the fort surrendered to the South on April 14, it represented a symbolic victory for Lincoln: he had forced the other side to fire first. Within days, his call for 75,000 new federal soldiers had been easily met, though the call to arms was enough to push Arkansas, North Carolina, Tennessee, and Virginia to secede. The Civil War had begun in earnest.

EMANCIPATION

From the beginning, both northerners and the Republican Party were divided over the war's meaning. To Democrats, moderate Republicans, and Lincoln himself, the main aim of the conflict was to preserve the Union. But to abolitionists, free blacks, and the so-called Radical Republicans, the war was about saving the Union and destroying slavery. At first, the former group—with its talk of gradually abolishing slavery over many years—predominated. But as casualties mounted in the first year of fighting, public and congressional opinion began to shift toward more immediate abolition, if only to punish the secessionist planters who most northerners felt had started the war.

Meanwhile, as Union armies pushed into the South, a new problem arose: runaway slaves. When three showed up at a Union army encampment on the Virginia coast in 1861, commanding officer General Benjamin Butler refused to return them to their masters, declaring them "contraband" of war, that is, property of the enemy. It was, in short, a legal cover for emancipation. With white southerners off at war, those three Virginia slaves were soon joined by thousands of African Americans.

In Washington, changing opinion and the problem of runaway slaves were forging an ever more radical antislavery coalition between Lincoln and congressional Republicans. In April 1862, slavery was outlawed in the District of Columbia; in June, it was outlawed in the territories. Neither act freed many slaves, but it showed a growing commitment to immediate abolition, a commitment bolstered by the Second Confiscation Act passed in July. Under this bill, all "contraband" was declared "forever free." The way was being paved for the most radical measure of all. On September 22, 1862, Lincoln issued the historic Emancipation Proclamation, declaring all slaves in rebel-held territories free as of January 1, 1863. Technically speaking, the proclamation did not free a single slave. Slaves in Union-held territory would remain in bondage (to maintain the support of border state leaders); and slaves held in rebel territory were out of reach of the act. But the proclamation forever changed the meaning of the war. From then on it was about abolishing slavery, and with every mile of territory captured by Union armies, African Americans would be emancipated by an act of the federal government.

AFRICAN-AMERICAN SOLDIERS

Just as African Americans had helped force emancipation by their decision to leave the plantations, so black leaders helped push into effect the recruitment of black soldiers into the Union army. At the beginning of the war, few people outside the abolitionist and free black communities believed in recruiting blacks. There

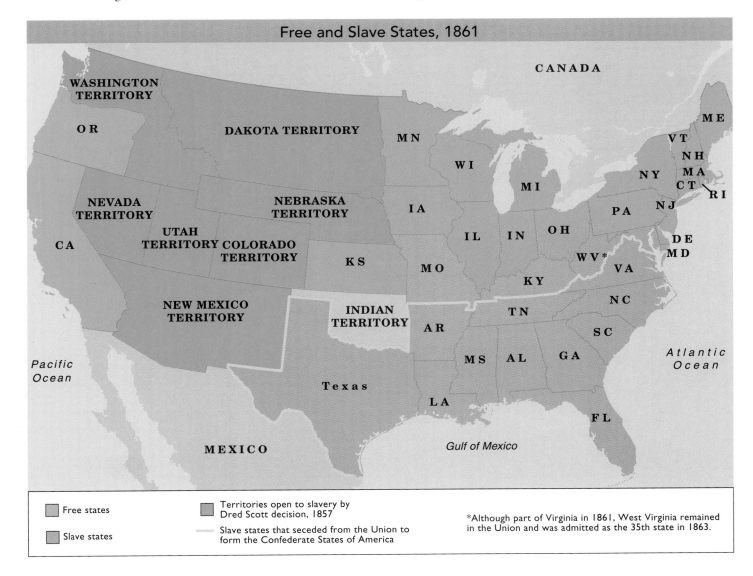

Free and Slave States, 1861

Free states

Slave states

Territories open to slavery by Dred Scott decision, 1857

Slave states that seceded from the Union to form the Confederate States of America

*Although part of Virginia in 1861, West Virginia remained in the Union and was admitted as the 35th state in 1863.

Recruitment of African Americans

STATE/DISTRICT	NUMBER OF ARMY RECRUITS
Kentucky	23,703
Missouri	8,766
Maryland	8,718
Pennsylvania	8,612
Ohio	5,092
New York	4,125
District of Columbia	3,269
Massachusetts	2,966
Rhode Island	1,837
Illinois	1,811
Other*	110,076
Union Total	**178,975**

*From the Confederacy and other northern states

Fifty-fourth Massachusetts Regiment storming Fort Wagner, South Carolina (Library of Congress)

was just too much prejudice. The racist thinking of the day considered blacks too cowardly and undisciplined for soldiering. And the notion of giving guns to blacks in order to kill whites—even if those whites were traitors to the Union—was anathema to the vast majority of northerners. But as the war ground on—and casualties mounted—the unthinkable became possible, then desirable.

On the other hand, from the moment southern guns fired on Fort Sumter in April 1861, African Americans clamored to serve in the military. Unlike whites, blacks understood from the beginning that the war would ultimately decide the fate of American slavery. This, they believed, was their struggle. And, as Frederick Douglass understood, "once let the black man get upon his person the brass letters, 'U.S.,' let him get an eagle on his buttons and a musket on his shoulder and bullets in his pockets, and there is no power on earth which can deny that he has earned the right to citizenship in the United States." Indeed, in 19th-century America, citizenship was often defined by one's willingness to serve one's country in the military.

Politicians hesitated, fearing northern public opinion and potential racial conflict in the ranks of soldiers. But public opinion in the North was changing and changing fast. As the idea that the war was about abolition—as opposed to simply preserving the Union—began to sink in, more and more whites came to accept the idea that if blacks were going to benefit by the war, they ought to share in the fighting and the dying. New technologies—including the grooved bore rifle that

allowed for greater accuracy over long distances—led to unprecedented carnage on the battlefield, as commanders were slow to adjust their tactics from older patterns of massed troop firing. Adding to the bloodshed was the recognition that the Civil War as a war of attrition. In other words, northern commanders were increasingly concluding that the only way to win the war was to grind down both southern armies and the South's ability to make war. Such a strategy required the North to sacrifice enormous numbers of soldiers and material, knowing that the region's greater population and resources would outlast those of the South.

Another factor in changing northern public opinion—and U.S. government policy—on recruiting African Americans was the field performance of black regiments. In January 1863, Thomas Wentworth Higginson, an abolitionist-turned-commander, wrote a well-read newspaper account praising the African-American First South Carolina Volunteers. "No [white] officer in this regiment," Higginson noted, "now doubts that the key to the successful prosecution of the war lies in the unlimited employment of black troops." Shortly thereafter, the War Department authorized the enlistment of troops from the free black community of the North and from among runaway slaves in the South.

At the same time, the abolitionist and free black communities of Boston organized the Fifty-fourth Massachusetts Regiment, an all-black regiment commanded by white abolitionist Robert Gould Shaw. At first, the Fifty-fourth was either kept in camp or ordered to perform routine noncombat duties. They were not even issued guns or ammunition. But protests by Shaw and his men—as well as drops in white recruitment—pushed higher-ups in the military to authorize combat duty for the regiment. In July 1863, during a heroic but doomed assault on South Carolina's Fort Wagner, black soldiers had finally proved to whites that they were able to fight and were willing to die in the cause of freedom. Nor could the pride and satisfaction in their new duties be disguised. One black soldier, seeing his former master among the prisoners he was guarding, greeted him with: "hello massa, bottom rail on top dis time."

Still, even as military commanders recognized the valor and discipline of black troops, racist attitudes prevailed. Black troops were kept in segregated camps and usually assigned to menial labor or guard duty. And, until mass protests by black troops in June 1864, they received little more than half the pay of white soldiers: $7 versus $13 a month. Even as black troops experienced discrimination within the Union army, they faced a threat on the battlefield that whites did not. That is to say, as the number of black troops rose, the Confederate government issued a dire warning: any blacks captured in war would either be executed or returned to slavery. When word came back that black prisoners of war were being routinely executed by southern military authorities, Lincoln cut off all prisoner exchanges, although he did not carry through on his own threat to begin executing southern POWs in retaliation.

Despite discrimination on the northern side and the executions on the southern side, blacks continued to flock to the military. By the end of the war, approximately 200,000 African Americans were serving in the Union army and navy, about 10 percent of the total fighting force. (Due to the close quarters of shipboard life, segregation was impossible in the navy and blacks and whites served together.) Their critical role in the war effort was recognized by Lincoln in an 1864 campaign speech, when he said that without black soldiers, "we would be compelled to abandon the war in three weeks." Nonetheless, prejudice in the North remained high. Many parts of the Midwest, largely inhabited by migrants from the South, were bastions of pro-southern sympathizers. These so-called copperheads—named after a particularly venomous snake of the region—turned increasingly against the Union war effort as it became associated with abolitionism.

New York City Draft Riots

Ironically, the most violent demonstrations against the war effort, abolitionism, and blacks took place far from the South: New York City. When the war began, New Yorkers—like the majority of northerners—supported the Union cause enthusiastically. The largely working-class and immigrant communities of the city had little sympathy for white planters, even if the city's economy was bound up with that of the South. Moreover, most New Yorkers—like most northerners—believed the war would be short, glorious, and relatively bloodless. When that proved to be far from the case, sentiment began to change and, by 1863, recruitments began to dry up. To maintain effective troop numbers, Lincoln and his War Department authorized two measures: one was the recruitment of black soldiers; the other was the Enrollment Act of 1863, the nation's first military draft. Among the provisions of the act was a commutation fee. Any draftee who could come up with $300—more than half a year's income for the average worker—could buy his way out of the war.

By the summer of 1863, when the draft was set to commence, tensions in working-class neighborhoods of the city were high. There was resentment. The largely Democratic population was not particularly fond of Lincoln and the Republicans, whom they saw as agents of the city's business leaders. There was also anger over high prices and war profiteering by the same merchants and factory owners who could pay the commutation fee. And there was fear. Immigrant and working-class New Yorkers believed that abolition would lead to a flood of southern black workers into the city who would drive wages down as they competed for the same unskilled positions.

Thus, when draftee names were announced in early July, the city exploded, particularly its Irish neighborhoods. The draft office was the first to receive the rioters' torch, then the mobs attacked buildings associated with the Republican Party and business elites. While the undermanned metropolitan police force was able to keep the rioters out of the wealthier residential neighborhoods, they lost control over most of the city. Ultimately, the mobs turned their wrath against the city's free black community, lynching dozens of African Americans and burning the Colored Orphans Asylum to the ground, forcing hundreds of terrified children to flee the city in the middle of the night. It took several days for Lincoln and the federal government to react, but when they did, they came down hard. Federal troops were rushed back from their battlefield victory over the Confederacy at Gettysburg to put down the rioting.

THE NEW YORK DRAFT RIOTS, 1863

July 13
① No-Draft demonstration and arson at 9th District draft office, 9:00–10:00 p.m.
② Riot, noon
③ 8th District marshal's office burned, 5:00 p.m.
④ Lexington Avenue, wealthy homes burned
⑤ 18th Ward arsenal raided for weapons, evening
⑥ Colored Orphans' Asylum burned, evening

July 14
⑦ Rioting spreads to 6th Ward Union Steam Works (East 21st Street)—crowds and troops clash, afternoon

July 15
⑧ Crowds and militia clash on First Avenue, afternoon

✖ **Blacks murdered**

The Emancipation Proclamation is celebrated. (Library of Congress)

had cost the lives of more than 600,000 Americans, far and away the bloodiest in the nation's history.

Historians have debated why and how the North won the war ever since. Most point to its vastly greater population and manufacturing capacity. Indeed, these were critical to winning the "first modern war" in world history, where the total destruction of the other side's capacity to make war was the ultimate object.

When the South went to war in 1861, it was largely to preserve slavery. For all the talk of state's rights, southerners would have not have gone to war unless they felt that slavery and white supremacy were threatened by the North. Ironically, by the end of the war, the South was fighting to preserve its existence, even if that jeopardized slavery. One of the last acts the Confederate Congress passed was a bill—never implemented, because the war ended first—to offer freedom to any slave that took up arms in defense of the Confederacy.

As with the South, the war started out as one thing for the North and ended up as another. In the beginning, it was fought to preserve the Union or, as Lincoln put it at Gettysburg, to ensure that "government of the people, by the people, for the people, shall not perish from the earth." But by the end, the North was fighting for an entirely different reason: ending slavery and bringing the long-postponed promise of freedom to the nation's African-American population. Sadly, the man most responsible for that transformation—President Abraham Lincoln—did not live to see it through to completion; he was assassinated just five days after the surrender at Appomattox. For the civil war he presided over was just half a revolution. It destroyed the slavery regime forever. But the struggle over the other half—that is, what would be constructed or, rather, reconstructed in its place—had just begun.

Dozens of rioters were shot and thousands were arrested. In the end, more than 100 people died in the New York City draft riots of 1863, making them the worst civil disturbance in American history.

THE NORTH VICTORIOUS

For all the bitter divisions within northern society, the ultimate outcome of the war was hardly in doubt after Gettysburg. By the end of 1863, the South was split in two down the Mississippi and effectively blockaded at sea. In 1864 and early 1865, Union armies under generals William Tecumseh Sherman and Philip Sheridan destroyed some of the most productive regions of the South, including much of Georgia and Virginia. Meanwhile, the main Union army, led by Ulysses S. Grant, was conducting a bloody war of attrition against the Army of Northern Virginia, under the command of Robert E. Lee. By early spring, Lee recognized that the struggle was lost. On April 9, at the courthouse in Appomattox, Virginia, he surrendered to Grant, ending the four-year-long war that

UP FROM SLAVERY
African Americans in the Late 19th Century

Between 1865 and 1877, the United States of America embarked on one of the greatest experiments in social transformation ever attempted in human history. The period—known as Reconstruction—has often been called the "second American Revolution," for its far-reaching efforts to fulfill the political and social promise of the first. Beginning during the Civil War and reaching its culmination in the decade that followed, Reconstruction saw the near total—albeit temporary—transformation of southern politics, economy, and society. Reconstruction involved several elements: reintegration of southern states into the Union, the punishment and rehabilitation of southern whites who had fought against their country in the Civil War,

and a battle between Congress and the White House for political supremacy. But, above all, Reconstruction was the story of African Americans and their struggle for integration into the mainstream of southern and American society.

RECONSTRUCTION

The pace of change during this period was breakneck. In 1861, 4 million African Americans in the South lived in bondage, the chattel property of their masters. Several hundred thousand other blacks—in both the South and North—lived in a twilight zone between freedom and servitude with, in the words of Chief Justice

African-American troops arrive home after the Civil War (Library of Congress)

A family of freedpersons (Library of Congress)

Roger Taney, "no rights which the white man was bound to respect." Less than a decade later, not only had 4 million slaves been removed from bondage, but all African-American males (black women—like their white counterparts—were still denied basic civil rights) had achieved political and legal equality with whites, including the right to vote. While it is true that this era of equality was short-lived—largely dying with the end of Reconstruction in 1877—it established the constitutional basis for the civil rights movement of the mid-20th century.

EMANCIPATION AND WARTIME RECONSTRUCTION

Reconstruction would have been impossible without the Civil War. And, of all the cataclysmic changes wrought by the Civil War on southern society, none was more important than the emancipation of African Americans from centuries of bondage and servitude. To understand the significance of emancipation, it is useful to examine what it was not. Emancipation was not a single event, but millions of individual events involving millions of individuals. Nor was emancipation primarily set in motion by Lincoln's Emancipation Proclamation, although that event has been used as the starting point for Reconstruction by the eminent historian Eric Foner. In most regions of the South, freedom was either seized by the slaves themselves or offered by advancing Union armies. Emancipation came whenever slaves sensed that the authority of the master no longer held sway. Emancipation, then, was not just a legal act, but a psychological and existential event in the lives of every African American emerging from bondage.

Among the first places to experience emancipation—more than a year before the Emancipation Proclamation went into effect—were the Sea Islands off the coast of South Carolina and Georgia. Occupied by the Union army as part of the North's wartime strategy of blockading the Confederacy by sea, the islands saw the white planter class flee at the first sign of trouble. When planters tried to force their slaves to follow them to the mainland, most of the latter refused. With northern armies coming, slaves understood that the disciplinary structure of the slave regime—and the authority of the slaveowners themselves—had crumbled. They were, in short, emancipated at that moment.

Emancipation meant many things to former bondsmen and bondswomen. On the Sea Islands, it meant liberation from the grinding gang labor of the cotton plantation. Indeed, one of the first things that the freedpersons did was destroy the cotton gins and other property of the former masters. As emancipation advanced across the South, so the freedpersons took advantage of their new-found freedom. Some shed their slave surnames and took on ones appropriate to the times, like Freeman. Others sought out local black preachers and Union army chaplains to legitimize the informal marriage arrangements of slavery times. Many took to the road—some for the purposes of finding loved ones separated on the auction block; others to experience the sheer joy of freedom of movement.

There were changes on the land as well. On most plantations, slave cabins were situated around the planter's house, so that the activities of the slaves could be easily monitored. With emancipation, many freedpersons moved their cabins to the far reaches of the plantations, to get away from white oversight. Former slaves also shifted their labor from cotton and other commercial crops to the raising of food for personal and family consumption. While planters and other apologists of the slave regime had long argued that African Americans would never work unless coerced, freedpersons proved them wrong. If hard work was necessary for survival or if it brought returns like a better diet or some cash in hand, then former slaves proved themselves more than willing to work hard. At the same time, absorbing the belief system of 19th-century America, the freedperson community also made it clear that they did not want their women to work in the fields. Thus, nearly half the labor force once available for commercial agriculture in the plantation South was lost.

Emancipation also meant the little things that might seem to trivial to anybody who had never been forced to do without them. In many towns and cities, African Americans took to promenading on streets and in neighborhoods where they had previously been banned. Freedpersons also began wearing more fashionable clothing, which was denied to them under slavery. And, most disturbingly to white southerners, blacks refused to pay their former masters the deference those masters had come to expect. "It is impossible to describe the condition of the city," one South Carolina planter said, describing postwar Charleston. "It is so unlike anything we could imagine—Negroes shoving white persons off the walk—Negro women drest in the most outré style, all with veils and parasols, for which they have an especial fancy."

The Sea Islands were not only where emancipation happened first; they were also where the first efforts at Reconstruction began. As one historian described them, wartime events in the Sea Islands represented a "rehearsal for Reconstruction." And, as would be the case in other parts of the South, the course of Reconstruction was determined by victorious white northerners as much as it was by liberated black southerners. Two groups of the former descended on the Sea Islands within months of their liberation. One included abolitionists who wanted to prove that black people were "reasonable beings" who had a "capacity for self-government." Alongside former

A Reconstruction school (Library of Congress)

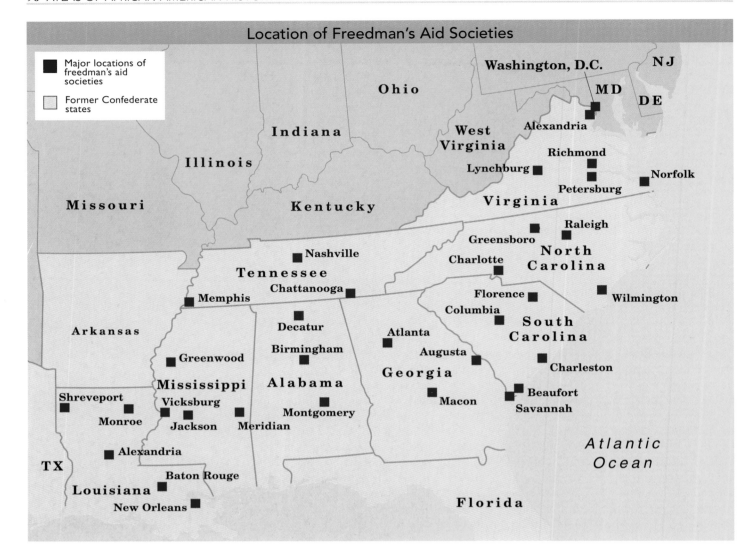

Location of Freedman's Aid Societies

Legend:
- ■ Major locations of freedman's aid societies
- ☐ Former Confederate states

slaves, the abolitionists established schools and churches, in order to prepare the freedpersons for eventual citizenship. Their dream—a goal that was shared by the former slaves—was to create a community of small land-owning farmers, harking back to the Jeffersonian ideal still widely held in much of America and shared by Lincoln himself—wherein political freedom was achieved through economic independence. Some modest steps in this direction were taken when several groups of blacks pooled their resources and bought several thousand acres of plantation land auctioned off by the federal government.

Other northerners had different ideas about the direction the Sea Island "rehearsal for Reconstruction" should take. Beginning in 1863—as the federal government began auctioning off lands that belonged to planters who had fled—northern investors came to the region. Believing that cotton was critical to the

South's future and to the American economy generally, they wanted to put the plantations back into production, not with slave labor, of course, but with wage labor, which they believed was more productive and profitable. Ultimately, the goals of these northern investors ran up against the aspirations of the former slaves who either refused to work for any white man—preferring subsistence farming without supervision—or demanded high wages that the northerners insisted they could not afford to pay.

A second experiment with wartime Reconstruction occurred in another area of the South occupied early by the Union army—Louisiana. As in the Sea Islands, the Bayou State quickly saw the arrival of abolitionist reformers from the American Missionary Association and other organizations who helped the former slaves found schools and churches. By the end of the war, the black community had founded more than 120 schools, serving some 13,000 students. Also, as in the Sea Islands, Lousiana's freedperson community made it clear from the beginning that they wanted land of their own. And once again they were thwarted by more conservative northern officials. In February 1863, military governor General Nathaniel Banks struck a deal with local planters: if the latter would abstain from physical punishment, provide decent food and clothing, and pay their black workers—either wages or a portion of the crop—the army would assure that the freedpersons "return[ed] to the plantations where they belong...to work diligently and faithfully for one year, to maintain respectful deportment to their employers and perfect subordination to their duties." As would be the case across much of the South after the Civil War, northern authorities' belief in the dominant wage labor ideology of the North, along with their racist assumptions that blacks would not work unless coerced, subverted the will of the African-American community of the South who wanted land of their own in order to work on their own.

Wartime controversies, however, were not confined to the South. In Washington, D.C., in the waning days of the conflict, Congress was beginning to assert its role in shaping Reconstruction. Dominated by Republicans, but divided between "radicals" who wanted to punish the South and establish full civil rights for blacks and "moderates" who sought southern white rehabilitation and limited black freedom, Congress established the Bureau of Refugees, Freedmen, and Abandoned Lands in March 1865. Popularly known as the Freedmen's Bureau, the agency took on the task of feeding and clothing black and white refugees, renting out confiscated planter land to "loyal" whites and freedpersons, and writing up and enforcing labor contracts between freedpersons and planters. In addition, the bureau worked with northern volunteer associations to establish schools and to send teachers throughout the South. By the end of the war, the Freedmen's Bureau had settled about 10,000 black and white families on lands seized from planters in Georgia and South Carolina. While it was not its intention, the bureau often encouraged blacks—in the hopes of gaining land of their own—to hold out against signing labor con-

tracts with their former masters. As one freedperson told South Carolina planter Thomas Pinckney, "we ain't going nowhere. We are going to work right here on the land where we were born and what belongs to us."

Land and labor were not the only wartime Reconstruction issues on the table. There were also the matters of political power and civil rights, questions that first came to the fore in Louisiana. With their base in New Orleans, the largest free black community in the South—allied with many antiplanter, pro-Union whites among the city's working class population—began to demand civil rights, including the vote, even before the war ended. At first, Lincoln made it clear that he hoped that the state government could be turned over to moderate white planters. In December 1863, the president announced his "10 percent plan." Under the proposal, any confederate state where 10 percent of the voters took a loyalty oath to the Union would be readmitted to the Union. But as black protests continued, Lincoln shifted his opinion, requesting that the state's 1864 constitutional convention grant the voting rights to "intelligent blacks" and black soldiers. Still, he did not make black voting rights a requisite for readmission to the Union.

Lincoln's assassination (Library of Congress)

Whether he would have shifted further in favor of black civil rights—as some historians claim—is impossible to ascertain.

On April 14, just five days after General Robert E. Lee surrendered to Ulysses S. Grant in Virginia, effectively ending the Civil War, Lincoln and his wife Mary Todd decided to relax by attending an English theatrical comedy at Washington's Ford Theatre. During the performance, a southern assassin named John Wilkes Booth put a bullet in Lincoln's head, killing the president within hours. The assassination was part of a larger conspiracy to avenge the Confederacy's defeat. Other targets included the Lincoln cabinet—Secretary of War William Seward was also stabbed—and Vice President Andrew Johnson, who escaped attack. In fact, Johnson, a southern loyalist whom Lincoln had selected as his running mate in 1864 in hopes of reconciling a postwar South—proved to be the best friend the planter class could possibly have had in Washington in the early years of Reconstruction.

ANDREW JOHNSON AND PRESIDENTIAL RECONSTRUCTION

While racism permeated 19th-century America, Andrew Johnson—a former Democratic senator and military governor of Tennessee—was in a class by himself. In one address to Congress, Johnson insisted African Americans had less "capacity for government than any other race of people.... [W]herever they have been left to their own devices they have shown a constant tendency to relapse into barbarism." Still, many Radical Republicans held out hope for a pro–civil rights, antiplanter policy in the early days of the Johnson administration, as the new president—a self-made man from the hill country of eastern Tennessee—was also known to hold deep suspicions and even animosity toward the planter class of the South. But when faced with a decision to back freedperson versus planter aspirations, Johnson sided with his fellow whites.

Like his predecessor in the White House, Johnson believed that the secession states had never legally left the Union and, therefore, their readmission did not require acts of Congress. Assuming executive branch control over the process, Johnson merely requested that southern states ratify the 13th Amendment—banning slavery—and revoke their acts of secession. Once southerners took an oath of allegiance to the Union, they would get back all of their civil rights and all their property, minus the slaves. Exempted persons—including high-ranking Confederate officials and officers and persons with taxable property exceeding $20,000—could personally petition Johnson, who turned virtually no one away. Southerners immediately moved to take back property seized by the Union army during and immediately after the war. In October, Johnson ordered Freedmen's Bureau head General Oliver Howard to tell Sea Island blacks that they had no legal title to the land they were working. When Howard reluctantly agreed, he was met with a barrage of protests. "Why do you take away our lands?" a petition from a group of dispossessed farmers begged to know. "You take them from us who have always been true, always true to the Government. You give them to our all-time enemies!" When blacks resisted, Union soldiers forced them off or ordered them to work for their former masters.

Despite interference from the federal government, the struggle over the two critical ingredients to the southern economy—land and labor—continued. Planters, of course, had lost much economically by the war—namely $3 billion in human property. Most had also seen their savings wiped out, as Confederate currency became worthless after surrender. Still, if they could regain control of their land and their labor, they felt they could return to economic health and political power. But they continued to meet black resistance. Many of the latter voted with their feet, moving to towns and cities where they could find better-paying jobs. Others retreated to subsistence farming, raising crops for their own consumption on small plots of land. And, as noted above, even where the labor force remained on the plantation, many black families insisted on pulling their women from the fields, thereby cutting the labor force significantly.

To counter these moves, the new postwar southern state governments—largely run by planters and their sympathizers—passed a series of strict new laws governing the freedperson population. The so-called black codes were essential-

President Andrew Johnson (Library of Congress)

TIMELINE OF RECONSTRUCTION

January 1863: President Abraham Lincoln's Emancipation Proclamation goes into effect.

July 1864: President Abraham Lincoln vetoes the Wade-Davis Reconstruction Bill, which proposes harsh penalties on the South if a Union victory is achieved.

March 1865: Congress establishes the Freedman's Bureau to feed, treat, shelter, and house the 4 million freed slaves of the Confederacy.

March: Lincoln is inaugurated for a second term as president. In his inaugural address, he promises a moderate peace policy toward the Confederacy.

April: Confederate general Robert E. Lee surrenders to Union general Ulysses S. Grant at Appomattox Courthouse, ending the Civil War.

April: Lincoln dies after being shot in the back of the head by Confederate sympathizer John Wilkes Booth. Vice President Andrew Johnson becomes president.

May: President Johnson announces his plan to offer full pardons to former Confederates who agree to take a pledge of allegiance to the Union.

December: The 13th Amendment is ratified by 27 states including eight southern states, ending slavery in the United States.

Februaury 1866: The New Freedman's Bureau bill, an attempt to enlarge the role of the Freedman's Bureau, is introduced in Congress. The legislation proposes to give the Bureau the power to try those accused of denying African Americans their rights. President Johnson vetoes the bill.

April: Congress passes the Civil Rights Act of 1866 over a veto by President Johnson. The law guarantees citizenship and "full and equal benefits of all laws" to African Americans. In 1883, the Supreme Court would find the act unconstitutional.

May: The Ku Klux Klan is founded in Pulaski, Tennessee, with former Confederate general Nathan Bedford Forrest as the first Grand Wizard. The goal of the organization is to destabilize Radical Reconstruction governments and establish white supremacy throughout the South.

November: The congressional elections of 1866–1867 strengthen the Radical Republican faction of Congress.

March 1867: Congress passes the Tenure of Office Act, which requires the president to get Congressional approval before firing members of his administration whose original appointments were confirmed by the Senate.

March: Congress passes the first Reconstruction Act over another of President Johnson's vetoes. The law divides the South into five military districts, each governed under martial law. Each state is called on to write a new constitution. Ex-Confederates are disqualified from voting.

July: Congress overrides Johnson yet again to pass a second Reconstruction Act, which allows the South's military governments to decide who is eligible to vote.

February 1868: Citing a violation of the 1867 Tenure of Office Act, Congress impeaches President Johnson after he fires Secretary of War Edwin Stanton. He is then tried and acquitted by a single vote.

June: Florida, Georgia, Louisiana, North Carolina, Alabama, and South Carolina are readmitted into the Union by Congress under the Omnibus Act.

July: The 14th Amendment, which grants citizenship to all persons born in the United States, becomes law when it is ratified by a three-fourths majority of the states. Former Confederate states had been required to ratify the amendment in order to be readmitted to the Union.

November: Union army hero Ulysses S. Grant is elected president with overwhelming support from more than 700,000 African-American voters.

December: In one of his last acts as president, Johnson grants amnesty to all but 300 former members of the Confederate government and military.

February 1869: Congress proposes the 15th Amendment, forbidding any state from depriving a citizen of his vote because of "race, color, or previous condition of servitude."

1870: Senator Hiram R. Revels of Mississippi and Representative Joseph H. Rainey of South Carolina become the first black members of Congress.

February: Congress passes the 15th Amendment, which gives black males the right to vote.

March 1871: President Grant begins passing the Ku Klux Klan Acts. The acts suspend habeas corpus—a safeguard against unlawful imprisonment—in some parts of the South and allow federal troops to arrest and imprison hundreds of Klansmen. Despite this clampdown, the Klan continues to operate.

June 1872: Congress closes the Freedmen's Bureau after heavy opposition in the South hampers its effectiveness.

1877: Following a disputed election, Democrats in Congress agree to accept Rutherford Hayes, a Republican, as president in return for the withdrawal of federal troops from the South. This agreement effectively ends Reconstruction.

ly designed to return the social and economic order of the South to a facsimile of antebellum times. Indeed, in writing the new laws, postwar southern legislatures often turned to the old slave codes, merely replacing the word *slave* with *negro* or *freedman*. Many of the laws concerning vagrancy were so loosely worded that they made it possible to arrest any black person who was not actually working at the moment when confronted by a law enforcement official. Faced with fines that they could not pay, the "guilty" parties were then hired out to employers, often the former masters. In some states, codes were passed setting long hours of work and onerous duties for freedpersons. Anybody who refused to abide by the

THE BLACK CODES

In the aftermath of the Civil War, southern state governments passed a series of strict new laws governing the freedperson population. The so-called black codes were intended to return the social and economic order of the South to the way it had been lived under slavery. Listed below are a number of black codes passed in Mississippi in 1865.

Penal Code
- Illegal for freedmen to carry firearms.
- Illegal for freedmen to sell liquor, participate in riots, use insulting language or gestures, or preach the Gospel without a license.
- Freedmen are liable for fines for the above, and if a freedman refuses to pay, he will be hired out to any white man who will pay for him.

Apprentice Law
- All freedmen under 18 years who are orphans or financially unprovided for by their parents, shall be forcibly apprenticed.
- If apprentice escapes and is caught, master may reclaim him. Apprentice faces imprisonment if he or she refuses to comply.
- Employer is legally allowed to punish freedman in any way a parent or guardian might their own child or ward.

- Apprentice shall be indentured until 21 years of age if male and 18 years if female.

Civil Rights of Freedmen
- Freedmen are forbidden to marry any white person upon penalty of life imprisonment.
- Reward offered to any person who catches a freedman who quits their employer's service prior to official termination.
- Penalty of up to $200 for any white man who employs or aids a runaway freedman.

Vagrancy Law
- All freedmen over the age of 18 who do not have written proof of employment at the beginning of each year are vagrants.
- All vagrants shall be fined up to $50 and jailed up to 10 days.
- If freedman cannot pay the fine, he shall be hired out to any white man who will pay it for him, with the amount deducted from his wages.
- Freedmen between 18 and 60 years of age will pay a tax up to $1 per year toward the Freedman's Pauper Fund.
- If a freedman cannot pay a tax, he is a vagrant and will be hired out to any white man who will pay it for him.

laws was deemed a vagrant. To keep blacks on the plantations, some states passed laws requiring licenses to take "irregular work," that is, jobs off the plantation. Legislation was also passed making it illegal for blacks to leave the plantation without a pass signed by their employer.

Harsh as the black codes were, they proved difficult to enforce. Supported by Freedmen's Bureau officials and Union army officers, many blacks refused to abide by them. Making things more difficult for planters was the overall postwar labor shortage. While laws might be passed making it illegal for one planter to entice another's labor force away, desperate planters often ignored the law. Still, the general tendency in the southern states in the first year after the Civil War, was a return—sanctioned by President Johnson—to the social, economic, and political order of the slavery regime, less the legal status of slavery itself.

But if the black codes were less than fully effective in maintaining tight control over the African-American labor force of the South, they had a more lasting and dramatic effect in Washington and the North generally. Seeing former Confederates back in power in the South and

passing laws aimed at overturning the objectives of the Civil War, many northerners—most of whom had had immediate family members killed or wounded in the fighting—were upset. In Washington, Radical and many moderate Republicans were outraged, especially as there was little any of them could do. Until the passage of the 20th Amendment in 1933, Congress was largely in recess during its second year. In the year after the Civil War, that meant Congress was not in session until December 1865. As the months rolled by, and the South was reconstructed under prosouthern rules set by President Johnson, frustration among congressmen grew and, with it, a consensus that Congress should take control of the Reconstruction process.

This feeling was nothing new. In July 1864, Radical and moderate Republicans in Congress had offered an alternative to what they saw as Lincoln's overly lenient Reconstruction policies. The Wade-Davis Bill set up a strict set of guidelines for a southern state's readmission to the union. Like Lincoln's plan, the states had to ratify the 13th Amendment. But rather than 10 percent signing oaths of allegiance, a majority of white adult males would have to do so. Furthermore, so-

U.S. Army officer protects freedmen (Library of Congress)

called ironclad oaths—whereby delegates to the conventions held to write new state constitutions had to swear they had never taken up arms against the Union—were required. This, of course, excluded the vast majority of southern whites. Finally, the Confederacy's military and civilian leaders were permanently disenfranchised. Lincoln—loath to turn over Reconstruction authority to Congress—had found the requirements too onerous and pocket-vetoed, or refused to sign, Wade-Davis, thereby postponing Congress's role in Reconstruction until well after the war.

CONGRESSIONAL RECONSTRUCTION

By December 1865, Republicans were itching for a showdown with Johnson over Reconstruction policy. While the Republican delegation was divided between minority Radicals—led by Pennsylvania congressman Thaddeus Stevens and Massachusetts senator Charles Sumner—and majority moderates—under senators William Fessenden of Maine and Lyman Trumbull of Illinois—it did agree on one thing: outrage at the arrival of former Confederate officials in Congress—including Confederate vice

president Alexander Stephens, as the new Senator from Georgia. As the Constitution mandates, "each House [of Congress] shall be the Judge of the Election, Returns, and Qualifications of its own Members." Congressional Republicans exercised that right by refusing to recognize the representatives sent to Washington by the southern states.

Next, Congress acted on the controversial issue of confiscated lands. While moderate Republicans voted down a measure by Thaddeus Stevens to turn over the "forfeited estates of the enemy" to freedpersons, they did move to countermand Johnson's orders to the Freedmen's Bureau evicting blacks from lands in the Sea Islands. And, in early 1866, Congress passed the Southern Homestead Act, opening up 45 million acres in the region to anyone—black or white—who cultivated 80-acre plots for five years. The legislation typified northern attitudes toward the freedpersons and Reconstruction. Where Radicals wanted active measures to guarantee black rights—including gifts of former planter estates—moderates believed in equality of opportunity, whereby both blacks and whites would be given a chance to earn their land. This fit in with both northern policy—as exemplified in the similar Homestead Act of 1862, which opened

Thaddeus Stevens (Library of Congress)

Celebrating passage of the Civil Rights Act of 1866 (Library of Congress)

up lands in the West—and averted Radicals' precedent-setting measures. After all, the reasoning of many moderate Republicans went, if southern property could be confiscated and given to the poor, so could northern factories and businesses, though this was hardly the intention of Stevens, himself the owner of an ironworks in Pennsylvania.

In February 1866, Congress's showdown with Johnson intensified when the president—citing the unconstitutionality of a "system for the support of indigent persons"—vetoed legislation extending the life of the Freedmen's Bureau. Unable to bring northern Democrats and conservative Republicans on board, the Radicals failed to override Johnson's veto. But then, adding fuel to the fire, an allegedly inebriated Johnson celebrated with prosouthern sympathizers in Washington, denouncing Radical Republicans as traitors in an impromptu speech. Both the veto and the ill-advised speech pushed many moderates into the arms of the Radicals. In March, Congress passed the Civil Rights bill. For the first time in its history, the federal government had passed legislation defining citizenship rights, including the right to own or rent property, the right to make contracts, and the right of access to the courts. In addition, the historic act authorized federal officials to sue on behalf of persons whose rights had been violated and guaranteed that civil rights suits would be heard in federal court.

Although advised by his cabinet that many of his moderate and conservative Republican allies were turning against him, Johnson vetoed the bill. To many, the justification he offered—that the bill offering immediate citizenship to former slaves violated the rights of white immigrants who had to wait five years—was far-fetched. And so this time, moderate Republicans—still stinging from Johnson's ill-advised remarks on the treasonous behavior of their fellow party members—overrode the president's veto. Now fully convinced that Congress had to take control of Reconstruction away from an increasingly reactionary and irresponsible president, moderate Republicans passed a watered-down version of the Freedmen's Bureau extension—requiring Sea Island blacks to buy, rather than be given, confiscated lands—and then overrode a second Johnson veto in July.

Meanwhile, the Joint Committee on Reconstruction—established by both houses of Congress to recommend further measures—was drawing up a plan to place the question of black civil rights and federal guarantees of citizenship beyond the law, that is, by anchoring them in the Constitution itself. In April, the committee submitted to the Congress the 14th Amendment. Although failing to offer guarantees of black suffrage—a key demand of Radical Republicans—the 14th Amendment represented perhaps the most far-reaching extension of federal powers in the history of the republic. Until its passage, the civil rights of all Americans were largely guaranteed by the states. The 14th Amendment put the federal government on record as the guarantor of the citizenship rights of "all persons born or naturalized in the United States." Moreover, the amendment made it unconstitutional for any state to abridge "the privileges or immunities of citizens of the United States" or deprive "any person of life, liberty, or property, without due process of law." Finally, the 14th Amendment penalized states that denied suffrage to any male by decreasing that state's representation in Congress proportional to the numbers of adult males denied the vote. (Much to the chagrin of women's rights supporters, this was the first time that gender-specified rights entered the Constitution.) Prompted by increasing violence against blacks in the

South, including rioting that left 48 persons dead—all but two black—in Memphis, Tennessee, Congress submitted the amendment for state ratification in June.

Johnson, needless to say, was outraged by what he considered to be a barely disguised black civil rights amendment to the Constitution. Under his urging, border states and former Confederate states refused to go along, denying amendment supporters the three-quarter state majority required for ratification under the Constitution. The president also attempted to create a political consensus against congressional control of Reconstruction by forming a new national party of Democrats and conservative Republicans. Violence was rising in the South, however—in New Orleans, a white, largely Democratic mob attacked a black suffrage convention in July, leaving 37 African Americans dead. Under the circumstances, Republicans refused to join Democrats, and Johnson's National Union Convention failed. Still, the president remained determined. In late summer, he sought to win support through a

railroad tour of the nation, even though personal campaigning by a sitting president was considered undignified at the time. Along the way Johnson himself damaged his case by drinking heavily and engaging in verbal shouting matches with hecklers, once again asserting his claim that the real root of treachery lay not in the South but in Congress.

Republicans responded in kind, initiating a political strategy that would prove successful through much of the late Nineteenth century. Known as "waving the bloody shirt," the strategy involved charging Democrats as the party of treason. It worked marvelously, especially in the congressional elections of 1866, when the party won a three-to-one majority in both the House and the Senate, as well as gaining control of the governorships and legislatures in every northern and most border states. Indeed, Republicans continued to "wave the bloody shirt" until the end of the 19th century, and the tactic proved successful up to and including the pivotal election year of 1896, when Republicans established a political hegemony over the national government that

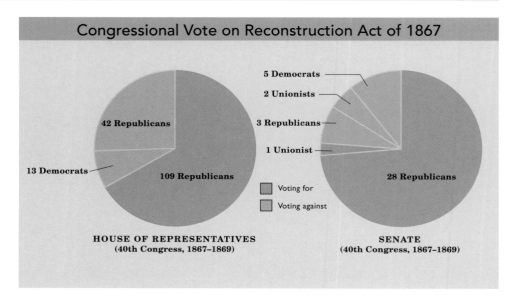

Congressional Vote on Reconstruction Act of 1867

5 Democrats

2 Unionists

3 Republicans

1 Unionist

42 Republicans

13 Democrats

109 Republicans

28 Republicans

Voting for

Voting against

HOUSE OF REPRESENTATIVES
(40th Congress, 1867–1869)

SENATE
(40th Congress, 1867–1869)

A freedman's first vote (Library of Congress)

would continue nearly unbroken until the rise of Franklin Roosevelt and the New Deal Democratic coalition in the 1930s.

With overwhelming control of Congress and state governments, the Republican majority gave its radical wing the lead in setting Reconstruction policy. First, in March 1867, came the Reconstruction Act, which divided the South into five military districts, each headed by Union army generals. Before a southern state could return to the Union, it had to ratify a constitution acceptable to Congress and ratify the 14th Amendment. Predictably, Johnson vetoed the bill and, just as predictably, Congress overrode the veto. To keep Johnson in line, Republicans on Capitol Hill passed the Tenure of Office Act, requiring congressional approval for the dismissal of any executive department official whose position required congressional ratification.

Deemed by many judicial experts then and now to be unconstitutional, the act was passed to protect Secretary of War Edwin Stanton, a Lincoln cabinet holdover who favored Radical Reconstruction measures and, as the man in charge of the Union army, was best-positioned to implement them. When Johnson decided to test the constitutionality of the act by formally dismissing Stanton in February 1868, the House voted to impeach him. As per the Constitution, the trial to remove Johnson from office then moved to the Senate. While Radicals were eager to do so, moderates feared establishing a precedent whereby a president could be removed from office for largely political differences with Congress. With presi-

dential elections coming up—and Johnson virtually neutralized politically already—the Radicals failed to win the two-thirds majority needed by just one vote. Johnson remained on as president for the remainder of his term, but largely as a figurehead.

The presidential-year elections of 1868 proved to be as successful for the Republicans as had the 1866 congressional elections. Not only did the party retain more than a two-thirds, veto-proof majority in Congress, but it gained a president in Union army commander Ulysses S. Grant, a man who shared the belief that stern measures were needed to assure black civil rights and to humble former secessionists. Within months of the election, Republicans pushed through yet another amendment to the Constitution, this one stripping states of the right to deny citizens the vote on the basis of race, color, or "previous condition of servitude." However, as in the case of land confiscation measures, radicals failed to get everything they wanted in the 15th Amendment, as the legislation failed to prohibit other voting restriction measures—such as literacy tests and poll taxes—that could effectively disenfranchise black (as well as poor white) voters without doing so by name.

Still, with the passage of the 15th Amendment, congressional reconstruction had reached its high water mark. Between 1868 and 1871, both the 14th and 15th Amendments were ratified and all 11 states of the former Confederacy had met the requirements established by Congress—including the granting of full civil rights to black males—and rejoined the Union. And just as the radicals in Washington were

The 15th Amendment (Library of Congress)

reaching the zenith of their power in these years, so too were their political allies in the South. For African Americans—freed from slavery just a few years earlier—were winning a degree of political power unprecedented in the nation's history, an achievement not to be repeated until the post–civil rights era of the 20th century.

AFRICAN-AMERICAN POLITICS IN THE RECONSTRUCTION ERA

As a historical drama, the so-called Radical Reconstruction of the South was momentous. And like a theatrical production, it had a stage—the South—a story line—the revolutionary transformation of the region's political, economic, and social order—and a cast of characters. While perhaps oversimplifying, it is possible to divide this cast of characters— the people of the Reconstruction—into four general groupings, each with their own motivation: African Americans, northerners, poor and middling white southerners, and planters. At the heart of the Reconstruction story were the freedpersons. More than 4 million in number—out of a total population of about 13 million—they included a majority of registered voters in five southern states:

Alabama, Florida, Louisiana, Mississippi, and South Carolina. The African-American community wanted land, economic independence from whites, a degree of political power commensurate to their numbers, and social equality, if not direct integration. Rallying behind the popular rallying cry "40 acres and a mule," the black community demanded that parcels of 40 acres of farmland be awarded to each freedman.

Closely allied to former freedpersons, but often with an agenda of their own, came northerners. The immediate post–Civil War South was both conquered territory and a region of enormous economic opportunities, and both conditions drew northerners. First, there were the administrators, both military and, later, civilian. With most southern politicians tainted by charges of treason, political advancement opened up for ambitious northern politicians willing to head South, such as Louisiana governor Henry Warmouth, a former judge from Illinois.

In greater numbers came the businessmen. From the cotton- and rice-growing Sea Islands of South Carolina and Georgia to the cattle-raising plains of Texas, northern business interests took advantage of land-poor southerners, that is, those people who owned land but had little money. With land cheap and cotton

African-American Political Power During Reconstruction

PERCENTAGE OF BLACKS IN STATE POPULATION, 1870

40–49%

50–59%

LH Percentage of blacks in lower house

UH Percentage of blacks in upper house

South Carolina
LH: 54%
UH: Not available

Louisiana
LH: 42%
UH: 19%

Virginia
LH: 21%
UH: 6%

Georgia
LH: 17%
UH: 7%

Mississippi
LH: 29%
UH: 15%

prices temporarily high due to war-induced shortages, many of these northern businessmen—as well as the politicians they helped elect—became quite rich. Southerners derisively referred to them as "carpetbaggers," for the expandable luggage they reputedly brought with them: the bags arrived empty and left full of money earned off southern land and labor.

A third grouping were poor and middling white southerners, most of whom had little wealth and little land before the Civil War. Finding themselves even more impoverished in the wake of the conflict, they represented the majority of the South's population and a critical group politically. Angry at the planters for starting the war—and, often, refusing to fight in it—many were enticed into supporting Republicans, northerners, and even the freedpersons by offers of a better economic deal. As examined below, the programs offered by the Radical Republican governments of the Reconstruction South included a host of programs—from public school building to progressive taxation—that poor whites could support. Still, many in this group could not overcome their lingering hostility to the North or their racist attitudes toward African Americans and remained stalwart supporters of planters and southern Democrats. In their eyes, white southern supporters of the new North-imposed Reconstruction governments were "scalawags," collaborators of a hated regime.

Finally, there were the planters. Once the unquestioned lords of southern politics and the southern economy, they had been crushed, at least temporarily, by the Civil War. Most had lost much of their wealth—either in the form of slaves or Confederate currency. Some had to sell their land and become overseers on plantations now owned by northerners. A few—unable to adjust to the new ways of the South—headed to a last bastion of slavery: Brazil. Not just economically crippled, the planters found themselves politically discredited and weak in much of the South. Still, they remained a potent force and would prove a formidable opponent to Radical Reconstruction regimes, using both violence and the ballot box to eventually regain political power and economic control in the region.

But that was still some years in the future. In the late 1860s, a new coalition of Republican Party forces—freedpersons, northerners, and progressive white southerners—had come to power in most of the South. Among these were a host of black politicians. With most blacks emerging from slavery illiterate and ignorant of the larger world, freedpersons often turned to more experienced men among the free black elite of pre–Civil War days. For example, both black senators from the South during Reconstruction—Blanche Bruce and Hiram Revels of Mississippi—were former slaves who had made their way out of the South before the Civil War and received an education in the North. Most of the 16 black representatives during the Reconstruction period were also free blacks in pre–Civil War days. An exception to the rule was Robert Smalls. A South Carolina slave impressed into the Confederate navy, Smalls seized control of his ship and delivered it to the Union navy in May 1862. The exploit won him acclaim throughout the North and the rank of captain in the Union navy. Smalls would serve as a representative from the state of South Carolina during most of the 1870s and 1880s.

Black politicians figured prominently at the state level in much of the South as well. Altogether some 20 African Americans served in statewide positions, including governor, lieutenant governor, secretary of state, treasurer, and superintendent of education. In addition, more than 600 African Americans won elections to serve in the various state legislatures. While they generally did not occupy seats in the various legislatures commensurate to their numbers in the population, they did for a time achieve a majority in the legislative lower house of South Carolina, a state where blacks

were in the majority among the population as well.

Along with their allies among northerners and progressive southern whites, these black politicians set forth an agenda that amounted to nothing less than the radical reconstruction of the South's social and economic order. The programs they promoted can roughly be divided into three areas: legal reform, economic modernization, and institution building.

The Radical Republican governments of the Reconstruction South rewrote their constitutions, extending the vote and making more offices elective. Laws were updated to northern standards. For example, in some southern states, statutes allowing for the imprisonment of debtors were still on the books in 1865. By the end of the Reconstruction period, those had disappeared. Women were aided by the new governments as well. Laws that turned over a married woman's property to her husband were done away with and divorce—virtually illegal in most southern states—was made fairer and easier to obtain.

The Radical Reconstruction governments also attempted to rebuild, diversify, and expand the southern economy.

Robert Smalls (Library of Congress)

The first African-Americans elected to the U.S. Congress were, from left to right, Robert Brown Elliot of South Carolina, Joseph Rainey of South Carolina, Jefferson Franklin Long of Georgia, Benjamin Turner of North Carolina, Robert DeLarge of South Carolina, Josiah Walls of Virginia, and Hiram Revels of Mississippi. (Library of Congress)

Prominent African-American Office Holders During Reconstruction

Name	Birth Status	Birthplace	State of Career	State Offices Held	Federal Offices Held
Bruce, Blanche	Slave	Virginia	Mississippi	None	Senator
DeLarge, Robert	Free	South Carolina	South Carolina	Chairman, S.C. House Ways and Means Committee	U.S. Representative
Elliott, Robert Brown	Free	New York	South Carolina	Assistant Attorney General	U.S. Representative
Gibbs, Jonathon	Free	Pennsylvania	Florida	Secretary of State, Superintendant of Schools	None
Long, Jefferson Franklin	Free	Georgia	Georgia	None	U.S. Representative
Pinchback, P. B. S.	Free	Georgia	Louisiana	President of State Senate, Lieut. Gov., acting Gov.	None
Rainey, Joseph	Slave	South Carolina	South Carolina	None	U.S. Representative
Smalls, Robert	Slave	South Carolina	South Carolina	State Rep., State Senator	U.S. Representative
Turner, Benjamin	Slave	North Carolina	Alabama	None	U.S. Representative
Walls, Josiah	Free	Virginia	Virginia	None	U.S. Representative

African-American Land Ownership in Rural Georgia, 1876

During the 1870s, African Americans made up just under half of the population of Georgia. Not surprisingly, however, they owned almost none of the land and held very few other assets.

Type of Asset	Percentage Owned by African Americans
Land	1.0%
City/town property	2.7%
Money/liquid assets	0.4%
Furniture	5.2%
Livestock	1.1%
Tools	4.9%
All other property	13.1%
Total taxable wealth	2.5%

The railroad network of the region was repaired and expanded and new manufacturing enterprises were promoted and subsidized. New roads were built into rural areas and city streets were paved. In addition, a host of new institutions—already familiar in most northern states—was introduced, including state hospitals, asylums for orphans and the insane, and more modern and humane prisons. Some southern states outpaced their northern counterparts, introducing social welfare programs that would not be seen in much of the country until the 1960s. For example, the Reconstruction regimes of South Carolina and Alabama respectively offered free medical care and legal counsel for the poor. (For the most part, the schools and other institutions created by the Reconstruction-era governments of the South remained strictly segregated along racial lines, prefiguring developments in the post-Reconstruction era.)

To pay for this vast expansion of government services, new taxes were passed. Not surprisingly, this served to create more opposition than almost anything else attempted by the Reconstruction governments. For years, the South had lagged behind the North in taxation. With their governments run by planters, land and personal property taxes were kept to a minimum. States balanced their budgets by offering almost no government services. But with their ambitious agendas, Reconstruction governments passed a series of property taxes. As with all progressive taxation schemes, those with more paid more. And, in the South, that meant the planters. The Reconstruction governments had a threefold agenda in imposing taxes on this group: to make them pay their fair share in rebuilding a backward and war-torn South; to diminish their economic power; and to force them to sell their land, making more land available to poor blacks and whites. Intensifying the hostility of the planters were the methods employed to assess and collect the taxes. Because counties with significant numbers of plantations usually had majority black populations, many of the new assessors and collectors were African Americans. Indeed, it was not unusual for a planter to find that the person forcing him to pay taxes—with the power of the state government behind him—was a former slave.

Nor was tax assessing unique in this regard. Just as some African Americans—largely freeborn elites—were gaining power during Reconstruction at the state and even federal level, many former slaves were winning office and gaining power at the local level. In fact, the freedpersons recognized early on that achieving social and economic gains depended upon who had power on the land. Thus, even as Reconstruction regimes were taking control of state governments, the Union (or Loyal) League was asserting power in localities throughout the South. Begun during the war as a northern organization to support the Union cause, the league quickly spread to the South when black and white organizers—often following in the wake of the Union army—founded chapters, largely in areas with significant African-American populations. These chapters soon became more than patriotic clubs. Many became self-help centers, helping to finance and construct local schools and churches. Most also had a political agenda, offering a civics education to newly freed slaves as well as promoting the candidacies of Radical Republican politicians at the local, state, and national levels. Finally, many Union League chapters—often filled with former Union army veterans, who retained their military rifles—formed militia companies to defend themselves against white violence and to protect those engaging in strikes against their landlords.

League chapters, militias, and local officials sympathetic to the plight of the freedperson were critical to the economic well-being of African Americans throughout the South. While some freedpersons migrated to southern towns and cities in search of work, the vast majority

of the population remained on the land. In some cases, they became agricultural laborers and were paid a wage for working a planter's land. As with northern factory work, there was a constant struggle during the Reconstruction period over wages and working conditions in the cotton fields, with strikes breaking out in various parts of the region. The existence of Union League chapters and militia companies meant that black—and poor white—strikers would not be met with violence or, at least, could defend themselves against it.

Still, while some freedpersons became agricultural laborers in the Reconstruction era, most turned to sharecropping. As its name implies, sharecropping was a system of sharing, whereby planters provided the land, while "croppers" added the labor. When the crop was harvested, the two shared the proceeds—usually on a fifty-fifty basis. "Cropping," as it was popularly called, provided a reasonable solution to the many problems facing southern agriculture in the immediate postwar years. For cash-poor planters, it offered a guaranteed labor force without the need for

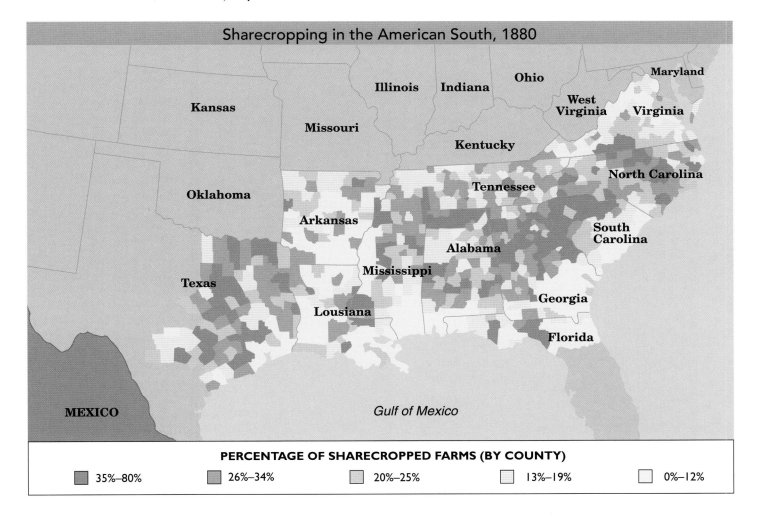

Sharecropping in the American South, 1880

PERCENTAGE OF SHARECROPPED FARMS (BY COUNTY)

35%–80% 26%–34% 20%–25% 13%–19% 0%–12%

Acres per Worker on White and Black Family Cotton Farms, 1880

The amount of land acreage available to African-American farmers was consistantly less than that available to whites.

Form of Tenure	White Farms	Black Farms
Owner-operated farms	12.5 acres	6.6 acres
Rented farms	14.5 acres	7.3 acres
Sharecropped farms	11.7 acres	8.0 acres
All farms	12.4 acres	7.5 acres

wages. (In fact, it often increased the labor force as croppers, eager to maximize their own returns, reintroduced women into the fields at critical periods in the crop cycle.) For the former freedpersons, it meant relative independence. Croppers worked the land at their own pace and without direct white supervision, two benefits of supreme importance to people who had known the lash and the auction block all of their lives.

At first, "cropping" effectively served all parties. Cotton prices remained high during the first years after the Civil War and so returns to both planters and croppers were good. At the same time, as long as there were local black militias and officials, the cropper could be assured of a fair deal. Since the system inherently favored the planter—who controlled the weighing of the crop and offered credit for seeds, tools, and food against next year's crop—it was critical that croppers could turn to the law to protect their interests. Under Republican Reconstruction regimes, black or pro-cropper sheriffs, judges, and other local officials made sure that croppers could turn to the courts and find justice in the law if they felt their landlord planters were trying to cheat them. Planters—so recently used to having absolute command over their labor force—found the new arrangements difficult to adjust to. Sharecropping, said one, "is the wrong policy. It makes the laborer too independent; he becomes a partner, and has a right to be consulted." Thus, from the very beginning of the post–Civil War era, the planter class of the South was determined to reassert its economic control over the region. But, as long as blacks, northerners, and their white progressive southern allies held the balance of political power, the planters were held in check. Not surprisingly, destroying that political power became the number one priority of the southern planter class during the Reconstruction era.

Scenes from a Union League parade in South Carolina, celebrating the anniversary of Emancipation Day (Library of Congress)

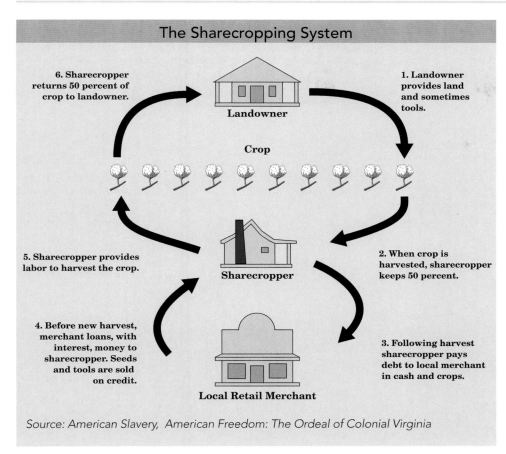

The Sharecropping System

6. Sharecropper returns 50 percent of crop to landowner.

1. Landowner provides land and sometimes tools.

Landowner

Crop

5. Sharecropper provides labor to harvest the crop.

Sharecropper

2. When crop is harvested, sharecropper keeps 50 percent.

4. Before new harvest, merchant loans, with interest, money to sharecropper. Seeds and tools are sold on credit.

3. Following harvest sharecropper pays debt to local merchant in cash and crops.

Local Retail Merchant

Source: American Slavery, American Freedom: The Ordeal of Colonial Virginia

Although black land ownership rose from 2 percent of farm families owning farms in 1870 to 21 percent in 1890, the vast majority of black farmers were sharecroppers.

REACTION AND "REDEMPTION"

Aside from the Civil War itself, the Reconstruction era is unquestionably the most violent period in American history, as planters and their allies among the white population of the region employed systematic terror to destroy black political power and the Republican Party in the South. The backlash began just one year after war's end. In 1866, a group of planters and other whites met in Pulaski, Tennessee, to form a secret organization dedicated to white power and white supremacy in the South. Led by Nathan Bedford Forrest, a vicious Confederate army leader who had massacred northern black troops after they surrendered in the 1864 Battle of Fort Pillow, the group called itself the Ku Klux Klan. Allied closely with the Democratic Party in the South, the Klan—the name derived from a Greek word for "circle of men"—quickly spread across the region and, by decade's end, was operating in every southern state. It was particularly active in

rural areas and in those parts of the South where the population of whites and blacks was relatively evenly balanced.

While most of the Klan's membership was drawn from the ranks of poor southern whites, its leadership was largely composed of planters, merchants, and other elites of the region, including large numbers of Democratic Party officials. As a white minister traveling in Alabama noted, the Klan was organized by "the leading men of the state. They had lost their property, and worst of all, their slaves were made their equals and perhaps their superiors to rule over them." This was a bit of an exaggeration—with little land of their own, freedpersons were hardly in a position to rule over the planters—but the minister's remarks captured the resentment permeating white society in the Reconstruction era.

At first, the organization was largely a social fraternity, focusing on ritualistic ceremonies that celebrated white southern heritage. The events of the mid-1860s—including the rise of the Republican Party in the South, as well as black economic and

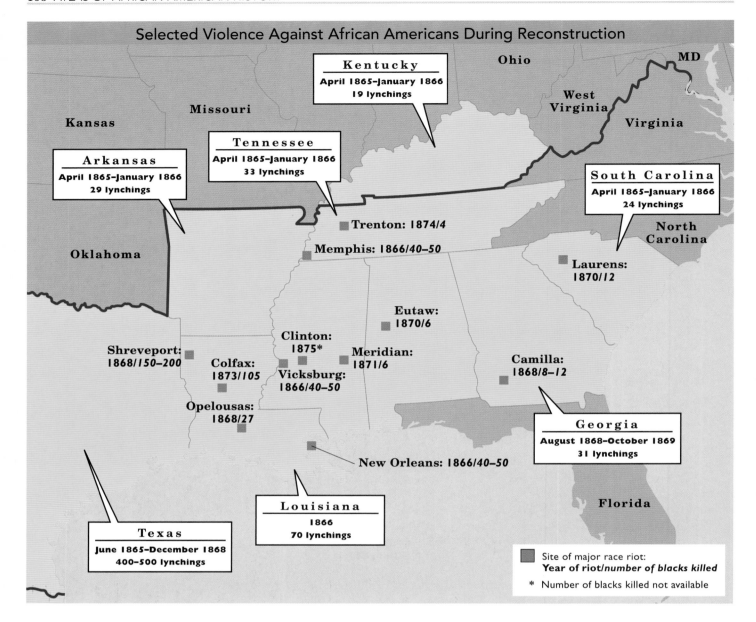

Selected Violence Against African Americans During Reconstruction

Kentucky
April 1865–January 1866
19 lynchings

Tennessee
April 1865–January 1866
33 lynchings

Arkansas
April 1865–January 1866
29 lynchings

South Carolina
April 1865–January 1866
24 lynchings

Trenton: 1874/4

Memphis: 1866/40–50

Laurens: 1870/12

Eutaw: 1870/6

Shreveport: 1868/150–200

Colfax: 1873/105

Clinton: 1875*

Meridian: 1871/6

Vicksburg: 1866/40–50

Camilla: 1868/8–12

Opelousas: 1868/27

New Orleans: 1866/40–50

Georgia
August 1868–October 1869
31 lynchings

Louisiana
1866
70 lynchings

Texas
June 1865–December 1868
400–500 lynchings

Kansas · Missouri · Ohio · MD · West Virginia · Virginia · Oklahoma · North Carolina · Florida

Site of major race riot:
Year of riot/*number of blacks killed*

* Number of blacks killed not available

political gains—soon turned the Klan into a vigilante organization that used violence and terror to achieve its ends, which included the return to power of the white planter class; the re-establishment of white social, economic, and political supremacy; and the resurrection of the Democratic Party in the South. By early 1868, with chapters throughout the South, the Klan had turned to physical intimidation and violence. While white Republicans and other pro-black sympathizers were attacked by the Klan, the group's primary targets were the black population of the South and freedmen's organizations, such as Union League chapters and local branches of the Republican Party. Indeed, Klan violence was rarely random. Singled out were black Union army veterans—most of whom were armed and many of whom were leaders in their local communities—as well as freedpersons who appeared to be succeeding economically, especially those who had been able to buy land of their own and thus escape the control of local planters.

Testimony gathered by federal investigators at the time provides a vivid depiction of Klan methods. "They took me to the woods and whipped me three hours or more and left me for dead," explained Abram Colby, a black member of the Georgia legislature, in 1869. "They said to me, 'Do you think you will ever vote for another damned radical ticket?'...I said, 'If there was an election tomorrow, I would vote the radical ticket.' They set in and whipped me a thousand licks more, with sticks and straps that had buckles on the end." Asked who attacked him, Colby testified, "Some are first-class men in our town. One is a lawyer, one a doctor, and some are farmers." Black women were also targeted for beatings, rape, and murder as a means of intimidating the black men, by showing them that they could not even defend their wives and daughters. "They came in; I was lying in bed," said Harriet Hernandes, a freedwoman from Spartanburg, South Carolina. "They took me out of bed…me and my daughter Lucy. [One] struck me on the forehead with a pistol…and kicked me over when I went to get over; and then he went to a brush pile, and they laid us right down there, both together." While the etiquette of the day did not allow Hernandes to go into detail, it is clear from her abridged testimony that she was raped alongside her daughter.

Not just individuals and families were targeted for attack. A Republican rally in Eutaw, Alabama, was assaulted in October 1870, leaving four African Americans dead and more than 50 wounded. For three weeks in 1873, Klansmen laid siege to Union League defenders of the predominantly black community of Colfax, Louisiana. On Easter Sunday, the Klan brought in a cannon and, despite a white surrender flag, went into the town and murdered 50 blacks and two whites. None of these, of course, were isolated incidents. Because the purpose of it was to end Reconstruction rule and prevent freedpersons and Republicans from voting, the violence was industrial in scale. While exact figures will never be known, it is estimated that as many as 10,000 southerners—largely black, but with a handful of pro-Reconstruction whites—were killed by the Klan between the late 1860s and the end of the Reconstruction era in 1877.

Not that there was not a counteroffensive. For example, Klansmen employed hoods not just for the purposes of intimidation—they mistakenly believed that superstitious blacks might mistake the night riders for ghosts—but for anonymity as well. With federal troops still patrolling the South—and with local government often under the control of Republican officials—Klansmen faced prosecution for their extralegal acts of violence, particularly after Congress passed the anti-Klan Force Acts in 1870 and 1871, which authorized federal prosecutions and the use of martial law to prevent vigilantism. Conviction under the

MAJOR WHITE RIOTS DURING RECONSTRUCTION

Locale and State	Year	Number of Blacks Killed
Memphis, Tennessee	1866	46
New Orleans, Louisiana	1866	40–50
Camilla, Georgia	1868	8–12
Opelousas, Louisiana	1868	27
Shreveport, Louisiana	1868	150–200
Eutaw, Alabama	1870	6
Laurens, South Carolina	1870	12
Meridien, Mississippi	1871	6
Colfax, Louisiana	1873	105
Trenton, Tennessee	1874	4
Vicksburg, Mississippi	1874	Unknown
Clinton, Mississippi	1875	Unknown
Hamburg, South Carolina	1876	Unknown

Force Acts or the Ku Klux Klan Act of 1871—the first laws in U.S. history that made crimes by private individuals punishable by federal law—deprived convicted Klansmen of the rights to vote, to hold elective office, and to serve on juries.

And for a time the federal government pursued the Klan vigorously. Agents infiltrated Klan chapters, gathering the evidence necessary for more than 3,000 indictments. In South Carolina, a virtual state of martial law was declared and some 2,000 Klansmen were driven from the state. Moreover, Union Leagues often pursued offending Klansmen and brought them before the law. Still, the odds against effectively destroying the organization were high. For one thing, the Klan enjoyed the support of much of the white South. Thus, it was relatively easy for fugitive Klansmen to find shelter or blend into the general population. Aside from white Republicans and African Americans—many of whom were effectively intimidated—it was difficult to find witnesses willing to testify or juries willing to convict. Ultimately, just 600 or so Klansmen were found guilty under the various federal acts aimed at the Klan,

CHRONOLOGY OF THE KU KLUX KLAN

April 1865: Confederacy surrenders; President Abraham Lincoln assassinated by southerner; Vice President Andrew Johnson, a southerner, becomes president.

December 1865: Congress passes 13th Amendment banning slavery.

March 1866: First Civil Rights Act passed by Congress.

June 1866: First Klan chapter organized in Pulaski, Tennessee; Congress passes 14th Amendment, guaranteeing equal civil rights to blacks.

July 1866: Tennessee becomes first Confederate state officially readmitted into the Union.

November 1866: Republicans sweep Congress.

March 1867: Congress passes Military Reconstruction Act, putting most of the South under martial law.

May 1867: Klan becomes national organization and elects former Confederate general Nathan Bedford Forrest its first Grand Wizard in Nashville, Tennessee.

Winter–Spring 1868: Klan quickly spreads across the South, from Virginia to Texas.

May 1868: U.S. House of Representative impeaches President Andrew Johnson. The Senate vote to remove him from office fails by one vote.

November 1868: Republican Ulysses S. Grant, the former commander of the Union army, is elected president.

February 1869: Congress passes 15th Amendment, giving black males the vote.

April 1871: Congress passes Ku Klux Klan Act, making violent anti–civil rights actions federal crimes.

Nathan Bedford Forrest
(Library of Congress)

Other Racist Organizations During Reconstruction

Constitutional Union Guard
 (North Carolina)
Knights of the Rising Sun (Texas)
Knights of the White Camelia
 (Louisiana)
Knights of the White Carnation
 (Alabama)
Knights of the White Cross
 (Mississippi)
White Brotherhood (North
 Carolina)
Young Men's Democratic Clubs
 (Tennessee)

and only a fraction of those were punished with significant jail time.

Northern Apathy

While Klansmen specifically targeted blacks and southern Republicans, they also effectively—if not entirely consciously—defeated another enemy: northern pro-Reconstruction Republicans. For all of blacks' political organizations, militias, and elected office holders, black political power in the South rested on a shaky

Early members of the Ku Klux Klan
(Library of Congress)

foundation: northern support. Ultimately, as a revolutionary from the 20th century noted, power comes from the barrel of a gun. As long as Union troops remained in the South—and as long as there was political will in the North to keep them there—the Radical Reconstruction regimes could remain politically viable in the face of a relentless surge in antiblack, anti-Republican violence. For a time, of course, that northern political will was strong, particularly after the Republican sweep in the 1866 elections. Indeed, many northern Republicans recognized that their hold over the national government depended upon their control of the South. Knowing full well that blacks and progressive southern whites were likely to vote for the Republican Party, it was in the party's interest to be sure that these persons could indeed vote. Moreover, in the immediate postwar years, there was widespread antiplanter sentiment in the North, and so support for the presence of Union troops and Radical Republican regimes in the southern states was widespread. Republicans in Washington and blacks in the South had discovered a marriage of convenience.

It did not last. For one thing, northern public opinion began to shift by the late 1860s. While antisouthern sentiment remained, there was a growing weariness with the "race question." The ongoing violence in the South left many northerners skeptical that the region could ever be changed. And though virtually all of the violence was directed against blacks and Republicans, this was conveyed poorly in the national press, leaving a feeling in many northerners' minds that both sides in the South were to blame. A commonly held sentiment was that it would be best to pull troops out of the region and let the locals fight it out amongst themselves.

At the same time, reports of corruption emerging from the South were turning northern opinion against the Republican regimes there. Indeed, there was an enormous amount of corruption in the South at this time. Planters and Democrats naturally blamed slick "carpetbagging" northern politicians and their "ignorant" black allies for the corruption. And with all of the new construction and new programs being initiated in the South, there was plenty of room for corruption. But the truth of the matter was that corruption tarnished every level of government and every region of the country in these years. It was endemic throughout the Union, North and South. Not for nothing have the decades following the Civil War come to be called the Gilded Age, an epithet coined at the time by Mark Twain and his writing partner Charles Dudley Warner to capture the gross excesses of wealth that characterized the period. In fact, the only real difference between northern and southern corruption during this period was scale: the pilfering of government funds in the North, the far richer region, vastly outpaced that in the South.

Growing northern frustration with the "race question" and southern corruption during the Reconstruction era was compounded by distractions. The late 1860s and early 1870s were marked by tremendous labor and social strife in the northern states. Finally, in 1873, the economy was rocked by a series of business failures that precipitated the worst depression in American history up to that time. Struggling to make ends meet on the farm—or battling factory bosses for a decent wage in industrial areas—made it hard for many northerners to feel much concern for the problems of distant blacks. Meanwhile, by the late 1860s, the Republican Party establishment in Washington was coming to the realization that it no longer needed the southern vote to stay in power. A Republican majority coalition of Civil War veterans and middle-class northerners had come into being. The results of this political alignment could be seen in a collapse of

Radical Republican leadership in Washington by the early 1870s.

Ultimately, growing northern frustration and apathy—induced by the interminable cycle of white violence and black appeals for help—played into the hands of Klansmen and white supremacists generally. Beginning in the upper South in the late 1860s and early 1870s—and then spreading to most of the Deep South by the middle part of the latter decade—Reconstruction governments fell throughout the South as intimidated black and white Republican voters were kept away from the polls. The process was euphemistically called "redemption" by white southerners, and it came first to Tennessee in 1869; North Carolina and Virginia in 1870; Georgia in 1871; Texas in 1873; Arkansas and Alabama in 1874; and Mississippi in 1876. By that latter presidential election year, only three southern states—Florida, Louisiana, and South Carolina—remained under Republican governments, and their days were numbered.

Cartoon of a northern carpetbagger (Library of Congress)

The End of Reconstruction

The Republican Party—in near complete control of the federal government since the election of Lincoln and the secession of the South in 1860–1861—was not looking forward to the centennial year

Despite the existence of the 14th and 15th Amendments, many African Americans were still denied participation in the political process. In this illustration, a group of blacks in Louisiana air their grievances to the state legislature. (Library of Congress)

A pro-Hayes political cartoon (Library of Congress)

electoral votes remained outstanding—19 in the remaining Republican-controlled southern states of Florida, Louisiana, and South Carolina, as well as a single disputed vote from Oregon. Both Republicans and Democrats quickly claimed that they had won the elections in the three southern states. As the Constitution offered no method for resolving such a circumstance, the nation was plunged into a period of anxiety and rising tensions between the November election and inauguration day in March 1877. Fears of a coup circulated in Washington. As individual congressmen argued and bartered their votes, Congress as a whole voted to create a commission of 15 to decide the outcome of the election, with seven Democrats, seven Republicans, and a presiding officer in Supreme Court Justice David Davis. At the last minute, however, the neutral Davis resigned from the court and was replaced by Joseph Bradley, a pro-Republican justice who voted along party lines, handing the election over to Hayes.

Democrats in general and southern Democrats in particular were outraged by the results and determined to use every means within their power to block the new president's inauguration. With the Senate in Republican hands and the House in Democratic hands, the balance of power lay with southern Democrats, and Hayes and other Republican leaders began to woo them in secret negotiations. Historians are not sure exactly who agreed to what—if anything—during these talks. But the outcome—the so-called compromise of 1877—led to the final dismantling of the Reconstruction governments of the South. Not only were Florida, Louisiana, and South Carolina turned over to Democratic rule, but the new president agreed to confine all federal troops in the South to their barracks.

Reconstruction—which had been undergoing a slow death since the late 1860s—was not killed off by the "compromise" but it was hastened to its end. Southern blacks would continue to vote and elect their own to local, state, and federal office through the end of the century. Segregation and the full imposition of the misnamed "separate but equal" doctrine were still a decade or more in the future. Still, the "compromise of 1877" did mark the end of the federal government's commitment to one of the most remarkable efforts at social reconstruction

election of 1876 with much enthusiasm. The two-term Grant administration had been rocked by corruption and scandal and the national economy was in the third year of economic depression. Businesses were failing by the thousands, the unemployed numbered in the millions, and, in places, there was real starvation. To hold onto the presidency, the Republicans had nominated Rutherford B. Hayes, a whistle-clean governor from Ohio and a moderate on Reconstruction. Democrats put up the corruption-fighting governor of New York, Samuel J. Tilden.

On election night, it appeared the Democrats had prevailed; Tilden had a slight majority of the popular vote and, more important, a 184-to-165 edge in the electoral college, the body that actually decides presidential elections. Still, 20 in the nation's history. And nowhere was the loss of that commitment more sharply felt than on the plantations of the South and in the economic relations between sharecroppers and their landlords.

As noted earlier, the presence of local politicians, judges, and law enforcement officials sympathetic to the plight of the freedperson was critical in assuring that fairness prevailed in the economic relations of sharecropping. It is not surprising, then, that the planter-led Ku Klux Klan specifically targeted African Americans, Republicans, and the candidates they voted for through intimidation, violence, and even murder. By destroying black political power in the South, the planters hoped to return the black population to economic subservience and assure that the bulk of the profits generated from sharecropping would accrue to those who owned the land. This goal became increasingly critical to cash-strapped planters as the price of cotton began to decline from the highs that prevailed in the immediate post–Civil War shortage years. Thus, even as the price of cotton and other commercial crops in the South declined, planters moved to take a bigger share of the profits that remained.

They did so through a system that came to be known as "debt peonage" or, as African Americans pointedly came to call it, "debt slavery." Croppers were usually forced to borrow from the planter to meet the farming and living expenses they accrued during the growing season. Sometimes this lending took the form of cash, but usually it was in goods such as seed, tools, foodstuffs, and cloth. The interest and/or prices charged by the planter were often exorbitant. A sharecropper might find that at the end of the season—when the crop was weighed and the profits divided—he or she owed more to the planter than the cropper's half of the crop was worth. Moreover, operating the scales and keeping the books—many croppers remained illiterate, especially after white "redemption" governments cut the budgets for public education—offered the planters many opportunities to cheat their tenants. If a tenant complained or threatened to find a better deal on another plantation, the planter could use law enforcement and the courts to keep the cropper in line. Laws were also passed at the state level to make it a crime to try

and induce croppers away from a planter, and local industrialists and railroads were warned not to recruit black workers, except for the lowliest, poorest-paying positions. Gradually, croppers—and this included both blacks and poor whites—found themselves so deeply in debt to their landlords that they could never leave. And if they tried, they could be arrested and rented out by the state to work on their former master's land.

THE LATE 19TH CENTURY

Given the conditions that freedmen in the South had to live under, it is not surprising that many African Americans who were able to leave the South in the years immediately following the collapse of Reconstruction did so. And, like many other Americans, some African Americans looked to the West for salvation. The so-called Exoduster movement of the late 1870s and early 1880s saw thousands of sharecroppers flee the South for the open farmlands of Kansas, Nebraska, and Oklahoma, where homesteading laws made it possible to stake out free claims on government land. Of course, the Exodusters were not the first blacks to head West. Although few in number, African Americans were critical to the history of the American West. Thus, before turning to the Exodusters, it is useful to examine the long, illustrious, and often overlooked history of blacks in the American West.

The first non–Native Americans to explore what would become the American West were the Spanish conquistadores of the 16th and 17th centuries. As discussed in chapter 2, one of the most famous of these "Spanish" explorers was Estéban Dorantes, a Moorish slave whose search for the mythical Seven Cities of Gold ended in his mysterious disappearance in the deserts of the Southwest. But the tradition of black exploration of the West did not die with Estéban Dorantes. Indeed, the African-American experience in the West followed the general outlines of the region's history—first exploration and surveying; then exploitation of natural resources and the military conquest of the Native American peoples; and finally the wholesale settlement of ranches and farms by westward migrating Americans.

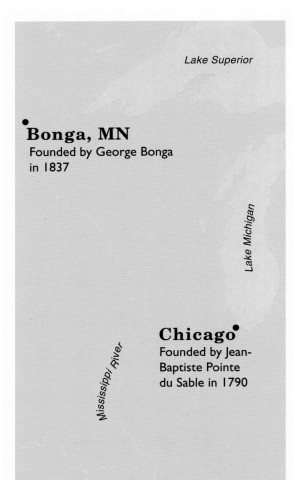

Lake Superior

Bonga, MN
Founded by George Bonga
in 1837

Lake Michigan

Chicago
Founded by Jean-
Baptiste Pointe
du Sable in 1790

Mississippi River

JEAN-BAPTISTE POINTE DU SABLE AND THE BONGA FAMILY

Jean-Baptiste Pointe du Sable was born in 1745 in Saint-Domingue. In 1773, he purchased a home and land in Old Peoria Fort, Illinois. Five years later, he founded a trading post at the mouth of the Chicago River. From that post, he established himself as a successful fur trapper and trader as well as a miller and cooper. In 1790, he built the first permanent settlement in what is now Chicago, Illinois. After selling his holdings in Chicago, du Sable retired in 1800 to a stone mansion in St. Charles, Missouri. He died in 1818.

Among the most important families in Minnesota history, Jean Bonga, his son Pierre, and his grandsons George and Stephen were instrumental in opening the Northwest Territories to settlement.

Jean Bonga, a former slave, opened the first inn on Mackinaw Island sometime after 1787.

His son, Pierre, was a renowned explorer and translator who joined the North West Company in 1803. Married to a Chippewa (Ojibway) Indian, he served as the chief guide during the British exploration of the Red River Valley.

Grandson Stephen was a skillful negotiator who helped convince Chippewa Chief Hole-in-the-Day to negotiate with the American government.

Of all the Bongas, grandson George had the most illustrious career. He too was a trader, negotiator, translator, and guide. In 1820, he helped lead the Cass expedition in search of the source of the Mississippi River. Standing 6'6" tall and weighing well over 200 pounds, George was a commanding presence whose half-black, half-Indian heritage won him the respect of Native American leaders.

In 1837, George founded a town in Cass County County, Minnesota, that bears his family name. His death in 1885 was noted in the U.S. Congress as well as in newspapers in New York, Chicago, and elsewhere.

AFRICAN AMERICANS IN THE WEST

Among the first black explorers in North America was Jean-Baptiste Pointe du Sable. Born in Haiti to a French sailor and African-American slave woman in 1745, du Sable was sent by his father to Paris for an education, eventually working as a seaman on one of his father's ships. Shipwrecked near New Orleans in 1765 and fearful of being enslaved, he fled the region for what was then the Old Northwest, working as a fur trapper. Like most in his profession, du Sable took an Indian woman for his wife. By 1779, he had built a cabin on the southern shores of Lake Michigan, at a site local Indians called Eschikagou, or "land of wild onions." Eventually, du Sable would buy land, on which he would establish a thriving farm and mill there, earning himself a historical claim as the founder of the nation's third largest city which, adapting the Indian name, would come to be known as Chicago.

Estéban and du Sable represented the black presence among Europeans in the American Midwest and West. But with the Louisiana Purchase of 1803, all of the land east of the Rocky Mountains came under American control. To learn what was there and to chart possible routes to the Pacific Ocean, President Thomas Jefferson recruited his personal secretary Meriwether Lewis and an army officer named William Clark to lead an expedition to the Pacific Northwest. Among the party was Clark's slave. Known to history by his Christian name only, York proved a critical member of the expedition. His great size, athletic prowess, and African features fascinated local Indians along the route, a phenomenon that greatly aided the progress of the largely white expedition as his presence often smoothed over relations with curious Native Americans.

While the Lewis and Clark expedition focused on exploring and mapping, those who soon followed were more interested in exploiting the resources of

James Beckwourth (Library of Congress)

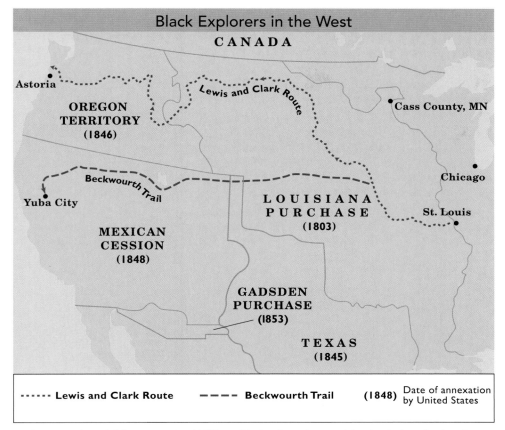

Black Explorers in the West

York, an enslaved African serving William Clark, played a crucial role during the Lewis and Clark expedition. The American explorers were guided by a Frenchman named Jean-Baptiste Charbonneau and his Native American wife Sacagawea. Because York spoke a little French as well as English, he served as company translator, not only within the company, but with Native Americans encountered along the way. The red line on the map above shows the westward route of the expedition. The Beckwourth Trail, forged by famed African-American mountain man James Beckwourth several decades later, is shown in green.

the region, even as they explored and mapped much of this territory. The trailblazers in this endeavor were the fur trappers, men who ranged far and wide across the plains and mountains of the West in search of beaver and other pelts. Generally working alone or in small parties, they often traded with, lived among, and even married Native Americans. Among the most famous of these trapper/explorers was James Beckwourth. Born in 1798 and, like du Sable, of mixed heritage, Beckwourth began his trapping days at age 19, working for the Rocky Mountain Fur Company. By the time of the California gold rush of the late 1840s, he was ranging as far west as the Sierra Nevada. In April 1850, he discovered one of the key passes through those intimidating mountains—a pass that still bears his name—and set up a farm and trading post at its western end, just in time to take

advantage of the many miners and settlers pouring into northern California after gold was discovered in 1848.

Indeed, among the forty-niners were a few African Americans, largely brought as slaves by southern gold seekers. But the freewheeling atmosphere of the mining camps and the instant metropolis of San Francisco made escape easy. Most slaves quickly broke free of their masters and worked on claims of their own, or as wage laborers for other miners—some white miners believed blacks were good luck—or in businesses that offered goods and services to miners. Some, like land speculator Biddy Mason, became entrepreneurs of their own. Others, like Mifflin Gibbs, who founded the state's first black newspaper, took on the role of civil rights activists. Nor were American blacks the first Africans in the Golden State. Many members of the state's

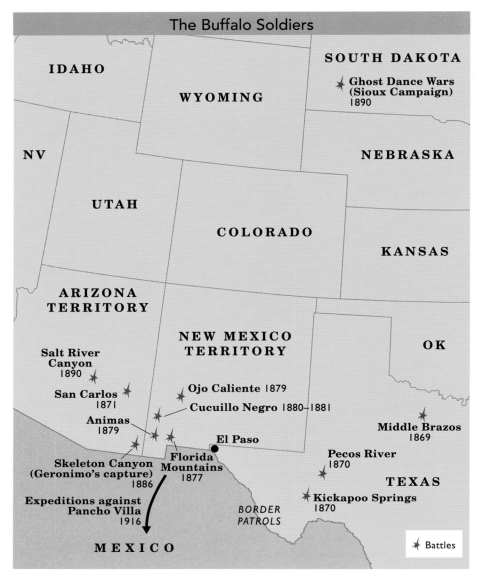

The Buffalo Soldiers

IDAHO

WYOMING

SOUTH DAKOTA

Ghost Dance Wars
(Sioux Campaign)
1890

NV

NEBRASKA

UTAH

COLORADO

KANSAS

ARIZONA
TERRITORY

NEW MEXICO
TERRITORY

OK

Salt River
Canyon
1890

San Carlos
1871

Ojo Caliente 1879

Cucuillo Negro 1880–1881

Animas
1879

Middle Brazos
1869

El Paso

Skeleton Canyon
(Geronimo's capture)
1886

Florida
Mountains
1877

Pecos River
1870

TEXAS

Expeditions against
Pancho Villa
1916

Kickapoo Springs
1870

BORDER
PATROLS

MEXICO

★ Battles

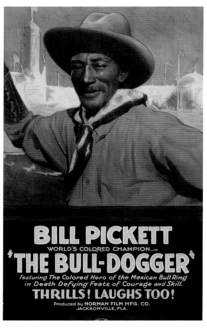

Bill Pickett (Library of Congress)

veterans of the Civil War—that Native Americans came to call Buffalo Soldiers, after their curly black hair, which the Indians believed looked like buffalo fur.

Divided into four regiments—two infantry and two cavalry, the latter making up 20 percent of all U.S. cavalry in the late 19th century—the Buffalo Soldiers patrolled the region between the Mississippi River and the Rocky Mountains. It was, of course, a physically and morally challenging task for many of the soldiers. For $13 per month, they divided their time between stays in rough-hewn forts and long, hard rides across the western landscape. They chased down outlaws and cattle rustlers and kept the peace in territories where sheep and cattle ranchers settled their differences with gunfire. Later, many of the black cavalrymen would see service in the Spanish-American War where they fought alongside Teddy Roosevelt's "Rough Riders" in the Battle of San Juan Hill. Black troops of the Ninth and 10th Cavalry overwhelmed a Spanish fort and cut though barbed wire, thus providing an opening for the Rough Riders to attack. In response, Roosevelt remarked, "Well, the Ninth and 10th men are alright. They can drink out of our canteens." The Buffalo Soldiers continued their service in the Philippines, helping to put down a revolt against American occupation in the early years of the 20th century, and Mexico, where they fought revolutionaries and bandits in 1916 after the latter conducted raids across the U.S. border.

But, mostly, the Buffalo Soldiers attacked Indians. Former slaves, they were given the task of forcing another oppressed people off the land to make way for a white population that had little respect for either group. Indeed, local whites often failed to pay the Buffalo Soldiers the respect that was given to other cavalrymen. In 1878, a major gunfight between white cowboys and black cavalry broke out in San Angelo, Texas, after the barroom murder of a Buffalo Soldier by a white cowhand who boasted that he committed the crime for "sport." Sometimes, they faced hostility from the army bureaucracy itself. Benjamin O. Flipper, West Point's first black graduate, was assigned to the 10th Cavalry, and was drummed out of the service after being caught riding with a white woman. As historian William Loren Katz noted, "it is

Mexican population were of mixed Spanish, Indian, and African heritage, including Pío Pico, a wealthy rancher and the first governor of California following its annexation after the U.S.-Mexican War.

The coming of the Civil War interrupted black migration to the West, just as it did for the population in general. But in the wake of the conflict a new surge of settlement began, particularly in the territories of the Great Plains and Mountain West. The intrusion of these settlers on their ancestral lands angered the Native Americans of the region and set off a series of wars between the U.S. Army and various Indian nations that would last until 1890 and the Wounded Knee Massacre in what is now South Dakota. Taking part in this bloody and oftentimes unjust struggle were several regiments of black soldiers—many of them ironic that these brave black soldiers served so well in the final and successful effort to crush American Indians, the first victims of white racism in this continent. But serve they did." In fact, they served with distinction, earning 23 Medals of Honor for their bravery in the Indian wars and the Spanish-American War.

Blacks in the West, however, were not always on the side of the law. A number of the more notorious outlaws of the old West were African American, including cattle rustler Isom Dart, gunfighter Cherokee Bill, and con man Ben Hodges, who once swindled the president of the Dodge City National Bank out of thousands of dollars.

Most black cowboys were honest, hardworking men. Making up an estimated 25 percent of all Texas cowhands in the late 19th century, black cowboys were such a part of the western scene that several became western legends. Bill Pickett is widely credited as the inventor of bulldogging, the popular rodeo sport of chasing down a steer on horseback, jumping off, and wrestling the animal to the ground. Pickett later went on to a

BLACKS IN THE SPANISH-AMERICAN WAR

Federal
Ninth Cavalry
10th Cavalry
24th Cavalry
25th Cavalry

State
Ninth Ohio
Third Alabama
Third North Carolina
Sixth Virginia
23rd Kansas
Eighth Illinois

Two Indiana infantry companies
Company L of the Sixth Massachusetts

Congressional Medal of Honor Winners
Pvt. Dennis Bell, 10th Cavalry, born in Washington, D.C.
Pvt. Fitz Lee, 10th Cavalry, born in Virginia
Pvt. William Thompkins, 10th Cavalry, born in New Jersey
Pvt. George Wanton, 10th Cavalry, born in Wyoming

lucrative career as a star of rodeo and the early movie screen. Nat Love—known as "Deadwood Dick"—was perhaps the most famous of the black cowboys, largely because of his autobiography which, in the tradition of western truth-stretching, painted Love as a man who could out-rope, out-shoot, and out-drink any man alive.

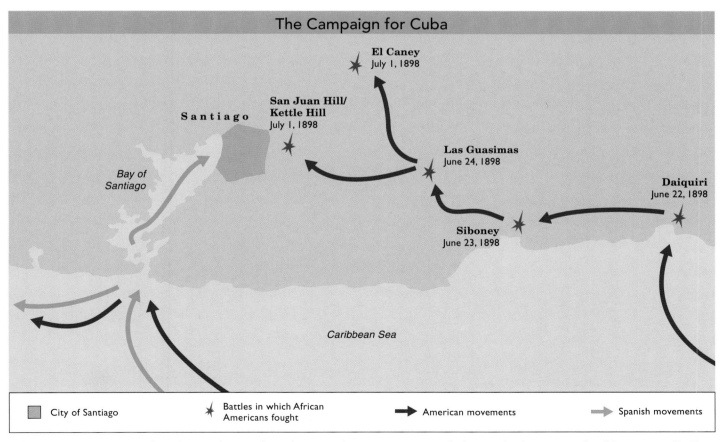

African-American troops played a significant role in the Spanish-American War, including at the famous Battle of San Juan Hill. The map shown here illustrates battles during the campaign for Cuba in which African-American troops played a part.

A recruitment sign for Singleton's
Homestead Association
(Library of Congress)

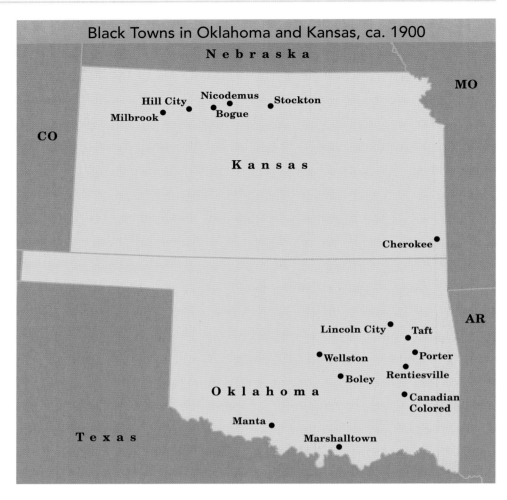

Black Towns in Oklahoma and Kansas, ca. 1900

"Pap" Singleton (Library of
Congress)

Still, the days of the open range—
for both blacks and whites in the
West—were numbered. Eventually,
farming followed ranching. As with
whites, many African Americans saw an
opportunity to improve their lot by
homesteading western lands. It also
offered—or so many blacks thought—an
escape from racism in the South. Rising
white violence and the collapse of pro-
black Reconstruction regimes in 1877
left many freedpersons in despair and
terror. Then, as in a religious revival,
promoters like Benjamin "Pap"
Singleton spread the word through
freedperson communities of the South
that there was free land and freedom
from white racism in the West.

During the spring of 1879, thousands heeded his call. By May, more than
6,000 Exodusters were camped out along
the St. Louis riverfront, awaiting river-
boats that would take them upriver to
Kansas and Nebraska. Many were impoverished, with no money for fares and little more than the clothes on their backs.
Still, by 1880, the U.S. Census reported

more than 40,000 black people in the
state of Kansas, making it the second-
largest black population in the West, after
Texas. Twenty years later, a second exodus
brought the black population of
Oklahoma to more than 130,000, including several thousand who lived in
"planned," all-black towns like Boley and
Langston City. As in other such real
estate ventures, streets were carefully laid
out on grids and lots set aside for parks,
schools, and other public buildings. Sadly,
both efforts at homesteading would be
largely defeated in the late 19th and early
20th centuries, broken by drought, low
crop prices, and racist institutions, including milling operations and railroads that
discriminated against black farmers.

THE RISE OF JIM CROW

While the end of Reconstruction came in
1877—with President Hayes's order to
end active federal army supervision of the
South—the impact of the nation's first
great experiment in racial equality lin-

gered on for at least another generation. Segregation—while widespread—was not absolute and had yet to be enshrined in law in the late 1870s and 1880s. In many regions of the South, for example, blacks continued to vote and elect other African Americans to local and state office through the end of the 19th century. In Mississippi and South Carolina, the two southern states with proportionally the largest black populations, voters sent African Americans to Congress through the end of the century.

Still, there were critical differences between the Reconstruction era and the "redemption" period of renewed white rule that succeeded it. During the former, blacks and white Republicans had political power somewhat commensurate to their numbers in the population, often vying with white Democrats for local and state government control. In the latter period, blacks and Republicans voted and won office as a distinctly minority force. Blacks continued to vote in large numbers in the late 1870s and 1880s but their vote was tightly controlled. Moreover, there was no institutional challenge to the rule of planters and other elites, as the Republican party—castigated as the party of northern carpetbaggers—virtually disappeared as a political force in the white South, not to be revived for another century. The South had become a one-party region and that party—the Democrats—had clearly become the voice of white supremacy and planter power.

Yet, despite the hegemony of the Democratic Party, there were deep divisions within southern society, and not just between blacks and whites. Resentment of planter wealth and political power ran deep even before the Civil War among many poor southern whites, particularly those who had been relegated to marginal hill-country lands. The huge losses suffered by white farmers in the war—a popular slogan of the day was that the conflict had been "a rich man's war but a poor man's fight"—added to the anger. But it was economic concerns that turned this resentment into political revolt, with enormous consequences for the black population of the South.

Following a postwar boost in the value of cotton and other commercial crops, prices began to fall in the 1880s. Many poor southern farmers fell into debt to local merchants who fronted them food and supplies for the growing

MADAME C. J. WALKER

Madame C.J. Walker, behind the wheel of her Model A Ford, in 1912. (A'Lelia Bundles/Walker Family Collection)

Among the host who migrated from the South in the 1880s was Madame C. J. Walker, an unschooled black orphan who became the world's first self-made female millionaire. Born Sarah Breedlove on a Louisiana plantation in 1867, she was married at age 14 and widowed by 20, whereupon she moved to St. Louis to join her brothers. After a scalp ailment left her temporarily bald, she became interested in hair tonics. In 1905, she moved to Denver, where she married Charles J. Walker and began her career as a door-to-door hair tonic saleswoman. Shortly thereafter, she founded her own business—the Madame C. J. Walker Manufacturing Company. The firm grew quickly, and by 1917 it was already the largest black-owned business in America. By then, she had relocated to Irvington-on-Hudson, a wealthy New York suburb, where she built a mansion called Villa Lewaro. Madame Walker used much of her wealth to promote the economic success of others, particularly African-American women. She was especially proud that her company employed thousands of black women, giving them a more rewarding form of employment than the domestic service jobs that so many were restricted to. She also gave handsomely to educational and social institutions like Bethune-Cookman College and the NAACP.

One key behind the company's success was "The Walker Method," a hair preparation technique for African-American women. Madam Walker's insistance on cleanliness was legendary. Many of her hygiene standards were incorporated into state and federal law after her death.

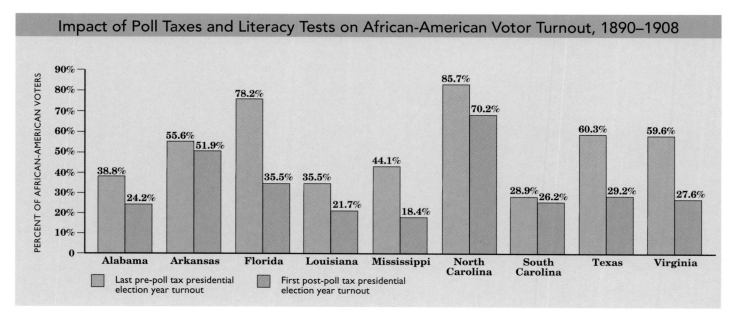

Impact of Poll Taxes and Literacy Tests on African-American Voter Turnout, 1890–1908

season. With prices for their crops falling, many farmers found themselves unable to pay their debts and were forced to sell their lands. The result was a burgeoning population of white sharecroppers across the South. As the economic distress grew, poor white farmers and sharecroppers formed the Southern Alliance, a populist-style movement aimed at addressing low crop prices and burdensome debt. Blacks followed suit with the Colored Farmers' Alliance. The organizations grew rapidly. By the late 1880s, the two organizations boasted a membership of 3 million between them.

Nor were the Southern Alliance and many poor white farmers generally slow to realize the obvious racial implications of their struggle. That is, poor white farmers and the Southern Alliance had far more in common with black croppers and the Colored Farmers' Alliance than they did with planters and the Democratic Party. As populist leader Tom Watson of Georgia remarked, "the accident of color can make no difference in the interest of farmers, croppers, and laborers. You are kept apart that you may be separately fleeced of your earnings." By 1890, both alliances were rallying behind the single largest challenge to the two-party system in the late 19th century—the Peoples' Party, also known as the Populists. This movement was designed to alleviate agricultural poverty through government action—including nationalization of the railroads, government purchase of crops, and inflationary

monetary policy (inflation, by lowering the value of money and raising the price of crops, makes it easier for farmers to pay back their debts). The Populists demonstrated enormous political appeal in both the South and Midwest.

Sadly, particularly for its black supporters, the Populist movement was broken in the South by the Democratic Party and its appeals to white supremacy. With money, power, and influence on their side, white elites and Democratic Party politicians appealed to the lowest instincts of poor white southerners. Arguing that economic and political cooperation with blacks would lead to social equality—and even sexual intermixing—southern political leaders were able to browbeat many poor whites into voting Democratic. Indeed, Democratic rallies often featured bevies of white women appealing to their menfolk to protect them from the black man. When visceral appeals to racial intolerance failed, white elites employed fraud, running up huge pro-Democratic tallies in the largely African-American counties that they controlled. As Frank Burkitt, a Mississippi populist, complained, "a class of corrupt office-seekers...hypocritically raised the howl of white supremacy while they debauched the ballot boxes...disregarded the rights of the blacks...and actually dominated the will of the white people through the instrumentality of the stolen negro vote." Sometimes, as in the case of the secret White Man's Union of Grimes County, Texas, the old, anti-Reconstruction methods of violence and intimidation were used to keep blacks from the polls in the late 1890s.

Yet, despite the shared economic concerns of blacks and poor whites, fraud and the appeals to white racism worked. Nationally, the Populist Party—torn by divisions over its national alliance with Democratic presidential candidate William Jennings Bryan—virtually disappeared as a political force after 1896. Regionally, future Populist threats to Democratic Party rule were met by reinforcing white supremacy and disenfranchising black voters. Segregation, or "Jim Crow" as it was called, once enforced by custom, became enshrined in law. All public places and conveyances were either strictly divided by race or restricted to whites only. At the same time, state after state in the South passed poll taxes and literacy tests to prevent blacks from voting.

Sometimes, these also had the potential to disenfranchise poor whites, but the rules were rarely enforced in white counties.

An even more effective method of disenfranchising blacks was the "grandfather clause," which denied the vote to anyone whose grandfather had not been free, preventing almost all blacks from voting, regardless of their finances or educations.

As with the retreat from Reconstruction, the white South's efforts to reverse black gains were abetted by northern apathy and acquiescence. During the 1880s and 1890s, a series of Supreme Court decisions virtually undid all of the civil rights laws of the Reconstruction era. In an 1883 case, the court virtually eliminated the "equal protection" clause of the 14th Amendment by exempting the actions of private citizens. That is to say, the court declared that the U.S.

SELECTED SEGREGATION LAWS

Separation in Railroad Cars by State

Separation in Railroad Cars by State	Year Law Passed	State	Year Law Passed
Georgia	1891	Louisiana	1902
South Carolina	1900	Arkansas, Tennessee	1903
North Carolina, Virginia	1901	Mississippi, Maryland	1904

Examples of Segregation Laws by State	Law	Year Law Passed
Alabama	Separate school system	1868*
Georgia	Separate parks	1905
Alabama	Separate streetcars	1906
Baltimore, Maryland	Separate neighborhoods	1910
Louisiana	Separate entrances and seating at circuses	1914
South Carolina	Separate entrances, working facilities, pay windows, water glasses, etc. in factories	1915
Oklahoma	Separate telephone booths	1915
Mississippi	Separate taxicabs	1922
Atlanta, Georgia	African-American barbers forbidden from cutting the hair of white women	1926
Atlanta, Georgia	White and black baseball teams banned from playing within two blocks of each other	1932
Texas	Whites and blacks forbidden from wrestling together	1933
Oklahoma	Whites and blacks forbidden from fishing or boating together	1935
Arkansas	Segregated racetracks	1937
Virginia	Segregated waiting rooms at airports	1944

* By 1885, all states in the South required separate schools for white and black children.

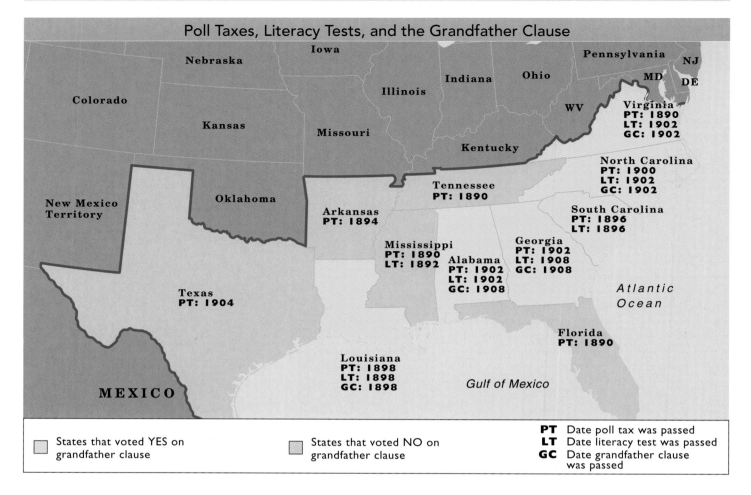

Poll Taxes, Literacy Tests, and the Grandfather Clause

Colorado

Nebraska

Iowa

Kansas

Missouri

Illinois

Indiana

Ohio

Pennsylvania

NJ

MD

DE

WV

Kentucky

New Mexico
Territory

Oklahoma

Virginia
PT: 1890
LT: 1902
GC: 1902

North Carolina
PT: 1900
LT: 1902
GC: 1902

Arkansas
PT: 1894

Tennessee
PT: 1890

South Carolina
PT: 1896
LT: 1896

Mississippi
PT: 1890
LT: 1892

Alabama
PT: 1902
LT: 1902
GC: 1908

Georgia
PT: 1902
LT: 1908
GC: 1908

Texas
PT: 1904

*Atlantic
Ocean*

Florida
PT: 1890

Louisiana
PT: 1898
LT: 1898
GC: 1898

Gulf of Mexico

MEXICO

▢ States that voted YES on
grandfather clause

▢ States that voted NO on
grandfather clause

PT Date poll tax was passed
LT Date literacy test was passed
GC Date grandfather clause
was passed

Constitution only applied in cases where the state itself discriminated. Thus, it was perfectly legal for a restaurant or a railroad to practice discrimination in its hiring or its offering of services to black citizens. The most infamous case reversing the gains of the Reconstruction era, however, was the 1896 *Plessy v. Ferguson* opinion in which the Court decided that governments—local, state, and even federal—could practice segregation, as long as they provided "separate but equal" facilities and services to both races. *Plessy v. Ferguson* resulted in the "separate" but not the "equal."

The 1890s and the early 20th century mark, perhaps, the nadir of post–Civil War racial tolerance. In the South, lynching—the arbitrary torture, execution, and even dismemberment of those suspected of disobedience or rule-breaking—flourished, with an average of 100 blacks killed every year between 1890 and 1910. In the North, where blacks remained few in number until the Great Migration of World War I and the 1920s, racism was equally widespread, based on the "scientific" principles of social Darwinism that deemed blacks genetically inferior to whites. Despite oppression, intimidation, and violence, individual blacks and black organizations continued to challenge the ideas and practices of late 19th- and early 20th-century racism. But the means to best accomplish that—separation or integration—created a rift in the African-American community that, arguably, has not healed to this day.

THE "NEW NEGRO"
African Americans from the Early to Mid-20th Century

At the threshold of the 20th century, the civil status of African Americans was severely eroded from the ideals put forth in the 13th, 14th, and 15th Amendments. While the 13th Amendment had abolished legal slavery, a system of debt peonage—in which black sharecroppers remained unable to pay off the loans fronted to them by their landlords—kept them tied to the cotton plantations as in antebellum times. The 14th Amendment ostensibly guaranteed black Americans due process and equal protection under the law, but new laws formalized and extended the daily racial segregation of southern life, in which separate but distinctly unequal facilities were provided for blacks and whites. The 15th Amendment gave African-American men the right to vote, but various methods disenfranchised blacks in southern states. Even as southern states passed discriminatory laws, decisions of the U.S. Supreme Court were upholding them, culminating in the 1896 *Plessy v. Ferguson* decision.

In the South, violence against blacks remained endemic; in the 1890s more than 1,100 blacks were beaten, hanged, or burned to death, often in festival-like surroundings. When not confronted by the direct violence of the lynch mob, most African Americans in the South—and the small minority who lived in the North—faced the day-to-day economic assault of poverty. In 1900 approximately half the African-American population were illiterate, handicapping their ability to improve their economic or legal standing.

THE EARLY CIVIL RIGHTS MOVEMENT

Widespread segregation and extreme discrimination were the context in which the civil rights leaders of the early 20th century tried to advance the interests of African Americans. One key to these efforts was the array of all-black colleges and universities established in the 19th century. Another was the use of journalism, book publication, and pamphlet-writing to publicize the extent of lynching and demand legal redress. A third was the establishment of political organizations to promote the cause of black civil rights. At the same time, the discoveries and inventions of African Americans made a lasting impact on U.S. life and culture.

BOOKER T. WASHINGTON AND AFRICAN-AMERICAN EDUCATION

Knowledge is a powerful tool for those who seek to equality and advancement. At the close of the 19th century, African Americans had far slimmer opportunities for education than their white counterparts. In higher education, however, oppor-

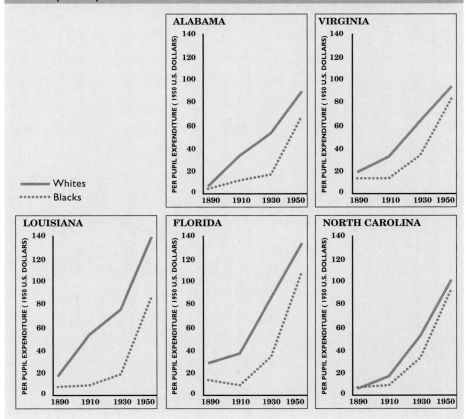

Per Pupil Expenditure for Selected States (in 1950 U.S. Dollars)

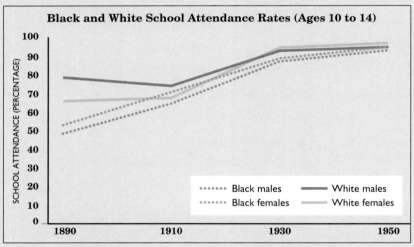

Black and White Illiteracy Rates (Ages 10 and Over)

ILLITERATE POPULATION (PERCENTAGE)

Black illiteracy

White illiteracy

80 70 60 50 40 30 20 10 0

1880 1900 1920 1940 1950

Black and White School Attendance Rates (Ages 10 to 14)

SCHOOL ATTENDANCE (PERCENTAGE)

100 90 80 70 60 50 40 30 20 10 0

1890 1910 1930 1950

······· Black males   —— White males
······· Black females   —— White females

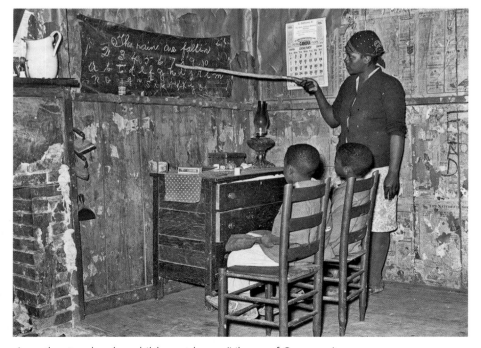

A mother teaches her children at home (Library of Congress)

tunities had expanded with the establishment of a number of all-black colleges and universities in the 19th century.

Cheyney University, the oldest of the so-called historically black colleges and universities (HBCUs), was founded in Pennsylvania in 1837. Lincoln University, also in Pennsylvania, followed in 1854. Hampton Institute, the first HBCU in the South, traces its roots to outdoor classes taught to local freedmen in 1861. Today, there are 105 HBCUs nationwide, mostly in the Northeast and South. In addition to Cheyney, Lincoln, and Hampton, the roster includes such highly regarded schools as Dillard, Fisk, Wilburforce, Howard, Spellman, and Morehouse.

Among those to benefit from a chance at higher education was a former slave named Booker T. Washington. Washington would become the most widely recognized black spokesperson since Frederick Douglass and easily the most influential African-American leader of the late 19th century. Born to a black mother and an unknown white father in rural Virginia, Washington was liberated by Union troops near the end of the Civil War. At 16, he left home for Virginia's Hampton Institute, one of the few higher educational facilities set up for blacks in the Reconstruction era. Under the guidance of Hampton's principal—a white former Union general named Samuel Chapman Armstrong— Washington imbibed a self-help philosophy as he received an education in both the liberal and manual arts. Armstrong also helped Washington financially, finding him a white benefactor who paid for his living and educational expenses. Both to Washington's later admirers and critics, this experience of white beneficence goes a long way in explaining the man's philosophy and his willingness to avoid challenging in any radical way the racial prejudices of his day.

In 1881, the state of Alabama asked Armstrong to recommend a principal for a new school for blacks to be opened at Tuskegee. Although Alabama asked for a white principal, Armstrong suggested Washington, and the state agreed. Apportioned just $2,000 for teachers' salaries—but nothing for land and buildings—Tuskegee quickly came to reflect the ideas for black education Washington picked up at Hampton. The emphasis was on manual skills, with boys learning carpentry, shoemaking, and other skills and girls being taught cooking and sewing. Students were also put to work raising money and helping construct buildings, aided by the donations of white philanthropists. Within a decade, Tuskegee was training 500 African Americans a year in the manual arts and agricultural sciences.

While Tuskegee earned Washington a modest reputation among wealthy white benefactors interested in black self-improvement, real prominence—and status as a national black spokesperson acceptable to the white community— came with his widely quoted speech at Atlanta's Cotton States and International Exposition in 1895, the year of Frederick Douglass's death. Speaking to a largely white audience, Washington advised his fellow African Americans to "cast down your bucket where you are." By this he meant that they should remain in the South, on the farm, and to accept the society as it was. "In all things that are purely social," he said of the two races, "we can be as separate as the fingers, yet one as the hand in all things essential to mutual progress." Washington did not, of course, blindly accept racial prejudice, discrimination, and intolerance. But he did believe that the best way to fight it was by improving the educational and economic level of black Americans, not by protesting or demanding civil rights.

Not surprisingly, the speech—which would later be criticized by civil rights advocates as the "Atlanta compromise"— won Washington both white acclaim and a large flow of donations for his Tuskegee Institute. Six years later, Washington published his autobiography *Up from Slavery*, a classic American tale of hard work and perseverance leading to success. With their emphasis on black self-help and tolerance of racial prejudice, the speech and autobiography were precisely what white Americans wanted to hear. To a small but growing coterie of educated civil rights activists in the North, however, Washington's philosophy was an

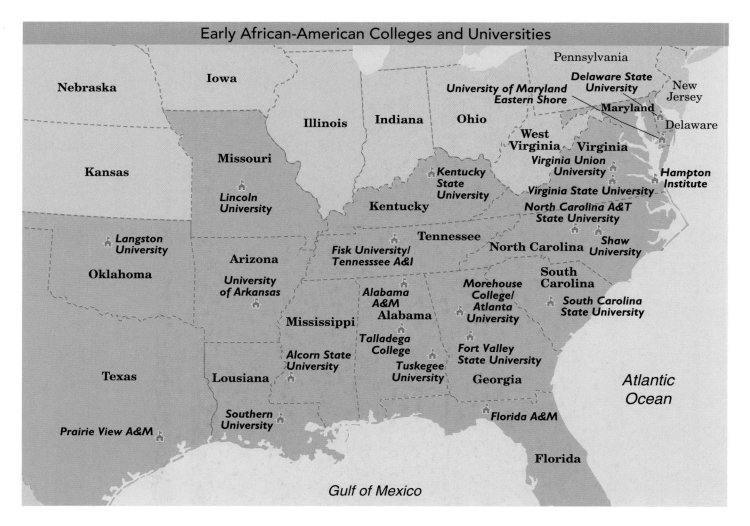

Early African-American Colleges and Universities

AFRICAN-AMERICAN INVENTORS

Following their freedom from slavery, African Americans were allowed to claim their inventions as their own. Whereas previously their inventions were automatically property of their owners, now they could patent their works and receive some of the recognition and benefits they deserved. More than 300 patents were recorded between 1871 and 1900, including inventions for folding beds, letter boxes, lawn mowers, and the electric lamp. Many of these products had a lasting impact on the lives, industry, and culture of the United States.

Elijah McCoy

McCoy worked on inventions for the lubrication of moving machinery. His most valued invention was the "drip cup" which enabled heavy-duty machinery such as steam trains and ocean steamers to be automatically lubricated without stopping them. He patented his invention in 1872, along with 56 other designs throughout his life. Most industrial machines with moving metal parts utilize this technology to this day.

Jan Matzeliger

Born in Dutch Guiana (present-day Suriname) in 1852, Matzeliger came to the United States in the early 1870s. While working at a shoe factory, he designed a machine that could cut, sew, and tack shoes, attaching the upper shoe to soles as accurately as a human in one minute's time. He sold his patent in 1883 to the United Shoe Manufacturing Company. The machine caused a 50 percent price reduction of shoes nationwide. Similar machines were quickly installed in shoe factories around the world.

Elijah McCoy
(Library of Congress)

Drip cup
(Library of Congress)

Jan Matzeliger
(Library of Congress)

Shoe-lasting machine
(Library of Congress)

Garrett Morgan

After successfully using the "gas inhalator," or gas mask, to help rescue several men trapped in a tunnel in Cleveland, Morgan received hundreds of orders for his invention. Although his gas mask was later used during World War I, Morgan did not enjoy immediate success, as many southerners canceled their orders when they discovered he was African American. Morgan sold his other major invention, the automatic traffic light, to General Electric for $40,000.

Granville T. Woods

Woods contributed to the growth of technological advances in the late 19th century. He patented several different inventions, including the electromechanical brake and different telegraphy systems that primarily involved sending telegraphs from moving trains. He also patented in 1887 a telephone system, which he sold to the American Bell Telephone Company.

Garrett Morgan
(Library of Congress)

Gas Inhalator (Library of Congress)

Granville T. Woods
(Library of Congress)

Electromechanical brake
(Library of Congress)

Booker T. Washington (center) with President William Howard Taft (left) and industrialist Andrew Carnegie (right) outside the White House. (Library of Congress)

accommodation to a grossly unfair system of political, social, and economic inequality. Increasingly, university-educated African Americans—many of whom came from the South but moved northward to gain an education and a relatively safe forum for expressing their views—were moving toward a more confrontational approach to America's racist order.

WELLS, TERRELL, AND THE NATIONAL ASSOCIATION OF COLORED WOMEN

Among these civil rights activists were two remarkable women—Mary Eliza Church Terrell and Ida Wells-Barnett—both born during the Civil War, both educated at black colleges, and both dedicated to the fight for black and women's civil rights. Born in Memphis in 1863, Terrell was educated at abolitionist-founded Wilberforce College in Ohio. A teacher turned homemaker, Terrell began to dedicate herself to the Colored Women's League, leading the organization as it merged with other black women's clubs to form the National Association of Colored Women (NACW) in 1896. A strong advocate of civil rights, Terrell praised Washington even as she gravitated toward the more civil rights–oriented politics of W. E. B. DuBois (see below), becoming a founding member of his National Association for the Advancement of Colored People (NAACP).

Wells-Barnett was born in Mississippi in 1862 and worked her way through Nashville's Fisk University as an elementary school teacher. In 1884, she won a circuit court case against a Tennessee railroad when she was forced out of an all-white car, though the suit was overturned by the state's supreme court. Seven years later, she was fired from her teaching position after writing an editorial criticizing the Memphis school board for inadequately funding black schools. Moving to the North, she dedicated herself full-time to journalism, writing scathing reports on lynching for black newspapers in New York and Chicago. In 1895, she published *A Red Record*, a closely researched statistical analysis of lynching in the South. Along with Terrell and others, Wells-Barnett went on to found the NACW and the NAACP.

W. E. B. DuBois

The towering civil rights leader of the age—and the most vocal critic of Booker T. Washington's accommodationist approach to American racial relations—was a Harvard graduate named William Edward Burghardt DuBois, better known by his initials W. E. B. DuBois. Born in the largely white community of Great Barrington, Massachusetts, in 1868, DuBois received one of the best educations available in his day to a man of any color. First attending Fisk University, he then received his bachelor's degree from Harvard, attended the University of Berlin for two years, and went on to earn his Ph.D. in sociology from Harvard, studying under the guidance of some of the leading intellectuals of the time, including philosophers George Santayana, William James, and Josiah Royce.

Despite this exceptional academic background, DuBois still faced the prejudice of his day and was forced to accept a low paying teaching position at Wilburforce College. Having moved on to Atlanta University, DuBois published *The Souls of Black Folk* in 1903, widely considered to be among the most important books ever published on African-American culture and American racial relations. The book passionately yet analytically examines the tortured role and

GEORGE WASHINGTON CARVER

George Washington Carver (Library of Congress)

George Washington Carver was born a slave during the Civil War, and died 80 years later an internationally renowned agricultural scientist. Carver was the most famous teacher at Booker T. Washington's Tuskegee Institute and is remembered for urging southern farmers to end their reliance on cotton, which left the soil depleted and worthless, and to start planting nutrient-rich, soil-renewing crops, such as peanuts and sweet potatoes. To further encourage the switch to peanuts and sweet potatoes, Carver created hundreds of money-making by-products of the crops, including coffee substitutes, flour, shaving cream, ink, dyes, plastics, vinegar, and more, giving small farmers hope for self-sufficiency. Throughout his career, Carver experimented with improved methods of cultivation. In his later years, he became a symbol of black achievement and was widely celebrated in the United States and throughout the world.

LUCY PARSONS, RADICAL

Although she is little known today, a former slave named Lucy Parsons played an important role in the radical labor movement of the late 19th century. Historians believe that Parsons was born on a Texas plantation in 1852. After the Civil War, she married Albert Parsons, a former Confederate soldier who had—unlike most southern white men—embraced the Radical Republican cause.

Forced to flee Texas because of their mixed marriage and Albert's efforts to register black Texas voters, the couple arrived in Chicago in 1873. Once there, Albert found work as a printer for the *Chicago Times*. Yet, a nationwide depression in 1873 had left millions of laborers unemployed, especially in industrial centers like Chicago. As they continued their efforts to improve the lives of the poor and disenfranchised, Albert and Lucy Parsons, like many other working-class Americans, became increasingly radicalized.

In 1877 Lucy Parsons opened a dress shop after her husband was blacklisted from his job. Writing articles about the homeless and unemployed, Civil War veterans, and working women, she also became known as a powerful speaker for workers' causes. In 1883 she cofounded the International Working People's Association (IWPA), an anarchist organization that preached violent action against industrial society and promoted a classless society based on racial and sexual equality. Parsons also condemned violence against blacks, though she saw racism as a symptom of capitalism's inequality. To Parsons, blacks were only victimized because they were poor, and that racism would inevitably disappear with the destruction of capitalism.

Together with other industrial trade unions, Parsons and the IPWA launched a general strike in May 1886 in support of an 8-hour workday. More than 40,000 workers in Chicago joined the strike. Then on May 3, Chicago police fired into a crowd of unarmed strikers at McCormick Harvest Works. In response, strike organizers called a strikers' meeting at Haymarket Square. When police attacked the strikers at that meeting, someone threw a bomb, killing one of the officers. Chicago authorities responded over the next few days by rounding up as many of Chicago's labor organizers and anarchists as they could find. Among those seized was Albert Parsons, who had not even been present at Haymarket Square. The following November, Albert Parsons and three other defendants were hanged.

After Albert's death, Lucy Parsons continued her work on behalf of radical causes. In 1905 she help found the Industrial Workers of the World (IWW), and in 1927 she joined the National Committee of the International Labor Defense, a communist-led organization that defended labor activists and unjustly accused blacks such as the Scottsboro Boys (see page 138). In 1939, she joined the Communist Party. Three years later, she died in a fire in her Chicago home. In the aftermath of the fire, Chicago police seized her personal papers and books from the rubble of her home.

Mary Church Terrell (Library of Congress)

place of black people in American history and society. He also used the book to criticize Booker T. Washington's philosophy of accomodation. "[When he] apologizes for injustice, does not rightly value the privilege and duty of voting, belittles the emasculating effects of caste distinctions, and opposes the higher training and ambition of our brighter minds," DuBois wrote, "we must unceasingly and firmly oppose [him]."

DuBois was as much a political activist as he was an intellectual. In 1905, he joined William Monroe Trotter, editor of the *Boston Guardian*, a radical African-American newspaper, in founding the Niagara Movement, named after the upstate New York town where it was begun. In a speech inaugurating the movement, DuBois laid out a series of demands, each of which was considered quite radical for the time: "First...we want full manhood suffrage...Second. We want discrimination in public accommodation to cease...Third. We claim the right of freemen to walk, talk, and be with them that wish to be with us. Fourth. We want the laws enforced...

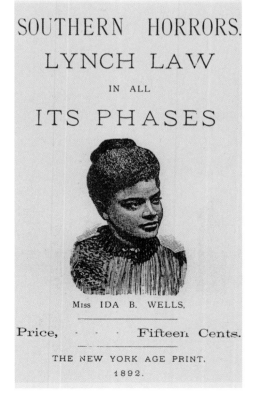

A groundbreaking study of lynching by Ida Wells-Barnett (Library of Congress)

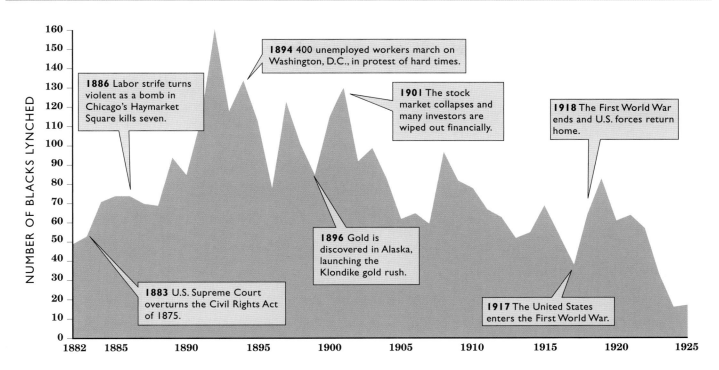

Annual Lynchings of African-Americans, 1882–1925

1886 Labor strife turns violent as a bomb in Chicago's Haymarket Square kills seven.

1894 400 unemployed workers march on Washington, D.C., in protest of hard times.

1901 The stock market collapses and many investors are wiped out financially.

1918 The First World War ends and U.S. forces return home.

1896 Gold is discovered in Alaska, launching the Klondike gold rush.

1883 U.S. Supreme Court overturns the Civil Rights Act of 1875.

1917 The United States enters the First World War.

NUMBER OF BLACKS LYNCHED

against white as well as black. Fifth. We want our children...trained as intelligent human beings should be."

While the Niagara Movement was short-lived, it laid the foundation for DuBois's most lasting contribution to the institutionalization of the struggle for African-American civil rights in the United States—the National Association for the Advancement of Colored People (NAACP). Unlike the Niagara Movement, the NAACP—which was founded in 1909—included members of all races. Indeed, much of its early leadership was white. In 1910, DuBois moved from Atlanta to New York City to take an assignment as the editor of the organization's magazine, *Crisis*. For the next 25 years, DuBois would use the publication as a forum for his views on civil rights.

Despite these notable accomplishments, DuBois was not above criticism. Many civil rights leaders charged him with elitism for his belief that the educated and "talented tenth" of African Americans were best suited to promote the interests of the race. In his later years, DuBois would increasingly come to embrace the cause of international communism. His controversial criticism of what he called American imperialism and his praise for the Soviet Union—which he

saw as a society free of racial prejudice and class distinctions—landed him in frequent trouble with the U.S. federal government during the height of the cold war years of the 1950s. Invited by the socialist government of Ghana to live in that country— the first black African nation to break free of European colonial domination— DuBois died in Africa in 1963, having lived for nearly a century.

By the time of his death, DuBois had long since given up hope that racial equality would ever be acheived in the United States. In an interesting twist of historical fate, the very same day he died, a young African-American minister from Atlanta, Georgia, Dr. Martin Luther King Jr., would deliver his famous "I Have a Dream" speech to a large multiracial crowd from steps of the Lincoln Memorial in Washington, D.C.

W. E. B. DuBois
(National Portrait Gallery)

WORLD WAR I AND THE GREAT MIGRATION

In *The Souls of Black Folk*, W. E. B. DuBois wrote with foresight that, "[t]he problem of the twentieth century is the problem of the color-line," thereby identifying racial relations as the most critical

Participants at the first meeting of the Niagara Movement (Library of Congress)

issue of the then-new 20th century. Indeed, as the history of the century proved, DuBois was right, not just for the United States but for the world generally. While the first great conflagration of the new century—the Great War as contemporaries called it, or World War I as it is better known today—was not directly about race per se, it had an enormous effect on relations between white and nonwhite peoples in the United States and around the world.

WORLD WAR I

Among the many causes of the war was the imperialist scramble for African colonies in the last two decades of the 19th century. At various points in that period, England, France, and Germany nearly came to blows over African territory, creating tensions that would play themselves out in European politics of the early 20th century. Moreover, the war itself would greatly debilitate the European imperialist powers. Not only was the loser—Germany—forced to cede its African colonial holdings, but even the winners found themselves substantially weakened vis-à-vis the nonwestern world. The idea that a superior European civilization was destined to rule the world

was forever destroyed in the barbaric carnage of World War I trench warfare. Indeed, many of the great independence leaders of the post–World War II era cite the beginning of the end of colonialism in the catastrophe of First World War.

For the United States, of course, World War I represented something altogether different. Rather than its world status being undermined by the war, the country found itself in a position of unrivaled power and prosperity in the wake of World War I, even if it failed to exploit that dominance and assert world leadership, as it would after World War II. Part of the reason the United States did not suffer as much from the war was its late entry. For nearly three years—beginning in August 1914—the United States watched the bloody struggle at a distance. Finally, after suffering enormous losses of ships to German submarines in the Atlantic—America continued to trade with Britain and France during the conflict—the country was drawn in to the war in April 1917.

As was the case in the Civil War, African-American soldiers hoped that their patriotic service in the war effort would help win them recognition, acceptance, and equality in American society. Even the critical and skeptical DuBois urged blacks to fight for their country. Resistance was great, particularly in the South, where whites feared that a uniform and a military record would make blacks unwilling to accept their inferior status in society. But the persistence of black leaders and the great need to fill the military ranks overcame these reservations and, by war's end, more than 365,000 blacks were drafted, virtually all of them into the army. (The U.S. Navy had few black sailors; the Marine Corps was white-only; and the air force did not yet exist.) At the same time, blacks were kept in the lowest ranks, with only 639 trained as officers at the Colored Officers' Training Camp, located at Fort Dodge, Iowa.

Prejudice also persisted against black soldiers off-base, particularly in the South. Protests and threats of violence against blacks training at nearby army facilities in Spartanburg, South Carolina, caused the military to send the unit—the soon-to-be highly decorated 369th U.S. Infantry—to France. Violence, however, was not avoided in Houston where black

Officers of the "Buffalos," the 367th Infantry, 77th Division, in France (National Archives)

troops—incensed by the abusive treatment they received from local whites—rioted, leaving 16 whites and four blacks dead. Ultimately, the military executed 19 black soldiers and sentenced dozens more to long prison sentences for their participation in the rioting.

By war's end, some 200,000 black American soldiers served in Europe. Although most were consigned to Service of Supplies units and labor battalions, several combat regiments were organized. Ironically, it was the prejudice of the American Expeditionary Force commander, John J. Pershing, that gave black soldiers their greatest opportunity to display valor and heroism. When France—desperate for soldiers to fill their depleted ranks—asked the Americans for more troops, General Pershing turned the 369th over to them. Spending more time on the front lines than any other American unit that served in the war, the men of the 369th earned an unprecedented 171 croix de guerre, France's highest military medal. (No U.S. Medals of Honor were awarded to black troops at the time, although one was bestowed posthumously in 1991.)

Despite their military service—and disappointing their hopes for equal treatment—African-American soldiers were met with disdain and even lynchings by

whites upon their return to the United States from Europe after the war. As one New Orleans city official in told black veterans, "you are going to be treated exactly like you were before the war; this is a white man's country, and we expect to rule it." Nor was the harsh welcome confined to the South. During the "Red Summer"—named after the fear of reds, or communist-sympathizing radicals, sweeping the country during the time—major civil disturbances broke out in two dozen cities nationwide, including a particularly violent one in Chicago that left 23 blacks and 15 whites dead, and another 520 persons injured. While the return of black soldiers was occasionally the spark that set off a riot, there also were much deeper social causes for the escalating postwar violence.

THE GREAT MIGRATION

In 1910, roughly 90 percent of all African Americans lived in the South, and nearly 80 percent of those worked in agriculture, figures not much changed from Civil War days. The next decade, however, would set in motion a dramatic demographic and geographic transformation that would see millions of blacks moving to northern cities by the 1960s. It has since been

MATTHEW HENSON, EXPLORER

Born in 1866, Matthew Henson was orphaned at the age of 8. At age 12, he went to sea as a cabin boy and spent six years learning the skills of a seaman. A meeting with Lieutenant Robert Peary in 1887 led to Henson's employment as the lieutenant's valet on a Peary expedition to Nicaragua. Peary recognized Henson's abilities and the two explored together for 22 years.

On April 6, 1909, the two Americans and their four Inuit guides became the first people ever to reach the North Pole. The achievement ended the friendship between Henson and Peary, however, due to tensions over proper recognition for the find. Because of his race, Henson did not receive the immediate honors that he deserved. Instead, he was ignored and forgotten. Today, however, Matthew Henson is officially recognized as codiscoverer of the North Pole. Henson's autobiography, *A Negro Explorer at the North Pole*, was published in 1912.

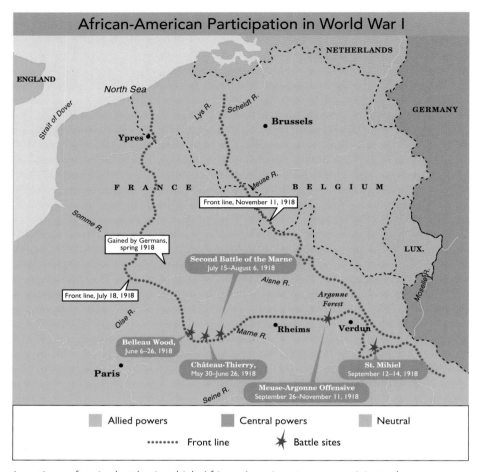

African-American Participation in World War I

ENGLAND

North Sea

Strait of Dover

NETHERLANDS

Lys R.

Scheldt R.

GERMANY

Ypres

• Brussels

F R A N C E

Meuse R.

B E L G I U M

Front line, November 11, 1918

Somme R.

Gained by Germans, spring 1918

LUX.

Second Battle of the Marne
July 15–August 6, 1918

Aisne R.

Moselle R.

Front line, July 18, 1918

Argonne
Forest

Oise R.

Marne R.

• Rheims

Verdun

Belleau Wood,
June 6–26, 1918

Château-Thierry,
May 30–June 26, 1918

St. Mihiel
September 12–14, 1918

Paris

Meuse-Argonne Offensive
September 26–November 11, 1918

Seine R.

| ☐ Allied powers | ☐ Central powers | ☐ Neutral |
| ········ Front line | ✦ Battle sites | |

Locations of major battles in which African-American troops participated

sharecroppers off the land in the second decade of the 20th century.

At the same time, there was a great demand for labor in northern and western factories. European immigration—the source of so much cheap labor in American history—had been cut off, first by the war and then by restrictive legislation. Adding to the shortage was America's entry into World War I. That is, just as the demand on industry was peaking to meet defense needs, millions of young men were drafted into the military. With wages rising correspondingly, word soon spread across the black South of unprecedented economic opportunities up North and out West. Moreover, while northerners held their own racial prejudices, discrimination was far less institutionalized there. Blacks in the North could vote; their children had a better chance of attending school; and there was far less violence directed against them. Many northern cities saw their black populations more than double in the 1910s. Where Chicago had roughly 35,000 African Americans in 1910, it claimed 90,000 ten years later. Southern planters and the newly revived Ku Klux Klan tried to stop the flow through violence, the banning of northern black newspapers—which promoted migration—and even the jailing of potential migrants.

But the draw was too strong and it only intensified in the decade following the war. With agriculture in a slump nationwide and relative prosperity buoying the urban economy, migration from the rural black South to the urban North and West accelerated. Nearly 1 million African Americans made the trek on the "chicken bone express"—named after the imagined trail of refuse left from the lunches packed for the migrants—in the 1920s. The demographic effects on northern and western cities was nothing less than transformative. Where Detroit's black population, for example, was a minuscule 6,000 before World War I, it stood at 120,000 by the time of the Great Crash in 1929. In New York, the numbers were 100,000 and 330,000 respectively.

The dramatic growth of the urban black population set off predictable fear and hostility among whites. During the war, there was intense competition for limited housing in growing industrial areas, one of the sources of white rioting in East St. Louis, Illinois, in 1917. Real

referred to as the Great Migration and, like other vast movements of humanity over the course of world history, it was triggered by both push and pull factors. Depressed cotton prices and infestations by the boll weevil—an insect pest that destroys the cotton plant—pushed many black (and white) tenant farmers and

African-American soldiers at women's club before leaving for Europe (National Archives)

estate interests and politicians responded with discriminatory housing practices, attempting to confine blacks to the worst parts of town. But housing was only one source of the friction. Many blacks were refused membership in unions and were thereby forced to work as "scabs," or strikebreakers, a trend exacerbated by industrialists who used racial differences to divide the labor force and forestall union solidarity. When the war ended, a wave of strikes spread across the country and further antagonized relations between nonunion black workers and unionized white ones. The recession of the early 1920s intensified the competition, although the boom of the latter half of the decade eased it somewhat.

For all the prejudice, hostility, and even violence blacks faced in the North, the Great Migration created something that had never existed before in American history—large, black urban communities. For the first time, great numbers of African Americans lived free of rural ignorance and oppression. It was, to use a term coined by African-American writer Alain Locke, the birth of a "new Negro," who proudly defied the old white stereotypes imposed on African Americans in favor of a new racial conciousness that celebrated black achievement on its own terms. The result of this liberation was a remarkable and unprecedented flowering of black political and artistic expression.

AFRICAN AMERICANS IN THE 1920s

Several trends came together to galvanize African-American politics in the 1920s. As in the case of the Civil War 60 years earlier and the Second World War a generation to come, World War I raised black expectations. Both service to country and the ideals for which the war was supposedly fought—"to make the world safe for democracy," in President Woodrow Wilson's high-minded words—led many African Americans to believe that a new dispensation of justice and equality was around the corner. However, unlike those two other wars, World War I resulted in little white acceptance for African Americans. That disappointment—combined with the confidence that came from their new

"YOUR COUNTRY IS SHOOTING AT YOU"

Tulsa's Greenwood section in flames (Tulsa Historical Society)

Known as "Black Wall Street," the segregated Greenwood section of Tulsa, Oklahoma, was home to African-American lawyers, doctors, pharmacists, and other prosperous black citizens. Then on May 30, 1921, a 19-year-old black shoe shiner named Dick Rowland was falsely accused of grabbing a 17-year-old white elevator operator.

The next morning, police arrested the young man, and by noon local papers were reporting that whites were forming lynch mobs to avenge the "attack." By that evening, a mob had formed at the courthouse where Rowland was being held. Around 9:00 p.m., a group of about 20 armed blacks arrived and offered to help the sheriff protect the young man. (The sheriff sent them home.) An hour later a second group of 75 renewed the offer. The mob, now swelled to about 2,000, observed the African Americans' weapons and readied their own.

A scuffle broke out when a member of the mob accosted a uniformed black World War I veteran, and the veteran's gun discharged into the air. A number of whites immediately began firing on the blacks, who returned fire before retreating toward Greenwood. Several whites and blacks lay dead. The mob pursued the blacks, stopping to loot local stores for more weapons. As news reached the Greenwood neighborhood, residents either prepared to leave town or armed themselves in defense of their community.

By 1:00 a.m., whites set fire to Greenwood's commercial center, which the rioters prevented local fire brigades from extinguishing. By 5:00 a.m., the mob, now numbering 5,000, poured into residential Greenwood. Some fired at any black person found trying to flee. Others rounded up blacks from their homes, forcing them into detainment centers, then looted and torched their homes.

Greenwood resident Olivia Hooker was six years old at the time of the riots. She remembers peeking from behind a curtain to see a sniper with a machine gun festooned with an American flag. Her mother pulled her to safety, saying to her, "Your country is shooting at you."

At about 9:00 a.m., martial law was finally declared and the violence came to an end. An estimated 300 innocent blacks had died and most of Greenwood had been destroyed. The mob caused more than $16 million in property damage in today's dollars, leaving more than 800 wounded and as many as 10,000 homeless. In the aftermath of the riot, a grand jury set free suspected mob participants. No whites were ever convicted of a crime.

demographic strength in the urban North—produced a political activism among African Americans unseen since Reconstruction days. It was a very different kind of politics, bent less on integrating into the majority white–controlled establishment and the Republican Party than on creating an independent and self-sufficient economic and political order within the black community itself. Something else in this period differed from the Reconstruction Era as well—

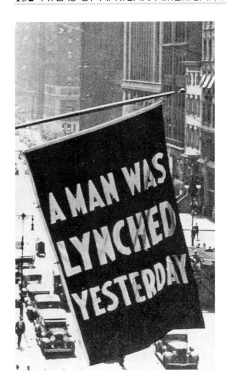

To bring attention to escalating violence against African Americans after World War I, the NAACP flew this flag outside of its headquarters office in New York (National Archives)

leadership. Unlike black politics in the post–Civil War era, the activism of the post–World War I years was largely influenced by one man, Marcus Mosiah Garvey.

MARCUS GARVEY AND THE UNIVERSAL NEGRO IMPROVEMENT ASSOCIATION

Born in rural Jamaica in 1887, Garvey moved to the island's administrative capital, Kingston, at age 16 and soon became involved in the anti-imperialist, black nationalist politics of the British colony. After traveling through Central America and Europe, Garvey settled briefly in England, where he worked on a pan-African journal. He returned to Jamaica on the eve of World War I. Initially influenced by Booker T. Washington's self-help philosophy, he founded the Universal Negro Improvement Association (UNIA) and attempted to build a Tuskegee-like institute in Jamaica. His efforts failed. Disappointed, Garvey then went on a speaking tour of North America, ending up in Harlem in 1917. There, influenced by the excitement of

the burgeoning center of black life in America, he restarted the UNIA. Garvey combined principles—economic self-reliance, political self-determination, and independence for black Africa—with panache. In the ritualistic style of the day, he held parades and created elaborate uniforms and insignias for organization members. A charismatic leader, Garvey soon founded chapters of the UNIA throughout the United States, Canada, the West Indies, Africa, Latin America, and Great Britain.

Garvey's most ambitious project, however, involved the establishment of the Black Star Steamship Line. The company aimed to fulfill two goals: first, to create an independent transportation network for black trade, and second, to provide passage to African Americans who wanted to return to the African homeland. A symbol of pride, the Black Star Line drew thousands more into the UNIA. In August 1920, the organization held a convention in New York's Madison Square Garden that drew 25,000 people. Delegates drew up *A Declaration of Rights of the Negro Peoples of the World*, voted on an anthem—the "Universal Ethiopian Anthem"—and elected Garvey president-general of the organization. Plans were also laid to develop a UNIA colony in Liberia, black Africa's only independent republic.

Heavy debt, poor management, constant criticism from DuBois and his integrationist allies in the NAACP, and—most critically—Garvey's indictment for mail fraud in 1922 sank the Black Star Line and permanently crippled the UNIA. A petition drive by Garvey's wife helped win the former UNIA leader a release from prison after three years, but he was immediately deported to Jamaica, where he tried to resuscitate the organization. Garvey moved to London in 1935 and died there of a stroke in 1940. While the UNIA barely remains alive as an organization today, its ideological legacy remains strong and Garvey is still a figure of great respect in many African-American homes. His emphasis on the pursuit of black economic independence and self-determination—as opposed to an emphasis on civil rights and integration—profoundly influenced the thinking and work of the Nation of Islam, Malcolm X, and the Black Panthers, among others.

An NAACP march against lynching during the "Red Summer" of 1919 (Library of Congress)

The Great Migration

WISCONSIN

MICHIGAN

NEW YORK

Detroit ■

IOWA

Chicago ■

Cleveland ■

Philadelphia

New York ■

PENNSYLVANIA

NJ ■

ILLINOIS

OHIO

Pittsburgh ■

Cincinnati ■

INDIANA

Washington, D.C. ■

MD ■

DE

Kansas City ■

St. Louis ■

KANSAS

WEST
VIRGINIA

Richmond ■

MISSOURI

KENTUCKY

VIRGINIA

OK

Nashville ■

NORTH
CAROLINA

TENNESSEE

ARKANSAS

Memphis ■

Atlanta ■

SOUTH
CAROLINA

Birmingham ■

*Atlantic
Ocean*

MISSISSIPPI

ALABAMA

GEORGIA

Savannah ■

TEXAS

LOUISIANA

FLORIDA

New Orleans ■

▢	Highest black population concentrations, 1900
■	Major African-American population centers and destinations
▢	Major routes of African-American migration

Gulf of Mexico

HARLEM RENAISSANCE

Along with black politics, the Great Migration had an enormous impact on the arts and culture of African Americans in the post–World War I era. Rural blacks from the Mississippi Delta region brought blues music—a hybrid of West African rhythms, slave field hollers, and gospel hymns that emerged at the turn of the century—to cities like St. Louis and Chicago, while musicians from New Orleans carried north a blues-influenced style of music known as jazz. While the basic blues structure is characterized by the use of a three-line stanza in which the words of the second line repeat the first, in a call and response pattern similar to

those found in West Africa, jazz used the blues form merely as a starting point, emphasizing the improvised interplay of weaving and contrasting elements. By 1920, Chicago had overtaken New Orleans as the center of jazz music in America. But the real center of black culture in the 1920s was neither the Crescent City nor the Windy City; it was New York.

The Harlem district of New York City—roughly that part of Manhattan stretching north a mile or so from Central Park—had become the unofficial "Negro capital of the world" by the beginning of the 1920s. As Reverend Adam Clayton Powell Sr., pastor of Harlem's influential Abyssinian Baptist

Marcus Garvey (Library of Congress)

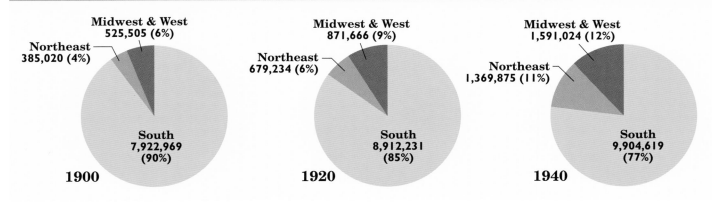

The Impact of the Great Migration on the African-American Population, by Region, 1900–1940

1900
Midwest & West 525,505 (6%)
Northeast 385,020 (4%)
South 7,922,969 (90%)

1920
Midwest & West 871,666 (9%)
Northeast 679,234 (6%)
South 8,912,231 (85%)

1940
Midwest & West 1,591,024 (12%)
Northeast 1,369,875 (11%)
South 9,904,619 (77%)

The Crisis (Library of Congress)

Jazz orchestra leader Cab Calloway, who like Ellington was a frequent headliner at the Cotton Club in Harlem (Library of Congress)

Church, put it, Harlem represented "the symbol of liberty and the Promised Land to Negroes everywhere." Here for the first time in American history was a large, confident, and vibrant urban black community, based in the cultural hub of the country. Its artistic flowering—popularly known as the Harlem Renaissance—was felt in music, dance, the visual arts, theater, and literature. Just as the Lost Generation of white writers of the 1920s represents, perhaps, the greatest literary decade of the 20th century, so the Harlem Renaissance—or the New Negro movement—stands, arguably, as the greatest artistic flowering in African-American history. Like the largely apolitical Lost Generation, the artists of the Harlem Renaissance—disappointed by the backlash against blacks in the wake of World War I—focused on artistry rather than politics in their writing and theater.

Several trends came together to produce the Harlem Renaissance. First was the vast expansion of Harlem itself, from a tiny black community of several thousand at century's turn to a city-unto-itself of a quarter-million African Americans by the end of the 1920s. The dynamism of Harlem could be seen everywhere, in the spread of street corner speakers, religious cults, and health fads. The excitement of the neighborhood's nightlife also drew white patrons eager to break free of the confining and straitlaced life of Prohibition America. Ironically, many of the hottest spots—like the premier showcase for black musical talent, the Cotton Club—were restricted to white patrons only who flocked uptown to hear the so-called jungle sound of Duke Ellington, as well as other jazz greats like Cab Calloway and Louis Armstrong.

Along with music, the greatest legacy of the Harlem Renaissance was in the field of literature. Two magazines—and the organizations that sponsored them—were primarily responsible for popularizing the literature of the period's black writers. The first was the NAACP's *Crisis,* edited by DuBois. DuBois both published the work of others and, in his editorials, stressed the need for a literature that emphasized black themes and an independent and assertive black voice. Even more critical to the movement was the National Urban League's journal, *Opportunity.* The National Urban League (NUL) was founded in 1911 to promote scientific social work in the black community. Under the editorship of the University of Chicago Ph.D. Charles Johnson, its journal not only published the works of young Harlem Renaissance writers but attempted to create a sense of community and purpose for the fledgling movement. In 1924, it hosted a gathering of white and black intellectuals and writers that, in the following year, turned into the movement's most important honors ceremony, the "Opportunity Awards." In 1926, literary critic Alain Locke—a contributor to *Opportunity*—edited *The New Negro,* an anthology that exposed Harlem Renaissance writers to a national audience.

Those whom DuBois, Johnson, and Locke sought to nurture and honor included a variety of poets, novelists, playwrights, and visual artists. Most prominent among the writers were Claude McKay, Jean Toomer, Countee Cullen, and Zora Neale Hurston.

Born in Jamaica in 1889, McKay moved to the United States in 1912 and attended Tuskegee Institute and Kansas

The Great Migration

WISCONSIN

MICHIGAN

NEW YORK

Detroit ■

IOWA

Chicago ■

Cleveland ■

Philadelphia

New York

PENNSYLVANIA

KANSAS

ILLINOIS

OHIO

Pittsburgh ■

NJ

INDIANA

Cincinnati ■

Washington, D.C.

MD

DE

Kansas City ■

St. Louis ■

WEST
VIRGINIA

Richmond ■

MISSOURI

KENTUCKY

VIRGINIA

OK

Nashville ■

NORTH
CAROLINA

ARKANSAS

Memphis ■

TENNESSEE

Atlanta ■

SOUTH
CAROLINA

Birmingham ■

*Atlantic
Ocean*

TEXAS

MISSISSIPPI

ALABAMA

GEORGIA

Savannah ■

LOUISIANA

New Orleans ■

FLORIDA

Gulf of Mexico

■ Highest black population concentrations, 1900
■ Major African-American population centers and destinations
■ Major routes of African-American migration

HARLEM RENAISSANCE

Along with black politics, the Great Migration had an enormous impact on the arts and culture of African Americans in the post–World War I era. Rural blacks from the Mississippi Delta region brought blues music—a hybrid of West African rhythms, slave field hollers, and gospel hymns that emerged at the turn of the century—to cities like St. Louis and Chicago, while musicians from New Orleans carried north a blues-influenced style of music known as jazz. While the basic blues structure is characterized by the use of a three-line stanza in which the words of the second line repeat the first, in a call and response pattern similar to

those found in West Africa, jazz used the blues form merely as a starting point, emphasizing the improvised interplay of weaving and contrasting elements. By 1920, Chicago had overtaken New Orleans as the center of jazz music in America. But the real center of black culture in the 1920s was neither the Crescent City nor the Windy City; it was New York.

The Harlem district of New York City—roughly that part of Manhattan stretching north a mile or so from Central Park—had become the unofficial "Negro capital of the world" by the beginning of the 1920s. As Reverend Adam Clayton Powell Sr., pastor of Harlem's influential Abyssinian Baptist

Marcus Garvey (Library of Congress)

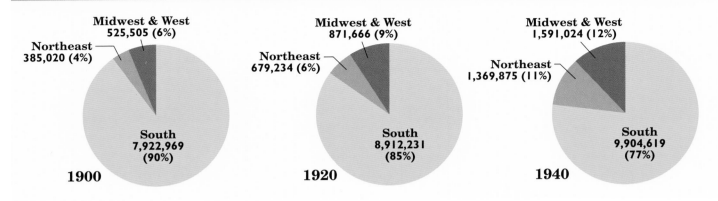

The Impact of the Great Migration on the African-American Population, by Region, 1900–1940

Midwest & West
525,505 (6%)

Northeast
385,020 (4%)

South
7,922,969
(90%)

1900

Midwest & West
871,666 (9%)

Northeast
679,234 (6%)

South
8,912,231
(85%)

1920

Midwest & West
1,591,024 (12%)

Northeast
1,369,875 (11%)

South
9,904,619
(77%)

1940

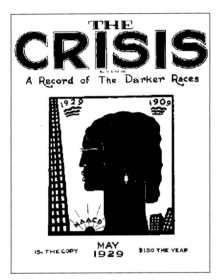

The Crisis (Library of Congress)

Jazz orchestra leader Cab Calloway, who like Ellington was a frequent headliner at the Cotton Club in Harlem (Library of Congress)

Church, put it, Harlem represented "the symbol of liberty and the Promised Land to Negroes everywhere." Here for the first time in American history was a large, confident, and vibrant urban black community, based in the cultural hub of the country. Its artistic flowering—popularly known as the Harlem Renaissance—was felt in music, dance, the visual arts, theater, and literature. Just as the Lost Generation of white writers of the 1920s represents, perhaps, the greatest literary decade of the 20th century, so the Harlem Renaissance—or the New Negro movement—stands, arguably, as the greatest artistic flowering in African-American history. Like the largely apolitical Lost Generation, the artists of the Harlem Renaissance—disappointed by the backlash against blacks in the wake of World War I—focused on artistry rather than politics in their writing and theater.

Several trends came together to produce the Harlem Renaissance. First was the vast expansion of Harlem itself, from a tiny black community of several thousand at century's turn to a city-unto-itself of a quarter-million African Americans by the end of the 1920s. The dynamism of Harlem could be seen everywhere, in the spread of street corner speakers, religious cults, and health fads. The excitement of the neighborhood's nightlife also drew white patrons eager to break free of the confining and straitlaced life of Prohibition America. Ironically, many of the hottest spots—like the premier showcase for black musical talent, the Cotton Club—were restricted to white patrons only who flocked uptown to hear the so-called jungle sound of Duke Ellington, as well as other jazz greats like Cab Calloway and Louis Armstrong.

Along with music, the greatest legacy of the Harlem Renaissance was in the field of literature. Two magazines—and the organizations that sponsored them—were primarily responsible for popularizing the literature of the period's black writers. The first was the NAACP's *Crisis*, edited by DuBois. DuBois both published the work of others and, in his editorials, stressed the need for a literature that emphasized black themes and an independent and assertive black voice. Even more critical to the movement was the National Urban League's journal, *Opportunity*. The National Urban League (NUL) was founded in 1911 to promote scientific social work in the black community. Under the editorship of the University of Chicago Ph.D. Charles Johnson, its journal not only published the works of young Harlem Renaissance writers but attempted to create a sense of community and purpose for the fledgling movement. In 1924, it hosted a gathering of white and black intellectuals and writers that, in the following year, turned into the movement's most important honors ceremony, the "Opportunity Awards." In 1926, literary critic Alain Locke—a contributor to *Opportunity*—edited *The New Negro*, an anthology that exposed Harlem Renaissance writers to a national audience.

Those whom DuBois, Johnson, and Locke sought to nurture and honor included a variety of poets, novelists, playwrights, and visual artists. Most prominent among the writers were Claude McKay, Jean Toomer, Countee Cullen, and Zora Neale Hurston.

Born in Jamaica in 1889, McKay moved to the United States in 1912 and attended Tuskegee Institute and Kansas

State University before moving to Harlem for seven years, where he wrote poetry while working on railroad dining cars. After a short stint in Europe, McKay returned to Harlem in 1921 and produced such memorable novels as *Home to Harlem* (1928) and *Banjo* (1929), where he explored issues of race, class, and the divisions between rural and urban black communities.

Toomer, a native of Washington, D.C., is best known for his novel *Cane* (1923), a tale of southern life that experimented with radical new forms of fictional narrative. *Cane* is considered one of the most important novels of 20th-century American literature, influencing the works of Alice Walker, Toni Morrison, and other black novelists to come.

A native of Kentucky, Cullen lived in New York City as a teenager, graduated from Harvard in 1927, and returned to Harlem to write poetry and help edit *Opportunity*. In such poetry volumes as *Copper Sun* and *The Ballad of the Brown Girl*, Cullen fused jazz and blues motifs with the written word.

Hurston, who was born in Alabama in 1891 and reared in rural Florida, attended Howard University before moving

Zora Neale Hurston (Library of Congress)

Harlem in the 1920s

1. Founded in 1809 as the Free Baptist Church of New York City, the **Abyssinian Baptist Church** became a center of civil rights activism when a young preacher named Adam Clayton Powell Sr. took over the pulpit a century later. The church building, dedicated in 1923, was a cavernous Gothic structure, featuring an Italian marble pulpit and imported stained glass windows. The congregation numbered more than 7,000.

2. Opened in 1922, the **Cotton Club** became the premier showcase in America for black musicians. The elegant interior, featuring primitivist decor, helped to inspire the "jungle sound" of Duke Ellington, who opened there in 1927. Other jazz greats who played there included Cab Calloway, Louis Armstong, and singer Lena Horne. Sadly, during the 1920s, black audiences could not listen to these musicians since the club was for whites only.

3. **The Harlem YWCA,** completed in 1919, offered some of the finest athletic facilities in New York City at the time. It also sponsored a host of conferences on subjects like women's suffrage, antilynching legislation, and civil rights activism. Among the figures who spoke there were Ida Wells, Mary McLeod Bethune, and Booker T. Washington.

4. **The Dunbar Apartments,** located at W. 149th and 150th Streets between Seventh and Eighth Avenues and financed by John D. Rockefeller Jr., were the first large cooperative built for African Americans. Among the prominent African Americans who lived at the Dunbar Apartments were W. E. B. DuBois, actor and singer Paul Robeson, labor leader A. Philip Randolph, and Arctic explorer Matthew A. Henson.

Duke Ellington (Library of Congress)

A SELECTIVE INTRODUCTION TO JAZZ

Scott Joplin   *Louis Armstrong*   *Bessie Smith*   *Fats Waller*   *Duke Ellington*   *Billie Holiday*   *Charlie Parker*

Louis Armstrong, who was widely regarded in his lifetime as not only the worldwide Ambassador of Jazz, but also one of its most revolutionary geniuses, once said, "If you have to ask what jazz is, you'll never understand." In its essence, however, jazz can be described as highly improvisational music that stresses syncopated rhythms and ensemble playing featuring weaving and contrasting elements. With roots in the West African rhythms and American slave field hollers and spirituals that formed that blues, jazz also has roots in European brass marching band music, ragtime, and other popular music of the late 19th and early 20th centuries. The chart below attempts to single out some of the major styles and figures that helped to shape the music uring the first half of the 20th century.

Style	Description	Era	Selected Major Figures
Minstrelsy	Music and comedy, mainly featuring whites in blackface, performing African-American songs, jokes, and impersonations for segregated audiences. Minstrelsy also provided work for a few blacks, such as Bert Williams, the first black recording star.	1890s–1920s	Bert Williams (1874–1922) Al Jolson (1885–1950) Emmett Miller (1900–1962)
Ragtime	Classically based, rhythmically bouncy music.	1890s–1910s	Scott Joplin (1868–1917) James Reese Europe (1881–1919)
New Orleans Traditional	The first true jazz style, born in New Orleans, and featuring use of clarinet and tuba. Commonly heard in celebrations and funerals. Dixieland jazz, an upbeat offshoot, added banjo to the mix.	1900s–1920s	Jelly Roll Morton (1890–1941) Louis Armstrong (1900–1971)
Female Blues Vocals/ Vaudeville Blues	Blues and pop vocal music set to jazz instrumentation, featured in the black vaudeville circuit of the 1920s and early 1930s. Although shows incorporated comedy performed by group acts, headliners were usually solo female vocalists, such as Bessie Smith.	1920s–1930s	Ma Rainey (1886–1939) Bessie Smith (1894–1937) Mamie Smith (1883–1946)
Harlem Stride	Highly rhythmic piano music.	1920s–1930s	James P. Johnson (1894–1955) Willie "The Lion" Smith (1897–1973) Fats Waller (1904–1943)
Swing/Big Band	Lush instrumental adaptations of popular song, played for dancing. The first jazz style to reach national audiences through radio and film soundtracks.	1930s–1940s	Duke Ellington (1899–1974) Benny Goodman (1909–1986)
Jazz Vocals	Classic vocalists interpreting popular standards and originals in a jazz style.	1930s–1950s	Billie Holiday (1915–1959) Ella Fitzgerald (1918–1996)
Bebop	A complex, innovative style emphasizing fast, highly improvised solos, and a stripped-down rhythm section. Often seen as a reaction against conventional Big Band orchestration.	1940s–1950s	Charlie "Bird" Parker (1920–1955) Dizzy Gillespie (1917–1993)

to Harlem in 1925. An anthropologist and novelist, she is famous for her pioneering studies of black folklore. Her best-known work, however, is the novel *Their Eyes Were Watching God* (1938), the story of the life and loves of a rural African-American woman.

Amidst this plethora of talent, the dominant figure of the Harlem Renaissance remains Langston Hughes. Born in Joplin, Missouri, in 1902, Hughes was first raised by his grandmother in Kansas and, as a teenager, lived with his mother in Cleveland. A poet even in high school, Hughes had his first piece, "The Negro Speaks of Rivers," published in *Crisis* when he was just 19; it remains one of his most beloved poems to this day. Hughes attended Columbia University but soon dropped out, drawn by the artistic excitement of nearby Harlem. (He would eventually receive his college degree from Lincoln University in Pennsylvania.) In 1930, he published his first novel, *Not Without Laughter.* Up to his death in 1967, Hughes remained prolific and versatile, putting out short story collections (*The Ways of White Folks*, 1934), plays (*Mulatto*, 1935, which is among the longest-running black plays in Broadway history), memoirs (*The Big Sea*, 1940), and weekly columns for the *Chicago Defender* for more than 20 years.

Some of more prominent visual artists of the Harlem Renaissance included Augusta Savage and Aaron Douglas. Born in rural Florida in 1892, Savage studied sculpting at Cooper Union in New York City, where she caught the attention of DuBois and Garvey. She even carved busts of them. After a brief sojourn in Paris, Savage returned to New York and opened the Savage School of Arts and Crafts in Harlem in 1932, where she taught classes and influenced future generations of black artists. Douglas, a native of Kansas, moved to Harlem in 1925 where he produced paintings and illustrations in the popular art deco style of the day. Perhaps Douglas's best known works are the illustrations he did for *God's Trombones: Seven Negro Sermons in Verse*, a collection of poetry based on the rhetoric of black preachers.

Like many great artistic movements, the Harlem Renaissance was relatively short-lived, a creature of a particular time and place. For all the excitement they generated at the time, the writers and artists of the Harlem Renaissance were often culturally and socially divorced from the needs and aspirations of the larger black community, an ironic situation given their desire to find an artistic voice that spoke for black America. Unable to connect with a black population that remained largely rural even during the Great Migration, they were dependent on white patronage for much of their livelihood and audience. When the economic climate soured following the stock market crash of 1929, white patronage dried up, leaving Harlem's writers and artists bereft. It would take the civil rights movement of the post–World War II era—and its emphasis on black cultural and historical studies—to revive interest in this great flowering of African-American artistic and literary talent.

THE GREAT DEPRESSION

The great economic boom of the 1920s did not affect all U.S. citizens equally. The rural United States, for example, where about half the population lived, remained mired in recession throughout the decade. Farmers were caught with excess capacity when World War I ended, resulting in a predictable collapse in commodity prices. With fully 80 percent of blacks living on farms as late as 1930, the ongoing agricultural slump hit them particularly hard. Fewer than 20 percent owned land and the per capita income was roughly $200 a year among rural blacks, less than a third that for urban whites. Nor were things much better in urban areas, where blacks were confined to the lowest-paying factory jobs, when they could find them. Unemployment rates among African Americans remained stubbornly high throughout the decade. The difference, then, between the Roaring Twenties and the depression of the 1930s was not nearly as sharp for the African-American community as the white. As one unemployed African-American worker noted in the 1930s, "it didn't mean too much to the [black man], the Great American Depression, as you call it. There was no such thing. The best he could be was a janitor or a shoeshine boy. It only became official when it hit the

Langston Hughes *(Library of Congress)*

Augusta Savage with one of her sculptures *(National Archives)*

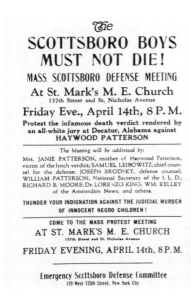

The
SCOTTSBORO BOYS
MUST NOT DIE!
MASS SCOTTSBORO DEFENSE MEETING
At St. Mark's M. E. Church
137th Street and St. Nicholas Avenue
Friday Eve., April 14th, 8 P.M.
**Protest the infamous death verdict rendered by
an all-white jury at Decatur, Alabama against
HAYWOOD PATTERSON**

The Meeting will be addressed by:
Mrs. JANIE PATTERSON, mother of Haywood Patterson,
victim of the lynch verdict; SAMUEL LEIBOWITZ, chief counsel for the defense; JOSEPH BRODSKY, defense counsel;
WILLIAM PATTERSON, National Secretary of the I. L. D.;
RICHARD B. MOORE; Dr. LORENZO KING; WM. KELLEY
of the Amsterdam News; and others.

**THUNDER YOUR INDIGNATION AGAINST THE JUDICIAL MURDER
OF INNOCENT NEGRO CHILDREN!**

COME TO THE MASS PROTEST MEETING
AT ST. MARK'S M. E. CHURCH
137th Street and St. Nicholas Avenue
FRIDAY EVENING, APRIL 14th, 8 P.M.

Emergency Scottsboro Defense Committee
119 West 135th Street, New York City

*Flyer in support of the Scottsboro
Boys (Library of Congress)*

white man." Or as Langston Hughes put it, "the Depression brought everybody down a peg or two. And the Negroes had but few pegs to fall."

HARD TIMES

Still, the Great Depression hit the black community with a double force. Not only were black workers subject to the same economic forces as whites, but they were often singled out for the first firings. By 1932, at the depth of the depression, approximately one half the black work force in most of the major industrial cities of the Northeast and Midwest were without jobs. In Pittsburgh, for example, the unemployment rate in 1933 was 48 percent for blacks and 31 percent for whites. It is estimated that nearly one out of three African-American families in 1932 was receiving some form of public assistance to get by.

Like much of working America, most African Americans were victims of the rising unemployment and waves of bankruptcies and foreclosures that accompanied the worst economic downturn in the nation's history—overall, output fell by 50 percent and corporate profits by 90 percent between 1929 and 1933. Yet they were also targeted for attack by angry and frustrated whites. Across the South, lynchings of blacks—which had steadily fallen through the 1920s to just seven in 1929—rose once again, to 20 in 1930 and 24 in 1933. Ironically, it was a case in which lynchings were avoided that focused the nation's attention—as it had not been since Reconstruction times—on the violence directed against southern blacks.

The incident began on March 25, 1931, when a freight train pulled into the small town of Scottsboro, Alabama. Like many such transports during the Great Depression, it was full of hoboes looking for work and fleeing hard times. A fight between white and black transients had been reported. As sheriff's deputies met the train and arrested nine black men, things turned decidedly ugly. Two white women suddenly came forward claiming they had been raped by the nine men. There was no worse accusation that could face a black man in the South in those days. Racist myths about uncontrolled black male lust for white female flesh

had always been one of the main justifications white southerners employed to defend their system of racial oppression. The scene in Scottsboro that day seemed ripe for multiple lynchings. Yet somehow the deputies held off the gathering mob and threw the men in jail.

The trial was a farce. An all-white jury and a white judge took almost no time—and heard virtually no corroborating evidence for the women's accusations—to find the men guilty and to sentence eight to death. (A ninth escaped the death penalty because he was a minor.) The Scottsboro case would probably have been just another case of racially prejudiced southern justice had it not been for the International Labor Defense (ILD), a labor group closely tied to the Communist Party of the U.S.A. (CPUSA), then experiencing an upsurge in membership and influence due to the collapse of the nation's capitalist economy. Bringing expert lawyers to bear, the ILD helped convince the Supreme Court to overturn the convictions and require a new trial, on the grounds the men had been denied adequate legal counsel. Despite the fact that the women's stories were riddled with contradictions—one of them eventually recanted her story—five of the men were convicted again, this time to long prison sentences. The cases dragged on for years, drawing the attention of the black press and public and the NAACP, which had initially been slow to react. Eventually, four of the convicted men were paroled in 1944, while one escaped to Michigan where the governor refused to extradite him back to Alabama.

The Scottsboro case helped galvanize black political activism at a moment in time when the nation's politics as a whole were undergoing one of the most dramatic transformations in history. In 1932, Democrat Franklin Roosevelt—promising a "new deal" for the American people—was elected president. Upon his inauguration in March of the following year—perhaps the lowest point of the Great Depression—the new president launched an unprecedented set of programs designed to save the nation's capitalist economy and put people back to work. A wide range of new programs—involving banking, manufacturing, and agriculture—were proposed and passed by a pro–New Deal Congress. The Federal Emergency Relief Administration doled out money to hungry families, while the Civilian Conservation Corps (CCC), the Public Works Administration (PWA), and the Civil Works Administration (CWA) offered millions jobs on public building projects.

While some of the programs undoubtedly aided poor and unemployed African Americans, there was no intent to use them to further civil rights. Roosevelt—never a strong civil rights advocate—feared that he would lose the support of crucial Southern Democratic support in Congress if he pushed too hard to promote black participation in the programs. Thus, CCC camps were segregated and jobs in the PWA and CWA usually went to whites first, especially in the South where most blacks still lived. Indeed, in one critical case, a New Deal program was positively detrimental to the interests of black Americans. That program was the Agricultural Adjustment Act, which paid farmers to cut production in the hopes of pushing up commodity prices. But the vast majority of payments in the South went to planters who reduced their cotton acreage. This meant that hundreds of thousands of African-American tenants and sharecroppers—who were largely ineligible for the program—found themselves thrown off the land.

As the New Deal gathered steam in 1935–1936, blacks began to benefit both directly and indirectly from the programs the Roosevelt administration fostered. African Americans, for example, constituted 18 percent of the workforce in the Works Progress Administration (WPA), the successor to the PWA and CWA. The Resettlement Administration—set up in 1935 to help tenants and sharecroppers buy their own farms—helped thousands of rural blacks in the late 1930s, until pro-planter southerners in Congress cut its budget. Moreover, the generally pro-labor climate of the Roosevelt years led to the formation of the Southern Farmers Tenant Union—an organization that conducted protests and strikes for higher farm wages—and the Congress of Industrial Organizations (CIO), a federation of unions in the mass production industries where many blacks labored.

In government circles, too, the Roosevelt administration appeared to be on the side of African Americans, although this had more to do with the advocacy of First Lady Eleanor Roosevelt than her husband. After prodding by the NAACP and other black organizations—as well as by his wife—Roosevelt and some of his cabinet officers agreed to appoint a number of African Americans to key positions, making sure that the many programs of the New Deal took black needs into consideration. Known as the Federal Council on Negro Affairs, but popularly called the "black cabinet," this coterie of officials was unofficially headed by Mary McLeod Bethune, a close friend of Eleanor Roosevelt's. Born in South Carolina in 1875, Bethune became an educator and founded the Daytona Educational and Industrial Institute in Florida, which eventually merged with the Cookman Institute to form Bethune-Cookman College in 1929. A civil rights advocate as well, Bethune founded the National Council of Negro Women in 1935, coordinating the activities of many black women's organizations to collectively push for a greater African-American voice in the federal government. In 1939, Bethune was appointed Director of Negro Affairs of the National Youth Administration, a New Deal program designed to promote jobs and education for young people.

HATTIE McDANIEL WINS AN OSCAR

Hattie McDaniel (Library of Congress)

Raised in Denver, Colorado, Hattie McDaniel first performed in her church choir and then spent a decade working in her brother's traveling minstrel show. In 1925 she toured with the stage musical *Show Boat* and later worked as a nightclub singer in Milwaukee. In 1932 McDaniel made her Hollywood debut in *The Golden West*. Although she worked in over 200 films, she only received credit for 60. However, her role as Mammy in 1939's *Gone with the Wind* earned her an Academy Award—the first ever given to an African American.

When some African Americans criticized McDaniel for her willingness to portray servants in the Hollywood movies she appeared in, she responded by saying, "It's better to get $7,000 a week for playing a servant than $7 a week for being one." While accepting Hollywood's racial limitations, she managed to broaden those boundaries, become wealthy and famous, and create characters that appealed to audiences of all races. She was also active in the struggle for civil rights, arranging for entertainment for segregated black soldiers during World War II and raising funds for education causes.

After her film career ended, she remained active on radio, particularly for her comedy show *Beulah,* which briefly appeared as a television show before McDaniel's death in 1952.

"Colored only" store, 1920s (National Archives)

WORLD WAR II

Although triggered in the United States by the crash of the stock market in 1929, the Great Depression was a global economic catastrophe that seemed to have its greatest impact on the most industrialized countries: Great Britain, the United States, Japan, and Germany. Like any great economic upheaval, the worldwide depression of the 1930s created political turmoil in the countries most affected by it. Whereas the long democratic traditions of England and the United States allowed those nations to weather the slump with their governing institutions largely intact—if greatly expanded to meet the emergency—the same was not the case with Germany and Japan. Both had little in the way of a democratic history and thus were vulnerable to dictators and militarists who argued that authoritarianism and conquest was the only way out of the depression. Adding to Germany's burden were the damage to the nation's industrial infrastructure in World War I and the huge reparations that the Treaty of Versailles forced the German government to pay following the war. In 1933, the same year Roosevelt became president, Germany installed Adolf Hitler and his Nazi Party to power. Two years earlier, the militarist government of Japan had invaded the Chinese province of Manchuria. In 1935, Italy—under the control of fascist dictator Benito Mussolini since the 1920s—launched a brutal war of conquest against Ethiopia, Africa's last remaining independent country, except for Liberia.

Hitler, Mussolini, and the Japanese justified their authoritarianism and aggression with racism. Each claimed that its own people were racially superior to others. In the case of the Japanese and especially the Germans, this ideology led to horrifying events. Japan perpetrated numerous massacres against the Chinese, while the Germans slaughtered millions of Slavic peoples, communists, and homosexuals and—most horrifying of all—attempted to wipe the Jewish and Roma (Gypsy) peoples from the face of Europe. The struggle against these brutal regimes—which the United States belatedly joined in 1941 after the Japanese attack on Peal Harbor, and partly justified as a crusade against racial intolerance—would have a

Eleanor Roosevelt was also a major figure in one of the most important symbolic victories for racial tolerance in the late 1930s. In 1939, the Daughters of the American Revolution—a politically conservative patriotic women's organization—refused the renowned African-American opera singer Marian Anderson the right to perform at its Constitution Hall in Washington because of her race. Eleanor Roosevelt—a member of the organization—resigned in protest and arranged for Anderson to perform at the Lincoln Memorial where 75,000 came to hear her lilting contralto voice.

Over the course of the 1930s, Franklin Roosevelt's New Deal programs and Eleanor Roosevelt's civil rights activism created a momentous shift in the political allegiance of black America. Ever since the days of Reconstruction, the vast majority of African-American voters—at least those who could safely exercise their right to vote—had supported the Republican Party—the party of Abraham Lincoln, emancipation, and radical reconstruction. This support even continued as African Americans flocked north to largely Democratic-controlled northern cities in the Great Migration. But by Roosevelt's second election in 1936, the majority of enfranchised blacks were casting their vote for the Democratic Party, a trend that continued through the end of the 20th century.

Mary McLeod Bethune
(Library of Congress)

critical effect on the postwar civil rights movement in the United States.

THE HOMEFRONT

Most historians agree that for all the innovation of the New Deal, the Great Depression finally ended because of World War II. Indeed, the amount of money the federal government pumped into the economy for the war effort dwarfed all of the programs of the New Deal combined. Unemployment—which still stood at more than 17 percent in 1939—dropped into single digits in 1941, as industry began pumping out armaments for Great Britain and the Soviet Union, the two major powers fighting Nazi Germany prior to Pearl Harbor. But for African Americans, the economic situation hardly improved. In the early years of the depression, they had been the first fired; now, as the country pulled out of the slump, it seemed like they were the last hired. For example, just 240 of the nation's 100,000 in 1940 aircraft workers were black, and most of those served in janitorial positions.

To address these economic inequalities, A. Philip Randolph—head of the Brotherhood of Sleeping Car Porters, the nation's largest black trade union—called for a march on Washington in the summer of 1941. Randolph, who questioned Roosevelt's commitment to civil rights, hoped that a mass demonstration might embarrass the president into action. He was right. Just days before the march's scheduled date of July 1, Roosevelt issued Executive Order 8002, banning "discrimination in the employment of workers in defense industries or government because of race, creed, color, or national origin." To implement the order, the president established the Fair Employment Practices Committee (FEPC) within the Office of Production Management, one of the key agencies involved in coordinating the wartime economy.

Neither Executive Order 8002 nor the FEPC was especially effective in battling discrimination. With little power to force compliance, the FEPC resolved only about one third of the 8,000 complaints it received. The fact that African Americans came to represent some 8 percent of all defense workers by 1944—the peak year for war-related production—had much more to do with industry's desperate need

for manpower than FEPC enforcement.

And yet in many encouraging ways, World War II was different from the previous conflict. For one thing, black leaders were far more assertive in demanding equal rights and fighting discrimination, pointing out the obvious parallels between Nazi anti-Semitism and American racism in their "Double V" campaign (victory against fascism abroad and victory over racism at home). Membership in the NAACP grew from around 50,000 in 1940 to more than 450,000 by 1945. And in 1942, Randolph established the Congress of Racial Equality (CORE), a more militant organization that took a direct, confrontational approach that included street protests and sit-ins. Presaging later civil rights–era actions, CORE forced a number of Washington restaurants to integrate, after picketing them with the slogan: "Are You for Hitler's Way or the American Way? Make Up Your Mind!" The war years also saw the publication of the most important academic study ever conducted on American racial relations, Gunnar Myrdal's 1944 *An American Dilemma: The Negro Problem and Modern Democracy*, a pathbreaking book that got many white Americans thinking about the problems of racism for the first time.

URBAN UNREST

The same forces that led to white backlash against blacks in World War I recurred during World War II. The Great Migration of blacks from the rural South to the urban North accelerated in the war years. This led to competition for

A. Philip Randolph (Library of Congress)

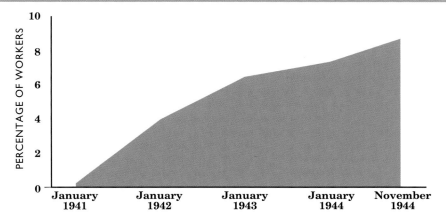

Percentage of Defense Workers Who Were African American

[Area chart. Vertical axis: PERCENTAGE OF WORKERS, ranging from 0 to 10. Horizontal axis showing dates: January 1941, January 1942, January 1943, January 1944, November 1944. The shaded area rises from near 0 in January 1941 to approximately 8–9 percent by November 1944.]

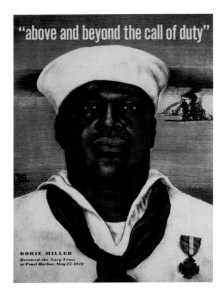

"above and beyond the call of duty"

Dorie Miller, a messman in the U.S. Navy, was awarded the Navy Cross for his heroism at Pearl Harbor. This poster, issued by the federal government, commemorates his actions. (National Archives)

scarce housing in industrial areas, which in turn set off riots in no fewer than 47 cities in 1943, including one in Detroit that left 25 blacks and nine whites dead, and yet another in Harlem.

The 1943 Harlem riot was triggered by a relatively minor incident. It began on August 1, when Private Robert Bandy, a 26-year-old soldier, overheard James Collins, a white policemen, use what he felt was inappropriate language while arguing with Marjorie Polite, a black woman, in front of the Braddock Hotel at 126th Street and Eighth Avenue. The soldier pushed to policeman to the ground. In response, the officer shot the soldier, wounding him. However, rumors quickly spread that a white policeman had killed a black serviceman, and the neighborhood exploded in rage. In the end, six people lay dead, 550 had been arrested, 1,450 stores had been damaged or burned to the ground, and total property damage reached $225,000. That same year, similar civil disturbances broke out in Mobile, Alabama; Beaumont, Texas; Los Angeles, California; and elsewhere.

AFRICAN AMERICANS IN UNIFORM

Despite the awareness by military planners that the manpower resources needed to defeat Germany, Italy, and Japan would be immense, discrimination prevailed, at least at first. On the eve of America's entry into World War II, the army's mobilization plan allowed for just 6 percent of recruits to be black, about half their proportion in the total population. There was no mention of integrating the armed forces. Most blacks were expected to fill menial positions. Yet, as the war progressed, things began to change and the history of African Americans in World War II offered a litany of firsts.

Messman Dorie Miller's story, though exceptional, captured the mixed record of blacks in the Second World War. Though ineligible for military training, Miller took over an anti-aircraft gun at Pearl Harbor, shooting down at least two and possibly more Japanese fighter planes. Ignored by the Navy, Miller was finally awarded the Navy Cross after a campaign on his behalf was conducted by the nation's black press. Yet, when his ship—the aircraft carrier USS *Liscome Bay*—was sunk a year later,

Miller was still a messman. Indeed, the Navy—which had a proud tradition of integrated crews through the Civil War—was the slowest to promote African Americans in its ranks and did not commission its first black officers until 1944.

The army was quicker to act. In 1941, it moved to integrate its officers' candidate school and by July 1944 prohibited discrimination in transportation and recreational facilities at all its bases, although bases in the South were sometimes slow to implement the policy. But it took the pressure of combat—specifically, the desperate Battle of the Bulge, Hitler's last-ditch effort in December 1944 to forestall Allied victory—to bring the first-ever integration of combat units. Perhaps the most illustrious achievement of African-American soldiers in World War II took place neither on sea or land but in the air.

Ever since the rise of military aviation in World War I, African Americans had demanded admission and training as airmen. These demands were dismissed out of hand. A 1925 Army War College study even offered "scientific proof" that blacks lacked the cranial capacity to operate sophisticated machinery like airplanes. Not until 1939 did the government—in expanding the air corps generally—authorize spending for pilot training programs at black colleges, including Tuskegee Institute, although only for support services and not combat. Still, resistance to the idea of black pilots persisted. Whites refused to serve with them and the army—which ran the air corps in those days—did not believe that blacks could make effective pilots. Thus, the airmen continued to train long after whites were sent into combat, and when they were finally permitted into combat, they remained segregated. Not surprisingly, the extra training made them especially effective pilots. By war's end, the all-black 332nd bomber escort group—of which the Tuskegee Airmen were a part—could claim a perfect record. In 1,578 missions and 15,552 sorties, they never lost a single bomber. The commander of the 332nd—Benjamin O. Davis—would go on to become the nation's first black three-star general.

Despite the many firsts and breakthroughs, the military remained a distinctly inhospitable place for African Americans during World War II. At no time did blacks constitute more than 8.7 percent of military personnel, and only 15 percent of all blacks in uniform ever served in combat. Still, World War II had a catalytic effect on racial relations both in the American military and in American society at large. The crusade against the racial superiority doctrines of Imperial Japan and Nazi Germany could not help but force some white Americans to question the racial practices in their own country. And, as in the Civil War, patriotism and military service contributed to a sense of pride in the black community and galvanized convictions that legal and political equality was their right as Americans. Moreover, the economic gains made by blacks during the war years—as well as in the prosperous decades to follow—created a confidence to take on the challenge of political activism. It is not too much to say that the great civil rights movement of the postwar era was born on the battlefields, army bases, defense plants, and homefront of World War II.

THE BIRTH OF A MOVEMENT

If World War II benefited African Americans by birthing the modern civil rights era, it is also true that black Americans benefitted economically from the war years as well. The war—with its enormous demand for manpower, as well as its upward effect on the value of agricultural commodities—offered unprecedented prosperity for civilian African Americans, both for those who sought work in northern factories and those who remained on southern farms. This economic bounty laid the foundations of a truly new phenomenon—an African-American middle class.

THE GI BILL AND THE BLACK MIDDLE CLASS

For thousand of American soldiers returning from Europe and the Pacific, the Second World War changed the way they saw the future. "All my relatives worked in factories. They didn't own any business. They worked with their hands. High school was as far as they went," said Jack Short, a white GI from suburban

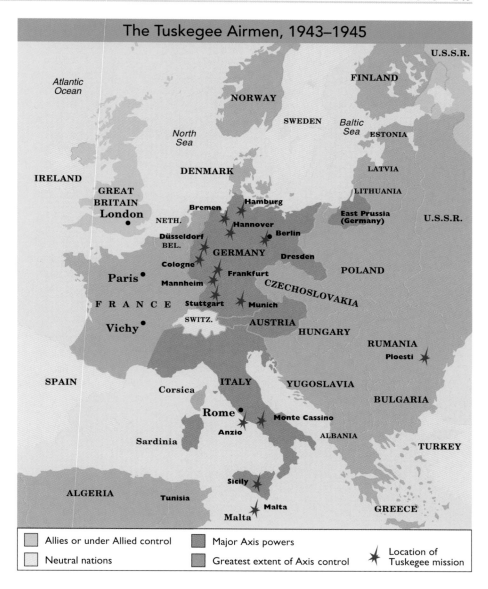

The Tuskegee Airmen, 1943–1945

Legend:
- Allies or under Allied control
- Neutral nations
- Major Axis powers
- Greatest extent of Axis control
- Location of Tuskegee mission

New York interviewed in Studs Terkel's history *The Good War*. Short participated in the invasion of Normandy shortly after D-Day. "The war changed our whole idea of how we wanted to live when we came back."

For Short, like thousands of others, a series of programs collectively known as the GI Bill of Rights widened horizons. The GI Bill paid tuition, purchased books, and granted stipends to cover living expenses for veterans who returned to either high school or college. Other programs provided home and business loans or employment assistance. Rather than settle for manual labor, thousands of young veterans used government assistance to go to college and build professional careers.

Though the law did not overtly advocate discrimination against blacks,

Colonel Benjamin O. Davis (Library of Congress)

neither did it contain any means of ensuring that blacks would receive equal benefits. The racial and social climate of the country in the 1940s almost guaranteed that black and white veterans would be benefit differently from the GI Bill. For example, only 12 percent of the black veterans using GI Bill benefits used them for higher education, compared with 28 percent of white veterans using the GI Bill.

Furthermore, many African Americans returned home to lives of poverty and, especially in the South, institutionalized racism, which made taking full advantage of the GI Bill difficult. For instance, in a 1947 survey of 13 cities in Georgia, *Ebony* magazine found that only two of 3,229 home and business loans had gone to blacks. As for going to college on the GI bill, black veterans with immediate demands for income were hard pressed to pursue a college education. Even those blacks who had the financial means to pay for higher education had more difficulty than whites gaining admission to colleges and universities. The University of Texas, for instance, denied Herman Sweatt admission to its all-white law school since an all-black, though inferior, law school already existed. (Sweatt would later be admitted to the school after the Supreme Court ruled that the separate black school was not equal to the white school, violating the *Plessy v. Ferguson* "separate but equal" doctrine.)

Those majority-white universities that did admit blacks had official or unofficial quotas on the number of blacks they would admit. Once on campus, African Americans encountered other problems. Blacks who were admitted to predominantly white schools usually faced a high degree of racism on campus. For example, G. W. McLauren, the sole black graduate student at the University of Oklahoma in 1950, was segregated from the rest of the student body—banned from sitting in the same classroom, library, or lunchroom when whites were present. (Ultimately, the NAACP brought McLauren's case to the Supreme Court, where justices ruled that segregating black students in classrooms or other facilities was illegal.)

Although the *McLauren* decision ended segregated facilities on university campuses, black students were still exceedingly rare at majority-white colleges and universities in the 1940s.

Ninety percent of the nation's black college students by 1950 attended HBCUs. Already short on resources following the Great Depression, HBCUs found themselves struggling to meet to meet the demands of their GI enrollees when the war ended. Traditionally, college-educated blacks often went on to teach or serve as religious ministers. Black veterans, on the other hand, required training for a broader array of professions that demanded wider curricula.

Despite the obstacles black veterans faced, the GI Bill did offer support to African Americans. While just over 1 percent of blacks attended college in 1940, that percentage had more that tripled by 1950. All told, more than 100,000 black GIs used the GI Bill to attend colleges and universities.

Even more blacks used their GI Bill benefits for trade and vocational training, or to finish high school. It is important to note that only 17 percent of black soldiers in World War II were high school graduates, compared with 41 percent of white soldiers, making black GIs less likely to go to college on the GI Bill. But they were not less likely to benefit from the bill. Although a higher percentage of whites used GI Bill benefits to attend college, a higher percentage of nonwhites used either the law's education or training benefits. Nationwide, according to Veterans Administration records, 49 percent of nonwhite GIs took advantage of these benefits, as opposed to 46 percent of white GIs.

Clearly, the GI Bill did not close the higher education gap between whites and blacks. Yet in the mid-20th century workers could more easily reach the middle class without college degrees than they can today. With vocational training, many black GIs could obtain working-class jobs that paid middle-class wages and benefits. While middle-class blacks were still unable to keep up with middle-cass whites, the healthy postwar economy fostered a broader, better-educated, and more confident black middle class.

JACKIE ROBINSON AND THE INTEGRATION OF BASEBALL

It is impossible to find a single date to mark the onset of something as profound and organic as the civil rights movement. But perhaps the best place to mark the starting point of the modern civil rights movement is with the integration of "America's favorite pastime"—baseball—by a college-educated World War II veteran named Jackie Robinson.

Baseball in the 1940s—as in most of the 20th century—was the all-American pastime. In its early days as an organized sport just after the Civil War, black and white players competed together. But by the latter part of the 19th century, a rigid color line kept blacks off white teams and black teams out of the white leagues. This exclusion, however, did not stop African-American athletes from playing professional baseball; they organized their own teams and leagues instead. Like many of the early white teams, the first black baseball squad was established by a business—New York's Argyle Hotel—for its employees and, no doubt, a few ringers from outside. A year later, in 1886, the Southern League of Colored Base Ballists was formed. It failed financially, as did several others, until the establishment of the Negro National League and the Eastern Colored League in 1920 and 1923 respectively.

While these black teams often had to accept inferior facilities—and had trouble finding accommodations on the road—there was nothing second-class about the ball they played. At least three teams—the Kansas City Monarchs, the Pittsburgh Crawfords, and the Homestead (Pennsylvania) Grays—were competitive with the best white teams, according to many sportswriters. And the stars of the African-American leagues—including outfielder James "Cool Papa" Bell; pitcher Leroy "Satchel" Paige; and Josh Gibson, arguably the greatest hitter, white or black, in baseball history, with a .362 lifetime batting average—could easily have played in the majors but for the prejudice of the day. Indeed, Jackie Robinson himself—the man to finally break major league baseball's color line—played briefly for the Monarchs at the end of World War II.

Robinson was born to sharecropping parents in rural Georgia but was raised in Pasadena, California. He attended UCLA, where he lettered in four sports. Upon graduation, he accepted a position as an athletic director with the National Youth Administration, a Great Depression–era agency that offered employment and educational opportunities for young people. In 1942, Robinson was drafted into the military and was court-martialed for refusing to sit in the back of an army bus at Fort Hood, Texas. After the war, Robinson played a season in the Negro Leagues before catching the eye of Dodger general manager Branch Rickey. Not only was Robinson a talented hitter and infielder, he was also a man of upstanding character and fortitude, two attributes that would prove essential in challenging the prejudice of white owners, white players, and white fans.

Jackie Robinson (Library of Congress)

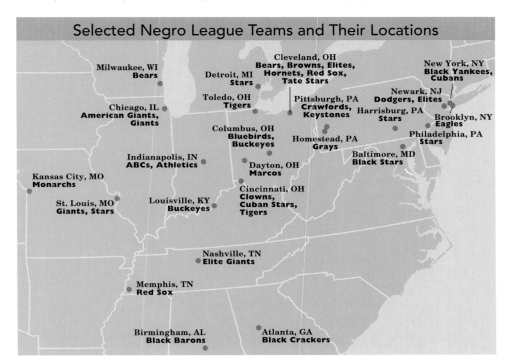

Selected Negro League Teams and Their Locations

Milwaukee, WI
Bears

Detroit, MI
Stars

Cleveland, OH
Bears, Browns, Elites, Hornets, Red Sox, Tate Stars

New York, NY
Black Yankees, Cubans

Toledo, OH
Tigers

Chicago, IL
American Giants, Giants

Pittsburgh, PA
Crawfords, Keystones

Newark, NJ
Dodgers, Elites

Harrisburg, PA
Stars

Brooklyn, NY
Eagles

Columbus, OH
Bluebirds, Buckeyes

Homestead, PA
Grays

Philadelphia, PA
Stars

Indianapolis, IN
ABCs, Athletics

Dayton, OH
Marcos

Baltimore, MD
Black Stars

Kansas City, MO
Monarchs

Cincinnati, OH
Clowns, Cuban Stars, Tigers

St. Louis, MO
Giants, Stars

Louisville, KY
Buckeyes

Nashville, TN
Elite Giants

Memphis, TN
Red Sox

Birmingham, AL
Black Barons

Atlanta, GA
Black Crackers

STARS OF THE NEGRO LEAGUES

**Cuban X-Giants, Leland Giants
Pitcher, Executive**

Andrew "Rube" Foster

Career: 1902–1926
Position: Pitcher, baseball executive
Teams: Cuban X-Giants, Leland Giants
Career Highlights: As a player, he defeated the Philadelphia A's star (and future Hall of Famer) Rube Waddell, thus earning his nickname. As an executive he is remembered as founder of the Negro National League.

**St. Louis Stars, Chicago Americans,
KC Monarchs, Pittsburgh Crawfords
Outfield**

James "Cool Papa" Bell

Career: 1922–1946
Position: Outfielder
Teams: St. Louis Stars, Chicago Americans, Kansas City Monarchs, Pittsburgh Crawfords
Career Highlights: A .330 lifetime hitter, Bell was so fast that he onced scored from first base on a single.

**Pittsburgh Crawfords,
Homestead Grays
Catcher**

Josh Gibson

Career: 1929–1946
Position: Catcher
Teams: Pittsburgh Crawfords, Homestead Grays, Mexican and Puerto Rican teams
Career Highlights: With an estimated 823 career home runs, Gibson is thought top have been an even more prodigious home run hitter than Hank Aaron or Barry Bonds. He also hit for average—with a .440 average in 1938, and .521 in 1943.

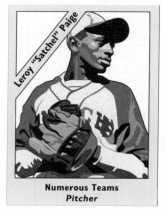

**Numerous Teams
Pitcher**

Leroy "Satchel" Paige

Career: 1926–1950, 1965
Position: Pitcher
Teams: Numerous, including major league baseball's Kansas City Atheletics, at age 59
Career Highlights: Crowd-pleasing theatrics made Paige perhaps the most popular (white or black) baseball player in America during the 1930s and 1940s. He first pitched in the major leagues in 1949.

Like many in major league baseball, Rickey recognized the enormous well of talent in the Negro Leagues. But unlike most of his colleagues, Rickey believed the time was right to challenge the major league baseball owners' unwritten "gentlemen's agreement" to keep black players off their rosters. At a secret 1945 meeting held to discuss the subject, Rickey's request to bring Robinson to Brooklyn (where the Dodgers played until their move to Los Angeles in 1958) was voted down unanimously by the owners. Rickey decided to challenge their decision, hiring Robinson to play for the Montreal Royals, a Dodger farm team, for 1946. His exceptional stats there—.349 batting average and 112 runs scored—convinced Rickey that Robinson was professionally ready for the majors, even if the majors were not ready for him.

In April 1947, "baseball's great experiment" began. Despite jeers from opposing players and fans, Robinson proved an exceptional ballplayer, winning Rookie of the Year honors that season and the National League's Most Valuable Player award in 1949. Other Negro League stars soon joined Robinson, including Willie Mays (often considered the best all-around baseball player of all time), Hank Aaron (lifetime home run champion), and Ernie Banks (winner of multiple baseball honors). Robinson's pioneering efforts had an impact far beyond baseball. As of 2005, no less than 69 percent of National Football League players and 77 percent of the National Basketball Association players were African American. Still, segregation continues to mar professional sports, with team owners, management, and coaches still predominantly white.

INTEGRATION OF THE NATION'S MILITARY

With the possible exception of the integration of professional sports, the integration of the U.S. military represents the most successful—and one of the earliest—efforts to fully integrate a major institution in the nation's history, though the struggle was a long and difficult one. As already noted, a number of significant gains and firsts were achieved by African Americans in the armed forces during World War II. Yet even at war's end, all branches of the military remained segregated and the generals and admirals seemed inclined to keep it that way. Military leaders in the mid-1940s feared that integration would stir up resentment among white soldiers and undermine combat readiness, a crucial consideration during a time of heightened cold war tensions. But the NAACP and other civil rights organizations maintained pressure on President and Commander-in-Chief Harry Truman, who in 1948 issued an executive order requiring integration of all branches of the military and the establishment of the President's Committee on Equality of Treatment and Opportunity in the Armed Services to monitor civil rights progress.

Resistance was stiff at first, but the onset of the Korean War in 1950 accelerated the process. By war's end, more than 90 percent of all black troops were serving in integrated units. The most surprising progress came in the Marine Corps, often considered the most elite—and once the most racist—service within the armed forces of the United States. At war's outset, blacks represented just 1.4 percent of the 75,000-man corps; by the end of the Korean conflict in 1953, the Marine Corps was approaching full integration. Indeed, Marine Corps and other military leaders quickly learned what civil rights groups had been saying—and common sense indicated—all along. In the heat of battle, skin color faded to insignificance. By the 1960s, the ranks of enlisted men were fully integrated, and while the officer corps lagged behind, even there significant progress had been made.

In the decades to come, the success of military integration would draw mixed reactions. In particular, the Vietnam War offered up a different kind of civil rights problem. While African Americans repre-

sented roughly 11 percent of the total military force in the war zone, they accounted for fully 20 percent of all battlefield casualties. It was, one African-American soldier remarked, "the kind of integration that could kill you." Many civil rights leaders, including Martin Luther King Jr., employed such statistics to bolster their arguments in favor of ending American involvement in the war. King and other African-American critics of the war also criticized American policy in Vietnam as an armed attack on a poor, nonwhite population—the Vietnamese—and as a drain on government financial resources that should have been spent on antipoverty programs.

Opposition to the Vietnam War was not limited to critics in the African-American community. The antiwar movement became a significant factor in not only shortening the war but also in establishing an all-volunteer military force. With higher unemployment levels, continued discrimination against them in private industry, and fewer economic opportunities in the rural South and inner-city North, blacks joined the military in far greater numbers than did whites. By 1979, 29 percent of the U.S. servicemen and women in the armed forces were African American. Although black enlistment began to level off beginning in the 1980s, African Americans continued to represent about 20 to 23 percent of American armed forces throughout the 1980s and 1990s. By 2000, the figure for the armed forces as a whole totaled roughly 20 percent, still significantly higher than the black proportion of the general population, which equaled roughly 12 percent the same year.

Most notable was the progress made in the officer corps of the various branches of the service, an achievement symbolized by the accession to chairman of the Joint Chiefs of Staff—the military's highest uniformed position—of General Colin Powell, the son of West Indian immigrants of African heritage. As General Powell himself noted, "The Army was living the democratic idea ahead of the rest of America. Beginning in the fifties, less discrimination, a truer merit system, and leveler playing fields existed inside the gates of our military posts than in any southern city hall or northern corporation."

Since the 1990s, however, fewer young blacks have shared Powell's view.

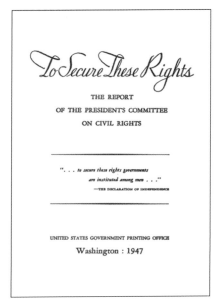

The commission report that recommended to President Harry S Truman that the U.S. military be desegregated (National Archives)

Integrated American troops in Korea (National Archives)

For example, a 2005 study by the Population Reference Bureau records black high school seniors' opinions of the military. In the 1970s and 1980s, only 10 percent felt that the military discriminated against African Americans "to a great extent" or "to a very great extent." That percentage had doubled by the close of the 1990s and stood at 15 percent in 2003.

The rate of African-American enlistment in the all-volunteer forces likewise began to slow, and during the first five years of the 21st century, it dropped rapidly. In 2000, about 20 percent of the new recruits were black. In 2005, only 15 percent of new recruits were black. That percentage is much closer to the percentage of blacks in the U.S. population as a whole, which was estimated at about 13 percent in 2005. Presumably, perceptions of descrimination in the military are just one factor in driving down black enlistments in recent years. The ongoing and increasingly unpopular Iraq War is likely another. Only time will tell if black enlistment will rise once more in peacetime.

INTEGRATION OF THE NATION'S SCHOOLS

In marked contrast to the military—where, all things considered, civil rights progress came relatively smoothly and quickly—the integration of the nation's schools proved to be one of the slowest, most difficult, and most controversial civil rights efforts in U.S. history. There are several reasons for this. First, the military is a highly centralized institution built on obedience and loyalty; it is expected that all personnel will obey an order from a superior, especially the commander-in-chief. America's schools, on the other hand, are a local affair and federal interference—in the name of civil rights or almost anything else—is often resented. Second, most military personnel live on bases far from home where local prejudices are likely to have less of an effect than in schools, which are situated in people's own neighborhoods. And finally the military consists of adults while schools consist of children. Southern

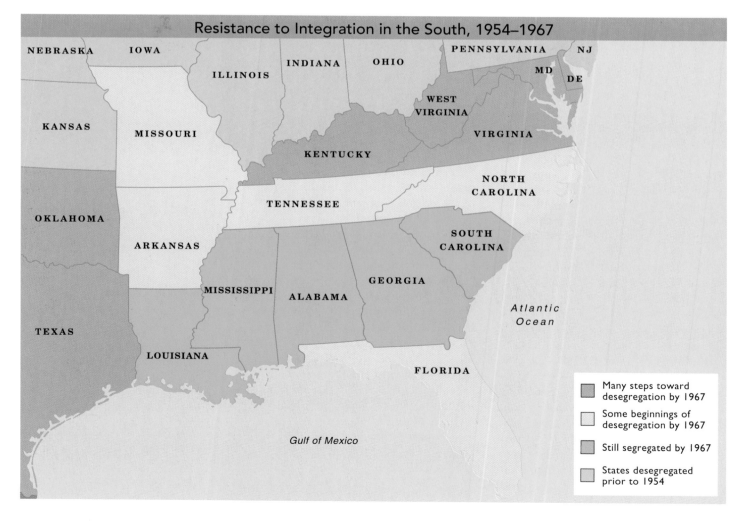

Resistance to Integration in the South, 1954–1967

Legend:
- Many steps toward desegregation by 1967
- Some beginnings of desegregation by 1967
- Still segregated by 1967
- States desegregated prior to 1954

SELECTED SUPREME COURT DESEGREGATION CASES, 1938–1950

Year	Case	Background	Outcome
1938	*Missouri ex rel Gaines*	After Lloyd Gaines was denied admission to University of Missouri Law School because of his race, his lawyers took their case to the Supreme Court, arguing that, counter to the "separate but equal" doctrine, Gaines had been denied an equal opportunity to become a lawyer in Missouri.	Although the Court did not strike down *Plessy v. Ferguson,* it ruled that because Missouri had no all-black law school, either Gaines must be admitted or the state would have to build an "equal" all-black school.
1950	*Sweatt v. Painter*	Following the *Gaines* case, states were faced with the choice of admitting black students to graduate programs or building new all-black schools. In this case, H. Marion Sweatt, a University of Texas Law School applicant, argued that although an all-black law school did exist, it was inferior to the white school.	Although the Court again refused to strike down *Plessy v. Ferguson,* it ruled that although the black school was separate, it was not equal. Sweatt, therefore, was allowed to enroll at the white school.
1950	*Henderson v. United States*	Elmer Henderson, a black man, had been separated from other diners on a train's dining car.	The Court ruled that dining cars on railroad cars had to end this Jim Crow practice.
1950	*McLaurin v. Oklahoma Board of Regents*	G. W. McLaurin was a black student who had been admitted to the all-white graduate school at University of Oklahoma. Once there, he was segregated from the rest of the student body by being forced to sit alone in classrooms, in the library, and in the cafeteria.	NAACP lawyers, led by Thurgood Marshall, brought his case to the Supreme Court, where the justices ruled that segregating black students was not allowed in classrooms or in any other graduate school facilities.

whites believed that they were defending their way of life when they stood against integration. And as raising children the way one chooses is one of the core values of the American way of life, it is not surprising that southern whites—and white parents in general—were incensed by efforts to integrate local schools.

In fact, since Reconstruction times, southern schools had been kept strictly segregated, a fact of life legally enshrined by the 1896 *Plessy v. Ferguson* Supreme Court decision which allowed for "separate but equal" educational facilities. As noted earlier, the practice of segregation was more about the "separate" than the "equal." Alabama, for example, spent $36 per white pupil but just $10 per black in 1929. Beginning in the 1930s, however, the Court began to whittle away at *Plessy,* beginning at the highest reaches of the educational establishment. In the latter half of the decade, the states of Maryland and Missouri were forced to open up their law schools to black students, while Oklahoma was required to admit an African American to its graduate school of education.

Still, at the primary, secondary, and college levels, segregation remained strictly enforced. At a conference in 1948, the NAACP pledged itself to challenge this policy, putting its legal staff—headed by future Supreme Court justice Thurgood Marshall—on the case. There were many groups of plaintiffs to choose from in the early 1950s, but, confusing the issue, a number of southern state governments pledged themselves to improving black education. Moreover, the NAACP wanted a case where spending was roughly equal between black and white schools, in order to challenge directly the "separate" part of the *Plessy* decision. They chose the school district of Topeka, Kansas, and thus in 1952 the most important case challenging school segregation in U.S. history was put in front of the Supreme Court as *Brown* (alphabetically, the first of the plaintiffs) *v. Board of Education* (of Topeka).

Marshall and his team of NAACP lawyers argued that segregation—or "separateness," as *Plessy v. Ferguson* called it—was inherently unequal even if the facilities for blacks and whites were identical down

*"Little Nigger at Central High
Has got mighty free with his eye
Winks at white girls
Grabs their blond curls
Little nigger sure is anxious
    to die."*

—Printed on a card circulated
among segregationist students
in Little Rock, Arkansas

THE LITTLE ROCK NINE

*Nine African-American teens deseg-
regated Central High in Little Rock.
The students are (top, left to right)
Gloria Ray, Terrence Roberts, Melba
Patillo, (center, left to right) Elizabeth
Eckford, Ernest Green, Minnijean
Brown, (bottom, left to right)
Jefferson Thomas, Carlotta Walls,
and Thelma Mothershed. (Library of
Congress)*

to the last nail. And because they were unequal, they were in violation of the equal protection clause of the 14th Amendment to the Constitution, an amendment ratified in the late 1860s to protect the newly won—and, then, quickly lost—civil rights of former slaves. Specifically, the lawyers argued, separate facilities for black schoolchildren ultimately created a second-class citizen.

To illustrate their point, they used the research of African-American sociologist Kenneth B. Clarke of Harvard University. Using two sets of dolls—one set with white features and one with black ones—Clarke asked black children to state their preferences. Virtually all chose the white dolls, which Clarke said indicated how segregated education lowers the self-esteem of black children, even when facilities at their schools matched those of whites'. That study—and the reasoned arguments of Marshall and the other NAACP lawyers—swayed the Court. Writing for the majority, Chief Justice Earl Warren argued that segregation "generates [in black children] a feeling of inferiority as to their status in the community that may affect their hearts and minds in a way unlikely to ever be undone." A year later, in a follow-up decision to the case commonly known as *Brown II*, the Court set out guidelines for dismantling segregated education in America.

But its choice of words—"with all deliberate speed"—was interpreted by many southern governments to mean "as slowly as possible." In 1956, more than 100 southern congressmen issued the "Southern Manifesto" denouncing *Brown* and urging their constituents to defy it. By 1957, more than half a million southern whites had formed White Citizens' Councils, organizations bent on blocking the implementation of civil rights measures. Confederate symbols and flags were officially adopted by southern state governments as demonstrations of resistance. More extremist southerners flocked to the Ku Klux Klan, swelling its numbers to the highest level since the 1920s. As the 1957–1958 academic year loomed, both sides—the civil rights organizations on one side and white anti–civil rights groups on the other—appeared ready for a confrontation.

In September 1957, the Little Rock, Arkansas school board tried to integrate nine black students in Little Rock's Central High School, an all-white institution. The nine students were met by crowds of jeering white students and parents who shouted insults and threw stones. Film crews captured the events and broadcast them night after night to the nation's TV viewers. Meanwhile, Governor Orval Faubus called in the National Guard, not to protect the students but to bar them from the schoolhouse. The combination of public pressure resulting from the newscasts and Faubus's challenge to federal authority forced a very reluctant president Dwight Eisenhower to act, nationalizing the National Guard and sending in an additional 1,000 federal troops, including the 101st Airborne Division, to integrate the school. Central High School was integrated, but it remained a rarity. Nonetheless, the fact that a U.S. president sent the 101st Airborne to protect the right of nine black teens to attend their local high school shows how much the nation had changed.

When the 20th century opened, thousands of Americans who had been born as slaves were still alive. Though no longer considered property, they, like all black Americans, remained shackled by a legalized system of segregation that kept them separate from white majority, with unequal opportunities for advancement. Yet in the early 20th century African Americans gradually loosened the binds placed upon them and asserted their citizenship. They served heroically in two world wars, helped to discover the North Pole, won Academy Awards, and built successful businesses. Their artistic achievements in music, literature, and fine arts burst forth in an unprecedented way, reshaping the cultural life of the nation, as well as the world. Along the way, leaders from W. E. B. DuBois and Marcus Garvey to A. Philip Randolph and Jackie Robinson demanded acknowledgment for their whole race through their individual acheivements and actions. As a result, African Americans gradually shifted the boundaries of their role in American life and forced their government to begin to treat them as equal citizens under the law.

THE CIVIL RIGHTS YEARS

In 1959 *Raisin in the Sun*, a drama produced, directed, and performed by African Americans, took to the Broadway stage. African-American playwright Lorraine Hansberry wrote the play as a reaction against what she saw as shallow, stereotypical treatment of black Americans onstage. The generally accepted view was that the play would fail, since plays featuring blacks were universally considered "death" at the box office. Hansberry proved naysayers wrong, however, and *Raisin in the Sun* earned her the 1958–1959 New York Drama Critics Award.

The play portrays the life of a black family in Chicago, centering around the different family members' conflicting opinions on how to spend money from the recently deceased father's life insurance policy. The issues the family faces were common to both blacks and whites, such as the generation gap between parents and children and the desire to establish a home in the suburbs as a means of achieving a better life. In addition to exploring generational conflicts, *Raisin in the Sun* explores the hurdles faced by black families in search of a better life in America. At its heart is a dilemma: How were blacks to achieve more economically prosperous lives in a majority-white culture without sacrificing identity, dignity, and pride?

An African-American moviegoer arriving at a segregated theater (National Archives)

How African Americans responded to this central question helped shape the direction of postwar American history. To some extent, the responses were generational. In the 1940s and 1950s, prominent African Americans demonstrated their worth—and the worth of people like them—through their success on stage, in print, on the athletic field, and elsewhere. Later leaders methodically demanded African Americans' rights as citizens. By the mid-1960s a younger, more confrontational generation of black leaders would emerge to challenge not only white resistance but also the older generation.

BLACK CULTURE IN POSTWAR AMERICA

As discussed in chapter 5, the United States faced a severe housing shortage after World War II. In response, the federal government gave developers financial subsidies to build affordable single-family homes and offered home buyers Federal Housing Authority (FHA) loans and income tax deductions for the purchase of new homes. These programs helped white working-class and middle-class families purchase houses. With this new purchasing power, millions of white families, many of them first- or second-generation immigrants from Europe, left the inner cities for suburbia.

Many blacks also moved during and after the war—America saw a revival of the Great Migration. Inner-city black neighborhoods in the North and Midwest and fast-growing western cities like Los Angeles gained new populations of rural southern blacks. At the time, mechanization of farm work—particularly cotton-picking machines—reduced the need for laborers in the fields. The promise of munitions factory jobs was what initially led to a surge in out-migration from the south at the start of World War II, but this migration continued throughout the 1940s and 1950s.

The postwar economic boom also enabled a growing number of African Americans and other minorities to purchase homes in the years after the war. But black Americans as a whole did not benefit as thoroughly as whites. The reason for this disparity lay, at least in part,

in government economic policy decisions of the era. Most of the new suburban developments springing up around the country excluded racial minorities. Many banks and the FHA itself practiced "redlining," which made certain neighborhoods off limits to blacks and other minorities. The relatively few black Americans who moved into the suburbs during this period usually moved into segregated communities. Most blacks either continued to live in rural areas or moved from the South to cities in the Midwest, Northeast, and West.

As families and businesses migrated to the suburbs, slum housing and vacant factories remained in the central areas. The Housing Acts of 1949 and 1954 granted funds to municipalities for urban renewal. Few of these federal dollars provided low-income housing, however. Mayors, bankers, and real-estate developers used the money to bulldoze slums and build gleaming office towers, civic centers, and apartment complexes for the affluent, leaving the poor to fend for themselves in the remaining dilapidated corners of the cities.

Although intended to revitalize cities, postwar urban renewal actually accelerated their decay and worsened conditions for the urban poor. Federally funded projects often disrupted or completely destroyed ethnic neighborhoods. In St. Paul, Minnesota, for instance, the construction of Interstate 94 during the 1950s allowed mostly white suburbanites to ease their commutes into and out of the city, but it also destroyed the thriving African-American neighborhood of Rondo. Prior to the highway's construction, the neighborhood centered around Rondo Avenue had been bustling with street vendors selling ice, coal, hot tamales, and other items. Social service agencies like Welcome Hall and Hallie Q. Brown Community Center—essential to the city's blacks since they could not frequent white-owned establishments—were all lost to the highway project.

Experiences such as these were the context of African-American daily life in the mid-20th century. Consequently, they infused the works black creative artists of the time—such as Lorraine Hansberry, the playwright of *Raisin in the Sun*—as well as other black writers, musicians, and performers. Although the social and legal structures of the day aimed to keep blacks separate from whites, the creative arts often found a wider audience. Despite segregation, the black experience had a profound impact on mainstream American culture.

BLACK WRITERS

The trends shaping American society in the mid-20th century also shaped the creative output that emerged from the black community during the period. In many ways, black artists of the period were reacting to economic and cultural racism that impacted their lives. They were also building on their African-American heritage to create new and often groundbreaking forms of self-expression.

Novelist and short-story writer Richard Wright created emotionally stirring tales protesting the fate that white America imposed upon black Americans. His first important work, *Uncle Tom's Children* (1938), painted a bleak picture of the prospects of blacks in a society that refused to recognize their humanity. His most famous novels—*Native Son* (1940), set in a Chicago ghetto, and *Black Boy* (1945), which described his own impoverished childhood in Mississippi—give eloquent voice to the African-American experience.

Wright abandoned the United States in the 1950s, settling in Paris until his death in 1960. But his legacy continued not only in the impact of his own writing but also in the friendships he cultivated with other black writers. Among them were Ralph Ellison and James Baldwin.

Even before releasing *Uncle Tom's Children*, Wright had already met and begun mentoring Ellison, then a young writer. Born in Oklahoma City, Ralph Ellison had attended the Tuskegee Institute on a music scholarship and made his way to New York. There he met Wright, who encouraged him to try writing fiction. For the next several years Ellison contributed a number of short stories and book reviews to various publications. After serving in the Merchant Marines in World War II, he returned home and began work on his masterpiece, *Invisible Man* (1953).

Invisible Man explored the struggle for personal identity and place in society. It centers on the life of a southern-born black man living in New York during the 1940s. The main character is figuratively "invisible" to those around him in that his full humanity as an individual black man is not recognized. Ellison's novel differs from Wright's work, however, in that its main character is articulate and educated. Alienated from the racist society around him, he is a detached observer who survives by withdrawing from attachment to this world. *Invisible Man* won the National Book Award for 1953.

Richard Wright also helped foster the career of another groundbreaking writer of the period, James Baldwin. Baldwin wrote impassioned novels, essays, and plays that, like the works of Wright and Ellison, protested the institutionalization of racism in America and undertook the search for personal identity. Baldwin had worked as a Pentecostal preacher in his native Harlem during his teens. Like Wright, he left the United States to live in Paris. There he wrote two semiautobiographical novels about an American in Paris, *Go Tell It on the Mountain* (1953) and *Giovanni's Room* (1956). Baldwin's key essay collections include *Notes of a Native Son* (1955), whose title is a clear reference to Wright's famous novel, as well as *Nobody Knows My Name* (1960) and *The Fire Next Time* (1963). The last is widely regarded as the most eloquent essay on the African-American civil rights movement ever written.

While his work shared many of the same themes as Wright and Ellison, Baldwin differed from them personally in that he was openly gay. Thus his work mined not only the theme of racial identity but also that of homosexual identity. Baldwin's status as a racial and sexual minority in a racially polarized nation where discussion of homosexuality was taboo was key in his departure from the United States. When he returned from his self-imposed exile in the early 1960s, however, Baldwin played an active role in the civil rights movement.

Mid-century black writers who had an impact on American culture were not all protégés of Wright, however; nor were they all male. The 1950s also saw the emergence of a generation of African-American women writers. Among the most prominent was Gwendolyn Brooks, who became the first African American to win a Pulitzer Prize for poetry. In 1950 she became the first African-American woman elected to the National Institute of Arts and Letters. Brooks's poetry collections

Ralph Ellison (Library of Congress)

James Baldwn (Library of Congress)

Gwendolyn Brooks (Library of Congress)

Janet Collins (Library of Congress)

include *A Street in Bronzeville* (1945), the Pulitzer-winning *Annie Allen* (1949), and *The Bean Eaters* (1956). Brooks's collections are praised for their sensitive portrayals of African-American urban life. For some Americans, these works resonated with their experience; for others they introduced the unfamiliar lives of their fellow Americans.

BLACK VISUAL ARTISTS

As is true of literature, the visual arts provide artists with a forum for expressing both their inner worlds and commenting on the world around them. In some cases, those artists were highly educated and trained in their techniques. In others, the artists were poor, sometimes illiterate and completely untrained.

The folk artist Clementine Hunter falls into the latter category. Born in 1866 on Little Eva Plantation near New Orleans, Hunter spent her life working as a cook in the kitchen of Melrose Plantation, which was a local gathering spot for Louisiana artists. After 50 years of cooking and picking cotton, she began painting for the first time, using a brush left behind by a New Orleans artist. A completely self-taught artist, Hunter depicted black life as she saw it in the rural South.

According to James Baldwin, the artist who influenced him more than any other was not a fellow writer but the artist Beauford Delaney, another African-American expatriate living in Paris. To Baldwin, Delaney was "the first living proof, for me, that a black man could be an artist." Primarily a pastel artist, Delaney's portraits of Baldwin, W. E. B. DuBois, Duke Ellington and others are considered classics.

Another major black artist of the mid-20th century was Romare Bearden. A painter and collage artist, Bearden created images filled with symbols and myths common to African-American culture. Beginning his career in the 1930s and working until his death in the 1980s, Bearden remained hugely influential. While his early work was mostly realistic paintings, his style became increasingly abstract by the early 1960s, as he became deeply influenced by the civil rights movement. At that stage of his career, he began creating collages of torn paper and

polymer paint to express abstract shapes and landscapes. These, he said, were "an attempt to redefine the image of man in terms of the black experience."

BLACK PERFORMING ARTISTS

The mid-20th century saw a major broadening in the audience for African-American contributions to classical dance and music. In the world of dance, African-American artists broke new ground. One of the most highly regarded classical dancers of the postwar period was the ballerina Janet Collins.

A dancer since the age of 10, Collins won an audition with the prestigious Ballet Russe de Monte Carlo and was offered a position in the company in 1932, at age 15. She turned down the offer, however, because the troupe insisted that she wear white face makeup while performing. Collins began a successful solo performance career and a tour with the noted Katherine Dunham group soon after and made her New York debut in 1949. She was the lead dancer in Cole Porter's 1950 musical *Out of This World*, and by 1951 she had become prima ballerina for the Metropolitan Opera.

While Janet Collins was employed by others as a featured dancer, Alvin Ailey founded his own company. In 1958 Ailey formed the renowned Alvin Ailey City Center Dance Theatre. The company has toured across six continents, and its dancers have won international acclaim for their vibrant performances. In 1965, during a highly successful European tour, the troupe received an unheard-of 61 curtain calls in Hamburg, Germany. Ailey later developed dances for Samuel Barber's opera *Antony and Cleopatra* (1966) and worked on the staging of Leonard Bernstein's *Mass* (1972).

In the realm of classical music, the popularization of African-American styles and performers actually dated back to the late 19th century with the Fisk Jubilee Singers. This vocal group toured the United States and Europe singing African-American spirituals in a classical style. In the early 20th century the gifted vocalist Roland Hayes further popularized the genre. Hayes, the son of a former slave, gave a triumphant European tour in 1921 and 1922, singing spirituals, classical works, operatic arias, and folk songs.

This blending of traditional African-American musical forms with European-based styles was also prominent in the extraordinary acting and singing career of Paul Robeson. Robeson first came to fame for his starring role in the 1925 stage revival of Eugene O'Neill's *The Emperor Jones;* he also starred in the 1933 screen version of the work. Robeson is perhaps best known for his version of the song "Ol' Man River" in both the theatrical and film versions of *Showboat.*

Robeson's career, however, was cut short by his outspoken condemnation of racism and, particularly, by his radical politics. He revived his role in *Othello* on the New York stage from 1943 to 1945, but by the late 1940s he had become almost as well known for championing communist causes as for his powerful bass voice. In 1952, at the height of the cold war, the Soviet Union awarded him the Stalin Peace Prize, effectively ending his career in America.

Robeson's career suffered not so much because of his race as because of his views. Racism hampered the daily lives of many African Americans in the 1950s, however, who were forced to live segregated lives. Despite this, many African-American artists in the postwar period gained increasing acceptance by audiences of all colors. In the 1930s, for example, the Daughters of the American Revolution had famously banned opera singer Marian Anderson from performing at the Lincoln Memorial; by contrast, Leontyne Price became one of the world's leading operatic voices by the late 1950s. After starring in a highly successful revival of George Gershwin's opera *Porgy and Bess,* Price went on to a spectacular career. In 1961 she debuted at New York's Metropolitan Opera in Verdi's *Il Trovatore,* and in 1982 she was invited to open the annual convention of none other than the Daughters of the American Revolution.

INNOVATIONS IN JAZZ

The success of black performers and vocal styles in the classical realm represented a significant inroads of black culture and talent into the American mainstream. But even these strides were dwarfed by the phenomenal influence of African-American contributions to American popular music. As discussed in chapter 5, jazz music first emerged out of New Orleans around the turn of the 20th century. Rooted in African-American musical styles that traced back to slave hollers and even to West African call-and-response singing styles, jazz incorporated the blues, syncopated rhythms, and especially improvisation.

Following the pattern of southern black migration to the North, jazz soon spread to other regions, where it took on a variety of styles. In Chicago, for instance, saxophones created a melody over a dance band rhythm, creating what became known as the "Chicago Jazz" sound. By the early 1920s, the young trumpeter Louis Armstrong had left New Orleans for Chicago, where he soon revolutionized jazz by emphasizing the importance of the soloist, and by improvising an innovative vocal style known as "scat" singing. At the same time, jazz played a central role in the Harlem Renaissance in New York as Armstrong's band, as well as other popular groups headed by artists such as Duke Ellington, gained enormous followings. By the 1940s, the big band sounds of artists like William "Count" Basie, Tommy Dorsey, Benny Goodman, and Glenn Miller had become the dominant form of American popular music. Many of these groups were fronted by popular vocalists, such as Ella Fitzgerald and Frank Sinatra.

During the early 1940s, however, a new, more experimental jazz form emerged. Known as bebop, it was pioneered by saxophonist Charlie Parker, trumpeter Dizzy Gillespie, pianist Thelonius Monk, and others. Rather than dance music, bebop was far more challenging, featuring complex sometimes atonal improvisation played at often lightning speed.

Initially a bebop trumpeter, St. Louis–born Miles Davis originated a new form known as cool jazz in the late 1940s and the 1950s. Later in his career he would help to launch a style known as jazz fusion, which fused jazz with another emerging postwar style known as rock and roll.

THE BIRTH OF ROCK AND ROLL

Despite the innovative new sounds of bebop and cool jazz during the 1940s and

1950s, those demanding styles had relatively limited audiences, particularly among those who wanted to dance to their music. To accommodate growing African-American communities in northern cities and out west in Los Angeles, musicians developed a style called jump blues. Jump blues took the horn-driven sound of big band jazz and melded it with the basic chord structures of traditional blues. They played pianos harder and louder, and their horns honked and squeaked. Jump blues vocalists like Big Joe Turner ("Shake, Rattle and Roll") and Tiny Bradshaw ("Train Kept a-Rollin'") shouted their songs, infusing them with the energy and spirit of black gospel music—albeit more secular.

At the same time, traditional blues music also underwent a major change—largely due to the growing urbanization of its black audiences. Whereas the early Mississippi bluesmen like Son House and Robert Johnson played acoustic guitars in the rural juke joints where they found their audiences, when the younger generation of Delta musicians moved north, they needed to make themselves heard in crowded urban nightclubs. For instance, when McKinley Morganfield, a young Mississippi guitarist, was recorded by the noted musicologist Alan Lomax, he was playing the acoustic guitar. By the time he moved north to Chicago and began performing under his lifelong nickname "Muddy Waters," he had plugged in and begun playing electric blues.

Whether horn-based jump blues or guitar-based electric blues, popular black music was generally known in the music industry as "race music" prior to the 1950s. But as the new decade opened, a *Billboard* magazine editor named Jerry Wexler renamed it "rhythm and blues," or R&B for short. R&B played a role in what would emerge a few years later as rock and roll.

But R&B was not the only form that contributed to the rock sound. Starting in the early 20th century, technologies such as wax records and radios had made it possible for music that was once largely confined to black communities to reach a larger audience. Likewise, early 20th-century black audiences were exposed to music that was more common to white communities, like Tin Pan Alley show tunes and country and western styles. As early as the late 1920s, country star Jimmie Rodgers recorded a blues-based country song that featured Louis Armstrong on the trumpet. Music crossed racial lines that were seldom crossed in other circumstances.

Like many art forms, rock and roll developed gradually, shaped largely by R&B and country western, as well as by other genres. What record constitutes the first rock record is a question that has been endlessly debated, but by 1954, when Bill Haley and the Comets covered the Big Joe Turner song "Shake, Rattle, and Roll," no one argued that it was rock and roll. Within the next few years, African-American musicians like Chuck Berry and Richard "Little Richard" Penniman joined white musicians like Elvis Presley and Buddy Holly to become stars with huge audiences of young people, white and black alike.

While white teens immediately embraced rock and roll, their parents were far more skeptical. It was well known that Elvis Presley's music had grown out of his love for black R&B that he heard on the radio. To white elders, his sneering, hip-shaking persona was alarming enough, but even more alarming was the unmistakable (though clearly racist) sense that there was something undeniably "Negro" about it all.

Despite parental disapproval—or perhaps because of it—music industry insiders knew rock and roll was here to stay. Yet the music industry then, as now, was an industry first and foremost. When some local citizens groups lobbied their local radio stations to ban rock music from the airwaves, industry executives moved to adapt. The need to do so became particularly acute when Elvis Presley enlisted in the army in 1958, temporarily ending his output of new music, and then Buddy Holly, the other top white star, was killed the following year in a plane crash.

As the decade came to a close, the new rock and roll stars were decidedly more clean cut and family friendly in appearance and style. White teen idols like Pat Boone recorded cover versions of songs that had originally been written and recorded by black artists. (Boone's far tamer version of the Little Richard hit "Tutti-Frutti," for example, easily outsold the original.)

As the 1960s opened, pop music continued to be dominated by white acts like

Boone, Frankie Avalon, and Bobby Rydell. Ironically, it would take the arrival of a Chuck Berry–loving wave of British acts like the Beatles and the Rolling Stones a few years later to reconnect rock with its roots in black music.

The birth and growth of rock music played a significant role in bringing black culture to mass audiences—in a way that literary works or classical music and dance could not. It is important to remember that these formative years of rock and roll were the same years that Jackie Robinson and other black baseball players ended segregation in the American pastime. They were also the years when the great period of African-American civil rights protests first took shape. Not coincidentally, resistance to rock music by white authorities took place at the very same time that African Americans were more actively asserting themselves in the struggle for equality.

CIVIL RIGHTS PROTESTS

As discussed in chapter 5, the integration of professional baseball, the *Brown* decision, and the events in Little Rock were three of the landmark events in civil rights history. Important as they were, each was a top-down gain for African Americans. That is to say, the efforts behind these achievements were usually spearheaded by the NAACP and other national civil rights organizations, often based far from the South in Washington or northern urban centers. Yet, above all else, the civil rights movement of the 1950s and 1960s was a grassroots affair, originating among the regular black folk of the South, albeit aided by northern white and black supporters. If the civil rights movement is measured by the criteria of southern black initiative and leadership—a bottom-up movement, as it were—then its origins go back to a simple but remarkable event of December 2, 1955.

Montgomery Bus Boycott

Rosa Parks—a Montgomery, Alabama seamstress and a member of the local NAACP chapter—was coming home from work on the bus one evening when she was asked to give up her seat to a white man, as per bus company rules and southern custom and law. Segregation of public facilities had been widespread throughout the South since the late 19th century and represented—in its indignity and even cruelty—a daily reminder to African Americans of their second-class status in society. This time, however, Parks refused to surrender her seat. While it is true that Parks's act of resistance was spontaneous, it was equally the case that local black civil rights activists—of whom Parks was one—were looking for an occasion to challenge Montgomery's segregation statutes. As a respected community leader, Parks represented the perfect candidate to rally around. Thus, the day after Parks's arrest for "disorderly conduct," the Women's Political Council, a local black women's civic group led by Jo Ann Robinson, issued 52,000 fliers calling for a one-day bus boycott to coincide with Parks's trial on December 5.

Meanwhile, after bailing Parks out of jail, local labor leader E. D. Nixon called two Montgomery ministers, Ralph Abernathy of the First Baptist Church

Rosa Parks being fingerprinted by a Montgomery, Alabama policeman following her arrest (Library of Congress)

A CHRONOLOGY OF THE CIVIL RIGHTS ERA

June 1946 In the case *Morgan v. Commonwealth of Virginia*, the U.S. Supreme Court bans segregated seating on interstate buses.

July 1948 President Truman issues an executive order banning segregation in the armed forces.

May 1954 The U.S. Supreme Court issues its *Brown v. Board of Education* ruling, declaring segregation in public schools to be unconstitutional.

December 1955 The Montgomery Bus Boycott begins. It ends one year later with the desegration of the city's bus system.

March 1956 Ninety-six southern members of Congress sign a "Southern Manifesto," pledging their opposition to school desegregation.

January 1957 Martin Luther King Jr., Ralph Abernathy, Joseph Lowery, and Fred Shuttlesworth organize the Southern Christian Leadership Conference (SCLC).

September 1957 President Dwight D. Eisenhower sends troops to provide security for black students trying to integrate Little Rock, Arkansas, Central High School.

February 1960 Black college students stage sit-ins at segregated lunch counters in Greensboro, North Carolina. Sit-ins spread to eight other southern states.

April 1960 Student Non-Violent Coordinating Committee (SNCC) is organized in Raleigh, North Carolina.

May 1961 Black and white freedom riders test the compliance of integration on interstate buses by traveling together.

October 1962 James Meredith becomes the first black student to attend University of Mississippi; his enrollment leads to the most violent campus riot of the decade.

April 1963 Civil rights protests hit Birmingham, Alabama; from jail, King writes his famous "Letter from Birmingham Jail."

June 1963 Civil rights worker Medgar Evers is murdered in Mississippi.

August 1963 The March on Washington brings 250,000 to demonstrate for civil rights; King makes his famous "I Have a Dream" speech.

September 1963 Four children die in the firebombing of a black church in Birmingham.

June 1964 The Freedom Summer project to register voters begins in Mississippi; civil rights workers James Earl Chaney, Andrew Goodman, and Michael Schwerner are murdered.

July 1964 President Lyndon B. Johnson signs the Civil Rights Act of 1964; the Democratic Party refuses to seat the Mississippi Freedom Democratic Party delegation at the convention.

February 1965 SCLC organizes the Selma-Montgomery (Alabama) voting rights march; civil rights workers Jimmy Lee Jackson, Viola Liuzzo, and the Reverend James Reeb are murdered.

August 1965 President Johnson signs the Voting Rights Act; rioting breaks out in the Watts section of Los Angeles.

and Martin Luther King Jr. of the Dexter Avenue Baptist Church, and told them of her arrest. This turn to centers of faith was not unusual, as the black church represented one of the few independent African-American institutions in most southern localities. Indeed, black churches were more than simply places of worship; they often engaged in civic and even political activities. And black churchmen—often more educated and worldly than most of their parishioners—traditionally served as community leaders in the black South. That was certainly the case with Abernathy and King. A graduate of Alabama State College, Abernathy became one of the founders of the Southern Christian Leadership Conference (SCLC) in 1957, among the leading civil rights organizations in the South. King had earned a Ph.D. in theology at Boston University

before accepting his post at the Dexter Avenue Baptist Church. The central figure of the civil rights movement for more than a decade, King would go on to cofound the SCLC, fight segregation and discrimination across the South, lead the largest civil rights march in American history, and win the Nobel Peace Prize for his efforts, all before being assassinated in 1968.

But in December 1955, King's focus was local—the Montgomery boycott. On December 5, the city's buses—usually full of black workers on their way to jobs in factories and white homes—ran almost entirely empty. White officials—convinced "Negro goon squads" were intimidating black riders—dispatched police to restore order. But there were no goon squads; the boycott had the support of the vast majority of Montgomery's black community. When Parks was found

guilty of violating the city's segregation ordinances, the boycott leaders organized the Montgomery Improvement Association, elected King as its president, and called for a continuing boycott to force an end to segregation on city buses. "There comes a time," King told an audience of 7,000 at the Holt Street Baptist Church, "when people get tired of being trampled over by the iron feet of oppression."

Reflecting King's philosophy of non-violence—which he had adopted from the teachings of Mohandas K. Gandhi, leader of the anticolonial movement in India—the Montgomery Improvement Association peacefully resisted police intimidation and white violence. As teams of black cab drivers and carpoolers were organized to take people to work—and routinely harassed and arrested for driving too fast or too slow—King and other black leaders met with Montgomery bus officials. But their demands—for an end to segregation and more black drivers—fell on deaf ears. White supremacists in the area—believing, incorrectly, that the movement was being orchestrated by outsiders including communists—targeted local black leaders, setting off bombs at their homes and churches. The following spring, Montgomery officials issued arrest warrants for King and other black leaders for organizing a boycott "without just cause or legal excuse." But when the arrestees turned themselves in, the national press came to cover the event.

By the summer, the civil rights movement had become a page one newspaper story, and King had appeared on the cover of *Time* and the *New York Times Magazine*. In June, a federal court ruled that segregated seating was unconstitutional, and although the case was appealed to the U.S. Supreme Court, the high court voted on December 20, 1956, to support the lower court's decision. Parks, Abernathy, King, the Montgomery Improvement Association, and the black community of Montgomery had won. As future events would bear out, the implications of the boycott were enormous—for the African-American community, the South, and the nation as a whole. "We have gained a new sense of dignity and destiny," King wrote. "We have discovered a new and powerful weapon—nonviolent resistance."

LUNCH COUNTER SIT-IN MOVEMENT

If the Montgomery bus boycott began as a spontaneous act of resistance, the lunch counter sit-ins—the next civil rights protest to gain national attention—were carefully planned and orchestrated. Like virtually all stores in the South, the Greensboro, North Carolina, Woolworth's maintained a strict segregationist policy. Blacks could shop there, but they were not permitted to eat at its lunch counter. It was a particularly insulting policy as it implied that blacks might somehow contaminate whites by their presence. And lunch counter segregation was only the tip of the iceberg; movie theaters, hotels, and restaurants of all kinds usually barred blacks or offered them distinctly inferior and separate sections. Nor was this policy always confined to the South. After black Hollywood movie star Dorothy Dandridge swam in a Las Vegas pool, the hotel drained and refilled it with water before allowing white patrons back in.

On February 5, 1960, four students from the all-black North Carolina Agricultural and Technical College— Ezell Blair Jr., Franklin McCain, Joseph McNeill, and David Richmond—sat down at the Woolworth's counter in Greensboro and ordered lunch. The staff refused to serve them and the four sat at the counter until the store closed, returning each morning for the next five days. As word of the protests spread, mobs of angry whites showed up, verbally and even physically abusing the students. Still, the four persisted, encouraged by hundreds of supporters on the streets outside. Over the course of 1960, the tactic of sit-ins would spread to no less than 126 towns and cities across the South, involving 50,000 participants. The most effective protests occurred in Nashville where the local student movement sat in at virtually all of the city's lunch counters, forcing storeowners to integrate their businesses.

While met by white violence and police intimidation—more than 36,000 protesters were jailed for disturbing the peace in 1960—the sit-ins proved very effective, as they cost the stores money. Not only did the protests disturb shoppers—and lead to a loss of black patronage—but TV and newspaper coverage spread the word across the country,

Martin Luther King Jr. (Library of Congress)

DIANE NASH

Diane Nash, a native of Chicago, was a 22-year-old student at Fisk University in Nashville when she became the chairperson of the central committee of the Nashville Student Movement. In that role, she led the local campaign to desegregate department store lunch counters. Nash organized sit-ins, trained students in nonviolent resistance, and later led a Nashville contingent of students during the Freedom Rides.

sparking boycotts of Woolworth's and other chain stores in northern cities as well. Older leaders of the civil rights movement soon realized the effectiveness of student idealism and activism, as well as certain freedoms youth afforded. Unlike their parents, students generally did not have families to support and did not have to fear losing their jobs, though many were expelled from their schools for taking part in the protests. In April, the SCLC sent Ella J. Baker—one of its top organizers—to work with the student protesters. The result was the formation of the Student Non-Violent Coordinating Committee (SNCC, pronounced "snick").

Still, for all their success in upper South states like North Carolina and Tennessee, the Deep South remained resistant to this kind of tactic. Some towns and cities simply outlawed the demonstrations and arrested protesters before they could begin a sit-in. In Montgomery, Alabama, store owners refused to serve blacks—and were supported in this decision by town officials—using the argument that the stores were their private property and they could make rules for them as they saw fit. The hard line failed, however, to dissuade civil rights activists who now tried a new tactic to integrate southern facilities.

FREEDOM RIDERS

Like the Montgomery bus boycott, the freedom rides—as they were called—were intended to challenge racial segregation in public transportation facilities, not at the local but at the interstate level. But where the earlier protest had kept African Americans off the buses, the freedom rides put them on them. The rides—inaugurated in the spring of 1961—were organized by the Congress of Racial Equality (CORE), an organization founded to protest segregated facilities in Chicago in 1942. A multiracial pacifist organization, CORE in its early days was the first civil rights organization to use the tactic of sit-ins. In 1947, CORE sent 16 white and black bus riders to the upper South to test segregation in interstate travel. The Journey of Reconciliation captured national attention, but it resulted in jail sentences for three CORE leaders, including Bayard Rustin, who were put to work on prison chain gangs in North Carolina. For several years after, CORE remained quiescent, although it increased its activities with the rise of the civil rights movement in the aftermath of the Montgomery boycott.

In May 1961—inspired by the lunch counter sit-ins of the previous year and a Supreme Court decision (*Boynton v.*

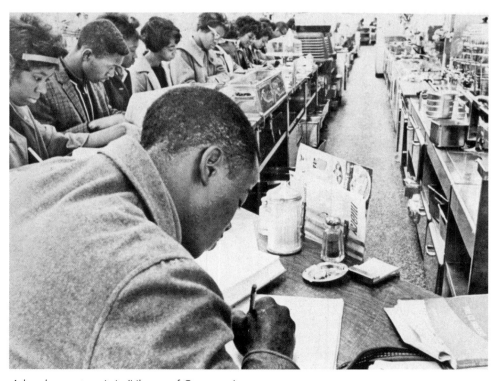

A lunch counter sit-in (Library of Congress)

The Sit-In Movement

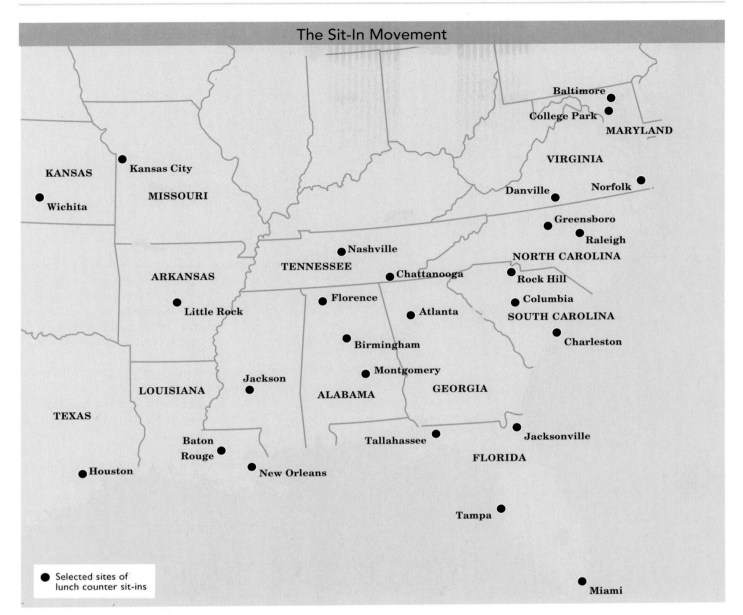

● Selected sites of lunch counter sit-ins

Virginia) prohibiting segregation in interstate transport facilities—CORE director James Farmer launched the freedom rides. The protest involved sending a small interracial group to challenge segregated restrooms, waiting rooms, and restaurants in bus terminals between Washington and New Orleans. The first bus, which set out on May 14, was set afire by a white mob in Anniston, Alabama, and a number of riders were beaten as they fled the burning vehicle.

With other riders being beaten in Montgomery and Birmingham, and Alabama governor James Patterson announcing he could not "guarantee protection for this bunch of rabble rousers," the federal government was forced to act. Attorney General Robert Kennedy sent federal authorities to guard the riders and ordered the Interstate Commerce Commission to enforce regulations against segregation in transportation facilities. With the weight of the federal government coming down on their shoulders, most southern municipalities accepted the orders and quietly integrated interstate bus and rail stations. CORE and the civil rights movement, meanwhile, had learned an important lesson. Practicing peaceful protest while provoking white violence produced powerful images that served the cause by stirring up national and international outrage at southern practices. As events in Birmingham would soon prove, white segregationists had failed to learn the same lesson.

THE FREEDOM RIDES, 1961

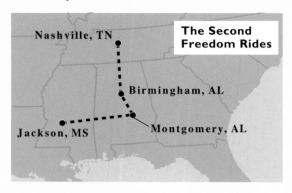

May 4 Seven blacks and six whites leave Washington, D.C., on one Greyhound bus and one Trailways bus.

May 7 Freedom rider Charles Perkins, an African American, attempts to get a shoe shine in a whites-only barbershop at a Charlotte, North Carolina, bus station. Although he is refused service, he remains in the shop until police place him under arrest.

May 9 In Rock Hill, South Carolina, a band of whites beat John Lewis after he attempts to enter the bus station waiting room. Albert Bigelow is also beaten. Although the police make no arrests, they allow riders to enter the waiting room.

May 11 In Winnesboro, South Carolina, freedom riders James Peck and Henry Thomas are arrested for attempting to integrate a bus station lunch counter.

May 14 Outside Anniston, Alabama, the Greyhound is surrounded by a mob, who break windows and slash the bus tires. One member of the mob tosses a torch through a window, filling the bus with smoke. As riders try to flee the bus, the crowd attempts to hold the doors shut, before beating passengers as they escape. The local hospital refuses to treat the injured riders. An hour later, the Trailways bus arrives in Anniston, where its passengers are also beaten before the bus leaves for Birmingham. There, whites board and attempt to force all blacks to the back of the bus. When two white riders attempt to intervene, they too are beaten. One, a 61-year-old retired teacher named Walter Bergman, is left close to death, with permanent brain damage. The other needs 56 stitches in the head.

May 15–17 Despite the attack, the riders vow to continue on to Montgomery, Alabama. When no driver will take them, the group abandons its plans. The Justice Department arranges for the freedom riders to fly to New Orleans, Louisiana. Although a bomb threat delays takeoff, the group flies to New Orleans.

May 17 Convinced that ending the freedom rides would reward racists for their violence, SNCC leader Diane Nash organizes a new group of freedom riders. Their bus leaves Nashville, Tennessee, bound for Birmingham, Alabama.

May 18 The freedom riders arrive in Birmingham. They are arrested and begin a prison hunger strike. Police respond by driving the riders 150 miles north to the Tennessee border and dropping them off near the state line. Diane Nash sends a car to pick them up and bring them back to Birmingham. There, they eat for the first time in two days and head for the bus station.

May 19 The state of Alabama issues an injunction to prevent "entry into and travel within the State of Alabama, and engaging in the so-called 'freedom ride' and other acts of conduct calculated to provoke breaches of the peace."

May 20 The freedom riders wait in the Birmingham bus station until a driver agrees to take them to Montgomery. They are met there by an angry crowd of several hundred, who begin to assault them with clubs. One passenger has his clothes set on fire. Assistant Attorney General John Siegenthaler, sent by the Kennedy administration to monitor the situation, is knocked unconscious after he attempts to assist one fleeing woman. Montgomery police allow the riot to continue for an hour before dispersing the crowd. In Washington, Attorney General Robert Kennedy orders 350 U.S. marshals into Alabama to quiet the situation.

May 21 U.S. marshals begin to arrive in Alabama. Martin Luther King Jr. flies into Mongomery. Governor John Patterson of Alabama threatens to arrest the marshals if they interfere, adding that the freedom rides were inspired by communists. That evening, a white mob forms outside of Reverend Ralph Abernathy's First Baptist Church, trapping inside 1,500 African Americans who are meeting there.

May 23 King, Abernathy, and Nash, as well as James Farmer and John Lewis of CORE, announce that the freedom rides will resume.

May 24 Escorted by Alabama National Guardsmen and the highway patrol, the riders leave Alabama for Jackson, Mississippi. When they arrive, Jackson police arrest them. Two days later, they are convicted and given suspended sentences. The riders elect to remain in jail, at notorious Parchman Penitentiary, where they remain for almost a month before they are released.

BIRMINGHAM, 1963

In 1963, King and the SCLC decided to turn their attention to Birmingham, Alabama's largest city and one of the industrial centers of the South. Local civil rights leader Fred Shuttlesworth, minister of the city's First Baptist Church, labeled it "the most segregated city in the United States." For six years, since civil rights organizers had begun to protest racial conditions in the city, there had been 18 unsolved bombings in the black community, earning the city the nickname "Bombingham." In early spring, the SCLC launched Project C (for "confrontation"), a series of demonstrations that brought thousands to downtown streets to protest the segregation and hiring practices of local department stores.

Civil rights activists were familiar with rough police tactics, but they had never seen anything like Birmingham. Under the leadership of Commissioner Eugene "Bull" Connor, the city's police used attack dogs, electric cattle prods, and high pressure fire hoses capable of stripping the bark off trees against the protesters, many of them children who had taken leave from school to participate. Once again, TV cameras were on hand to convey images of peaceful demonstrators being met with overwhelming violence for simply demanding their constitutional rights. As President John F. Kennedy noted, "the civil rights movement should thank God for Bull Connor. He's helped it as much as Abraham Lincoln." After securing a court order barring further demonstrations, Connor arrested King. While in jail, the SCLC leader penned a response to a group of white clergymen who criticized him for moving too fast on civil rights. "[I have] yet to engage in a direct-action campaign that was 'well-timed' in view of those who have not suffered unduly from the disease of segregation," King wrote in his famous essay "Letter from Birmingham City Jail." "For years now, I have heard the word 'Wait!' ring in the ear of every Negro with piercing familiarity. This 'Wait' has almost always meant 'Never.'" Meanwhile, protesters continued to pour into the streets and continued to be arrested, with more than 2,000 in jail by May.

With the city on the verge of a full-scale race riot, local business leaders asked the Kennedy administration to intervene. A federal mediator negotiated an agreement calling for an end to segregation in downtown stores. More bombings prompted the dispatch of federal troops. Birmingham proved a watershed for Kennedy on civil rights. Although widely supported by black voters, the young president had been reluctant to return the favor during his first few years in office. He and his brother, Attorney General Robert Kennedy, had even asked the Federal Bureau of Investigation to conduct surveillance on King's private life, leading to revelations of extramarital affairs by the civil rights leader. Most

MAJOR CIVIL RIGHTS ORGANIZATIONS

NAACP Legal Defense and Educational Fund
DATE FOUNDED: 1939
MAJOR LEADER: Thurgood Marshall
AIMS: To use the courts to fight discrimination and segregation
ACCOMPLISHMENTS: Helped win *Brown v. Board of Education* ruling outlawing segregation in public education

Congress of Racial Equality (CORE)
DATE FOUNDED: 1942
MAJOR LEADERS: James Farmer, Roy Innes
AIMS: To fight discrimination and racism through sit-ins and other nonviolent direct action
ACCOMPLISHMENTS: Sponsored freedom rides to end segregation in interstate transport

Southern Christian Leadership Conference (SCLC)
DATE FOUNDED: 1957
MAJOR LEADERS: Martin Luther King Jr., Ralph Abernathy
AIMS: To work for civil rights through direct nonviolent action
ACCOMPLISHMENTS: Helped get the 1965 Voting Rights Act passed

Student Non-Violent Coordinating Commitee (SNCC)
DATE FOUNDED: 1960
MAJOR LEADERS: John Lewis, Stokely Carmichael
AIMS: To fight segregation and discrimination through direct action, including jail-ins
ACCOMPLISHMENTS: Helped register voters during Freedom Summer in Mississippi; fought to integrate delegations at the Democratic National Convention

Black Panthers
DATE FOUNDED: 1966
MAJOR LEADERS: Bobby Seale, Huey Newton
AIMS: To fight racism in northern cities; defend the black community against racist police officers; provide social services for inner-city black communities
ACCOMPLISHMENTS: Established several day-care centers and clinics in black communities

Segregationist Alabama governor George Wallace ran for president in both 1968 and 1972. (private collection)

Birmingham police turn fire hoses on protesters. (Birmingham News)

important, like Franklin Roosevelt before him, Kennedy had an ambitious legislative agenda and feared alienating conservative southern Democrats in Congress. But the gathering momentum of the civil rights movement—and fears that internationally broadcast images of American racism were hurting the country's image at a crucial moment in the cold war—prompted Kennedy to act. On June 12—the day Alabama governor George Wallace stood in the doorway of the University of Alabama to bar newly admitted black students—Kennedy went on national TV to announce a major federal initiative to enforce anti-segregation court rulings. Yet that very same evening came news of another act of white violence—the murder of Mississippi NAACP organizer Medgar Evers.

MARCH ON WASHINGTON

To rally support for Kennedy's proposal, as well as to demonstrate the broad coalition of forces that stood behind the civil rights movement, leaders of the "big six" organizations decided to sponsor a massive march on Washington for the summer of 1963. The six included Whitney Young of the National Urban League (NUL); Roy Wilkins, head of the NAACP; James Farmer, founder and president of the CORE; SNCC head John Lewis; and King of the SCLC. But while these leaders put the march together, the idea came from the old warhorse of the civil rights movement, A. Philip Randolph, president of the Brotherhood of Sleeping Car Porters and Negro American Labor Council. As noted in the previous chapter, Randolph had planned a civil rights march on Washington in 1941 but was dissuaded when President Roosevelt signed legislation creating the Fair Employment Practices Committee to assure equal opportunities for African Americans in the burgeoning defense industry.

In December 1962, Randolph met with Bayard Rustin, a civil rights veteran famous for his early freedom ride in the 1940s, to discuss a new march to coincide with the 100th anniversary of the Emancipation Proclamation. As a labor leader, Randolph wanted to focus on jobs but Rustin suggested "freedom." In June, King—in the midst of his Birmingham struggle—signed on, urging that the march be used as an expression of the strength of the growing civil rights

movement. Still, there remained deep divisions in the movement about the efficacy of such an action. More conservative civil rights organizations like the NAACP insisted that the march be nonviolent and nonconfrontational. Younger and more militant members of CORE and SNCC wanted to incorporate civil disobedience and more forceful language in the declarations surrounding the march. But King—increasingly the man other civil rights activists looked to for leadership—sided with the conservative groups. Soon, liberal white religious organizations—like the National Council of Churches, the National Conference of Catholic for Interracial Justice, and the American Jewish Congress—had come on board.

Working out of offices in Harlem, Rustin—now the chief organizer of the march—organized the complicated logistics of transportation, health and safety,

and publicity—all on a limited budget made possible by thousands of small cash contributions and the sale of buttons. There were the normal organizational fears that few people would show up and the march would be a washout. But in the days leading up to August 28, tens of thousands of people poured into Washington by car, rail, and plane. One man even roller-skated there from Chicago. The sheer size of the crowd—some 250,000 persons attended—as well as its ethnic and religious diversity was perhaps the best demonstration of the widespread support the civil rights movement enjoyed across America. The audience listened as Rustin read the march leaders' ten demands, which included an end to housing and school desegregation, more job training, and a raise in the minimum wage. Later, organizers met with a supportive President Kennedy.

The March on Washington (Library of Congress)

Dr. King and fellow marchers in Washington. King can be seen second from the left, in the front row. (Library of Congress)

The bombing of the Sixteenth Street Baptist Church in Birmingham (Birmingham News)

the state of Mississippi, a state sweltering with the heat of injustice and oppression, will be transformed into an oasis of freedom and justice. I have a dream that my four little children will one day live in a nation where they will not be judged by the color of their skin but by the content of their character." Then he ended the speech with the words of an old Negro spiritual, "Free at last! Free at last! Thank God almighty, we are free at last!"

While King's eloquence had long been familiar to civil rights activists in the field, this was the first time many ordinary Americans—both black and white—had had a chance to hear him and the speech established the SCLC leader as one of the towering figures in 20th century U.S. history. As for the march, it was an enormous success, demonstrating through a peaceful gathering of hundreds of thousands of white and black Americans the power of nonviolent protest. Sadly, that Gandhian concept would soon be tested. Just three weeks after the March, a bomb was set off at the Sixteenth Street Baptist Church in Birmingham, killing four young African-American girls. Two months after that, on November 22, 1963, President Kennedy was assassinated in Dallas.

But if the 1963 March on Washington is remembered for one thing, it is the stirring words of King. "I have a dream," he told the assembled thousands, "that one day on the red hills of Georgia the sons of former slaves and the sons of former slaveowners will be able to sit down together at the table of brotherhood. I have a dream that one day even

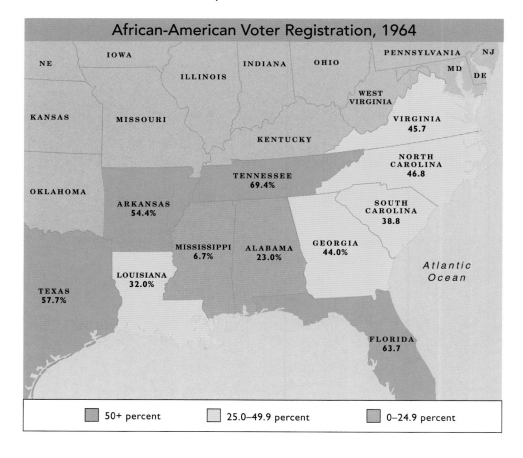

African-American Voter Registration, 1964

NE IOWA INDIANA OHIO PENNSYLVANIA NJ

ILLINOIS MD DE

KANSAS MISSOURI WEST VIRGINIA

VIRGINIA
45.7

KENTUCKY

NORTH CAROLINA
46.8

OKLAHOMA ARKANSAS
54.4%

TENNESSEE
69.4%

SOUTH CAROLINA
38.8

MISSISSIPPI
6.7%

ALABAMA
23.0%

GEORGIA
44.0%

Atlantic Ocean

LOUISIANA
32.0%

TEXAS
57.7%

FLORIDA
63.7

50+ percent   25.0–49.9 percent   0–24.9 percent

CIVIL RIGHTS ACT OF 1964 AND FREEDOM SUMMER

The rise to the presidency of Vice President Lyndon Baines Johnson worried King and other civil rights leaders. Johnson was a southerner, from Texas, and had shown little commitment to black issues in his long political career in the House and Senate. But the new president surprised the African-American community. From the beginning, he put civil rights high on his agenda and told Congress that passage of the Civil Rights Act would serve as a memorial to the slain president, a rather ironic appeal given Kennedy's lukewarm support of civil rights. In June 1964, Congress passed and Johnson signed the Civil Rights Act, the first major civil rights bill since Reconstruction times. The key provision of the act was Title VII, which outlawed segregation in public accommodations and job discrimination on the basis of race, national origin, religion, or sex. Southerners in the Senate had tried to filibuster, or talk the bill to death, while local officials in the South vowed to obstruct the new law. But the legislation had teeth. It allowed the attorney general of the United States to withhold federal funds from any state program that practiced discrimination. Moreover, it permitted aggrieved persons to petition the federal Equal Employment Opportunity Commission—an agency that President Kennedy had authorized—for redress.

Still, it was a recognition of continuing white political power and intransigence that convinced CORE, SNCC, and the NAACP that a major black voter registration drive was needed in the South, in order to make the power of the African-American vote felt. As discussed in earlier chapters, African-American men had won the right to vote with passage of the 15th Amendment in 1869. (Black and white women won the vote in 1920.) For the next few years, they were able to exercise that right and send more than a dozen black representatives to Congress, as well as electing hundreds of state and local officials across the South during Reconstruction. But in response to the multiracial, antiplanter appeal of the radical Populists in the late 19th century, white southern officials disenfranchised blacks through measures like poll taxes and literacy tests, which were rigorously

A CHRONOLOGY OF THE CAREER OF MARTIN LUTHER KING JR.

1951–55 Attends Boston University doctoral program; earns Ph.D. in theology

1953 Marries Coretta Scott, a student at the New England Conservatory of Music

1954 Is appointed minister of Dexter Avenue Baptist Church in Montgomery, Alabama

1955–56 Leads a successful one-year boycott of Montgomery's bus system

1957 In early January, helps organize Southern Christian Leadership Conference (SCLC); a bomb is thrown at the King house, but it does not explode.

1958 Meets with President Dwight D. Eisenhower at the White House; he is arrested in Montgomery (first charged with loitering, a charge that is dropped and replaced with "failure to obey an officer"). King publishes *Strive Toward Freedom*, an account of the Montgomery bus boycott. While on tour to promote the book, he is stabbed in the chest. His condition is serious but not critical.

1960 Is arrested in February on charges that he failed to pay his Alabama state taxes in 1956 and 1958. He is later acquitted by an all-white jury. In June, he meets with President John F. Kennedy. In December he is arrested at an Atlanta sit-in.

1961 Arrives in Albany, Georgia, to participate in an unsuccessful desegregation campaign. In December, he is arrested in Albany for obstructing the sidewalk and leading a parade without a permit.

1962 Is arrested again, at a July prayer vigil in Albany, and charged with failure to obey a police officer, obstructing the sidewalk, and disorderly conduct. In October, he meets once more with President Kennedy.

1963 In March and April, leads sit-in demonstrations in Birmingham, Alabama. In jail, he writes his "Letter from Birmingham Jail." That summer he leads the historic March on Washington and delivers his famous "I Have a Dream" speech.

1964 Joins demonstrations in St. Augustine, Florida, in May and June and is arrested. His book *We Can't Wait* is released in June, and in July, he attends the ceremony at which President Lyndon Johnson signs the Civil Rights Act of 1964. In September, he meets with Pope Paul VI at the Vatican, and, in December, he receives the Nobel Peace Prize in Oslo, Norway.

1965 The Southern Christian Leadership Conference organizes a civil rights march from Selma to Montgomery, Alabama. On March 7, the marchers are beaten by Alabama state troopers when they attempt to cross Selma's Edmund Pettus Bridge. Two weeks later, joined by 3,000 supporters from around the nation, and protected by federal troops, they begin their march again. En route, they are joined by another 25,000 supporters. When he and the other marchers reach Selma, King addresses the marchers from the Montgomery capitol building.

1966 In Chicago, meets with Elijah Muhammad, leader of the Nation of Islam, and leads an unsuccessful protest against job discrimination, poor schools, and slum housing

1967 King's book *Where Do We Go From Here* is published. At a speech in Chicago, he denounces the war in Vietnam. In November, he announces that the SCLC will launch a Poor People's Campaign to address the problems of poor blacks and whites.

1968 Is assassinated after leading a sanitation workers strike in Memphis

An FBI poster released after the disappearances of civil rights workers Andrew Goodman, James Chaney, and Michael Schwerner (Federal Bureau of Investigation)

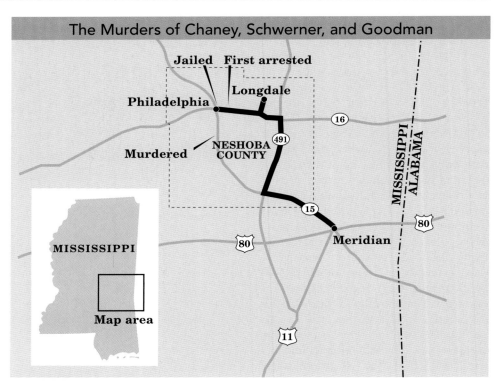

On June 21, 1964, three civil rights workers—Mississippian James Chaney and New Yorkers Michael Schwerner and Andrew Goodman—were arrested for alleged traffic violations outside of Philadelphia, Mississippi. After being held for several hours in a Philadelphia jail cell, the three were released. Fearing for their lives, the three young civil rights workers headed for the nearby Alabama state line. Before they reached it, however, the three were stopped by local Klansmen and murdered.

enforced in areas with large numbers of African Americans and laxly enforced where poor and uneducated whites lived. If a black person insisted on their constitutional rights, rougher measures—including beatings and lynchings—were employed. For roughly three-quarters of a century, then, only a tiny percentage of African Americans were permitted to register and vote in the South.

Between 1961 and 1963, CORE and SNCC had led efforts to register black voters in the region but had met with intimidation and violence. In 1964, they decided to intensify their efforts by focusing on the state that seemed to present the biggest obstacle to black political participation—Mississippi, where barely 6 percent of eligible African Americans were registered to vote, the lowest rate in the country. They called the plan Freedom Summer. Under the leadership of SNCC volunteer Robert Moses, hundreds of local blacks were organized and taught how to register voters. In addition, SNCC sent young white volunteers from the North to aid

them; the idea being that the presence of whites would draw national press attention and provide a modicum of protection to the black organizers. The first part of the plan worked as dozens of TV and newspaper reporters flocked to cover the story; the second element, however, was not as successful.

On June 21, three SNCC volunteers—two whites from the North named Andrew Goodman and Michael Schwerner, along with James Chaney, a local African American—were sent out to investigate the bombing of a black church near Philadelphia, Mississippi. Arrested and held for several hours for alleged traffic violations, the three were released that evening, only to disappear. For six weeks, state and federal authorities conducted a massive search for the three, which ended in the discovery of their bodies buried in a nearby earthen dam. Autopsies revealed Goodman and Schwerner were killed by a single bullet; Chaney had been beaten to death.

The murders—as well as dissension in the ranks as local blacks complained that the white volunteers were usurping leadership positions—failed to stop the drive. Nor did the more than one thousand arrests, 80 beatings by white mobs, and 67 bombings of black homes and churches. Despite fear of white reprisals, more than 80,000 black Mississippians registered to join the Mississippi Freedom Democratic Party (MFDP). At that year's Democratic convention in Atlantic City, New Jersey, however, party officials refused to recognize the MFDP's delegation, choosing the all-white regular Mississippi Democratic Party to represent the state. But MFDP delegation leader Fannie Lou Hamer—who had been evicted from the farm she had sharecropped for 18 years for her organizing efforts—won a ban against racially discriminatory delegations at future conventions.

Meanwhile, in Mississippi, the Freedom Summer volunteers set up 30 Freedom Schools throughout the state. The schools had a dual purpose: first, to highlight the gross inequalities between the state's white and black schools; and second, to provide classes for the children of impoverished black Mississippians. Again, using local black volunteers and white college students from the North as teachers, the schools offered courses in civil rights, black history, and leadership development, as well as more basic instruction in reading, writing, and arithmetic. Expecting about a thousand students, the Freedom Schools eventually enrolled more than 3,000. Beyond educating and registering thousands of Mississippi's African Americans, Freedom Summer—as well as the Selma-Montgomery (Alabama) march of the following year—paved the way for perhaps the greatest political accomplishment of the civil rights era, the Voting Rights Act of 1965.

THE SELMA MARCH AND THE VOTING RIGHTS ACT OF 1965

On February 18, 1965, Jimmy Lee Jackson—timber worker, church official, and voting rights activist from Marion, Alabama—attended a rally at a local church to protest the jailing of a local SCLC official. As the congregation left the church, they were attacked by local police and state troopers. Jackson was beaten and shot in the stomach as he tried to protect his mother and grandfather; he died in

Fannie Lou Hamer (Library of Congress)

March Route Through Selma, March 7, 1965

Route of march

FANNIE LOU HAMER

To civil rights advocates, the struggle to register African Americans to vote was a direct assault on the entrenched political white power structure that had enforced the Jim Crow system for a solid century. Those that led the fight literally risked everything they had—including their lives. Once such leader was Fannie Lou Hamer.

Hamer spent much of her life as a poor sharecropper in Mississippi. In 1962, workers with the Southern Christian Leadership Conference (SCLC) and the Student Nonviolent Coordinating Committee (SNCC) arrived in Montgomery County, Mississippi, where she lived. Her life changed dramatically. After Hamer not only registered herself, but then joined the organizing efforts to help others register, she was evicted from the farm she sharecropped. Then after one demonstration, she was arrested and beaten so badly that her eye and kidneys were permanently damaged.

Still, Hamer refused to back down. In 1964 she helped found the Mississippi Freedom Democratic Party (MFDP) and led a delegation to the national Democratic presidential convention to press the cause of black political representation. Although the MFDP delegation was not recognized as Mississippi's official delegation, the party won a ban against racially discriminatory delegations at future conventions.

In the years after the 1964 convention, Hamer continued to fight for her people. She launched the Freedom Farm Cooperative, which allowed people to grow their own food; she founded a garment factory to provide jobs; she helped start a day-care center; and she raised money for housing. By her life's end in 1977, Hamer, who had only six years of formal education, held numerous honorary university degrees acknowledging her important work.

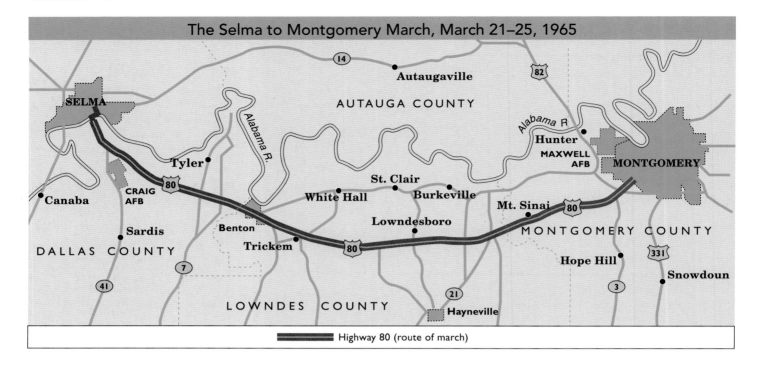

The Selma to Montgomery March, March 21–25, 1965

14 · Autaugaville · 82 · AUTAUGA COUNTY · Alabama R. · Hunter · MAXWELL AFB · MONTGOMERY · SELMA · Alabama R. · Tyler · 80 · St. Clair · Burkeville · Mt. Sinai · 80 · Canaba · CRAIG AFB · White Hall · Lowndesboro · MONTGOMERY COUNTY · Sardis · Benton · Trickem · 80 · Hope Hill · 331 · DALLAS COUNTY · 7 · Snowdoun · 41 · 3 · LOWNDES COUNTY · 21 · Hayneville

▬▬▬▬ Highway 80 (route of march)

hospital eight days later from his wounds. On March 3, King came to speak at Jackson's funeral and, in one of his first public criticisms of President Johnson, asked why the government could spend millions defending the South Vietnamese but could not protect one of its own citizens on American soil. Jackson's death—which many said was linked to his voter registration activities—helped convince King and other civil rights leaders that a dramatic gesture was needed to prod the federal government on voting rights legislation.

Two months earlier, King and the SCLC arrived in nearby Selma to help SNCC organizers and the local Dallas County Voters League in their two-year effort to register local African-American voters. A series of marches—designed to draw media attention to the violence and discrimination that barred black political participation—had met with violence from white mobs and police. On March 7, just four days after Jackson's funeral, a four-day march was organized from Selma to Montgomery—some 50 miles to the east—to petition Governor Wallace directly. Wallace forbid the march, saying that he could not protect the safety of the marchers. In fact, the governor was being disingenuous. It was not that he could not defend them, but that he would not. For as the marchers made their way across the Edmund Pettus Bridge on the outskirts of Selma, they were attacked not by white mobs, but by police on horseback, and forced back into town. Television cameras captured the violence of Bloody Sunday—as civil rights activists called it—and broadcast it on the evening news to horrified viewers nationwide.

Eight days later, President Johnson himself went on national TV to announce

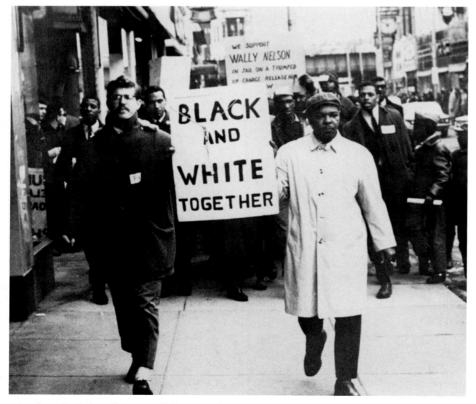

Marchers in Selma (Library of Congress)

that he was submitting a comprehensive voting rights bill to Congress. "Their cause," he said of the marchers, "must be our cause, too. Because it's not just Negroes, but it's really all of us who must overcome the crippling legacy of bigotry and injustice." Appearing to speak to Wallace and other white Alabamans, he insisted, "It is wrong—deadly wrong, to deny any of your fellow Americans the right to vote in this country." Then, borrowing the rallying cry of the movement, he ended his speech, "And, we shall overcome." Never before had a president identified himself so closely and unapologetically with the cause of civil rights. King, it was said, cried as he listened to the speech. On March 21—accompanied by federal marshals and troops—King led 25,000 people across the Edmund Pettus Bridge and all the way to Montgomery without any violent incidents to speak of. They camped out along the way and reached Montgomery on March 25.

The Voting Rights Act signed into law by President Johnson on August 6, 1965, was the second and last major piece of legislation of the civil rights era. It was a sweeping and powerful bill that banned literacy tests and put Washington in the business of voter registration for the first time, by sending federal examiners to register voters in any county where more

King confers with President Johnson prior to passage of the Voting Rights Act of 1965. (Library of Congress)

than 50 percent of the voting age population failed to show up on the registration lists. Together with the 24th Amendment of 1964, which banned poll taxes, the act ended all the legal ruses that southern states had employed to stop blacks from registering to vote.

Together, the Voting Rights Act of 1965 and the Civil Rights Act of 1964 fulfilled the promises of equal protection made by the 14th Amendment during

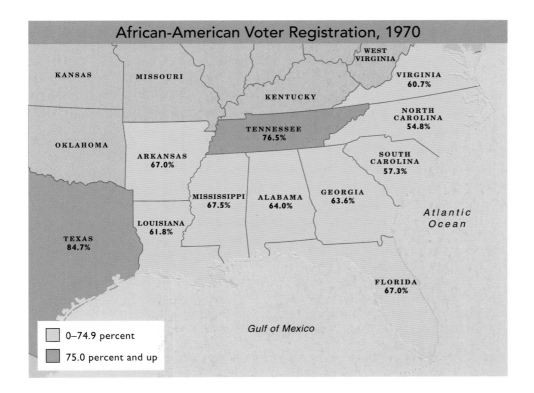

African-American Voter Registration, 1970

KANSAS

MISSOURI

WEST VIRGINIA

VIRGINIA
60.7%

KENTUCKY

OKLAHOMA

NORTH CAROLINA
54.8%

TENNESSEE
76.5%

ARKANSAS
67.0%

SOUTH CAROLINA
57.3%

MISSISSIPPI
67.5%

ALABAMA
64.0%

GEORGIA
63.6%

Atlantic Ocean

LOUISIANA
61.8%

TEXAS
84.7%

FLORIDA
67.0%

Gulf of Mexico

0–74.9 percent

75.0 percent and up

Reconstruction. They reversed nearly a century of Jim Crow laws, though it would take another decade or so to finally end the practice of southern segregation. But just as these bills represented the high water mark of civil rights legislation, so too the Selma-Montgomery march marked the culmination of nonviolent protest as the centerpiece of the civil rights struggle. Less than six months later and just five days after Johnson signed the Voting Rights Act, violence exploded in a city as far from Alabama and Mississippi as it could be: the Watts Riots of Los Angeles. Born of a more subtle de facto segregation—that is, segregation through practice rather than law—and triggered by routine police brutality, the Watts Riots signaled a new and more violent phase of black unrest, and one that was not confined to the South.

MALCOLM X AND THE RISE OF BLACK NATIONALISM

Throughout the 20th century, two conflicting tendencies have permeated African-American political thought. One traces its lineage back to the writings of W. E. B. DuBois and the founding ideals of the NAACP: an integrated, multiracial United States, free of prejudice and discrimination, where African Americans enjoy equality of economic opportunity and full political participation. The means to reach these ends included political advocacy, nonviolent protest, Christian love, an appeal to constitutional protections, rigorous use of the legal system, and an acceptance of liberal, well-meaning whites within the ranks of the movement. The integrationist tendency, as it has been called, reached its highest peak in the civil rights movement of the 1950s and early 1960s and found its greatest leader—and martyr—in the Reverend Martin Luther King Jr.

But there has been another school of thought and action among black activists in this century, one that traces its lineage back to Marcus Garvey and his Universal Negro Improvement Association. While the integrationist approach to black freedom and equality was premised on the idea that white America could be changed and redeemed, the separatist approach—as it is sometimes referred to—condemned white America as unalterably hostile to the aspirations of blacks. Where the integrationists believed that nonviolence was the most effective means to deal with white violence, black nationalists—who believed that even the best-intentioned whites should be excluded on principle—advocated "a fight fire with fire" approach, not a Christian turning of the cheek but a militant and, if necessary, armed defense of life and liberty. The ends of the two schools were as different as their means. With white America irredeemably racist, nationalists argued, blacks must withdraw into their own social, economic, and political space. This separatist tendency achieved its own peak in the Black Power movement of the late 1960s and early 1970s and found its greatest leader—and martyr—in Malcolm X.

The two movements existed in an uneasy tension with each other, characterized by the mutual respect and mutual suspicion in which King and Malcolm held each other. Deep down both shared fundamental ideals: political equality for blacks, racial self-respect and dignity, and economic justice. Indeed, both shared a basic distrust of capitalism as the best means to achieve economic equality. And each admired the undeniable bravery of the other. But they disagreed about much, too. King felt that the nationalists—by engendering fear in whites—were in danger of provoking violent retribution against themselves and the black community generally. For his part, Malcolm ridiculed the nonviolent ideals of the integrationists as futile and even self-destructive. He likened the differences between the two tendencies to the old divisions of the plantation South. The integrationists, he said, were the "house niggers" who—feeling privileged by living in the master's house—identified with it and hoped to ameliorate its worst aspects. The nationalists, on the other hand, were the "field hands," living separate from whites, with no illusion of ever being accepted in the white man's world.

However much one accepts or rejects the metaphor, there was an underlying truth to Malcolm's point—the two movements were fundamentally different, both in the physical and spiritual sense. Where the civil rights movement came out of the rural (and urban) South, the separatists were largely a northern and urban phe-

THE BASIC TENETS OF THE NATION OF ISLAM

Although the Nation of Islam has roots in the Islamic faith, and shares some of its principles, it is an entirely separate religion. Below, some of the main tenets of each are discussed.

Basic Tenets of Islam

1. Islam's central feature is its devotion to the Koran, believed to be the revelation of God, or Allah, to the prophet Muhammad.
2. Allah is all powerful, just, loving, merciful, and good.
3. No creature is to be compared to Allah, who is preeminent.
4. Allah has made revelations known through a series of chosen prophets, and when man has fallen away from these revelations, Allah has sent new prophets.
5. Early prophets included Adam, Noah, Abraham, Moses, and Jesus. Muhammad is the last prophet and when man falls from him, the end of the world will arrive.
6. Christians and Jews have corrupted the meaning of the Old Testament.
7. Muslims are forbidden to touch or eat pork, drink wine, gamble, or commit usury, fraud, or slander. They are also forbidden to make images.
8. The Muslim has five duties: First, once in his life, a follower must say with absolute acceptance, "There is no god but God and Muhammad is his prophet"; second, he must pray five times a day; third, he must give alms generously; fourth, he must keep the fast of Ramadan; and fifth, once in his life, if he is able, he must make a pilgrimage to Mecca.

Basic Tenets of the Nation of Islam

1. W. D. Fard was an incarnation of Allah who had come to free the "Lost-Found Nation of Islam in the West," or African Americans.
2. By listening to Fard, African Americans will learn the truth about themselves, defeat their white "slave masters," and be restored to a position of primacy among the peoples of the world.
3. According to the teachings of Elijah Muhammad, and later Louis Farrakhan, black men are destined by Allah to assume their rightful cultural and political leadership of the earth.
4. Christianity is a white man's plot to enslave nonwhites.
5. The white race is a race of devils, whose reign is soon coming to an end.
6. In preparation for the final battle between good and evil, there is a need for blacks to work together to heal their fallen, such as drug addicts and criminals, and to strive for economic independence from white society.
7. Adherents of the Nation of Islam are prohibited from touching or eating pork, using intoxicants, and practicing sexual promiscuity.

nomenon. And where the integrationists placed their faith in a Christian god, separatists often looked to Allah and Islam, which—along with Marcus Garvey's Back-to-Africa movement of the 1920s—is where the history of 20th-century black nationalism begins.

THE NATION OF ISLAM

When Africans were brought to American shores as slaves in the 17th and 18th centuries, most practiced local ancestor-based indigenous faiths, while a minority followed Islam. Traumatized by the enslavement process, severed from their local cultural traditions, mixed together with Africans of varied backgrounds, thrust headlong into a dominant European-based society, and often worked to the point of exhaustion and death, the vast majority of enslaved Africans in North America lost touch with their African faiths or Islam, embracing Christianity in its stead. For hundreds of years, through slavery and the nominal freedom they won in the Civil War, African Americans utilized the Christian faith to sustain their spirit and hopes for a better life in the next world, even as they developed Christian institutions that served as centers of cultural, political, and social life in this one.

But to Wallace Fard, a door-to-door silk salesperson in early 1930s Detroit, Christianity represented the faith of the oppressor and its worship by African Americans a symbol of their exile and servitude. While pitching his wares, Fard also preached a new Islamic-based faith. Islam held several attractions. Although tainted by its own connections to the slave trade, Islam was not associated in most African-American eyes with racism. Indeed, it was an alternative faith to Christianity, with the two in historically hostile competition with each other. At the same time, Islam was related to Christianity (it considered the Bible a holy book and Jesus a prophet, though not the son of God), so it was not entirely unfamiliar to African Americans. And finally, perhaps foremost among its many doctrines, it preached an equality of mankind, in submission to an almighty god, Allah. But Fard's Islam was hardly orthodox; it was heavily infused with biblical scripture (which was often employed

Elijah Muhammad (Library of Congress)

to criticize Christianity), an Afrocentric view of humanity's creation, and denunciations of western civilization and white people, whom Fard called "blue-eyed devils."

Like many new religions, it began informally. But as it grew in numbers, it developed both written texts and an organizational infrastructure. Fard called the new faith the Nation of Islam (NOI) because he hoped to create an "independent" black Islamic nation—not necessarily geographically removed from America—but spiritually, culturally, and even economically separate. Fard wrote two manuals to guide the faithful and established two schools—for men and women—to teach the precepts of the faith. He also created a kind of religious police force—the Fruits of Islam—who acted as his bodyguards and enforced NOI laws.

With its militancy and strong antiwhite message, the NOI soon attracted the attention of white authorities, who tried to frame Fard in 1931 for a murder committed by one of his followers. Fearing prison, or worse, Fard prepared his right-hand man Elijah Muhammad (born Elijah Poole) for leadership. But the transfer of power did not go smoothly; the NOI split into two mutually suspicious groups and Muhammad led his followers to Chicago where they established the Temple of Islam Number 2 as the faith's national headquarters. Under Muhammad, the NOI grew rapidly, attracting legions of urban blacks, newly arrived from the rural South. Bewildered and frightened by their new environment, many found solace in NOI teaching and its emphasis on a highly structured way of life. The NOI preached the sanctity of marriage and family and, like its parent faith, Islam, advocated strict behavioral rules about diet, hygiene, and abstinence from alcohol and drugs. Muhammad emphasized both the importance of women and their subservience to men, a principle that would come to be heavily criticized, not only during the women's liberation movement in the 1970s, but for decades to come.

At the same time, Muhammad put Fard's ideas about economic nationalism into practice. With their adherence to principles of clean living and hard work, black Muslims were often economically successful and most donated a large portion of their salary to the NOI. This

allowed it to build more than 100 temples nationwide which, in turn, supported shops, restaurants and other small businesses in black neighborhoods. During the 1930s and the 1940s, the Nation of Islam became an institution within much of urban black America and began to adopt the trappings of the nationalism it preached. The Nation of Islam adopted a flag, an anthem, and salutes and it periodically conducted military parades. It was, in the description of one historian, a kind of "military theocracy." Unlike integrationist organizations, such as the NAACP, it offered more than politics; it offered an alternative way of life, free from whites. Its rituals, its emphasis on black pride, and its insistence on clean living often appealed to those African Americans most victimized by white society—particularly the ghetto poor and prisoners. In the late 1940s, the Nation of Islam recruited its most famous convert—an imprisoned former drug dealer and petty thief named Malcolm Little. After joining the Nation of Islam, Little abandoned what he considered his "slave name" and changed his name to Malcolm X.

MALCOLM X AND BLACK NATIONALISM

In many ways, Malcolm X's story is the classic American tale of a person remaking their life after hitting rock bottom. And, in his redemption from a life of crime to a life dedicated to a fight for racial justice, he has inspired millions of black—and white—Americans. Born in Omaha in 1925, he grew up in a household shattered by the effects of white racism. Malcolm's father—Earl Little—was a local Baptist preacher and disciple of Marcus Garvey. While Earl's beliefs influenced his son, they also got the family in trouble with the Ku Klux Klan, which burned their new home in Lansing, Michigan, to the ground. Later, Earl was killed under mysterious circumstances, allegedly being forced under a streetcar by white toughs. Louisa Little—Malcolm's mother—was committed to a mental institution and the children were placed in foster homes, with Malcolm ending up the ward of a racist white couple. In his early teens, he fled Michigan for Boston, where he moved into the home of his half-sister Ella.

In the black Roxbury district of Boston, Malcolm discovered a world of people who lived by their wits and enjoyed all of the diversions of urban life. Malcolm danced the popular lindy hop, wore loud and colorful zoot suits, and had his hair "conked" (or straightened), the latter decision one he would condemn later in life as a sad and self-degrading attempt to look more white. While not particularly political, he could not help hearing about the World War II–era, antiblack race riots in Detroit and elsewhere and did his best to avoid the draft into a "white man's war." To support himself, Malcolm soon turned to crime, including drug-dealing, pimping, and gambling, a way of life he continued after his move to Harlem. In 1946, however, Malcolm was arrested and convicted for burglary and other crimes and sent to prison.

It was in prison that Malcolm found the NOI and dedicated himself to the teachings of Wallace Fard and the leadership of Elijah Muhammad. In the NOI tradition, he immediately set out to improve himself, delving deeply into the Bible and the Koran, and reading widely in literature and history. To improve his vocabulary, he once read a dictionary from cover to cover. First an acolyte, Malcolm soon became an advocate, preaching the message of the NOI and honing his rhetorical skills. He even led the prison's debating team to victory over a squad from the Massachusetts Institute of Technology (MIT), arguing against capital punishment.

In 1952, Malcolm was released from prison and went to work for the NOI. He also changed his name. Calling his surname "Little" a "white man's name," he adopted "X" to symbolize his lost African heritage. (After his pilgrimage to Mecca in 1964, he adopted the Islamic name El-Hajj Malik El-Shabazz.) With his intense energy and charisma, his fiery rhetoric, and his devotion to Elijah Muhammad, Malcolm quickly rose within the NOI ranks, becoming minister of its Harlem temple and founder of its first national newspaper, *Muhammad Speaks*. Indeed, Malcolm's introduction into NOI leadership circles came at a fortuitous moment. For years on the cutting edge of black militancy, the NOI found itself in the mid-1950s competing with the civil rights movement for the hearts and minds of African Americans. Speaking around the country and through the media, Malcolm denounced the integrationist ideals of King and other civil rights leaders. "It is not integration that Negroes in America want," he insisted, "it is human dignity." Why, he asked, should blacks strive to fit into a society that detested them when they could use their talents building an independent black "nation"?

In 1958, Malcolm married Betty Sanders (later Betty Shabazz), a fellow NOI disciple, and would eventually father four daughters. Like his beloved Muhammad, Malcolm believed in traditional gender roles and insisted that his wife not overstep her bounds as mother and homemaker. Yet, in other ways, Malcolm was creating a certain intellectual distance between himself and Muhammad in the late 1950s. He questioned the latter's firm belief that all white people were "devils," and he quietly broke with the NOI's principle of not becoming involved in politics. Malcolm supported boycotts and marches called by civil rights organizations and increasingly became an advocate of the decolonization of nonwhite peoples around the world. He especially came to advocate pan-Africanism—a political belief that preached the unity of black people around the world—after a trip to the continent in 1959.

This independence of thought and action did not sit well with Muhammad, who feared that his famous follower's popularity was eclipsing his own, and he began looking for ways to reassert his authority. The opportunity arose in November 1963, with President Kennedy's assassination. Asked by a reporter for his thoughts on the events in Dallas, Malcolm said it was a case of "the chickens coming home to roost," meaning Kennedy's unwillingness to stop racist violence in the South had created the conditions for his own murder in a southern state. The uproar that greeted these remarks led Muhammad to demand Malcolm make no more public statements. This move—combined with disturbing revelations that Muhammad had fathered several illegitimate children—led Malcolm to make a formal break with the NOI. On March 8, 1964, he announced both his resignation and his founding of a new Islamic movement—the Muslim Mosque, Inc.—which would commit itself to political activism and cooperation with civil rights leaders.

Malcolm X (Library of Congress)

Black Panthers march in New York. (New York Public Library)

He also took time off to make the pilgrimage to Mecca, a requirement of all able-bodied Muslims, and to several newly independent African countries. Both had a profound impact on the last remaining year of his life. Claiming to have witnessed the brotherhood of man at Mecca, Malcolm returned to the United States committed to establishing alliances with liberal and left-leaning whites. His visit to Africa inspired the formation of the Organization of Afro-American Unity (modeled after the Organization of African Unity), which advocated both independent black institutions and black participation in electoral politics. Where these new ideas and this new organization were heading is anyone's guess. For on February 21, 1965, while speaking at Harlem's Audubon ballroom, Malcolm died in a hail of bullets, allegedly fired by NOI assassins.

Like King's, Malcolm X's legacy is profound. His warning to white America that African-American frustration would turn to anger and violence was borne out within months of his death, in the rioting in the Watts section of Los Angeles. His

rhetoric of black militancy and self-defense was picked up by radical groups like the Black Panthers and his calls for African-American self-dignity bore fruit in the "black is beautiful" movement of the late 1960s. His autobiography—dictated to *Roots* author Alex Haley—was read by millions of young blacks and whites as both a paean to self-improvement and as a primer in radical political education. Ironically, like many radical icons of the 1960s, Malcolm's name and image would eventually be co-opted and mass-marketed in the 1990s, with the "X" logo appearing on everything from shoes to baseball caps. And yet, at the same time, Malcolm's legacy remains unclear. For just as King was moving toward a more all-encompassing radical critique of American society—including denunciations of capitalism and the war in Vietnam—at the time of his assassination in 1968, so Malcolm was shifting toward a more inclusive political orientation upon his murder three years before in 1965. Their untimely deaths elevated both men to the status of martyrs but left their full potential to change America unrealized.

BLACK POWER MOVEMENT AND THE BLACK PANTHERS

Nowhere was Malcolm X's legacy more immediately and more powerfully felt than in the Black Power movement of the mid to late 1960s. More an ideology and way of life than an institutionalized movement, the idea for Black Power arose out of the maturing civil rights movement in the South. With the passage of the Civil Rights Act of 1964 and the Voting Rights Act of 1965, segregation rules and discriminatory statutes had virtually been wiped from the legal record, thanks to the activism of CORE, SNCC, and the SCLC and the legal strategies of the NAACP and other civil rights groups. Despite these hard-fought successes, de facto discrimination as opposed to de jure—or legal—discrimination remained very much a part of the southern (and northern) way of life. This discrepancy frustrated many activists within the civil rights movement, particularly the younger members of SNCC and CORE. Taking a page from Malcolm's rhetoric, they argued that further progress depended on independent black political action.

In early 1966, Stokely Carmichael (later Kwame Turé), a black Trinidadian immigrant who was raised in the Bronx, New York, and educated at Howard University in Washington, D.C., led a radical coalition to power within SNCC. He then moved to oust white members of the organization. In June, SNCC joined a broad-based civil rights march to protest the shooting of James Meredith, the University of Mississippi's first African-American student. While marching, Carmichael and other SNCC members took up the call-and-response chant: "What do you want?...Black Power!" The media immediately focused on this militancy as a new angle on the civil rights movement story.

In fact, the Black Power ideology had been coalescing for over a year and involved much more than a political strategy of economic self-reliance and independent black politics. In the tradition of many 1960s-era protest movements, it offered a cultural agenda as well. For many African Americans like poet Amiri Baraka (LeRoi Jones), it meant a pride in black America's African heritage. While black intellectuals called for a resurrection of Afrocentric literature and arts—as

THE BLACK PANTHER PARTY PROGRAM

1. We want freedom. We want power to determine the destiny of our Black Community.
2. We want full employment for our people.
3. We want an end to the robbery by the white man of our Black Community.
4. We want decent housing, fit for shelter of human beings.
5. We want education for our people that exposes the true nature of this decadent American society. We want education that teaches us our true history and our role in the present-day society.
6. We want all Black men to be exempt from military service.
7. We want an immediate end to POLICE BRUTALITY and MURDER of Black people.
8. We want freedom for all Black men held in federal, state, county, and city prisons and jails.
9. We want all Black people when brought to trial to be tried in a court by a jury of their peer group or people from their Black communities, as defined by the Constitution of the United States.
10. We want land, bread, housing, education, clothing, justice, and peace. And as our major political objective, a United Nations–supervised plebiscite to be held throughout the Black colony in which only Black colonial subjects will be allowed to participate, for the purpose of determining the will of Black people as to their national destiny.

well as demanding the establishment of black studies courses and departments at universities—ordinary African Americans expressed the Black Power message by sporting the Afro hairstyle, characterized by a round shape and tight curls, and wearing dashikis, a billowing and colorful West African upper garment. As the popular expression of the day had it, "black is beautiful."

Yet many veteran civil rights leaders had mixed feelings about Black Power. King, for one, appreciated its emphasis on African pride but feared it would commit the "error of building a distrust for all white people" and stray from the path of peaceful protest. Indeed, a leading proponent of Black Power and a future SNCC chairman—H. Rap Brown—was quoted as saying "violence is as American as apple pie." But perhaps the most serious challenge to King's integrationist, nonviolent philosophy came not from his SNCC allies in the South, but from a radical new organization arising on the West Coast—the Black Panther Party (BPP).

The Panthers were founded in Oakland, California, in October 1966 by activists Huey Newton and Bobby Seale who became, respectively, the new organization's defense minister and chairman. As with most urban African Americans in

Former SNCC leader Stokely Carmichael changed his name to Kwame Turé upon converting to Islam. (Library of Congress)

A CHRONOLOGY OF THE BLACK PANTHER PARTY

1966

October 15 Huey Newton and Bobby Seale organize the Black Panther Party and draft a ten-point program for economic, social, and political development in black neighborhoods.

1967

January 1 The party opens its first official headquarters in Oakland, California.

February 21 Betty Shabazz, widow of Malcolm X, visits San Francisco; the Panthers provide armed security; they are stopped by police but cite their right to bear arms and are not arrested.

April 27 The first issue of the Panther paper, *Black Community News Service*, is published.

May 21 The Panthers show up in the state capital of Sacramento bearing arms; they read a statement, proclaiming their right to bear arms.

June 29 Stokely Carmichael, former chair of Student Non-Violent Coordinating Committee (SNCC), joins the Panthers.

October 28 Returning home from a party, Newton is stopped by police; a shootout erupts and an officer is killed; Newton is wounded and charged with murder, though no gun is found on his person.

1968

February 17–18 Two "Free Huey" rallies, featuring H. Rap Brown and Stokely Carmichael, lead to an alliance between SNCC and the Panthers.

March 4 FBI issues secret memos to fight Panthers.

April 4 Martin Luther King Jr. is assassinated; the Panthers plead for calm in Oakland.

April 6 Panther Bobby Hutton is killed by police; Eldridge Cleaver is wounded.

September 28 Newton is sentenced to 2–15 years; Oakland police officers, outraged by the light sentence, shoot out the windows of the Panther headquarters.

1969

January 17 Two leaders of the Southern California Panther Party are slain; police conduct raids on several Panther offices in Los Angeles.

April 2 Twenty-one Panthers in New York City are arrested for conspiring to bomb local department stores; all are acquitted in May 1971.

July 18–21 The Panthers sponsor an anti-fascist conference in Oakland, attended by SNCC, the Young Lords, and the Students for a Democratic Society.

December 4 Panther leaders Fred Hampton and Mark Clarke are slain by Chicago police.

1970

January 9 The Boston Panther Party starts free clothing program.

July 25 The Panther Party office in Omaha is bombed.

August 5 Newton is released from jail.

August 7 Hoping to liberate his brother George, Panther Jonathan Jackson assaults a courtroom in Marin County, California; Jackson, two other Panthers and the judge are killed in the shootout.

September 3 Panther leader Cleaver opens an international section in Algeria.

November 7 Southern California Panthers start a free breakfast program; they provide 1,700 meals a week to the poor.

1971

January 16 The Panthers establish a legal assistance program in Toledo, Ohio; the Chicago Panthers start a door-to-door health program.

August 21 Panther leader George Jackson is slain in San Quentin prison; guards say he was trying to escape.

February Newton publishes *To Die for the People*.

1974

Summer Newton goes into exile in Cuba to avoid trial for murder of a female barroom customer.

Fall After converting to born-again Christianity, Cleaver returns to the United States from Algeria.

the North and West, the party itself had southern roots. For example, its logo, a crouched black panther, was adopted from the Lowndes County (Alabama) Freedom Organization, a black political party founded by Carmichael and SNCC in March 1966. The symbolic connection aside, the BPP had a very different agenda, advocating black self-defense—particularly against the police—and the restructuring of U.S. society along more economically, politically, and socially egalitarian lines.

In a ten-point program, Newton and Seale demanded—among other things— "full employment"; "decent housing, fit for shelter of human beings" ; exemption for blacks from military service; an end to police brutality; and "the power to determine the destiny of our Black Community." More than just a political party and a self-defense organization, the Panthers also organized food, health, and education programs in the many black communities where they operated. While not admitting whites into their ranks, the

Panthers nevertheless established alliances with the antiwar movement, including the Students for a Democratic Society and the radical Weather Underground. Just eight months after its founding, the Panthers drew national media attention when they showed up in Sacramento, California's capital, to protest a law that banned the bearing of arms in public. Wearing their uniform black berets and black leather jackets, the Panthers also came armed with rifles. Seale and 30 others—including future Panther leader Eldridge Cleaver—were arrested.

From that moment, the BPP became the most controversial and widely feared organization in the country, at least as far as the white community and the government were concerned. This became especially the case after nationwide urban rioting in the summers of 1967 and 1968, which some police officials blamed on the Panthers. Calling the group the "greatest threat to internal security in the country," FBI director J. Edgar Hoover launched COINTELPRO (short for counterintelligence program). Using infiltrators, informers, and agents provocateurs (spies who would break the law on purpose to implicate the party), the FBI worked with local police to destroy the organization. By 1970, more than 25 Panthers had been killed by police, including activists Fred Hampton and Mark Clark, killed in a raid on the party's Chicago headquarters in December 1969. Hundreds of others were prosecuted for a range of crimes and either sent to prison or forced into exile, such as Cleaver, who escaped to Cuba. No fewer than 21 BPP members in New York were charged with conspiring to kill police officers, blow up buildings, and even assassinate President Nixon. Many of the charges were based on the testimony of informants with criminal records, and a number of convictions—including Newton's for the shooting of an Oakland police officer—were overthrown on appeal.

The following year, three Panthers, George Jackson, Fleeta Drumgo, and John Cluchette, known as "the Soledad Brothers," went on trial in Marin County, California. During the trial, the three attempted to escape, causing a bloody shootout in which the judge and four others were killed. Among those arrested was a controversial University of California at Los Angeles philosophy professor named Angela Davis. Davis, a member of the Communist Party, was well known. California governor Ronald Reagan had campaigned to have her fired for her political views. In the wake of her arrest, Davis was found guilty of providing weapons used in the escape. She spent 16 months in jail before public pressure won her release.

Ironically, the BPP's commitment to a broad multiracial alliance of revolutionary groups served to isolate it. Its connections to SNCC—formed during the "Free Huey (Newton)" crusade of 1968—came apart over Newton's decision to end all ties to white activists, as did the BPP's relationship with US, a Southern California-based black nationalist organization founded by Maulana Karenga, the creator of the Kwaanza holiday. Indeed, this latter break turned fatal when the two groups fought a gun battle on the UCLA campus that left two Panthers dead. With much of its leadership imprisoned, in exile, or dead, the BPP shifted to a less confrontational style and agenda in the early 1970s, epitomized by Seale's near-successful run for the mayoralty of Oakland. Despite such efforts, the Panthers continued to decline, a victim of isolation from other black political organizations and unprecedented government repression.

VIOLENCE IN THE STREETS

The growth of organizations like the Nation of Islam and the Black Panthers reflected, in part, a massive demographic shift within black America. Continuing a trend that began in the early part of the century, rural African Americans from the South had been making their way to urban centers in the North and West in ever greater numbers. By 1960, more than 40 percent of all U.S. blacks lived outside the South and nearly 75 percent resided in cities. There they faced very different challenges. While legal segregation was rare, de facto separation of the races was a way of life. Most urban blacks lived in ghettoes, poor inner-city neighborhoods that had once been inhabited by immigrants from southern and eastern Europe. But as these white ethnics prospered, they often moved to the suburbs, a trend accelerated by a phenomenon known as "white flight." As blacks moved in, whites—fearful of racial mixing and convinced that the

CIVIL DISTURBANCES OF THE 1960s

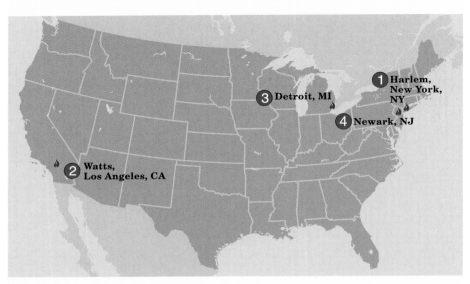

❶ Harlem (1964)

In July, a policeman shot and killed a 15-year-old Harlem boy. Police then forcibly broke up protest meetings being planned by the African-American community. Fights broke out, one person was killed, 500 arrests were made, and more than 100 stores were looted or burned. Violence soon spread to other cities.

Dead: 1
Arrests: 500
Property Damage: 112 stores looted or burned

❷ Watts (1965)

Violence erupted in the Watts section of Los Angeles after an angry crowd of African Americans began gathering around two white traffic police, who were in the process of arresting an African-American driver. Police called for help, and 80 additional police arrived on the scene. People began looting nearby stores, stoning passing buses and cars, and fighting with the police. The disturbances lasted for six days.

Dead: 34
Injured: 900
Arrests: 4,000
Property Damage: $225 million

❸ The Long, Hot Summer (1967)

During the summer of 1967, temperatures were in the 90s Fahrenheit all across America. In the urban ghettoes of the nation's cities, tempers were also running high. Within weeks of each other, major riots took place in Newark, Detroit, and other cities. All told, more than 150 racial disturbances broke out during the first nine months of the year alone. In the wake of the riots, President Lyndon B. Johnson ordered that a special commission look into the causes of the violence. In 1968, the Kerner Commission released its findings.

❹ Detroit

Dead: 43
Arrests: 7,200
Property Damage: 2,700 stores looted or burned

Newark

Dead: 21
Arrests: 1,600
Property Damage: $10 million

jobs, social services, and local businesses grew increasingly scarce.

Adding to the plight were poorly thought through urban renewal programs. Interstate highways were extended through minority communities, dividing and destroying neighborhoods, while hundreds of thousands of poor blacks and Hispanics were crowded into soulless high-rise towers. The results were predictable: high unemployment, alcoholism, drug abuse, crime, and a growing sense of frustration. The response of local police forces did not help. Largely made up of white ethnics, police departments around the country—sometimes openly racist and nearly always insensitive to blacks whose personal history made them suspicious of authority—used increasingly intrusive and even brutal tactics to maintain order in the ghettoes. The frustration of inner-city black communities was boiling over by the mid-1960s.

The first great explosion of African-American anger erupted in Los Angeles. On the evening of August 11, 1965—in the midst of a summer heat wave—police officers arrested an African-American man for drunk-driving in the predominantly black community of Watts. As crowds taunted the police, one of the officers—according to eyewitnesses—began hitting people with his baton. As word of the alleged police brutality spread through the community, rioting erupted. By the next day, hundreds of area stores and businesses had been looted and torched. With some 35,000 people taking part in the unrest, it took more than 16,000 police, sheriff's deputies, and National Guardsmen to return the area to calm. But the five days of violence had left 34 dead, 1,000 wounded, and some $200 million in property damage. The "long, hot summers" of the 1960s had begun. In 1966, rioting tore through Cleveland and Nashville. The following year, full-scale rioting broke out in Washington, Atlanta, Chicago, Newark, and, most violent of all, Detroit.

Motown—as it was called—offered the quintessential urban black experience. Drawn to the high-wage automobile industry, rural southern blacks had been flocking to Detroit since the second decade of the 20th century. During World War II, major riots broke out between whites and blacks over scarce housing, leaving 34 dead. Despite the violence, and with the auto industry booming, blacks

presence of African Americans drove down housing values—left. Left in the wake of "white flight" were predominantly black and Hispanic communities, where

In this photograph, looted buildings line a Newark street in the aftermath of the July 1967 rioting. It took more than 4,000 police and National Guard troops to end the violence. (Library of Congress)

continued to move there through the 1950s and 1960s, as whites slowly made their way out. While employment remained low, a lack of black businesses, poor housing, dilapidated schools, and, most troubling, ongoing police abuses fueled a sense of frustration and anger. On the morning of July 23, 1967, police raided a bar in a black neighborhood frequented by African-American patrons. As the customers were led out in handcuffs, a crowd gathered and the police retreated. Looting and arson—first aimed at white-owned businesses—spread to all establishments. Again, National Guardsmen quelled the violence, but not before 43 African Americans had died, along with nearly 1,200 wounded and over 7,000 arrested. Whether or not white flight was one of the causes of the violence, it was most definitely a result. By the 1980s, the vast majority of nonblacks had fled the city

and, with them, much of the tax base that supported municipal services and schools.

In the wake of Detroit, President Johnson appointed a commission—headed by Illinois governor Otto Kerner—to look into the causes of the violence. After seven months, the commission issued a report, both factually detailed and brutally honest in its conclusions. Blame was placed squarely on a racist society that failed to address the needs of impoverished inner-city blacks, including a lack of jobs, poor schools, inadequate health care, low-quality housing, and systematic police prejudice and brutality. Warning that the nation was "moving toward two societies, one black, one white—separate and unequal," the commission made sweeping recommendations: new initiatives in urban education, housing, job programs, and a "national system of income supplementation." King called the report a "physician's warning of approaching death, with a prescription for life."

But the solutions the report offered were stillborn. While Johnson had instituted a number of antipoverty initiatives as part of his Great Society plan in the mid-1960s—including Medicaid and Head Start—much of the money destined for these domestic spending programs was siphoned off to pay for the war in Vietnam. Indeed, in his last year of life, King had turned against his erstwhile ally in the White House and begun denouncing U.S. involvement in Southeast Asia. Moreover, the same forces that produced white flight also fostered white political backlash. In 1968, Republican Richard Nixon won the presidency on a "law and order" platform that many blacks and white liberals felt was a coded and racist message calling for a police crackdown on neighborhoods in the inner city. As president, Nixon ignored the Kerner Commission's recommendations.

Just months after its release, another wave of violence wracked the urban United States. On April 4, 1968, Martin Luther King Jr. was assassinated by a white gunman named James Earl Ray Jr. in Memphis, Tennessee. While the identity of his killer would not be known for weeks, news of the murder set off rioting in more than 100 cities across the country. In Chicago, Mayor Richard Daley—a hard-nosed machine politician who would unleash his police against antiwar protesters at the Democratic Party convention in August—instituted a "shoot to kill" policy. In Washington, it took thousands of National Guard troops to protect the

THE KERNER COMMISSION REPORT

Following particularly violent disturbances in Newark and Detroit in 1967, President Lyndon B. Johnson, created the National Advisory Commission in Civic Disorder, or the Kerner Commission, after its leader, Governor Otto Kerner of Illinois. After studying 164 *civil disturbances, which took place nationwide during the summer of 1967, the Kerner Commission released its findings concerning the general causes and recommended a series of solutions. The Kerner Commission findings are quoted below:*

Causes of Disturbances

1. Pervasive discrimination and segregation in employment, education, and housing;
2. Black in-migration and white exodus, which had provided a growing crisis of deteriorating facilities and services and unmet human needs;
3. The black ghettoes, where segregation and poverty converged on the young to destroy opportunity and enforce failure;
4. The expectations aroused by the...victories of the civil rights movement have led to frustration, hostility, and cynicism in the face of the persistent gap between promise and fulfilment
5. A climate that tends toward the approval and encouragement of violence...created by white terrorism...and by some protest groups engaging in civil disobedience who...resort to violence in an attempt to compel alteration of laws and policies with which they disagree.
6. Negroes...lack the channels of communication, influence, and appeal that traditionally have been available to [white ethnic minorities]...which enabled them—unburdened by color—to scale the walls of white ghettos in an earlier era.
7. These conditions have created a volatile mixture of attitudes and beliefs which needs only a spark to ignite mass violence. Strident appeals to violence, first heard from white racists, were echoed and reinforced last summer in the inflammatory rhetoric of black racists and militants.

8. Almost invariably the incident that ignites disorder arises from police action...All the major outbursts of recent years were precipitated by arrests of Negroes by white police for minor offenses.

Recommendations

1. Increased job opportunities through the creation of two million new jobs by the Federal government. The Commission also recommended that the government support job training programs through direct sub sidies and tax incentives;
2. Increased educational opportunity through sharply increased efforts to eliminate de facto segregation, the extension of early childhood education to every disadvantaged child in the country, and substantial federal funding of compensatory education programs at schools serving disadvantaged children;
3. A reform of the welfare system, accomplished by a huge infusion of federal dollars, so that the amount of supplementary income each recipient received from the government might be...increased.
4. An increased supply of adequate housing, through the expansion of a rent supplement program, the creation of new programs to make home ownership possible for low income families, and the expansion of Federal public housing programs, with a particular emphasis on placing low and moderate-income housing outside of ghetto areas.

White House and Capitol building from attack by angry rioters.

The 1960s, then, came to an end with an increasingly polarized United States. There had been progress. Generations of legalized segregation and discrimination in the South had been swept away by the civil rights movement and federal legislation. With the elimination of legal barriers, the way was set for the growth of the black middle class. Still, more fundamental problems remained. The nation was indeed "moving toward two societies" divided not by law but by practice. U.S. urban centers were growing increasingly segregated, with an impoverished inner city inhabited by blacks and belts of suburbs where middle-class whites lived and increasingly worked, oblivious to, and frightened of the problems plaguing the nation's downtowns. The results were urban rioting and increasingly militant black nationalism, the former contained by massive shows of governmental force and the latter destroyed by ruthless police repression.

The nation's politics reflected this picture of progress and poverty. Southern electoral politics was on the eve of sweeping change, as black voters flocked to the polls and elected unprecedented numbers of African-American officials at the local, state, and federal level. At the same time, however, many white southern Democrats grew disenchanted with their party's pro–civil rights platform and perceived leniency toward inner-city unrest. They first flirted with racist Alabama governor George Wallace in his independent 1968 run for the presidency before turning to the Republicans in ever greater numbers, a true tidal shift given the white South's historical enmity for the party of Lincoln and Radical Reconstruction. For black voters the shift to the Democrats had occurred decades earlier with Franklin Roosevelt. But it was not until the pro–civil rights presidencies of Kennedy and especially Johnson that the Democrats effectively reciprocated that loyalty. In 1972, liberal whites and blacks would seize the party, leading to a disastrous defeat and Nixon's reelection. For the next 20 or so years, the Democrats—though in command of the Congress—often remained a party in opposition, fighting rear-guard actions against an increasingly conservative white majority and a Republican White House.

CULTURAL EMPOWERMENT

Cassius Marcellus Clay Jr. was born in Louisville, Kentucky, in 1942. In 1960, he won an Olympic gold medal for boxing and decided to turn professional. Clay gained attention for his boxing skills and his constant reminder: "I am the greatest!" He knocked out Sonny Liston in 1964 and became the world heavyweight champion. The next day, he announced that he was joining the Nation of Islam and changing his name to Muhammad Ali. In 1967, when he refused his military draft for religious reasons, Ali was stripped of his boxing title. He returned to boxing in 1971, only to be defeated by Joe Frazier. Ali regained his title in 1974, defeating George Foreman, but he lost it again to Leon Spinks in 1978. Ali retired from boxing in 1981.

Muhammad Ali is one of those rare athletes whose impact exceeded the confines of his individual sport. Ali's reputation as a boxer was for his extraordinary quickness and his graceful ability to "float like a butterfly" around the ring, exhausting his opponents in the chase. But his outsize persona, complete with rhyming boasts and outspoken bravado, were what caught the general public's attention. Here was a black man competing on his own terms, powerful, boastful, afraid of no one. On top of that, his willingness to sacrifice his status as heavyweight champion of the world because of his moral views on the Vietnam War only added to that stature.

Ali was by no means the first gifted black athlete, and not the first to possess a strong sense of self or a healthy ego. Nonetheless, most black athletes before Ali were careful about being too outspoken. Even an icon like Jackie Robinson did most of his talking on the field during his career. Only after Robinson left baseball in 1956 did he serve on the board of the NAACP and proclaim his support for Dr. King (in his own syndicated newspaper column). But Robinson recognized the cultural revolution around him. Before his death in 1972, he warned the Nixon White House that the younger black generation was not nearly patient as his had been in seeking change.

As a member of that younger generation, Muhammad Ali personified its impatience. His public persona also highlighted

Muhammad Ali (Library of Congress)

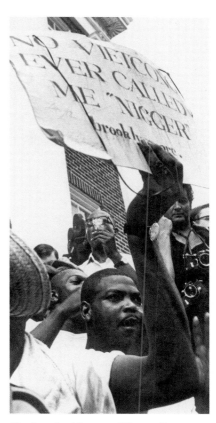

During the Vietnam War, a disproportionate number of African-American youths were drafted, which added increased urgency to antiwar demonstrations in the black community. (New York Public Library)

KWANZAA

Created in 1966 by African studies professor Maulana Karenga, Kwanzaa (which means "first fruits" in Swahili) is a celebration of African culture. The annual seven-day holiday falls between December 26 and January 1. Each evening during that period, family and friends gather to eat and drink together, sing, pray, and light candles, and rejoice in their collective bond and blessings. Each evening is committed to one of the Seven Principles, and celebrants commit themselves to honoring the message behind each principle throughout the year. At the heart of Kwanzaa is the belief that through cultural unity and a knowledge of traditional African heritage, African Americans can better effect social change in the community.

Seven Principles of Kwanzaa

The *nguzo saba*, or seven principles, represent African-American values, which are the product of tradition and present-day needs. A different candle is lit each day of the holiday, bringing focus to the principle represented, and commitment to uphold the responsibility of its practice.

kujichagulia, **self-determination:** importance of defining common goals and interests, and making decisions based on the collective good of the family and community

umojo, **unity of family and community:** reflected in the African motto "I am because We are"

ujima, **collective work and responsibility:** a reminder of the past, present, and future and the role of the African-American community in society and the world

ujamma, **cooperative economics:** collective economic power which encourages mutual support to achieve common needs

nia, **purpose:** a reminder of the need to look within to determine goals for the good of the community

kuumba, **creativity:** use of creative energies to build a strong and lively community

imani, **faith:** emphasizes self-worth and belief in the ability to succeed in the struggle for higher life for humankind

KUUMBA · UJAMMA · KUJICHAGULIA · UMOJO · UJIMA · NIA · IMANI

the changing social climate that the civil rights movement had helped bring about. Increasingly, young black public figures were bringing their private and political views—once taboo—into the public arena. In a particularly famous incident, Tommy Smith and John Carlos, both African Americans, raised their fists in the Black Power salute while receiving their medals at the 1968 Olympic Games, Black atheletes, entertainers, and other creative artists could now express their personal views more freely and speak out on social issues ranging from racism and poverty to the Vietnam War.

LITERATURE OF THE LATE 1960S AND EARLY 1970S

The new and powerful black consciousness borne of African Americans' civil rights struggle quickly found expression in literature, music, and other arts. While James Baldwin continued as perhaps the best-known African-American novelist and essayist of the decade, the Black Power movement of the late 1960s spawned a literary movement of politically infused, radically race-conscious new voices. One of the first of these was the publisher, poet, music critic, and playwright LeRoi Jones.

After the assassination of Malcolm X, Jones moved from Manhattan's Lower East Side uptown to Harlem, where he founded the Black Arts Repertory Theatre/School (BART/S). Around the same time, a number of Lower East Side writers, such as Steve Cannon, Ishmael Reed, and the musician-writer Archie Shepp, emerged from a writers' association called the Umbra Workshop. Umbra's writers produced *Umbra* magazine. The *Umbra* poets are considered the first post–civil rights era African-American literary group to establish their own voice and following outside of the dominant white literary establishment.

Another group of black writers, known as the Harlem Writers Guild, included Maya Angelou. Angelou would eventually be asked to read a poem at President Bill Clinton's inauguration. At that time, however, she and the other members of the group focused on fiction and other prose.

Poetry, however, was the form most frequently associated with the leading, politically motivated black writers of the day. This was because poetry could be performed out loud and could incorporate chants, anthems, and slogans far more easily than fiction.

One black poet to make memorable use of the rhythmic cadences of poetry was Nikki Giovanni. Giovanni graduated from Fisk University in 1967 and founded her own publishing company by 1970. Her work often comments on the need for blacks to proclaim their identities in the face of a white-majority culture. Together with Etheridge Knight, Don L. Lee (later known as Haki R. Madhubuti), Larry Neal, and Sonia Sanchez, she formed the group of black poets known as the "Broadside Quartet."

Earlier in her career, Sanchez had also belonged to a Lower East Side writing workshop with LeRoi Jones. Although she had initially believed in integration, once she became aware of Malcolm X, she grew to feel that blacks would never be fully accepted by whites.

Unlike their fiction-writing contemporaries, many of the black poets of the day saw poetry as a political weapon. Jones's 1965 poem "Black Art" was explicit: "We want poems that kill," read one line. This call to arms was not merely metaphor, either. Jones would become closely allied with the call for armed self-defense against the white power structure. In 1967, the same year Jones changed his name to Amiri Baraka, he visited Los Angeles and met with Maulana Karenga, the creator of Kwanzaa, as well as Black Panthers Bobby Seale and Eldridge Cleaver. Later that year, he would be beaten and arrested by Newark, New Jersey police, charged with inciting a riot and illegally possessing a gun.

The following year, a group of poets associated with the East Wind Writers Workshop met in East Harlem's Marcus Garvey Park to form a spoken word and music group called the Last Poets. In 1970, four members of this group—Jalal Mansur Nuriddin, Umar Bin Hassan, Abiodun Oyewole, and percussionist Nilaja—released a self-titled debut album that reached number 40 on the *Billboard* charts. Although the group's sales faded with subsequent releases, today they are remembered as the forerunners of today's rap music. As Amiri Baraka wrote of the group, "The Last Poets are the prototype Rappers . . . the kina nigger you don' never wanna meet!"

MUSICIANS AND THE MUSIC INDUSTRY

Few black musical artists of the 1960s were as openly radical as the Last Poets; most attempted to appeal to more mainstream taste. Even so, black popular music grew more overtly political as the 1960s wore on. Popular music written and performed by blacks during that tumultuous decade can be divided into two categories: music for blacks, and music that aimed at the widest possible commercial acceptance.

As discussed earlier, the first years of rock and roll gave way by the late 1950s to tamer versions of teen pop, aimed largely at the young white audiences. At the same time, music by and for black audiences continued to thrive in black communities. During the 1950s, traditional R&B continued to evolve, frequently blending with elements of gospel and pop music. At the forefront of this movement was a blind singer and pianist from Georgia named Ray Charles. Today, Charles's 1954 hit "I Got a Woman" is widely recognized as the first song that can can be classified as "soul music." By the start of the 1960s, Charles had been joined by other soul singers, including Sam Cooke (who had begun his career as a gospel artist), Jackie Wilson, and James Brown.

As the 1960s progressed, soul arrangements became more and more complex, often featuring smooth group harmonies. Although many of the songs were love songs, the lyrics tended to be more mature, complicated, and bittersweet than the R&B love songs of the previous decade. Far and away the most successful form of soul music during the 1960s was the style identified with Detroit-based Motown Records. Featuring legendary performers such as Smokey Robinson, the Temptations, the Supremes, Marvin Gaye, Stevie Wonder, the Four Tops, the Jackson Five, and

Amiri Baraka (Corbis)

Aretha Franklin (Corbis)

many more, the "Motown Sound" was the preeminent voice of black popular music in the 1960s and early 1970s.

Motown was founded in 1959 and tightly controlled by the pioneering executive Berry Gordy Jr. Particularly in the early 1960s, Motown executives carefully molded its groups, instructing its artists in not only singing technique and dance moves but also what to wear and how to behave. In recent years, critics have accused Gordy and his Motown team of being too formulaic and smooth, and overly concerned with appealing to white audiences. Such criticism ignores the fact that Motown was even more popular with black audiences than it was with white ones. Besides that, the wide-ranging variety of hits that emerged from the company's studios remain undeniable classics.

Motown's only major competition in soul music was the Memphis-based Stax/Volt Records. Stax/Volt artists like Booker T. and the MGs, Otis Redding, and Sam and Dave featured a bluesier, more horn-based sound than Motown soul. In the late 1960s, Stax/Volt was purchased by Atlantic Records, by this time headed by the same Jerry Wexler who had coined the term "rhythm and blues" back in the 1950s. Like Stax/Volt, Atlantic's soul artists, including a preacher's daughter from Detroit named Aretha Franklin, shared the same horn-based, rougher sound as Stax/Volt.

By the end of the 1960s, soul music was undergoing dramatic change, as was the country as a whole. Motown stars like the Temptations released the more psychedelic album *Cloud Nine*, and Marvin Gaye and Stevie Wonder broke away from the Motown hit-machine model and began writing more expressly personal and political full-length records. Aretha Franklin's cover of the Otis Redding song "Respect" sounded a battle cry for black and female empowerment, while her record *Young, Gifted, and Black* did the same. Meanwhile, the "Godfather of Soul," James Brown, continued to evolve his sound, pioneering a new bass-heavy genre called funk. His 1969 album title proclaimed, *Say It Loud, I'm Black and I'm Proud*—a fitting summation for an era in which African-American culture and identity politics asserted itself in the larger culture.

BLACKS IN FILM

If African Americans in music, literature, dance, and sports all gained greater mass exposure in the postwar period, the same was certainly true for black actors in film and television. Prior to World War II, blacks in film generally played either characters in subservient, often racially offensive, roles that were meant as comic relief or smiling song-and-dance men included for pure entertainment. Though there were exceptions, such as Paul Robeson's role in 1933 film *The Emperor Jones*, the depiction of the authentic black experience on film was rare.

After World War II, however, African Americans featured in more films. Notably, in 1949 Hollywood released two important films dealing directly with racism. *Home of the Brave*, with James Edwards, Steve Edwards, and Lloyd Bridges, concerned a black soldier in World War II, while *Pinky*, starring Jeanne Crain and Ethel Waters, dealt with the issue of light-skinned blacks "passing" for white. In 1950, Sidney Poitier emerged in his first starring role as Dr. Luther Brooks, the head of a successful middle-class black family. Poitier became the first major African-American film star, and he became the first African American to win the Oscar for Best Actor, awarded for his 1963 performance in *Lilies of the Field*.

This was not to say that postwar Hollywood became color-blind. In 1953, Harry Belafonte and Dorothy Dandridge starred together in *Bright Road*. Belafonte, a gifted singer as well as actor, would go on to a long and successful career and play an important role speaking out for civil rights causes. Dandridge, by contrast, had a far more difficult road. Hollywood casting directors recognized Dandridge as both a stunning beauty and a real talent. Indeed, she was nominated for an Academy Award in 1954 for her lead role in *Carmen Jones*. But leading roles for beautiful black women, no matter how talented, were hard to come by in the 1950s and early 1960s. Struggling under the weight of her unfulfilled promise, Dandridge died in 1965 from an overdose of antidepressants.

Besides Poitier and Belafonte, Hollywood still lacked any major black film stars before the early 1970s. In 1970,

however, the veteran film and stage actor Ossie Davis produced *Cotton Comes to Harlem*, starring Godfrey Cambridge. Screening to virtually all-black audiences, the film took in $9 million, proving that a market existed for films produced, directed, and starred in by black Americans. The next year, a film by a young director named Melvin Van Peebles underscored this fact. Van Peebles wrote, produced, directed, distributed, and starred in *Sweetback*, a low-budget film whose main character was pitted against the white establishment and won.

The success of *Sweetback* was followed by the even more successful *Superfly*, directed by the noted African- American photographer Gordon Parks, as well as *Shaft*, directed by Parks's son, Gordon Parks Jr. Suddenly, generally low-budget movies about powerful black men sticking it to "the man" were everywhere. The genre came to be known by the derogatory term "blaxploitation films" because critics believed the testosterone-heavy lead characters in the films—often drug dealers, pimps, and other criminals—played off of negative stereotypes of African Americans. Black audiences, however, lined up in droves.

BLACKS IN TELEVISION

Even as black actors became a more visible presence in film during the early 1970s, many of those films played to largely black audiences. Television was a different matter.

Some of the earliest appearances of blacks on television were, like many early television shows, updates of popular radio programs that dated from the 1930s and 1940s. As such, the earliest black TV shows traded on stereotypes such as the lazy and ignorant *Amos 'n' Andy*. Beginning in 1956, the popular singer Nat "King" Cole had his own variety show, but otherwise, blacks had few opportunities on television before 1965.

In that year, stand-up comedian Bill Cosby broke ground as the first realistically portrayed lead character on television, costarring in the show *I Spy*. Three years later, he was followed by Diahann Carroll as the title character in *Julia*. During the early 1970s black comedians such as Godfrey Cambridge, Nipsey Russell, and Moms Mabley began to make appearances on television, and Flip Wilson hosted a popular variety show.

The most influential black comedian of the era (and one of the most influential comedians of all time) had limited opportunity on the small screen. Richard Pryor was born in a brothel in Peoria, Illinois, the son of a prostitute mother and pimp father. After his mother deserted him at age 10, he was raised by his grandmother. Expelled from school at 14, he joined the army at 18 but spent most of his tour of duty in army prison for participating in the nonfatal stabbing of a white soldier.

By 1963, Pryor had made his way to the nightclub stages of New York, where he found himself opening for performers like Bob Dylan and Woody Allen. At this stage of his career, Pryor modeled his then noncontroversial act on that of Bill Cosby. Soon he was landing prestigious TV gigs on *The Tonight Show* and *The Ed Sullivan Show* and appearing regularly in Las Vegas. That stage of Pryor's career came to an abrupt end one night in Las Vegas, when he walked up to the microphone, peered out at the sold-out, celebrity-studded audience and said, "What the #$%$ am I doing here?" before walking off.

From then on, Pryor began working more profanity into his act, using the word "nigger" and directly commenting on race relations in his act. No longer welcome in front of the television camera, he found work writing for Flip Wilson's and other shows, while also releasing a string of hugely popular comedy albums. By the mid-1970s, Pryor had also begun a highly successful film career. Although he struggled with drugs and alcohol (and suffered major burns while smoking cocaine), Pryor cemented his status as an outspoken comedic legend long before his death in 2005.

Richard Pryor used his biting comedy to highlight the uncomfortable truth of racism in America—all the while gaining millions of fans of all races. If popular culture is a product of a society's values and mores, Pryor's success illustrates just how far the nation had come since World War II.

In the 1940s and 1950s, African Americans had quietly disproved stereotypes by their remarkable achievements. Some prominent individuals allowed their

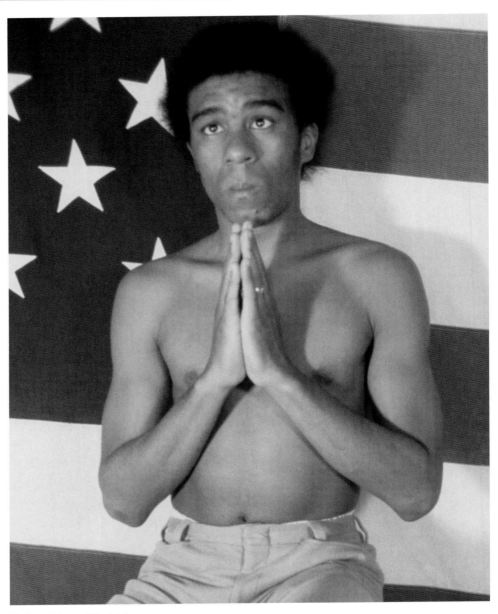

Richard Pryor (Corbis)

considerable talents to speak for themselves. Millions of others discredited hypocritical laws and sought social acceptance and integrations using passive resistance, as advocated by Dr. King and others.

But in the 1960s and early 1970s, another, vastly different style of public life became possible. Leaders like Malcolm X and organizations such as Nation of Islam were arguing that blacks should reject America's unequal society and establish separateness on their own terms. In this spirit, black writers of the day expressed their growing impatience, and a more prosperous, more empowered African-American population supported them. African-American figures could openly comment on their society and its politics—in Richard Pryor's case, even capitalizing on outspoken criticism—and maintain successful and lucrative careers.

Like other Americans, blacks of the civil rights era sought a better life. And like other Americans, they identified many paths to this goal and disagreed, often along generational lines, on the best approach. Despite these disagreements, one thing is certain: Because of the civil rights struggle of the mid-20th century, more African Americans have been able to achieve better lives.

BACKLASH AND RETRENCHMENT
The Post–Civil Rights Era

There is no better proof that history often repeats itself than the story of American race relations in the second halves of the 19th and 20th centuries. In the Reconstruction era, the federal government passed and enforced a wide range of new laws intended to make American society more racially egalitarian and just. Similarly, the civil rights protests of the late 20th century produced a host of new laws that ended legalized segregation and eliminated restrictions on the right to vote.

Both periods, however, were followed by decades of social and political retreat: African Americans' white allies began to lose interest in or grow hostile to new demands for justice and equality. This political falling out was followed by judicial retreat. In the late 19th century, the Supreme Court authored a series of rulings that undermined federal enforcement of civil rights laws and legitimated segregation. In the late 20th century, the courts stepped in to invalidate affirmative action laws designed to assure minorities equal representation in many of the nation's institutions. As Justice Thurgood Marshall put it in 1989, the country's conservative courts were conducting a "deliberate retrenching of the civil rights agenda."

One result of the country's failure to live up to the ideals of the civil rights era was continued racial conflict in the mid-1970s through the mid-1990s, the hostility stemming from both black frustration and nonblack racism. But the circumstances did not stop the progression of black influence. African-American politicians gradually took office in nearly the full spectrum of American political life. At the close of the millennium, cultural critics

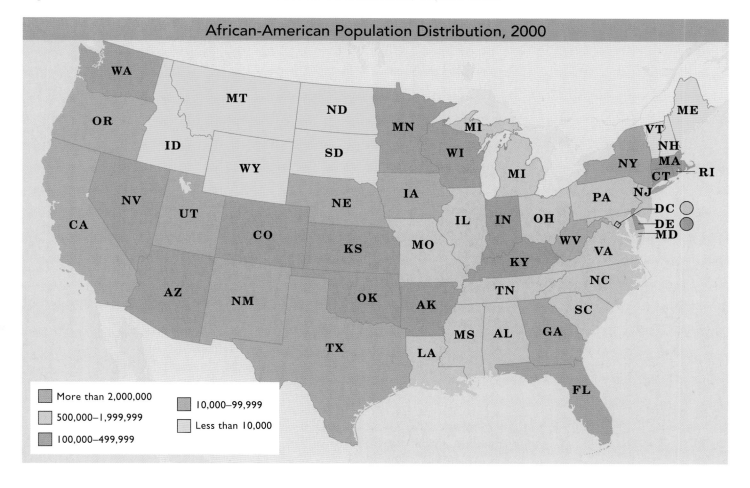

African-American Population Distribution, 2000

Legend:
- More than 2,000,000
- 500,000–1,999,999
- 100,000–499,999
- 10,000–99,999
- Less than 10,000

were arguing about the "authenticity" of representations of black experience, but unarguably, African-American creative artists occupied a prime cultural place.

DESEGREGATION, AFFIRMATIVE ACTION, AND WHITE BACKLASH

The 1970s owed much to the legacy of 1968, a year that was critical in the history of U.S. racial relations. In April, Martin Luther King Jr. had been assassinated, leading to riots in cities across the country. Two months later, Senator Robert Kennedy—a Democratic aspirant for the presidency and one of the few national figures who appealed to both white and black voters—was also gunned down. Meanwhile gaining ground in the democratic presidential contest was Alabama's segregationist governor George Wallace, whose calls for "law and order" were seen by many as a barely concealed appeal to white racism. Wallace did not win the nomination, but his impact on U.S politics and race relations would be felt for decades to come.

With the Democrats in disarray over the Vietnam War, Republican presidential candidate Richard Nixon narrowly defeated Vice President Hubert Humphrey, the Democratic nominee. Adopting a page from Wallace's political playbook, Nixon made "law and order" the centerpiece of his campaign. Realizing that he had little chance of winning black and white liberal voters, Nixon openly appealed to what he called "the silent majority"—white suburban voters frustrated with the perceived breakdown in social order caused, in their minds, by hippies, antiwar protesters, and black radical activists. This strategy succeeded, and Nixon won the presidency. In this increasingly conservative social and political climate, the country began to scale back its formerly ambitious plans for desegregation and affirmative action.

School Desegregation and Busing in the 1970s

President Nixon had no interest in furthering the civil rights agenda advanced by his Democratic predecessors Kennedy and Johnson. Indeed, internal memos within the Nixon White House that were leaked to the press in 1971 used the term "benign neglect" to describe the administration's approach to African Americans generally and to civil rights specifically. All manner of social programs launched by Johnson to fight poverty had their budgets cut. Nixon also moved to put more conservative judges on the nation's courts, though his first attempt to do so on the Supreme Court backfired: It was revealed that one of his appointees—G. Harrold Carswell—had worked to prevent the integration of a golf course in Florida. In the end, though, Nixon's succeeded in moving the court to the right, and his appointees—particularly Chief Justice William Rehnquist—were generally hostile to expanding the federal government's role in the enforcement of civil rights. This policy would accelerate during the Republican administrations of Ronald Reagan and George Bush during the 1980s and early 1990s.

Still, most of the federal courts remained in the hands of pro–civil rights liberals throughout the Nixon administration. Allied with liberal congressmen and leaders of the civil rights movement, many of these judges saw equality in education as the most pressing priority in the fight for equal opportunity for all over the long term. Thus, many liberals were particularly frustrated at the glacial pace in which local and state governments moved to implement the *Brown v. Board of Education* decision of 1954—which called for integration of the nation's schools "with all deliberate speed." Out of this frustration, pro–civil rights judges began to force the issue. In 1971, a federal judge ordered the Charlotte-Mecklenburg school district in North Carolina to desegregate by means of busing children. Specifically, children in predominantly or all-black schools would be bused out of their neighborhoods to predominantly or all-white schools in other parts of the district. A more radical plan to merge the predominantly black inner-city and predominantly white suburban school districts into one unit, however, was rejected by the court in 1974. Yet, in the same decision, the court upheld the ruling that largely racially segregated systems would have to use busing to integrate their schools.

Ironically, one such system was Boston. The center of antislave and

Cities with Failed Desegregation Policies Since 1994

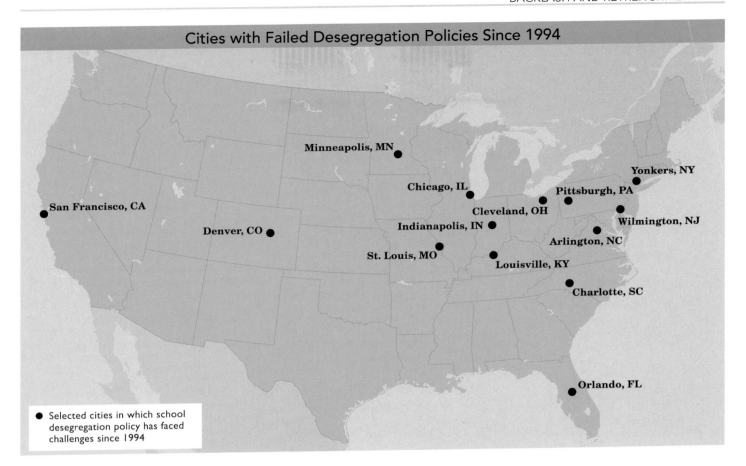

Minneapolis, MN

Yonkers, NY

San Francisco, CA

Chicago, IL

Pittsburgh, PA

Cleveland, OH

Denver, CO

Indianapolis, IN

Wilmington, NJ

Arlington, NC

St. Louis, MO

Louisville, KY

Charlotte, SC

Orlando, FL

● Selected cities in which school desegregation policy has faced challenges since 1994

abolitionist sentiment before the Civil War and one of the most liberal cities in America, Boston was—and continues to be—among the most segregated. Beginning in the 1960s, black civil rights activists and their white allies had moved to integrate the city's schools. In 1965, the state legislature passed the Massachusetts Racial Imbalance Act to do just that. Then, in the late 1960s and early 1970s, integrationist forces developed plans for "magnet" schools, or schools with extra funding and services designed to draw white and black students from around the city. There was even talk of forming a single district, uniting white suburban and black urban schools. But all of these plans met with resistance, particularly from the residents of Irish-American working class enclave of South Boston. In 1974, in the face of this resistance, Judge Arthur Garrity ordered that students from the predominantly black neighborhood of Roxbury be bused to South Boston High School. Meant only as a temporary measure, the order was bitterly resented by South Boston residents.

In scenes reminiscent of the integration of Little Rock, Arkansas's Central High School in 1957, the first black students at South Boston High in the fall of

1974 were greeted by whites shouting racial obscenities and throwing rotten eggs and stones. Only the presence of hundreds of riot police prevented angry mobs from attacking the students and destroying the buses. (In Michigan around the same time, school buses used for integration were indeed torched by whites.) And although integration occurred at South Boston High, tensions remained high for years. As Phyllis Ellison, one of the first blacks at the school recalled, "the black students sat on one side of the classes. The white students sat on the other side. . . . In the lunchrooms, the black students sat on one side. The white students sat on the other. . . . If the blacks wanted to play basketball, the whites wanted to play volleyball. So we never played together."

Ellison's observations reflected the fundamental obstacle to integration in post–civil rights era America. Although it had taken a great struggle and cost the lives of dozens of courageous black (and white) citizens, ending legal segregation and discrimination had been relatively straightforward. The Constitution was clear on the matter and the power of the federal government eventually trumped

MAJOR DESEGREGATION COURT CASES, 1954–1995

Year	Case	Ruling
1954	Brown v. Board of Education	Outlawed school segregation and declared racially separate schools inherently unequal.
1971	Swann v. Charlotte-Mecklenburg Board of Education	Held that federal courts could order that students be bused from one neighborhood to another in order to desegregate Mecklenburg schools. At the same time, the court ruled that once legally enforced segregation was eliminated, single-race schools were permitted, as long as agencies of the government had not deliberately resegregated them.
1974	Millikin v. Bradley	After a federal court order that the city of Detroit would have to integrate its schools with 53 surrounding districts, the Supreme Court overturned the decision, stating that suburban districts could not be ordered to desegregate a city's schools unless those suburbs had been involved in illegally segregating them in the first place. In his dissenting opinion, Justice Thurgood Marshall, who had successfully argued the Brown v. Board of Education case 20 years earlier, argued that the ruling would permit "our great metropolitan areas to be divided up each into two cities—one black and one white."
1990	Board of Education of Oklahoma City v. Dowell	Declared that a school district may be declared "unitary," or be freed from court supervision, once it eliminates the vestiges of segregation "to the extent practicable."
1992	Freeman v. Pitts	Stated that districts can be declared "unitary" "before full compliance has been achieved in every area of school operations." To do so, a district must demonstrate a "good faith commitment" to the desegregation program.
1995	Missouri v. Jenkins	The Supreme Court overturned the decision of a federal judge who ordered the Kansas City, Missouri School District to create a system of "magnet schools" to attract white suburban students to inner-city schools.

This cartoon pokes fun at President Richard Nixon, who occupied the White House when the implementation of federally mandated busing began. (Library of Congress)

the resistance of racist state governments. Yet it was one thing to force the integration of schools where students were kept apart by law; it was quite another to integrate schools and neighborhoods where segregation resulted from settlement patterns that had emerged over generations. In the end, court-ordered busing solved little in Boston, as many white parents pulled their children out of the schools and put them into largely segregated religious or private ones, thereby reinforcing segregation in the city's schools. By the late 1970s, an increasingly conservative federal court system backed away from busing as a means to integrate the nation's schools.

Ultimately, the failure of busing pointed out the profound difficulties of trying to undo centuries of racism and discrimination through laws and court orders. Once overtly racist legislation was eliminated from the nation's law books,

the far more difficult—but just as morally and constitutionally necessary—task of redressing historically racist patterns in housing, college enrollment, business, and employment began. The method employed by the government to do this was called "affirmative action." And while it did not meet with the same violent resistance as busing did, it nevertheless was resented by many whites.

THE AFFIRMATIVE ACTION DEBATE

Throughout the 1950s and early 1960s, civil rights leaders had emphasized that their goal for America was a "color-blind" society or, to put it in King's mellifluous phrasing, a nation where a person would "not be judged by the color of their skin but by the content of their character." Nonetheless, by the mid-1960s, King and other civil rights leaders had come to recognize that centuries of racist attitudes and discriminatory practices could not be undone as easily as all that. As President Johnson noted in 1965, "[y]ou do not take a person who for years has been hobbled by chains and . . . bring him up to the starting line of a race and then say, 'you are free to compete with all the others' and still justly believe that you have been completely fair." As early as 1969, the Nixon administration—though not normally associated with civil rights initiatives—instituted the first federal affirmative action program. Called the Philadelphia Plan, it required companies seeking federal contracts to develop goals for hiring minority employees.

In 1971, the Supreme Court—still largely liberal—ruled that Title VII of the 1964 Civil Rights Act—which banned discrimination in employment and public accommodations—also outlawed "practices that are fair in [legal] form but discriminatory in operation." The court that even if a predominantly white business had violated no laws in its hiring practices, it could still be found guilty of discrimination. Thus, to avoid discrimination lawsuits, that same business should redress past hiring practices by specifically seeking out minority applicants. (In 1972, Title VII was expanded to educational institutions as well.)

For all its noble intentions, however, affirmative action was problematic in practice. It raised legal and constitutional problems because programs or policies that favored blacks at the expense of whites would not pass constitutional muster. The courts, then, were forced to deal with a thicket of complicated legal cases arising from affirmative action. During the 1970s, the Supreme Court generally ruled in favor of affirmative action, but only on very narrow grounds. In the 1979 *United Steelworkers v. Weber* decision, the court permitted the continuation of a training program that gave preference to minorities so long as it remained short-term and voluntary. But when it came to quotas—that is, the establishment of numerical goals for minority hiring or enrollment—the Court was less agreeable. In the landmark 1978 *Regents of the University of California v. Bakke* ruling, the Court decided that a quota system that set aside a certain number of places for minority students at the

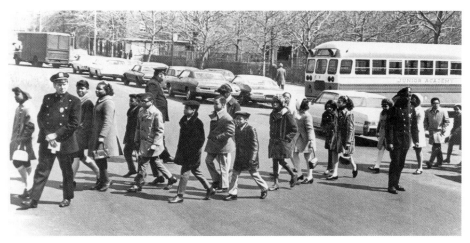

Policemen escort African-American children off a bus into school. (Library of Congress)

University of California at Davis School of Medicine was unconstitutional in principle and discriminatory in practice against white applicants.

As conservative justices appointed by Republican presidents Ronald Reagan and George Bush began to take their place on the Court's bench during the 1980s and early 1990s, rulings further limited the use of affirmative action. In the 1986 *Wygant v. Jackson Board of Education* ruling, the court threw out a plan that protected minority teachers from layoffs at the expense of white teachers with more seniority. Then, in 1989, the Court ruled that local governments do not have the power to create "set-asides," or quotas, for minority businesses competing for government contracts. Six years later, the justices ruled that even federally mandated "set-asides"—in this case, a law that required 10 percent of contracts on federal highway construction projects be reserved for businesses owned by "socially and economically disadvantaged individuals"—were unconstitutional unless they were "narrowly tailored" to serve a "compelling government interest."

Proponents of affirmative action faced more than just legal and constitutional hurdles. They faced major political opposition as well. While many whites could appreciate the principles upon which affirmative action was based—and even support them in the abstract—affirmative action in practice rubbed many people the wrong way. First, it seemed to be a case of "two wrongs not making a right." If redressing past discrimination against blacks meant present discrimination against whites, then most whites were against it. This became obvious during the 1980s, when downsizing corporations and governments laid off millions of workers. As it became more difficult to find employment, many whites came to believe—despite the evidence of much higher unemployment rates among minority workers—that they faced discrimination because of affirmative action. Second, affirmative action seemed to violate the principle of equality before the law upon which the country had been founded. Although, as many African Americans pointed out, whites—who had not only tolerated racial inequality for centuries but positively benefited from it—only raised a ruckus about equal rights when they felt their own rights were being threatened.

Still, whites dominated the political process and no politician could effectively ignore their rising sense of resent-

ment. In 1995, the regents of the University of California voted to end all affirmative action programs in hiring and employment. A year later, a federal district court ordered the same thing in Texas. Defenders of affirmative action found little solace in the fact that their direst warnings—that black and Hispanic enrollment in the two state university systems would drop precipitously—proved correct. Meanwhile, California governor Pete Wilson—who had pressured the regents in their decision—worked to expand his crusade against affirmative action statewide. In 1996, he helped sponsor Proposition 209, a successful ballot referendum that put a stop to all state-sponsored affirmative action programs. According to a July 2006 study in the Journal of Blacks in Higher Education, the black percentage of all

KEY MOMENTS IN THE AFFIRMATIVE ACTION DEBATE

First Year Enrollments of African-American Students at the University of Texas School of Law

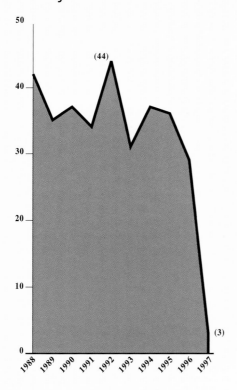

Source: University of Texas

The *Bakke* Decision (1978)
In 1978, Allan Bakke, a white applicant to the University of California at Davis School of Medicine, was denied admission due to the school's affirmative action policy. He sued on the grounds that his outstanding academic record was ignored through "reverse discrimination." In 1978, the U.S. Supreme Court ruled in his favor and ordered the university to enroll him.

Proposition 209 (1996)
This California law prohibits the state, local governments, districts, public universities, colleges, and schools from giving preferential treatment to any individual or group in public employment, public education, or public contracting on the basis of race, sex, color, ethnicity, or national origin.

The *Hopwood* Ruling (1996)
In this decision, the Fifth Circuit Court of Appeals forbade the University of Texas from accounting for race in law school admissions. As more graduate programs enforced race-neutral admissions policies, the number of African-American enrollees declined.

Grutter v. Bollinger (2003)
In this decision, the Supreme Court upheld the constitutionality of the University of Michigan law school's admission policy, a process designed to create a diverse student body that considered race as only one of several factors. But in the related *Gratz v. Bollinger* decision, the Court declared the university's undergraduate admission policy unconstitutional on the grounds that it was not narrowly defined.

new faculty hires at Berkeley and UCLA—the two most prestigious schools in the state's system—dropped dramatically between 1996 and 2005.

California was not alone in challenging the policy. In 1998, Washington State voters overwhelmingly passed Initiative 200, which prohibited all local governments from granting "preferential treatment" based on race, sex, color, ethnicity, or national origin in public employment, education, or in awarding government contracts. In 2003, the Washington State Supreme Court interpreted Initiative 200 to mean that it forbid affirmative action programs that promoted a "less qualified" applicant over a "more qualified" applicant. At the same time, the Washington court maintained the constitutionality of laws that aimed to promote diversity without considering individual merit. Programs established to achieve greater diversity persist, even in states that, like Washington, have passed anti–affirmative action laws.

In the late 1990s, supporters of affirmative action feared that developments in California and Washington presaged a nationwide move to repeal all affirmative action laws. But this turned out not to be the case. Between 1996 and 2000, legislatures in at least 13 states voted down or refused to act on bills modeled after California's Proposition 209, while in Houston the voters themselves rejected a 209-like proposal in a referendum. At the federal level, President Bill Clinton reiterated his support for affirmative action in principle by adopting Jesse Jackson's slogan "mend it, don't end it."

The affirmative action debate continued into the presidency of George W. Bush. In 2003, an important new challenge to the practice reached the Supreme Court—the first such case the Court had agreed to hear since *Bakke* in 1978. The case, *Grutter v. Bollinger*, involved admission policies at the University of Michigan Law School, which considered race as part of an student's overall application in order to improve diversity. The Bush administration supported an alternative plan—a type sometimes called a percentage plan—in which all applicants who graduated near the top of their respective classes would be admitted to state universities, regardless of the quality of the schools they graduated from. Such plans were already in place in California, Texas,

and Florida. The Court, however, upheld the law school's narrowly defined practice of affirmative action in *Grutter v. Bollinger*.

Despite this outcome, affirmative action remains open to legal challenge because the Constitution bans even indirect racial discrimination. Ignoring race is an unsatisfactory way to promote diversity, however. According to Harvard Law professor Lawrence Tribe, "If one tries to do it under the table, that has all the vices and none of the virtues of a candid acknowledgment that in our society race still matters." Clearly, the use of affirmative action to legislate equal opportunity is an issue that will continue to divide Americans.

THE STATE OF BLACK EDUCATION

School desegregation, busing, and affirmative action are issues that focus not so much on what happens in the classrooms as on the various means of opening the schoolhouse door for all. But the end result of such efforts—increased diversity—is not a signifier of academic success in and of itself. On the contrary, America's increasingly diverse cultural, ethnic, linguistic, and socioeconomic school-age population has only increased the number of challenges faced every day by the nation's teachers.

Particularly in America's inner cities, elementary and high school classes often include students from households with just one parent, or in poverty, or where English is spoken as a second language or not at all. Traditionally, students who fall into one or more of these categories are labeled "at risk." Since the 1960s, a so-called compensatory education movement has worked to provide at-risk students with extra help to "compensate" for these disadvantages.

One way of compensating for disadvantages is by placing students into classes or other academic groupings according to their abilities, talents, or prior academic records. For example, a 12-year-old who can compose a fluidly written, coherently argued essay would be placed in a more advanced group than a 12-year-old who struggles with basic sentence structure. Some of these groups are temporary and change throughout the school year. In other cases, these

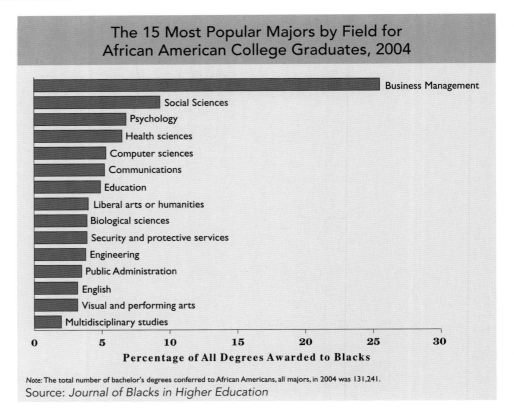

The 15 Most Popular Majors by Field for African American College Graduates, 2004

Business Management
Social Sciences
Psychology
Health sciences
Computer sciences
Communications
Education
Liberal arts or humanities
Biological sciences
Security and protective services
Engineering
Public Administration
English
Visual and performing arts
Multidisciplinary studies

0   5   10   15   20   25   30

Percentage of All Degrees Awarded to Blacks

Note: The total number of bachelor's degrees conferred to African Americans, all majors, in 2004 was 131,241.

Source: *Journal of Blacks in Higher Education*

groups can become almost permanent. This broader use of academic grouping is known as tracking.

Tracking is most common in high schools, where some students are placed in a rigorous college-preparatory track while others are assigned to vocational tracks with the more limited aim of workplace readiness. Proponents of tracking argue that grouping students by ability allows teachers to better serve the needs of individual children. According to child psychologist Richard Slavin, when children of differing abilities are in one mixed group, teachers have difficulty maintaining a environment that permits everyone to learn. If slower learners are removed from a class, the remaining students are free to learn at their own faster pace, and these advanced students then tend to do even better academically.

But critics point out that tracking is not so beneficial to lower-level students. Grouped with other low-achieving students, they tend not to improve and generally have a less positive attitude about school. When students with perceived lower abilities are placed into a lower track, they tend to remain there for all subject areas, especially once they reach high school. This is a particular risk for black and other minority students. According to data from the Department

of Education's Office of Civil Rights, black and Latino students are only half as likely as whites to be placed in gifted and talented classes.

Statistics suggest that this discrepancy reflects the quality of education in inner-city public schools. According to the National Center for Education Statistics (part of the U.S. Department of Education), schools with the highest percentage of minority, low-income, and limited-English-proficiency students are more likely to employ beginning teachers than other schools. In addition, teachers in high-poverty schools are less likely to have master's degrees and more likely to be teaching in subject areas outside their own major fields of study. In his 2002 book *All Talk No Action: Putting an End to Out-of-Field Teaching*, researcher Craig Jerald found that teachers in high-poverty schools were 77 percent more likely than other educators to teach subjects outside of their area of academic expertise. Similarly, teachers in majority-nonwhite schools were 40 percent more likely to be teaching outside of their subject area than teachers in majority-white schools.

Teachers in high-minority, high-poverty schools are also more likely to leave their schools. According to the Texas Center for Educational Research, the turnover rate at low-income, majority

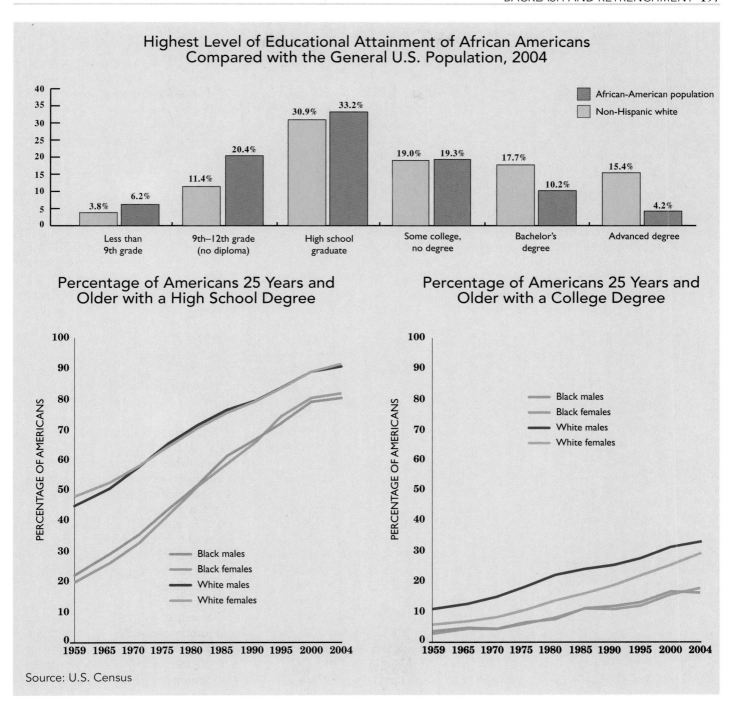

Highest Level of Educational Attainment of African Americans Compared with the General U.S. Population, 2004

- African-American population
- Non-Hispanic white

Less than 9th grade	9th–12th grade (no diploma)	High school graduate	Some college, no degree	Bachelor's degree	Advanced degree
3.8% / 6.2%	11.4% / 20.4%	30.9% / 33.2%	19.0% / 19.3%	17.7% / 10.2%	15.4% / 4.2%

Percentage of Americans 25 Years and Older with a High School Degree

- Black males
- Black females
- White males
- White females

Percentage of Americans 25 Years and Older with a College Degree

- Black males
- Black females
- White males
- White females

Source: U.S. Census

nonwhite schools is one third higher than the rate for all schools. The main reason for this high turnover is lack of resources, ranging from facilities, books, and supplies to administrative support and staff. Staff shortages result in larger class sizes. Moreover, studies show that the more minorities there are in a given classroom, the more likely the class is to be overcrowded. According to a 2003 report by the National Center for Education Statistics, a class with a 75 percent minority population is about 10 percent more likely to number more than 25 students than a class where less than 10 percent are minority students.

These facts highlight the need to address the quality of America's high-minority schools. Although public school reform is generally the province of local communities, the federal government has taken steps in recent years to address the situation.

In 2001, President George W. Bush signed the No Child Left Behind Act (NCLB), a law meant to improve the performance of the nation's elementary and high schools. Based on the idea that setting

MARIAN WRIGHT EDELMAN

A graduate of Spelman College and Yale Law School, Marian Wright Edelman was the first African-American woman to be admitted to the Mississippi Bar Association. She spent her early legal career in the cause of civil rights and worked for the NAACP Legal Defense Fund, the Poor People's March on Washington, and a number of other civil rights organizations. Her concern for economic issues, especially the poverty of black children, grew and in 1973 Edelman founded the Children's Defense Fund (CDF). CDF is one of the nation's leading child advocacy and research groups. The organization's motto is "Leave No Child Behind," and its mission is lobbying the federal and state governments on behalf of children.

In 2001, the CDF's signature public policy initiative, the Dodd-Miller Act to Leave No Child Behind, was introduced in Congress. The bill proposed a comprehensive suite of programs to combat child hunger and poverty, improve education, and provide health insurance and affordable child care for every child. Congress ultimately adopted the Bush administration's No Child Left Behind Act (2002) instead, which took its name from the CDF motto but differed significantly.

high expectations and goals will lead to success for all students, NCLB has increased national education standards for states, local school districts, and individual schools, and it promotes a greater emphasis on reading. It has also attempted to give parents of all races more ability to choose which schools their children will attend.

According to the U.S. Department of Education, the results have proven NCLB a success. The National Assessment of Education Progress, released in July 2005, reported that reading and math scores for African-American and Hispanic nine-year-olds had reached an all-time high, as had math scores for African-American and Hispanic-American 13-year-olds. According to the same report, 43 states and the District of Columbia either improved academically or held steady in all categories.

Critics, however, suggest that these test results are faulty. They note that the law's system of incentives and penalties creates a strong motive for schools to manipulate results. A number of schools have been shown to exclude the results of minority students and to use creative methods to reclassify student dropouts so as to improve the school's statistical success rate.

Whatever impact NCLB is having, African Americans have made steady educational progress that began long before the law was instituted. For example, in 1980, just 51 percent of all African Americans over the age of 25 had a high school diploma, versus 72 percent of whites. By 1999, high school graduation rates were 77 percent for blacks versus 87 percent for whites, meaning that African Americans had cut the gap in half. By 2004, the rates were 81 percent for blacks versus 91 percent for whites. This remaining gap is expected to shrink further in coming years, because the highest percentage of African Americans without a high school diploma are those over the age of 50.

College graduation rates show similar gains. While just 8 percent of blacks over the age of 25 had college diplomas in 1980, that figure had increased to 15 percent by 1999 and 18 percent by 2004. For the white population, the figures were 18 percent in 1980, 28 percent in 1999, and 31 percent by 2004. In other words, the black college graduation rate was less than half that of whites in 1980 but was approaching 60 percent by 1999.

Of course, income—as well as race—helps determine who goes to college. One of the main explanations for the relatively low black college graduation rate is that blacks have less money to pay for college. According to the U.S. Department of Education, more than two thirds of all blacks who dropped out of college did so for financial reasons. In 2004, nearly 57 percent of all black undergraduates came from families that had incomes under $40,000. For whites, the figure was just 24 percent.

In the final decades of the 20th century, Americans' commitment to the civil rights agenda waned. Consequently, U.S. efforts to provide both equal access to education and equal quality of education for minorities were gradually scaled back. As indicated by the history of school desegregation, busing, affirmative action, and NCLB, these more modest efforts to extend the benefits of a quality education to all have met with mixed success.

THE RISE OF BLACK OFFICEHOLDERS

While African Americans continued to lag behind whites in educational attainment and economic success in the late 20th century, they made tremendous strides in the political arena. These are even more visible when one takes a longer view of black progress in American history.

One difference between the Reconstruction and 20th-century civil rights era concerns black political power. While Reconstruction represented a temporary high water mark in the number of black officeholders, the civil rights era led to few immediate election wins for blacks. It has, however, spawned a substantial and permanent African-American presence in local, state, and national government. Most of the nation's major cities are or have been run by black mayors; blacks are represented in every legislature of every state where there is a significant black presence; the number of African Americans in Congress approaches the proportion of blacks in the national electorate; and numerous appointive offices—including cabinet positions—have been awarded to African Americans in the administrations of both Democratic and, to a lesser extent, Republican presidents.

For all of this success, there are limitations. The fact that very few blacks have been elected to high statewide office—notably governor or senator—indicates that many whites remain reluctant to vote for a black candidate. Moreover, in recent decisions, the Supreme Court has ruled that the creation of districts designed for the purposes of creating black majorities cannot go too far in violating geographic conformity. For example, districts that cobble together two of a city's black neighborhoods while excluding a white neighborhood that lies between them might violate this ruling.

AFRICAN-AMERICAN MAYORS

Nowhere have African Americans made more gains in holding office than in the city halls of the nation's largest metropolises. Part of the explanation for this comes from the Great Migration. The vast majority of rural blacks who fled the South during the 20th century migrated to the large cities of the Northeast, Midwest, and Far West. Yet that alone cannot explain how African-American politicians have been elected to the mayoralty of cities with nonblack majorities such as New York, Chicago, and Los Angeles. In such ethnically polyglot cities, coalition-building is essential, and African-American politicians who have won the highest office have been masters at the give-and-take of urban politics.

Still, it was not until the civil rights movement of the 1960s that black politicians were taken seriously as contenders for city hall. The first breakthroughs came in the gritty industrial cities of the Midwest. In 1967, Richard Hatcher, a city councilman in Gary, Indiana, became the first black mayor of a major American city. He was followed later that year by Carl Stokes in Cleveland, Ohio. Stokes's term in office was short, just four years. Although he accomplished some basic improvements in city services, his mayoralty was plagued by conflicts between police and black nationalists.

In 1973, Coleman Young and Tom Bradley were elected mayors of Detroit and Los Angeles respectively. Both would serve in office through the early 1990s, but the two men were very different in temperament and style.

Young—a native of Tuscaloosa, Alabama, and a member of the Tuskegee airmen in World War II—had worked in the auto plants of his adopted city after the war and later helped found the National Negro Labor Council. Coming to office in the early 1970s, Young faced a city in serious decline. Riots six years earlier had destroyed downtown businesses and accelerated white flight, leaving the city's tax base depleted. Still, he helped keep the major auto manufacturers in the city and did much to integrate the police force and city government. Critics said Young was dictatorial and corrupt, and his abrasive style of speech alienated many white suburbanites and the city's media. But he was popular among the largely working-class citizens of Detroit, who reelected him four times, until ill health forced him to retire in 1993.

Bradley, the son of Texas sharecroppers, moved with his family to Los Angeles when he was seven. After attending UCLA, Bradley joined the Los Angeles Police Department. He served for 20 years and rose to the rank of lieutenant, then the highest LAPD position reached by an African American. After retirement, he entered politics and served 10 years as a councilman before being elected mayor on his second try. Unlike Detroit, Los Angeles was a predominantly white city at the time, and the largest minority was Mexican Americans. Although racial tensions were still sore eight years after the Watts riots, Los Angeles was emerging as a global city, a trend Bradley encouraged

Adam Clayton Powell Jr. (Library of Congress)

Marion Barry (courtesy Marion Barry)

Andrew Young (Library of Congress)

David Dinkins (Mayor's Office, New York City)

SELECTED AFRICAN-AMERICAN POLITICAL LEADERS, 1964–1996

John Conyers Jr. (1929–) In 1964 John Conyers Jr. ran for Congress on the platform of "Jobs, Justice, Peace." The Detroit Democrat was elected and for the next 38 years has made social justice and economic opportunity a priority. He is an active opponent of violence against women, has helped write the Hate Crimes Statistics Act, and is a strong advocate of health care reform. Conyers is an original cofounder of the Congressional Black Caucus.

Unita Blackwell (1933–) The daughter of Mississippi Delta sharecroppers, Unita Blackwell risked her safety as a field worker for the Student Nonviolent Coordinating Committee in the "Freedom Summer" of 1964. That year, she also served as a delegate of the Mississippi Freedom Democratic Party, which went to the Democratic National Convention in Atlantic City. During the late 1960s and early 1970s, Blackwell worked as a community development specialist with the National Council of Negro Women. In 1977, Blackwell was elected mayor of the town of Mayersville, Mississippi, becoming the first black woman in Mississippi history to serve as a mayor. After her election as mayor, she was invited to participate in President Carter's Energy Summit at Camp David. In 1992, she was awarded the prestigious MacArthur Foundation Fellowship.

Maxine Carr Waters (1938–) Maxine Waters was one of 13 children raised by a single mother in St. Louis, Missouri. By 1966 Waters lived in Los Angeles with two young children of her own barely surviving on low-paying jobs. That year she was hired by Head Start and her interest in politics and activism was born. In 1976 she was elected to the California State Assembly. Her success at passing important legislation such as preventing police from strip-searching people for a minor offense helped to get her elected to the House of Representatives in 1990.

Carol Moseley-Braun (1947–) Born, raised, and educated in Chicago, Carol Moseley-Braun served as assistant U.S. attorney after graduating from the University of Chicago Law School. She then became an Illinois state representative and a county executive. Angry about the manner in which the Senate handled the Anita Hill hearings in 1991, Moseley-Braun was inspired to run for the Senate herself to help facilitate change. Without much funding or support from fellow politicians, Carol Moseley-Braun was elected senator in 1992. Moseley-Braun lost in her reelection campaign against Senator Peter Fitzgerald. In 1999 she was appointed ambassador to New Zealand.

Kweisi Mfume (1948–) A Democrat born in Baltimore, Maryland, Kweisi Mfume was a civil rights activist and the recipient of many community awards. He served on the Baltimore Council of Foreign Affairs and in 1986 he was elected to Congress, representing the 7th Congressional District of Maryland for 10 years. While a member of Congress, Mfume served on the Banking and Financial Services Committee. In 1995 he was elected president of the NAACP. As president and CEO Mfume eliminated the NAACP's debt and helped inspire a new generation of civil rights leaders.

Alan Keyes (1950–) Alan Keyes was born in New York City and received a Ph.D. in government from Harvard University. Keyes served as U.S. ambassador to the United Nations Economic Council and also as the Reagan administration's assistant secretary of state for international organizations. Keyes was twice the Republican nominee to the U.S. Senate for the state of Maryland. In 1996 and 2000 he campaigned as the Republican candidate for president in the primaries. In addition to his accomplishments as a politician he is an acclaimed writer, public speaker, and media personality.

through his conservative, pro-business policies. Though he saw himself as a builder and a racial healer, Bradley presided over the most violent and destructive episode in the city's history, the massive 1992 rioting that followed the acquittal of the four policemen accused of beating black motorist Rodney King. Later that year, Bradley announced that he would not run for a sixth term.

Another long-serving black mayor—Marion Barry of Washington, D.C.—had a far more checkered career than his counterparts in Detroit and Los Angeles. Born poor in the rural South, Barry was the first in his family to attend college. He went on to become an activist in various civil rights organizations, helping to stage nonviolent sit-ins at segregated Nashville restaurants. In 1965, Barry moved to the nation's capital where he organized youth groups and a political coalition trying to win home rule for the district, which was largely run by Congress at the time. In 1974, he was elected to the city council and then ran successfully for mayor in 1978, winning with support from many of the city's liberal whites. Barry proved a poor administrator, however, and the city soon found itself in a fiscal crisis. Yet it was his personal shortcomings that led to his downfall. Caught in 1990 smoking crack cocaine by FBI cameras, Barry was removed from office and sent to jail. Upon his release from jail six months later, he began a remarkable political comeback, winning a seat on the city council and then the mayoralty once again in 1994, claiming he had experienced religious redemption. But a fiscal crisis led Congress to reassert its control over the city's budget and the voters to turn him out of office.

Although serving far shorter terms in office, mayors Harold Washington of Chicago and David Dinkins of New York City also had significant impacts on their cities. A longtime Democratic politician, Washington had served in the Illinois legislature and the U.S. Congress before winning the mayor's office in 1983. Left-leaning and blunt-spoken, Washington moved to diversify city government and city contracting, bringing many women and minorities into his governing coalition. A successful politician with a bright future ahead of him, Washington's life was cut short in 1987 by a fatal heart

attack. David Dinkins, a longtime Democratic politician in city government, was elected mayor of the nation's largest city in 1989. A civil and dignified man, Dinkins was accused of indecision and mismanagement, especially when he failed to respond to racial flare-ups. He was defeated after just one term in 1993.

Following the defeats or retirements of Young, Bradley, Barry, and Dinkins, most of the nation's cities were once again governed by white mayors during the rest of the decade. However, a new generation of black mayors has arrived in northeastern and southern cities from Newark to New Orleans. Among them are John Street of Philadelphia, Shirley Franklin of Atlanta, and Kwame Kilpatrick of Detroit.

AFRICAN AMERICANS IN CONGRESS

Throughout most of its history, the U.S. Congress has been largely a white man's institution. Of the 11,000 representatives who have served there since 1789, fewer than 100 have been African American. Their history has often been divided into two waves. The first occurred during and after Reconstruction, when some 22 African Americans—20 congressmen and two senators—represented southern states with large black constituencies. With the fall of Reconstruction in 1877, black membership in Congress dwindled to a handful, with the last representative— George White of North Carolina—leaving office in 1901.

From that year until 1929, when Republican Oscar DePriest of Chicago was elected, not a single African American served in the U.S. Congress, even though black Americans represented some 12 percent of the total U.S. population.

The second wave of African-American congressional representation was different from the first in a number of ways. First, unlike the sudden burst of black political power during Reconstruction, it took several decades for black representatives to establish themselves as a significant presence in Congress. Second, Oscar DePriest notwithstanding, most black congressional representatives in the 20th century have been members of the Democratic party. And third, African-American congressional representation

began in northern urban rather southern rural districts.

Of the black representatives from the pre–civil rights era, the most important and best known was Adam Clayton Powell Jr. of New York City's Harlem. The son of a well-known local minister, Powell served on the New York City Council before assuming his seat in Congress in 1945. An outspoken critic of racial segregation and discrimination, he became the first African American to chair a major congressional committee— Education and Labor—and was instrumental in the passage of the Medicaid, Medicare, and Head Start programs of the 1960s. Plagued by scandal in 1967, however, Powell was denied his seat by an act of Congress. Although he won it back on an appeal to the Supreme Court, he was badly weakened politically and in 1970 lost his seat to Charles Rangel, who remains Harlem's congressional representative to this day.

In the wake of the civil rights movement—and the Voting Rights Act of 1965—black representation in Congress increased significantly and spread to southern states. (At the same time, the three black senators of the late 20th and early 21st centuries—Republican Edward Brooke of Massachusetts and Democrats Carol Mosely-Braun and Barack Obama, both of Illinois—came from urban-dominated northern states.) In addition, the early 1970s witnessed the arrival of the first black women representatives in Congress. First came Brooklyn's Shirley Chisholm, followed by Barbara Jordan of Houston, Texas, and Yvonne Burke of Los Angeles, all Democrats.

In 1971, the 13 African-American representatives in Congress established the Congressional Black Caucus (CBC). With its motto "Black People have no permanent friends, no permanent enemies, just permanent interests," the CBC set itself several missions: to push for more black representation in Congress, to fight for more power for black representatives in Congress, and to sponsor and support legislation of importance to African Americans generally. Denounced by black conservatives as too liberal and by white liberals as racially divisive, the CBC immediately gained a name for itself by presenting the Nixon administration with a list of 60 foreign and domestic policy recommendations. At the National

Edward Brooke (Library of Congress)

Shirley Chisholm (Library of Congress)

Barbara Jordan (Library of Congress)

Jessie Jackson (Rainbow Coalition)

Black Political Convention in 1972, the CBC issued the Black Declaration of Independence, calling on the Democratic Party to work for complete racial equality. In 1977, the CBC formed TransAfrica, an organization lobbying on behalf of African countries. In the 1980s, TransAfrica served a critical role in winning sanctions against the apartheid regime in South Africa. Although divided over many issues, the CBC—with 43 members in 2006—is now recognized as one of the most influential caucuses within the Congress.

PRESIDENTIAL CAMPAIGNS OF JESSE JACKSON

While black mayors have made their mark on municipal government and the Congressional Black Caucus has represented a consistent voice for predominantly black constituencies around the country, no individual has done more to raise awareness of black issues on a national level than Jesse Jackson, an achievement made even more remarkable by the fact that this minister and civil rights activist has never won elective office. Born to a teenage single mother in South Carolina in 1941, Jackson graduated from the historically black North Carolina Agricultural and Technical State College and then from the Chicago Theological Seminary. In 1965, Jackson took part in the historical civil rights march in Selma, Alabama, an event he says changed his life. He became active in the Southern Christian Leadership Conference, and after King's assassination in 1968, which Jackson witnessed, he formed Operation PUSH (People United to Serve Humanity) to empower blacks economically.

Still, Jackson is best known for his presidential campaigns. In 1983, he announced his candidacy for the Democratic nomination. Pledging to build a "rainbow coalition" of all races and ethnic groups in America, Jackson ran on a progressive platform that criticized both Republicans and mainstream Democrats for their unwillingness to seriously tackle the problems of poverty, racism, and corporate economic dominance. Although he won many black votes and far more white votes than expected, Jackson faced a barrage of criticism after he made an anti-Semitic remark about New York City. A

gifted orator and wordsmith, Jackson—who failed to win the nomination—moved and electrified the delegates at the 1984 Democratic convention with his call to "keep hope alive."

Two years later, he formed the National Rainbow Coalition, both as a vehicle for promoting progressive politics and for his second presidential run in 1988. Once again, Jackson demonstrated a remarkable ability to motivate poor and minority voters that were alienated from the political process and win large blocks of delegates. Nonetheless, he ultimately lost the Democratic nomination to Michael Dukakis, the governor of Massachusetts. Since 1988, Jackson has continued efforts to increase minority hiring by corporations, to inspire African-American parents to take a more active role in their children's education, and to achieve statehood for Washington, D.C. He has also led unofficial diplomatic missions to win the release of American prisoners abroad and to settle conflicts in West Africa. In 2000, President Bill Clinton awarded Jackson the Presidential Medal of Freedom, the nation's highest civilian honor. His son, Jesse Jackson Jr., won election to the U.S. House of Representatives in 1994.

BLACK CONSERVATIVES

No constituency in America has been more consistently liberal in its political ideology than African Americans, who regularly vote for Democratic Party candidates by margins of five or even ten to one. Since the Reagan era of the 1980s, however, a new and more conservative—if still politically marginal—voice has emerged in black America. It criticizes the affirmative action demands of the mainstream civil rights establishment and has called for the end of a host of government programs—such as welfare and low-income housing—that disproportionately benefit minority citizens. Specifically, these black conservatives say that affirmative action not only runs counter to U.S. principles of equality before the law but stigmatizes blacks because whites will assume they got their place in college or their job through racial favoritism rather than intelligence, hard work, or skill. Like their white counterparts, black conservatives have attacked welfare programs as encouraging dependency and penalizing marriage. (Under pre-1996 welfare reform law, only single women with children could receive aid from the government.)

Their critics, however, point to the many contradictions in black conservatism. Some charge black conservatives with hypocrisy. Having benefited from affirmative action programs, critics say, the conservatives want to end them now that they themselves have become successful. Others claim that black conservatives are largely a creation of the Republican Party and conservative media groups, looking to dispel charges of racism and prejudice by bringing in blacks. Whatever the case, black conservatives have achieved a level of recognition that is hard to ignore, even if their views are more likely to appeal to white rather than black America.

Black conservatives of the late 20th century ran the gamut of public and private life and included intellectuals such as Stanley Crouch, radio talk show hosts such as Ken Hamblin, and politicians like Republican Oklahoma congressman J. C. Watts. Two of the most prominent and influential black conservatives in America of the 1990s—Clarence Thomas and Ward Connerly—are in neither media nor elected office. Thomas is an associate justice on the Supreme Court, and Connerly is a California businessman who in the 1990s led the movement to end affirmative action.

Thomas was born in rural Georgia in 1948 and raised by his grandparents. A graduate of Holy Cross College and Yale University Law School, Thomas developed increasingly anti–affirmative action views, which caught the attention of the incoming Reagan administration in the 1980s. He was appointed to head the Equal Employment Opportunity Commission (EEOC). President Bush appointed Thomas to the U.S. Circuit Board of Appeals in 1989 and the U.S. Supreme Courts in 1991. The latter caused great controversy when Anita Hill, a former staff member at the EEOC, accused Thomas of sexual harassment. Subsequent congressional hearings tarnished Thomas's name, but he nevertheless won Senate approval and has proved to be one of the more conservative members of the court.

Connerly was born in rural Louisiana in 1939 and earned his bachelor of arts degree in political science from California's Sacramento State College in 1962. After working as a civil servant and government consultant—winning some $140,000 in affirmative action contracts— Connerly became a fundraiser for Republican governor Pete Wilson, who appointed him to the University of California Board of Regents in 1993. There, he became an anti–affirmative action advocate and helped persuade the board to end affirmative action in 1996. At the same time, Connerly organized a movement to win passage of the California Civil Rights Initiative of 1996, or Proposition 209, effectively ending affirmative action in the state. In the wake of this success, he founded the American Civil Rights Initiative to spread the battle against affirmative action nationwide. But a first effort in Florida was stymied by opposition from both Republican and Democratic state leaders.

In 2003, Connerly initiated a California ballot measure aimed at prohibiting the state government from classifying any person by race, ethnicity, color, or national origin, with some exceptions. Critics were concerned that such a ban would make it hard to track housing discrimination and racial profiling activities, and that it would harm legitimate medical and scientific research. The ballot measure was defeated.

Clarence Thomas (U.S. Supreme Court)

RACIAL CONFLICT IN THE 1990s

Starting in the late 1960s, as discussed in chapter 6, blacks in America's northern and western cities rose up to protest racial discrimination, poverty, the Vietnam War, the assassination of Martin Luther King Jr., and—most frequently—police brutality. One momentous outcome of these disturbances was the literal retreat of whites from inner cities to suburbia, which depleted the urban tax base and economically crippled many inner-city areas. Another was increased political activism among African Americans who remained in the cities. This state of affairs led to both the election of African-American mayors and the development of more ethnically diverse police forces. Despite these changes, however, police brutality and the rioting that it sparks have posed a persistent problem in urban America in the decades since the 1960s.

COLIN POWELL

Colin Powell (Department of Defense)

Colin Powell, retired Commander of the Joint Chiefs of Staff, is the most prominent recent example of African-American achievement in the Armed services. The son of Jamaican immigrants, Powell was born in New York City's Harlem in 1937. He enrolled in infantry school as a lieutenant in 1958 and later served two tours in Vietnam. In 1972, he was chosen as a White House Fellow and served as military aide to top civilian officials in the Pentagon. Powell served as National Security Adviser to Ronald Reagan during the 1980s and became a four-star general in 1988. The following year, he was promoted to Chairman of the Joint Chiefs of Staff, and two years later, during the Persian Gulf War, he became the first African American to lead a U.S. war. Following the war, President George H. W. Bush nominated Powell for Secretary of Defense, a position he held for the remainder of Bush's presidency and the beginning of Bill Clinton's first term. Touted as a possible presidential candidate in 2000, he opted not to run. He then served as Secretary of State during George W. Bush's first term.

AFRICAN AMERICANS AND THE POLICE

In 1980, the city of Miami erupted in violence after five white policemen were acquitted of the murder of a black motorist after a high-speed car chase. Police maintained that Arthur McDuffie died after his motorcycle crashed, but popular opinion put the blame on the officers who allegedly beat the man to death. The May 1980 verdict sparked violence, including rock and bottle assaults on white motorists passing through the predominantly black Liberty City section of Miami. A night of rioting was finally quelled by Miami police and National Guard units, but only after 855 persons had been arrested and $80 million in property damage incurred. Most observers of the Miami scene agreed that McDuffie's death alone would not have led to violence had there not been a history of unpunished police brutality and malfeasance in the city.

Twelve years later, the situation repeated itself on a much greater scale in Los Angeles. South Central Los Angeles, like the predominantly black sections of many other U.S. cities, had seen a flight of manufacturing jobs since the 1960s, leaving joblessness and poverty in its wake. The resulting crime, gang, and drug wave was met with increased police activity. While many South Central residents appreciated the crackdown on crime, they were often dismayed by the heavy-handed and often brutal tactics employed by the police. As in Miami, a single incident seemed to encapsulate their fears and frustrations.

On the evening of March 3, 1991, a black motorist named Rodney King was pulled over for speeding. A nearby amateur video cameraman then captured on film four police officers striking and kicking King 56 times, as well as administering several shocks from their stun guns, even after King appeared to be lying helpless on the ground. Broadcast on national television, the video outraged both black and white citizens and led to the trial of the four officers. Their April 1992 acquittal by an all-white suburban jury was the final straw for a black and Hispanic populace who had long protested police brutality. In the nation's worst rioting since the 1863 New York City draft riots, more than 50 people were killed and nearly 400 injured. Fires and looting spread across the city, causing more than $1 billion in property damage. Particularly distressing to the city's many new immigrants were the open clashes between Korean businesspeople and black protesters. In the end, it took 4,500 U.S. Army troops and 17,000 arrests—many of which did not lead to trials or convictions—to end the three days of violence.

As was the case in the Watts riots of 1965, the 1992 rioting produced much soul-searching on the part of Angelenos, both white and black, as well as calls for more civilian control over the police and more investment in the African-American community. Yet in Los Angeles, the problem of police indifference to minority concerns and their apparent targeting of nonwhite people persisted. Los Angeles itself was later rocked by one of the worst police corruption scandals in U.S. history. Charges leveled against members of the force included planting evidence, lying under oath, and stealing drugs and money. Indeed, dozens of convictions were overturned and the city faced hundreds of millions of dollars in false arrest, false imprisonment, and other civil suits.

Nor was Los Angeles alone in dealing with police corruption and brutality against minority citizens. In 1998, Human Rights Watch, a respected international monitor of government abuse, issued a report on 14 U.S. cities concluding that "police brutality is persistent [and] that systems to deal with abuse have had similar failing in all the cities."

Indeed, the nation's largest city—New York—has been plagued by a string of police brutality cases. In 1997, several officers beat and sodomized a Haitian immigrant named Abner Louima in a Brooklyn police station. Although the police were tried and convicted for that case, four officers responsible for the 1999 killing of West African immigrant Amadou Diallo—involving 41 shots that police say resulted because they mistook a wallet for a gun—were acquitted by a jury in Albany, where the trial was relocated for fear that the accused could not get a fair trial in the Bronx. Then, just weeks after the Diallo verdict, yet another Haitian immigrant—Patrick Dorismond—was shot down after refusing to buy drugs from an undercover antinarcotics team in Manhattan. Police again angered the black community by using excessive force in the shooting deaths of 19-year-old Timothy Stansbury in 2004 and of 23-year-old Sean Bell in 2007.

To many black Americans, these events are not isolated incidents but the inevitable result of the practice of racial profiling, whereby police single out blacks and other minorities as more likely crime suspects. A number of police forces—including the New Jersey State Police—have since also come under investigation for their profiling practices.

WHITE HATE GROUPS

U.S. police forces are not racist organizations in and of themselves. Since the 1960s, many have become highly integrated. Even critics of the police agree that the majority of officers try to do their duty in a color-blind fashion. This, however, does not apply to the many white hate groups that have emerged in the United States over the past few decades. According to the Southern Poverty Law Center (SPLC), a nonprofit organization that tracks and often works to destroy such groups and their activities, there were some 157 branches of neo-Nazi organizations in dozens of states in 2005, no fewer than 179 branches of the Ku Klux Klan, and more than 56 racist skinhead groups. Another estimate by the

Anti-Defamation League, a Jewish organization that monitors racist and anti-Semitic organizations, put the number of racist skinhead groups at 110 in 2006. (In addition, there are many right-wing militias and survivalist organizations, which focus on antigovernment activities but often spout antiblack rhetoric as well.)

Of these groups, the Ku Klux Klan is probably the most infamous and certainly the oldest. The most recent incarnation of the KKK is actually its third, following its original Reconstruction-era origins and then its 1920s revival as an anti-immigrant, anti-Catholic, antiblack organization. The latest incarnation of the KKK began in the 1950s and 1960s as a response to the civil rights movement and, while diminished in number since those days, remains active in much of the South and elsewhere.

Nazi sympathizers have been around since the 1930s, rising with the Nazi regime in Germany. Following Hitler's defeat in World War II, many neo-Nazis went underground, only to emerge in the 1960s, as a response to the various protest movements of the era, including the civil rights movement. But it was not until the 1980s that the various neo-Nazi groups began to recruit members in significant numbers. Like the Ku Klux Klan, neo-Nazi groups argue that the United States should be a "white man's country."

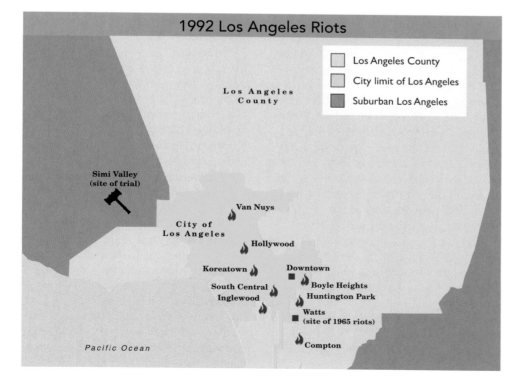

THE O. J. SIMPSON TRIAL

In June 1994, O. J. Simpson, one of the most successful running backs in professional football history, was charged with the murders of his former wife, Nicole Brown Simpson, and Ronald Goldman, a friend of hers, after the two victims were found stabbed to death outside Nicole Simpson's Los Angeles condominium. Although no witnesses to the crime came forward, prosecutors presented blood evidence found at the crime scene, in Simpson's car, and at his home, and used these samples to argue for Simpson's guilt. Simpson's lawyers argued that the evidence had been planted by racist police, and they buttressed their case by producing witnesses and a taped interview that showed police detective Mark Furhman held racist beliefs and that he had lied about these beliefs on the witness stand. On the night of the murder, Furhman had scaled a wall at Simpson's estate and found the bloody glove that was at the center of the prosecution's case. Prosecutors claimed that hair, fiber, footprints, and other circumstantial evidence all proved Simpson's guilt. Simpson's defense team maintained that this evidence had been contaminated by sloppy police procedure and was therefore unreliable.

O. J. Simpson (Corbis)

At the end of the sensational, racially charged nine-month trial, the jury deliberated for just three hours before acquitting Simpson. The verdict was celebrated by a majority of African Americans, many of whom viewed the acquittal as an indictment against a U.S. justice system that in their view discriminated against African Americans. The majority of white Americans, however, saw Simpson as clearly guilty and were stunned by the verdict. The trial thus revealed the deep schism between white and black views of the basic fairness of the U.S. justice system. In 1996, in a separate civil trial, Simpson was found liable for causing the deaths of his wife and Goldman and was ordered to pay a large fine. No other suspects have been charged with the murders.

Permeated with anti-Semitism, as well as racism, many of these groups believe that there is a secret conspiracy—perpetrated by Jews—to destroy the white race through racial intermingling and marriage. Neo-Nazi organizations often include, or are loosely affiliated with, so-called skinhead groups. These groups usually consist of young men in their teens or early twenties who shave their heads and engage in racially motivated violence.

Among the earliest racist skinhead groups was White Aryan Resistance (WAR), set up in California in 1983. In 1988, a group of WAR-affiliated skinheads murdered Mulegeta Seraw, an Ethiopian man attending college in the United States. The SPLC launched a civil suit against Tom Metzger, WAR's leader, charging that WAR had encouraged acts of violence. The jury returned what was then the largest civil verdict in Oregon history—$12.5 million—effectively bankrupting WAR.

During the late 1990s, many hate groups, including WAR, began using the Internet to raise money—and their public profiles. Web sites have made it easier for those sharing racist views to contact each other and to attempt to recruit new members. According to the Simon Wiesenthal Center, a human rights organization, the number of hate group Web sites rose from just one in 1995 to more than 2,000 by 2000. More recent studies suggest that the Internet may not be as effective a recruiting tool as hate site operators had initially hoped. The SPLC estimates that the number of sites leveled off at roughly 400 by 2007.

Though U.S. society remained resistant to minorities' demands for equality and justice, most Americans did not go so far as to support racist hate groups. Still, some black leaders viewed withdrawal from U.S. society as the best response to the racism and rejection that African Americans faced.

FARRAKHAN AND THE MILLION MAN MARCH

In the early 1960s, CBS Television broadcast "The Hate That Hate Produced," a news report about the Nation of Islam (NOI). In that documentary, reporter Mike Wallace reviewed various antiwhite statements and beliefs of the NOI and its chief spokesperson Malcolm X, who was interviewed for the program. With Malcolm's assassination in 1965 and the NOI's eclipse by more mainstream civil rights organizations in the 1960s and 1970s, the black nationalist organization largely disappeared from the nation's media and consciousness. In 1978, the organization split in two, with the larger, more radical wing keeping the NOI name and coming under the leadership of Louis Farrakhan. Under this charismatic but highly controversial leader, the NOI gained new prominence, especially as its appeal grew for young African Americans—many of whom were frustrated by an aging and increasingly moderate civil rights leadership.

Farrakhan was born Louis Walcott in the Bronx in 1933 and attended Winston-Salem Teachers College, before taking up a brief career as a nightclub singer. In 1955, Malcolm X recruited Walcott for the NOI. Like Malcolm, Walcott adopted the surname replacement "X"—symbolizing an African name lost to slavery—before adopting the Muslim name Abdul Haleem "Louis" Farrakhan. While Farrakhan sided with Malcolm during the latter's dispute with NOI leader Elijah Muhammad in 1963, he turned against the renegade NOI spokesperson when Malcolm broke with the organization in 1965. Indeed, many claim that Farrakhan had a part in Malcolm's assassination, a charge never proved in court and denied by Farrakhan himself.

After taking control of the NOI in 1978, Farrakhan went to work building new mosques around the country. But it was his fiery rhetoric—which fused a message of black self-reliance and a strong distrust of white people—that gained the organization many new recruits among young black Americans. They adopted his call for responsible living—no drugs, no alcohol, and responsibility to spouse, family, and community—and appreciated his willingness to speak out candidly against what he perceived to be an inherently racist society. Farrakhan, however, was also prone in the 1980s to both antiwhite and anti-Semitic rhetoric, including statements that called Judaism a "gutter religion" and praised Hitler as a great leader. But the condemnation he received from whites and most black civil rights leaders only seemed to reaffirm his standing among many urban youths, who viewed the attacks as part of a plot against independent black thought and activism.

Still, Farrakhan bristled at the criticism and by the early 1990s was trying to distance himself from his earlier remarks. Attempting to refurbish his image—as well as promote his ideas of black self-reliance and responsibility—Farrakhan organized what he called a Day of Atonement, whereby the nation's African-American men would agree to take responsibility for themselves, their families, black women, the black community, and the nation as a whole. Popularly known as the Million Man March, the October 16, 1995 event brought some 900,000 black men to Washington. Although primarily organized by Benjamin Chavis of the NAACP, the

A Ku Klux Klan cross burning in suburban Maryland in 1980 (Library of Congress)

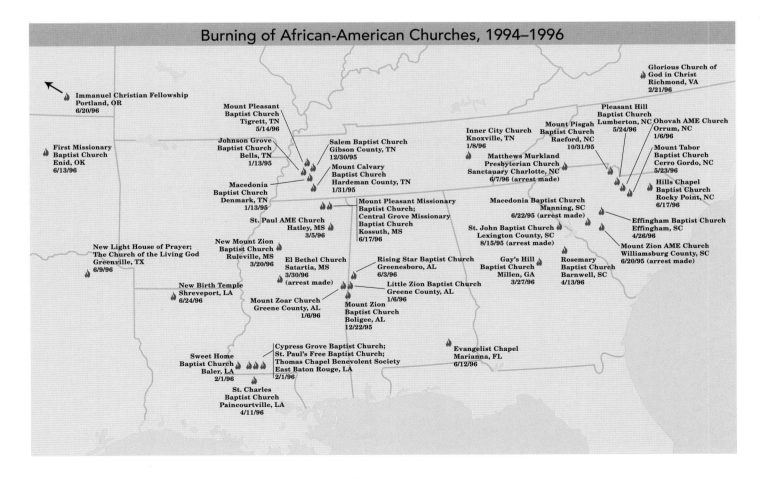

Burning of African-American Churches, 1994–1996

Glorious Church of God in Christ
Richmond, VA
2/21/96

Immanuel Christian Fellowship
Portland, OR
6/20/96

Mount Pleasant
Baptist Church
Tigrett, TN
5/14/96

Pleasant Hill
Baptist Church
Lumberton, NC
5/24/96

Ohovah AME Church
Orrum, NC
1/6/96

Inner City Church
Knoxville, TN
1/8/96

Mount Pisgah
Baptist Church
Raeford, NC
10/31/95

Johnson Grove
Baptist Church
Bells, TN
1/13/95

Salem Baptist Church
Gibson County, TN
12/30/95

Mount Tabor
Baptist Church
Cerro Gordo, NC
5/23/96

First Missionary
Baptist Church
Enid, OK
6/13/96

Matthews Murkland
Presbyterian Church
Sanctauary Charlotte, NC
6/7/96 (arrest made)

Mount Calvary
Baptist Church
Hardeman County, TN
1/31/95

Hills Chapel
Baptist Church
Rocky Point, NC
6/17/96

Macedonia
Baptist Church
Denmark, TN
1/13/95

Mount Pleasant Missionary
Baptist Church;
Central Grove Missionary
Baptist Church
Kossuth, MS
6/17/96

Macedonia Baptist Church
Manning, SC
6/22/95 (arrest made)

Effingham Baptist Church
Effingham, SC
4/26/96

St. Paul AME Church
Hatley, MS
3/5/96

St. John Baptist Church
Lexington County, SC
8/15/95 (arrest made)

Mount Zion AME Church
Williamsburg County, SC
6/20/95 (arrest made)

New Light House of Prayer;
The Church of the Living God
Greenville, TX
6/9/96

New Mount Zion
Baptist Church
Ruleville, MS
3/20/96

El Bethel Church
Satartia, MS
3/30/96
(arrest made)

Rising Star Baptist Church
Greenesboro, AL
6/3/96

Gay's Hill
Baptist Church
Millen, GA
3/27/96

Rosemary
Baptist Church
Barnwell, SC
4/13/96

New Birth Temple
Shreveport, LA
6/24/96

Little Zion Baptist Church
Greene County, AL
1/6/96

Mount Zoar Church
Greene County, AL
1/6/96

Mount Zion
Baptist Church
Boligee, AL
12/22/95

Sweet Home
Baptist Church
Baler, LA
2/1/96

Cypress Grove Baptist Church;
St. Paul's Free Baptist Church;
Thomas Chapel Benevolent Society
East Baton Rouge, LA
2/1/96

Evangelist Chapel
Marianna, FL
6/12/96

St. Charles
Baptist Church
Paincourtville, LA
4/11/96

Louis Farrakhan (Corbis)

march was associated in the public mind with Farrakhan. While the march—the largest gathering ever in the nation's capital—was viewed favorably by most Americans for its message and its peacefulness—many black women criticized Farrakhan and other event organizers for excluding them. Three years later, a smaller Million Woman March was organized in Philadelphia, and in 2005, Farrakhan launched the Millions More Movement to commemorate the tenth anniversary of the original march. A march was held on October 15, 2005, this time open to men, women, and children. Its goal was to strengthen relationships between individuals, faith-based organizations, and community institutions.

Despite these efforts to accentuate the positive, Farrakhan remained controversial into the 2000s, coming under criticism for visiting and praising countries like Libya and Nigeria—the former deemed a terrorist state by the U.S. government and the latter considered a human rights violator by both the State Department and many black leaders.

In 1999, NOI confirmed reports that Farrakhan was suffering from cancer. Although he survived, Farrakhan's health continued to decline, and he turned over control of NOI to an executive committee in August 2006. In February 2007, he made what was billed as his final address.

Questions loomed about who would succeed Farrakhan and the direction that NOI would head. Critics like Warith Deen Muhammad predicted that NOI's isolationist days were numbered. Muhammad, a son of Elijah Muhammad, had himself broken with NOI in 1975 in favor of more traditional Sunni Islam beliefs. Sunni teachings differ from NOI teachings by embracing diversity and the unity of all believers, regardless of race. Muhammad had approximately 3.6 million African-American followers as of 2006, while the active membership in NOI was estimated at 50,000.

In a 2007 interview with the *New York Times*, Warith Deen Muhammad's senior aide Imam Muhammad Sideeq argued that NOI would have to embrace a more inclusive, traditional form of Islam to survive. This idea was dismissed by NOI representative Ismael Muhammad, who is another son of Elijah Muhammad and Farrakhan's possible successor. Integration with the white majority, he said, "has left the masses behind." However blacks may choose to respond to the situation, racial conflict in America has not gone away.

BLACK CULTURE IN THE 1980s AND 1990s

As discussed in chapter 6, the 1960s witnessed a tremendous surge in African-American literature, music, and dance. By the early 1970s, black artists had left their mark on television and film as well. These trends continued, and in the 1980s and 1990s, numerous other African-American creative artists also achieved mainstream notice and success. In this epoch of creativity, more Americans than ever before were exposed to the wealth that black Americans were infusing into American culture. Although it is impossible to generalize across or even within the wide spectrum of artistic genres, black creative artists—ranging from writers, actors, and musicians to television producers and filmmakers—reached larger audiences than ever before during the 1980s and 1990s. Some of those artists produced work aimed at a select, smaller audience, while others sought out the widest possible audiences across racial and cultural lines.

LITERATURE

In the 1960s, African-American writers like Amiri Baraka, Ishmael Reed, and Nikki Giovanni had produced a forceful and distinctly political body of literature. Because they aimed to establish their own voice and following outside of the dominant white literary establishment, the audience for their work lay largely in the black community.

By the 1970s, however, a number of books by black women found large audiences across the racial spectrum. In addition to exploring the black experience in the face of racism, some of these books also explored the relationships between the sexes. Maya Angelou's 1971 autobiography, *I Know Why the Caged Bird Sings*, dealt not only with racism, but also with the isolation and loneliness of her childhood as well as sexism and rape.

Another writer who became well known in the 1970s is poet, essayist, and novelist Alice Walker. In 1973, Walker and literary scholar Charlotte Hunt located the unmarked grave of Zora Neale Hurston in Florida. Although Hurston was one of the leading black writers of the 1930s, her work had been largely forgotten by the time of her death in 1960. In 1974, Walker gained wide attention for an essay on Hurston's 1937 novel *Their Eyes Were Watching God*, published in *Ms.* magazine. The article revived interest in Hurston's work as an authentic literary expression of the black experience.

Like Hurston's novels, Alice Walker's 1982 novel *The Color Purple* focused only in part on racism. The book tells the story of Celie, a young woman who, at 14, is sexually abused and impregnated by her stepfather and later forced to marry an abusive widower. Through a relationship with her husband's mistress, Celie gradually becomes empowered to express her identity as an independent woman. The book, which, like Hurston's novels, uses black vernacular English, was praised for the depth of its female characters, and it won both the National Book Award and a Pulitzer Prize. The book's impact was so great that it was later dramatized as both a feature a film (directed by Steven Spielberg in 1985) and a Broadway play (produced by Oprah Winfrey in 2005).

As a Random House editor, Toni Morrison had promoted the success of African-American writers like Toni Cade Bambara and Gayl Jones in the 1960s, but in the 1970s and 1980s she became an even more successful writer herself. Her first novel, *The Bluest Eye* (1970), dealt with a young black girl's journey through adolescence. Like *The Color Purple*, the book also deals with incest and abuse, as well as self-hatred, since the protagonist comes to feel that her problems would be solved if she only had blue eyes.

Song of Solomon (1977) and *Beloved* (1987) have placed Morrison among the most important authors of the 20th century. The first tells the story of Macon "Milkman" Dead, a young man alienated from himself and estranged from his family, his community, and his historical and cultural roots. The novel recounts Milkman's journey of coming to terms with himself and his heritage over a 30-year period. The novel *Beloved*, the complex tale of a murdered child, a runaway slave, and a deep family secret, is widely considered Morrison's masterpiece. In 1993, she won the Nobel Prize in literature in recognition of what the Nobel committee called "her epic power, her unerring ear for dialogue, and her poetically charged and richly expressive depictions of Black America."

Other important writers of the 1980s and 1990s include novelists Jamaica Kincaid, Randall Kenan, and John Edgar Wideman. For Kincaid, an Antiguan-American, frequent themes include conflicts between mother and daughter, the search for black female identity, and the impact of colonialism. Kenan's work has focused on what it means to be black and gay in the American South. Wideman first gained attention for *Brothers and Keepers* (1984), a memoir that focused on his relationship with his brother Robbie, who was convicted of murder and sentenced to life in prison.

Because the authors cited here come from diverse backgrounds and experience, it is risky to attempt to group them together under the literary umbrella of "black literature." Certainly race plays a role in all of their work, but so to do other factors—the legacy of history, gender, family, colonialism, and sexual identity to name a few. That the work of these talented writers are not simply defined by race but can explore the full range of individual human identity is a sign of progress.

African-American poets of the mid-1970s to mid-1990s likewise garnered attention for the range of experience they portray. Rita Dove, who won a Pulitzer Prize and served as Poet Laureate of the United States from 1993 to 1995, dealt with the lives of her maternal grandparents in her most famous work, *Thomas and Beulah* (1987). In his *Soul Make a Path Through Shouting*, Cyrus Cassells dealt with a global array of tragedy, ranging from the Holocaust and AIDS to environmental desecration and the Spanish Revolution. The book won him a nomination for a Pulitzer Prize in 1994.

Readers responded to this literary wealth, and from the mid-1990s well into the 2000s, the market for books aimed at African-American readers grew steadily. A small army of self-published authors rose up to tap this swelling market, as did publishers—both small black presses and large New York houses. By 2006, black book–focused imprints were thriving at Ballantine, Doubleday, Harlequin, HarperCollins, Hyperion, and Simon &

SELECTED AFRICAN-AMERICAN WRITERS, 1965–1996

Name	Selected Works
Maya Angelou (1928–)	Autobiography: *I Know Why the Caged Bird Sings* (1970); Poem: "On the Pulse of Morning" (1992)
Rita Dove (1952–)	Poetry: *Thomas and Beulah* (1985)
Ernest J. Gaines (1933–)	Novels: *The Autobiography of Miss Jane Pittman* (1971); *A Gathering of Old Men* (1983); *A Lesson Before Dying* (1993)
Alex Haley (1921–1992)	Biography: *The Autobiography of Malcolm X* (co-written with Malcolm X) (1965); History: *Roots* (1971)
Michael S. Harper (1938–)	Poetry: *Dear John, Dear Coltrane* (1970); *Images of Kin* (1977)
Charles Johnson (1948–)	Novel: *Middle Passage* (1990)
Jamaica Kincaid (1949–)	Novels: *Annie John* (1985); *Lucy* (1990); *The Autobiography of My Mother* (1996)
Terry McMillan (1951–)	Novels: *Mama* (1987); *Waiting to Exhale* (1992)
Toni Morrison (1931–)	Novels: *The Bluest Eye* (1970); *Beloved* (1987)
Gloria Naylor (1950–)	Novel: *The Women of Brewster Place* (1983)
Walter Mosely (1952–)	Novel: *Devil in a Blue Dress* (1990)
Alice Walker (1944–)	Poetry: *Once* (1968); Novel: *The Color Purple* (1982)
John Edgar Wideman (1944–)	Memoir: *Brothers and Keepers*; Novel: *The Cattle Killing* (1996)
August Wilson (1945–2006)	Plays: *Ma Rainey's Black Bottom* (1984); *Fences* (1987); *Joe Turner's Come and Gone* (1988)

Novelist Toni Morrison (AP Images/Kathy Willins)

Schuster. Publications ranged widely, from new African-American fiction and classics to self-help and scholarly works. At Kensington Publishing alone, the African-American category represented a strong 11 percent of the publishing house's 2005 revenues and, according to Kensington president Steven Zacharius, sales and revenues were expected to continue their upward trend.

TELEVISION AND "AUTHENTICITY"

The single most influential literary work by an African American in the post-1960s era was Alex Haley's semiautobiographical book *Roots*. The book traced Haley's ancestry from Africa through the early days of the American slave trade. Most Americans, however, became familiar with Haley's book through the 12-hour television miniseries that was broadcast in 1977 and watched by an astounding 130 million Americans. Televised on eight consecutive nights, *Roots* attracted an unprecedented number of viewers unmatched by any miniseries since, including its own 1979 sequel, *Roots: The Next Generation.* The 1977 miniseries did more than simply entertain. It provided an engaging history of race relations and sparked an interest in genealogy among millions of African Americans. And for millions of white viewers, *Roots* put a human face on what had been an abstraction—the painful legacy of slavery.

By the time *Roots* appeared on television, a growing number of blacks had found work on the small screen. Following in the paths charted by Bill Cosby's *I Spy* and Diahann Carroll's *Julia*, mid-1970s sitcoms such as *Good Times* (1974–1979), *The Jeffersons* 1975–1985), and *Sanford and Son* (1972–1977) reached wide audiences. Black faces also began appearing in television commercials, as contestants on game shows, as sports announcers, and as news commentators.

What lay behind the increase in black representation on TV during the 1970s and early 1980s? Was it because blacks were more readily accepted on TV by that time, making their appearance less controversial? Or did their growing prominence on the small screen promote increased acceptance? The answer to both questions is most likely "yes." On the one hand, when the Kerner Commission issued its report on the state of race relations in the aftermath of nationwide civil disturbances in 1968, one of the recommendations it made was that "Negroes should appear more frequently in dramatic and comedy series."

The Commission had also recommended that broadcast news do more to shed light on urban issues and to hire more blacks to report those stories. Over the next decade, television news divisions responded. Among the most notable African-American television journalists of the 1970s were Tony Brown, host of *Tony Brown's Journal*, and Carl Rowan and Julian Bond, who regularly appeared as panelists on news programs. By the early 1980s, the first African-American news anchors arrived on television. Max Robinson cohosted ABC News from 1978 to 1983, and Bernard Shaw served as lead anchor for CNN. Even more prominent was Ed Bradley, longtime reporter for *60 Minutes*.

Bradley, who died in 2006, served as a role model and mentor for a generation of black journalists who followed him. Bradley attributed his success not to the added attention he brought to "black" issues, but to the fact that he never allowed himself to be restricted to only "black stories." He was, he argued, a journalist, not a "black journalist," and hard work and journalistic skill, not race, were behind the acceptance and trust that he won with audiences of all races.

While skilled journalists like Bradley helped open the door to other black journalists on television, television is a business like any other. The fact is *Sanford and Son* and *The Jeffersons* stayed on network television because they were popular, not because of enlightened racial awareness. When ratings for those shows began to decline, their runs came to an end.

In the 1980s, lead roles for blacks in television shows were scarcer. Black actors found supporting roles in early 1980s shows such as *Barney Miller* and *WKRP in Cincinnati*. But shows that featured African American actors—such as *Diff'rent Strokes* and *Gimme a Break*—cast them in roles that many regarded as demeaning stereotypes. The dearth of accurate depictions of blacks on 1980s television reflected a problem behind the cameras: By the end of the decade, fewer than 100 out of the 4,000 Writers Guild/West members were black, and 90 percent of all black sitcoms were written by whites. At the same time, two African-American TV personalities became arguably the most beloved of all television stars—Oprah Winfrey and Bill Cosby.

Winfrey began her first media job, working at a local radio station, while she was still in high school. In college, she accepted a position as a TV newscaster in Tennessee. Soon after, she worked as a cohost on the TV show *People Are Talking*, and in 1985 a station in Chicago offered Winfrey her own talk show. *The Oprah Winfrey Show* quickly achieved national syndication and Oprah soon became a household name. One of the highest-paid television personalities in America, Winfrey has acted in films and runs her own production company, Harpo ("Oprah" spelled backward). When she purchased the Harpo production facilities in 1988, she become the first black woman to own a film or television studio. Oprah's Book Club, through which Winfrey spotlights favorite books on a segment of her television show, has enormous influence on the American book publishing industry since its launch in 1996. A spot on her program generally guarantees best-seller status for any book. In 2000 she launched a new women's magazine known simply as *O*.

After a long and varied career, Cosby began his most successful project yet—*The Cosby Show* (1984–1989), which he wrote, produced, and frequently directed. The show broke new ground by portraying an upper-middle-class black family headed by a doctor (Cosby) and a lawyer. The success of *The Cosby Show* opened new opportunities for blacks on television. *A Different World* (a spin-off of *The Cosby Show*) took place at a fictional historically black college called Hillman, while *The Fresh Prince of Bel Air*—starring Will Smith, then a rap star—portrayed a wisecracking teen from inner-city Philadelphia who moves in with his wealthy aunt and uncle in suburban Los Angeles. Both shows broke with prevailing stereotypes by depicting educated, well-off black families.

Perhaps surprisingly, critics faulted *The Cosby Show* for the upper-middle-class life that it depicted, arguing that it did not accurately reflect the lives of most African Americans. Some said the show

Hip-hop artist Will Smith launched his highly successful acting career in the early 1990s by starring in The Fresh Prince of Bel Air. (Corbis)

gave the impression that all blacks might be just as successful if they only worked hard to assimilate with mainstream white culture. Others criticized the show's very popularity. The fictional Huxtable family decorated their home with African art; the parents danced to jazz and blues and wore sweatshirts advertising historically black colleges; and their grandchildren were named after the South African icons Nelson and Winnie Mandela. None of this satisfied radical black critics, for whom the show's popularity with whites proved that the Huxtables were somehow "not black enough."

What then does it mean to be "black enough" in contemporary society? Is there a litmus test? Although some African-American social critics have argued that black creative artists have an obligation to present the "authentic" black experience, how does one begin to define the "authentic" experiences of more than 30 million Americans?

If, on the other hand, "authenticity" in arts and entertainment is based on depicting the complex identities of individuals in their daily experience, then there is no one single barometer of the authentic black experience. How the black experience is depicted depends on the intended purpose of the work being produced. Is George Jefferson's comical social climbing and inflated ego any more authentic to the black experience than the Machiavellian treachery of *Dallas*'s J. R. Ewing is to the "white experience"? Can't black actors play roles that are simply meant to entertain?

To be fair, the long history of black entertainers playing stereotyped secondary roles on radio, television, and film gives advocates for African-American creative arts cause for concern. While Jimmy Walker's J. J. on *Good Times* or Gary Coleman's Arnold on *Diff'rent Strokes* surely entertained, they have also been criticized as little more than updated minstrel acts, playing stereotypes for laughs.

While debates over what is authentic may never be properly settled, it should be noted that the executives behind shows like *Good Times*, *Sanford and Son*, and *Diff'rent Strokes* were white. So too were a majority of the writers on those shows. In truth, it is doubtful that a sitcom can depict "authentic" experiences of anyone, but one way to ensure scripts that are closer to the real lives of viewers is to have

writers for the screen write out of experience. Under that rationale, *The Cosby Show* may actually have been more authentic to the black experience than any other program on 1980s television.

THE BLACK FILM MOVEMENT

Another medium where black experiences were memorably dramatized in the 1980s and 1990s was film. Several African-American directors made a name for themselves, among them Robert Townshend, whose *Hollywood Shuffle* (1987) skewered the U.S. entertainment industry and its biases, and Spike Lee, who made several films including *She's Gotta Have It* (1986) and his masterpiece *Do the Right Thing* (1989). The latter film, a fictional story inspired by the real-life murder of a black man in the Howard Beach neighborhood of New York City, unflinchingly portrayed the volatile racial divides of inner-city life. John Singleton's powerful *Boyz N the Hood* (1991) explored the similar theme of gang life in inner-city Los Angeles. By contrast, Julie Dash's *Daughters of the Dust* (1992) portrayed rural challenges. Set in the Sea Islands off the coast of South Carolina, the characters must choose between preserving their threatened Gullah cultural heritage and pursuing opportunities outside the islands.

As black producers and directors made more films in the 1980s and 1990s, opportunities for African-American actors increased. These decades saw the rise to stardom of Danny Glover, Whoopi Goldberg, Eddie Murphy, Denzel Washington, Samuel L. Jackson, and Halle Berry. Increased acclaim followed, as when Whoopi Goldberg (1991) and Denzel Washington (1989) won Academy Awards as supporting actors. Washington went on to win an Oscar for best actor in 2001, and in 2002 Halle Berry became the first black woman to win the Academy Award for best actress.

These actors have performed in a diversity of film genres, from comedy to drama to action. While some have appeared in films with black themes, such as Denzel Washington's starring role in *Malcolm X*, others have acted in films in which their race was not central to the plot. In the 2001 film *Swordfish*, for example, Halle Berry romanced Hugh Jackman and John Travolta, both white actors, eliciting little public reaction regarding race. Today, black stars are among the most popular actors in Hollywood, and their popularity cuts across racial lines.

THE ROOTS OF RAP

In the mid-1970s, black popular music was dominated by R&B bands like Earth, Wind & Fire and funk groups like Sly and the Family Stone and George Clinton's ensembles Parliament and Funkadelic. African-American singers and musicians were also playing a role in the creation of disco music. Kool & the Gang, Gloria Gaynor, and especially Donna Summer all had enormous disco hits.

Yet away from the ears of white audiences, a new form known as hip-hop or rap was emerging. With its roots in Bronx, New York block parties, hip-hop arose as one of the key elements in a rebellious new scene. As disc jockeys spun records, MCs introduced the tracks. One of the most important figures in this early hip-hop scene was Jamaican-born Clive Campbell, better known as DJ Kool Herc. Campbell was the first DJ to began isolating bass, percussion, and vocals from records and repeating them in new ways to form insistent, danceable beats. Over these beats, MCs improvised more complex vocal arrangements, or raps.

The first commercially issued hip-hop recording was released in 1979. "Rapper's Delight" by the Sugarhill Gang became a Top 40 hit on *Billboard*'s U.S. pop singles chart. With its dance-heavy beat and boastful lyrics ("Well, my name is known all over the world/By all the foxy ladies and the pretty girls"), "Rapper's Delight" perfectly encapsulated the infectious, good-time party atmosphere of early hip-hop music.

Another early track showed hip-hop's potential to address weightier themes. Released in 1982, "The Message" by Grandmaster Flash and the Furious Five sounded an alarm: "Don't push me 'cuz I'm close to the edge/I'm trying not to lose my head/It's like a jungle sometimes/It makes me wonder how I keep from goin' under." This blunt statement of barely contained black anger was a breakthrough hit.

Even mainstream black artists such as Michael Jackson, Lionel Ritchie,

Whitney Houston, and Prince dominated the 1980s airwaves, hip-hop spread out. From New York it went nationwide, encouraging artists in cities like Miami, Chicago, and in particular Los Angeles to develop their own styles.

As early as 1983, hip-hop also began to attract young white fans. One draw was three young white New Yorkers calling themselves The Beastie Boys, who put a funky beat behind a recording of a crank call to a Carvel Ice Cream store and called the combination "Cookie Puss." The next year, they signed a contract with the hip-hop label Def Jam Records, co-founded by a concert promoter from Queens named Russell Simmons.

Among Def Jam's other important early hip-hop acts was Run-DMC, a trio made up of Russell Simmons' younger brother Joseph "Run" Simmons, Daryl "D.M.C." McDaniels, and Jason "Jam Master Jay" Mizell. Run-DMC helped spread hip-hop to a large, mainstream, interracial audience. In 1985, the group played at Live Aid, the famous benefit concert for African famine relief. The next year they performed a rap cover version of "Walk This Way," originally recorded by the rock band Aerosmith. MTV gave massive airtime to the song's video, featuring Steven Tyler and Joe Perry of Aerosmith, and the song became a *Billboard* Top 10 single, a first for a rap recording.

By the late 1980s, however, listeners were gravitating toward a harder-edged, political brand of rap. The New York group Public Enemy offered up a politically radical consciousness, rooted in the black separatism of Malcolm X and the Nation of Islam. Their song "Fight the Power!" was prominently featured in Spike Lee's film *Do the Right Thing*.

At the same time, the group N.W.A. (Niggaz With Attitude) highlighted the reality of gang life in South Central Los Angeles. Led by O'Shea Jackson—better known as "Ice Cube"—N.W.A. spouted controversial antipolice lyrics. Born and raised in South Central himself, Ice Cube appeared in *Boyz N the Hood* in 1991.

While mainstream opinion condemned Public Enemy and N.W.A. for their provocative lyrics, music critics embraced them—as did a growing legion of fans in both the inner cities and the predominantly white suburbs. By the early 1990s, a new genre known as "gangsta

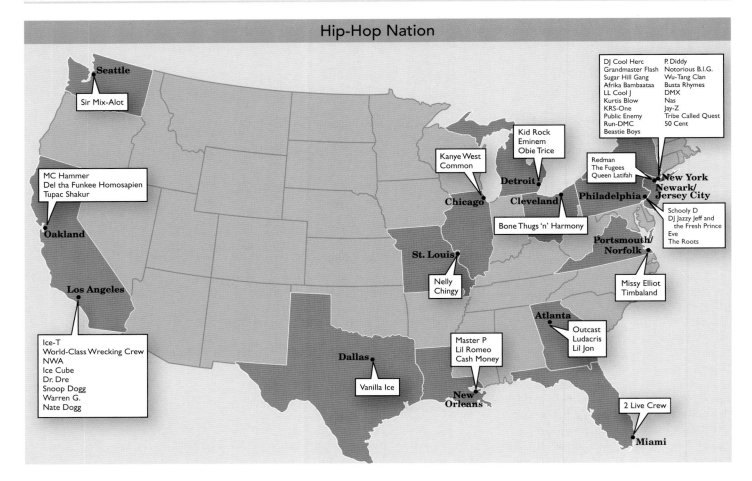

Hip-Hop Nation

DJ Cool Herc — P. Diddy
Grandmaster Flash — Notorious B.I.G.
Sugar Hill Gang — Wu-Tang Clan
Afrika Bambaataa — Busta Rhymes
LL Cool J — DMX
Kurtis Blow — Nas
KRS-One — Jay-Z
Public Enemy — Tribe Called Quest
Run-DMC — 50 Cent
Beastie Boys

Seattle
Sir Mix-Alot

Kid Rock
Eminem
Obie Trice

Kanye West
Common

Detroit

New York
Newark/
Jersey City

Redman
The Fugees
Queen Latifah

MC Hammer
Del tha Funkee Homosapien
Tupac Shakur

Chicago — Cleveland — Philadelphia

Bone Thugs 'n' Harmony

Schooly D
DJ Jazzy Jeff and
the Fresh Prince
Eve
The Roots

Oakland

St. Louis

Portsmouth/
Norfolk

Los Angeles

Nelly
Chingy

Missy Elliot
Timbaland

Ice-T
World-Class Wrecking Crew
NWA
Ice Cube
Dr. Dre
Snoop Dogg
Warren G.
Nate Dogg

Atlanta

Outcast
Ludacris
Lil Jon

Dallas

Master P
Lil Romeo
Cash Money

Vanilla Ice

New
Orleans

2 Live Crew

Miami

rap" dominated the hip-hop music scene, and reputed former gang members and drug dealers such as Ice T, Tupac Shakur, and Notorious B.I.G. filled the charts.

Politically and socially, the mid-1970s to the mid-1990s was a period of racial retrenchment in America. The successes of the civil rights movement did enable millions of blacks to elect city councilors, mayors, and even members of Congress to represent them in record numbers. But at the same time, the country abandoned the 1960s War on Poverty, leaving the poorest African Americans and other minorities behind in decaying inner cities.

However, the influence of black culture was felt more strongly—and affected a broader cross-section of Americans—than ever before. On television and film, in literature, and especially in music, African-American impact was evident everywhere.

BLACK AMERICA TODAY

On August 31, 2005, the worst hurricane to hit a major U.S. city in 100 years swept along the Gulf Coast region and struck New Orleans, Louisiana. After Hurricane Katrina passed, two sections of the New Orleans levee system gave way, flooding 90 percent of the historic city, which is below sea level. Most people with cars had already evacuated the city before the hurricane made landfall. Those remaining were the elderly, the poor, the sick, and their family members who stayed to care for them. The vast majority were black.

Over 1,800 people died, many due to heat and dehydration, as local and state emergency plans were overwhelmed and the federal government failed to act in a timely manner. For many Americans, the heart-wrenching images that came out of New Orleans put a face on America's poor. Because the vast majority of the New Orleans poor were black, the hurricane also highlighted a continuing racial divide. Television news reports showed predominantly poor, black residents of the city left stranded, waiting endlessly for government assistance that for some never came. Americans watched as the city's very social fabric seemed to collapse: Dead, swollen bodies floated in flooded streets, and city police deserted their posts even as roving gangs looted abandoned shops.

Media coverage also focused on the social ills that had long plagued New Orleans. The city's population, which was 67 percent black before Katrina, was also one of the nation's poorest, with 30 percent living below the poverty line. Only a handful of other urban populations had lower average household incomes, and a majority of the city's poor had no health insurance. In addition, New Orleans had a serious crime problem. In 2004, it had the highest crime rate of any large U.S. city.

Many Americans were outraged that society's poorest and most vulnerable seemed to have been abandoned by their government. For some, the racial disparities spotlighted by Hurricane Katrina were especially disturbing—and government neglect was only the beginning. On September 3, rapper Kanye West gave voice to the anger of many black Americans during a live television appeal for Red Cross donations. Dispensing with his scripted comments, he railed against the Bush administration's slow response

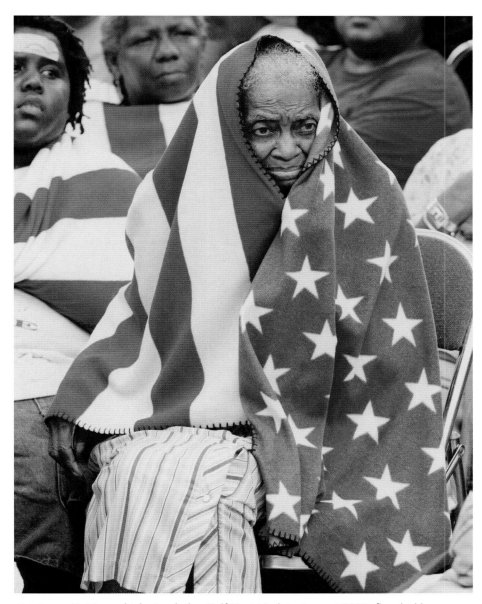

Hurricane Katrina, which struck the Gulf Coast in late August 2005, flooded large portions of New Orleans. As federal, state, and local officials blamed each other for the slow governmental response, poor and elderly residents of the Crescent City found themselves stranded. Above, an elderly citizen waits to be evacuated. (Corbis)

and the way the news media were covering the crisis. "I hate the way they portray us in the media," he protested. "You see a black family, it says, 'They're looting.' You see a white family, it says, 'They're looking for food.'" Ignoring his flustered cohost, West proclaimed, "George Bush doesn't care about black people!"

Two weeks after Katrina hit, President George W. Bush pledged that his administration would oversee a massive rebuilding program that would not only rebuild lost property, but also create new job training programs and other antipoverty efforts. In this way, he argued, he would help to close the economic gap between the Crescent City's haves and have-nots. But this effort would cost. The storm caused an estimated $86 billion in damage, a vast sum, and the nation's budget was already straining to pay three times that much to finance wars in Iraq and Afghanistan. Members of President Bush's own party were already alarmed by surging federal spending under a Republican president and Congress. In the months after the hurricane, they began to insist upon deep cuts in other areas of the federal budget to offset the costs of reconstructing New Orleans. At the close of 2006, few promised programs had actually been passed by Congress, and many questions remained about the government's response and long-term plans for New Orleans.

CONTEMPORARY SOCIAL AND ECONOMIC TRENDS

While New Orleans may be one of the nation's most troubled cities, the socioeconomic divisions between blacks and white Americans are not limited to that city. The social stresses in New Orleans—so visible to the nation in the days, weeks, and months after Katrina—have long been apparent in any close reading of

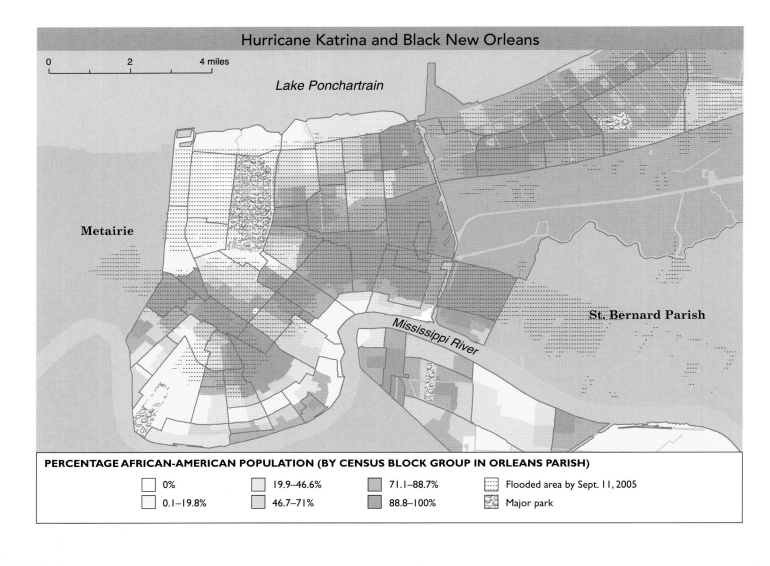

Hurricane Katrina and Black New Orleans

0   2   4 miles

Lake Ponchartrain

Metairie

St. Bernard Parish

Mississippi River

PERCENTAGE AFRICAN-AMERICAN POPULATION (BY CENSUS BLOCK GROUP IN ORLEANS PARISH)

0%	19.9–46.6%	71.1–88.7%
0.1–19.8%	46.7–71%	88.8–100%

Flooded area by Sept. 11, 2005

Major park

nationwide demographic studies. All too often, measures of social well-being break along racial lines, with the average African American trailing the average white American in most areas. Crime and criminal justice are a case in point.

CRIMINAL JUSTICE

Crime and the criminal justice system have long been two of the most dominant issues in the lives of African Americans and other minorities, and their influence has been hugely destructive to the quality of life in many minority communities. A 2004 study by the U.S. Department of Justice, for example, showed that between 1976 and 2004, African Americans were more seven times likely to commit murder than whites. All told, over 52 percent of all murders in the United States during those years were committed by black Americans.

African Americans make up only about 13 percent of the total U.S. population, but more than half the murders in the United States since the 1970s have been committed by blacks. This is alarming, yet equally alarming is the fact that nearly 47 percent of all murder victims have also been black. Since 1974, blacks have been about 20 percent more likely than whites to be victims of either violent crimes or property crimes. Fully 94 percent of all murders in 2004 involving African Americans involved both a black offender and a black victim.

Why does race play a role in whether an individual will be involved, as perpetrator or victim, in a crime? The answer is housing and poverty. According to the U.S. Census Bureau, blacks are far more likely than whites to live in poor neighborhoods that lack educational and employment opportunities. Most murders involving black Americans take place in black neighborhoods. These facts underline the still-segregated nature of American communities. In addition, the violent crimes that take place in poor neighborhoods are often drug related. To a large degree, the drug in question has been crack cocaine.

Crack first emerged in America's inner cities during the mid-1980s, launching what became popularly known as "the crack epidemic." Although its use has moderated somewhat since the mid-1990s, crack cocaine remains common in many inner-city neighborhoods because it is potent and cheap, a dangerous combination. Five- and ten-dollar quantities of crack, known as "nickels" and "dimes," make the drug more affordable than cocaine in its powdered form. Dosages known as "blasts" are often sold for as little as a dollar.

The crack epidemic in America's inner cities had a dramatic impact on crime, especially among young men lured into drug-dealing by the promise of "easy" money. Competition for this drug money sparked turf wars among dealers and a dramatic increase in murder and other violent crime, usually involving the black teenage males who served as street-level drug dealers. According to the National Institute for Justice, between 1985 and 1992, the murder rate for defendants aged 18 and under nearly doubled after 15 years of near stability, even as the rate for other age groups stayed the same. The crack epidemic abated somewhat during the 1990s, but as of 2005 homicide remained the leading cause of death among black males between the ages of 15 and 34, according to the Centers for Disease Control. By contrast, the leading cause of death for same-age males of other races was accidental death.

The fact that blacks are more likely than other Americans to be the victims of violent crime has led many people to demand more resources for adequate policing. But simply putting more police on the beat may not be enough. According to the U.S. Justice Department, the solution lies in the kind of policing that is practiced.

During the early 1990s, a handful of cities, including Houston, Boston, and New York, began using a strategy known as "community policing." Community policing programs work to establish individual police and police departments as hands-on members of the community. Rather than simply patrol neighborhoods in cars, police walk a beat and often live in the neighborhoods in which they work. Officers attempt to understand local issues by listening to the concerns of community members—and even possible suspects—in an unbiased and nonjudgmental manner. In that way, they can create a sense of trust between themselves and the residents.

Community policing programs require effective training—and the financial resources for this training. During the early 1990s, the Clinton administration initiated a plan to support community policing programs across the country. The administration's COPS initiative, passed as part of the 1994 Crime Bill, provided funding for more than 11,000 law-enforcement agencies to hire or redeploy more than 100,000 police officers over five years. The increased number of police on the beat—and their new emphasis on working more closely with the communities they served—seemed to work. For a decade following the program's passage, overall crime rates dropped every year in the longest continuous drop on record. As of 2000, urban crime in the United States was at a 26-year low.

Despite the statistical improvements, winning the trust and confidence of local communities has not been a universal success for the nation's local police forces. Residents of inner-city neighborhoods still tend to view the police as a force that unfairly targets blacks, especially young black males. Many African Americans accuse police of using illegal "racial profiling" techniques, by which police use a person's race as one factor in assessing whether that person is likely to have committed a crime.

Although the U.S. Supreme Court has declared racial profiling unconstitutional, observers believe that many police forces still use it. Statistics bear out this claim. For instance, according to the *Dallas Morning News*, 36 percent of all motorists pulled over in 2006 by Dallas police were black, despite the fact that African Americans make up only 26 percent of Dallas's population. Likewise, 45 percent of all automobiles searched were those driven by blacks, while only 22 percent of the cars searched were owned by whites. Similarly, in 2005, police in Anne Arundel County, Maryland, which includes the state capital of Annapolis, pulled over a disproportionately high percentage of black drivers: African-American drivers accounted for 24 percent of all cars stopped, even though only 13.9 percent of the county's population are black. Both the Dallas and Anne Ardundel County police deny any intentional policy of racial profiling. However, critics argue that unofficial racial profiling often exists, sometimes on the initiative of the individual police officer. Those so targeted refer to their supposed offense as "driving while black."

Racial disparities are also evident in criminal sentencing, raising suspicion of racial bias in the justice system. For example, U.S. federal drug laws are far harsher for those convicted of dealing crack cocaine than for those who sell powdered cocaine. Possession of more than 500 grams of powdered cocaine carries a minimum sentence of five years' imprisonment; the same minimum sentence applies for possession of just 5 grams of crack. And according to a 2005 study by the U.S. Sentencing Commission, African-American drug offenders were 20 percent more likely to be sentenced to prison than white drug offenders. Blacks were also more likely to receive far longer jail sentences. According to U.S. Justice Department statistics, the average sentence for those convicted of selling 25 grams or less of crack cocaine was 65 months in 2002. Those caught selling a similar amount of powdered cocaine, on the other hand, received just 14 months on average.

Racial disparities are also evident in criminal sentencing, raising suspicion of racial bias in the justice system. For example, U.S. federal drug laws are far harsher for those convicted of dealing crack cocaine than for those who sell powdered cocaine. Possession of more than 500 grams of powdered cocaine carries a minimum sentence of five years' imprisonment; the same minimum sentence applies for possession of just 5 grams of crack. And according to a 2005 study by the U.S. Sentencing Commission, African-American drug offenders were 20 percent more likely to be sentenced to prison than white drug offenders. Blacks were also more likely to receive far longer jail sentences. According to U.S. Justice Department statistics, the average sentence for those convicted of selling 25 grams or less of crack cocaine was 65 months in 2002. Those caught selling a similar amount of powdered cocaine, on the other hand, received just 14 months on average.

In 2002, 10.4 percent of black males between the ages of 25 and 29 were in prison, and more than one in every four black men (28.5 percent) could expect to serve time in a state or federal prison at some point in his life. Mandatory

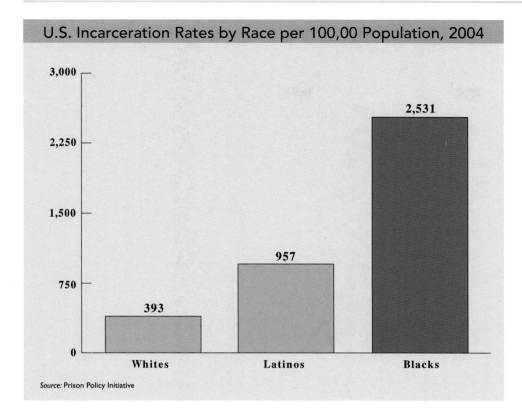

U.S. Incarceration Rates by Race per 100,00 Population, 2004

Source: Prison Policy Initiative

sentencing laws and "three strikes" regulations, which stipulate long sentences for third offenses, have contributed to huge increases in percentage of black males serving time. In many instances, these disparities in jail times are due to politically popular, though controversial mandatory sentences for crack that do not apply to powdered cocaine.

The resulting large prison populations strain local and state government budgets. In 2003, however, the Bush administration cut funding for community policing programs. Critics assert that these cuts are responsible for a renewed growth in crimes rates since that year. Critics also argue that policies that ease the re-entry of convicts into their communities, families, and the job market are critical if these young men are to remain out of jail.

The potential long-term impact of these statistics is dramatic. As of 2004, only 35 percent of black children were growing up in two-parent homes, according to the U.S. Census Bureau. These families must make do without the potential income of an absent, incarcerated father. With limited incomes that sometimes require them to take more than one job, these single mothers often cannot afford health insurance and have little time to attend their children's school func-

tions or to supervise their children after school. Thus, high crime and poverty, paired with poor health and poor employment opportunities, can trap poor African Americans in a vicious cycle.

HEALTH

Little progress has been made toward closing the health gap between blacks and whites. According to the National Center for Health Statistics, the only health indices where blacks outscored whites were suicide and Alzheimer's disease. The disparities are particularly evident for African-American males. For example, a black male child born in the year 2003 is likely to live just 69.2 years, while a white male born in the same year can expect to survive beyond his 75th birthday. This gap of nearly six years was only marginally better than the eight-year gap recorded in 1970. For females, the racial health gap is slightly smaller. Black females born in 2003 can expect to live to be over 76, while white females born the same year are likely to live to be about 80, a gap of just four years. Similarly, black women aged 65 in the year 2000 could expect to live nearly another 18 years, while white women were projected to live another 19.5 years on average, a gap of less than two years.

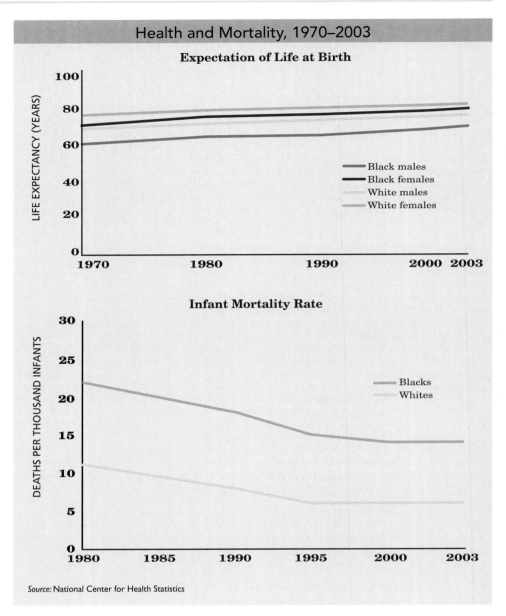

Health and Mortality, 1970–2003

Expectation of Life at Birth

Black males
Black females
White males
White females

Infant Mortality Rate

Blacks
Whites

Source: National Center for Health Statistics

In other health-related areas, the racial gap is wider. For example, infant mortality rates among blacks in 2003 were 13.6 per 100,000 live births versus just 5.7 for whites, or about 140 percent higher. Similarly, African-American teens are twice as likely to deliver low-birth-weight babies and 1.5 times more likely to have premature babies than white teens. In virtually every other category, the picture remains the same. The most glaring discrepancies emerged in the areas of violence and sexually transmitted disease. And with a rate of 93.3 per 100,000, African Americans were more than six times as likely to be suffering from AIDS.

These categories aside, there are a number of factors that help explain why African-American health indices lag so badly behind those of whites. First and perhaps foremost is poverty. While 14.3 percent of white children under the age of 18 lived in poverty, the rate for black youths was 34 percent in 2004. Poverty and lack of steady employment also means less health care coverage. According to the U.S. Census, non-Hispanic white children (7.2 percent) were less likely to be without health insurance than black children (12.5 percent) in 2005. Not surprisingly, this translates into lower physician contact rates. Thus, blacks were less likely to have visited a doctor's office over the course of a year than whites, and more likely to see a doctor in an emergency room. In addition, young black children between the ages of 19 and 25 months lagged behind white children of the same age in receiving vaccinations. This gap leaves millions of children susceptible to preventable diseases like measles, tuberculosis, diphtheria, and hepatitis B, among others.

A 1999 survey of 720 physicians conducted by the National Heart, Lung, and Blood Institute considered the role of doctors' behavior in African-American health. The authors of the study, which was reported in the *New England Journal of Medicine*, recorded doctors' responses to patients complaining of chest pains. They found that doctors were only 60 percent as likely to order cardiac catheterization for black patients as for white patients. Catheterization is considered the best diagnostic procedure for determining heart problems. This finding suggests that prejudice in the health care community contributes to the higher mortality rates of African Americans.

INCOME

As recorded by the U.S. Bureau of the Census, the income gap between blacks and the general population has by no means disappeared, with blacks actually falling further behind since 1980. For example, in 1980, median black household income averaged $24,153 in stable 2005 dollars, well below the median household income of $39,606 for all races. After reaching a high of $30,434 (in 2005 dollars) in 2000, the median black household income fell to $29,026 by 2002 and then to $30,248 in 2005. The median incomes for all households between 2000 and 2005 also fell, though not as far.

Meanwhile, there were far fewer black than white households in the upper income reaches. While more than 18 percent of all white households in the United States had incomes over $100,000 in 2005, less than 1 percent of black households had this much income.

Not surprisingly, lower black income levels are directly related to the kinds of jobs African Americans perform. According to the U.S. Census Bureau, African Americans are less likely than whites to hold managerial or professional jobs, where pay tends to equal or exceed the U.S. median. While fully 34.7 percent of the total population were engaged in managerial or professional work in 2005, only 8.1 percent of blacks worked in this category. At the other end of the job ladder, blacks were nearly a third more likely to be working in the low-paying, low-skill service sector (23.1 percent) than whites (15 percent).

Consequently, a far greater proportion of black families than white lived in poverty, though the situation improved somewhat between 1980 and 2005. In 1980, 31.1 percent of all black families and 10.3 percent of white families lived at or below the poverty level. In 2000, rates fell to a low of 21.4 percent in for black households and 7.8 percent for white, then increased again to 23.8 percent for blacks and 8.6 percent for whites by 2005. At the same time, income levels rose modestly and employment rates climbed significantly for all Americans. Declining from double-digit rates throughout the 1980s and early 1990s, black unemployment fell to 8.4 percent in December 2006, when the unemployment rate for Americans as a whole was 4.5 percent.

THE NEW BLACK PROFESSIONAL

The average income gap between blacks and whites has not diminished since the 1960s. That, however, is not to say that African Americans have made no significant economic strides. Although households earning less than $25,000 still make up the largest single income bracket of African Americans, the number of these households dropped markedly between 1994 and 2005. At the same time, the number of black households in middle- and upper-income brackets increased.

The growth of a vibrant black middle class has been called one of the greatest legacies of the civil rights years. Prior to the 1960s, employment options even for the most highly educated African Americans were limited to fields that served the black community, such as small businesspeople, ministers, teachers, and undertakers, as well as a handful of doctors, lawyers, and pharmacists. African Americans working outside of the black community were relegated to unskilled labor or service jobs. Black women were employed almost exclusively as domestic servants.

In the 1960s, economic growth, the civil rights movement, and governmental action combined to spur the growth of the African-American middle class. By the end of the 20th century, African

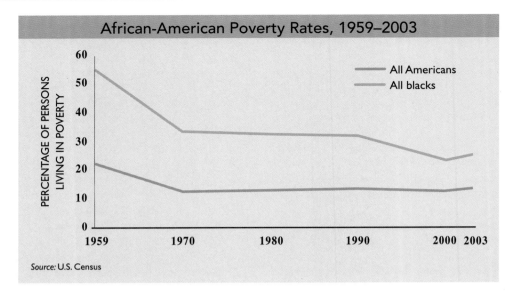

Americans held an expanded range of jobs. Blacks now manage department stores that they once were not allowed to shop in and serve as mayors in towns and cities where they once were denied the vote. Thanks in large part to governmental affirmative action policies, African Americans have been particularly successful in finding middle-income employment in the public sector. In 2003, blacks were twice as likely as whites to work for the city, state, or federal government.

Some analysts worry, however, that the middle-class blacks face a number of economic social hurdles that middle-class whites do not. While their numbers have grown rapidly since the 1980s, middle-class black households tend to be more heavily dependant than white households on income from women. Although many families, regardless of race, depend on two incomes, black wives are more than twice as likely to work full-time than their white counterparts. Because the income gap between white and black women is much smaller than that between white and black men, it is all the more important for black women to work in order to lift their households to middle-class status.

Analysts point to another economic concern in surveying the black middle class—a shortage of assets. As Hugh Price, former president of the National Urban League, put it, "Many of us have been laboring under the false comfort that the expansion of the black middle class and the creation of individual black millionaires has moved African Americans closer to economic parity. The reality is, no matter how great incomes become for individual blacks, our wealth is not sustained because we have very few assets that can be passed on."

In other words, those blacks who are the first in their families to reach the middle class are there based on their incomes

BLACK HOUSEHOLD INCOME, 1994 VERSUS 2005

Income	Number of African-American Households	
	1994	2005
less than $25,000	6.4 million	5.8 million
$25,000 to $50,000	3.0 million	3.5 million
$50,000 to $75,000	1.3 million	1.7 million
$75,000 to $100,000	4.3 million	8.0 million
more than $100,000	3.0 million	10.9 million

Source: U.S. Census Bureau

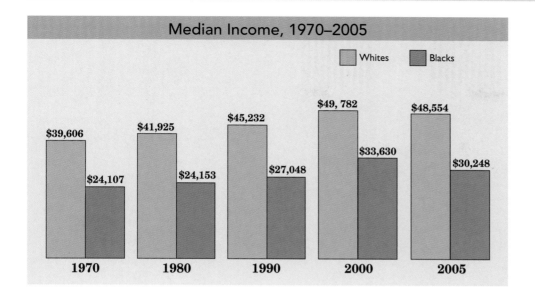

Median Income, 1970–2005

rather than assets like real estate, investments, or inheritance. A study by Robert
L. Harris Jr. of the Africana Studies and
Research Center at Cornell University
estimates that black married couples have
about 80 percent of the assets of white
couples but only 25 percent of their total
net worth. Harris also argues that elderly
whites are more likely to receive Social
Security and pension checks than elderly
blacks. This means that adult black children are more likely to have the financial
responsibility of caring for their parents
instead of receiving an inheritance from
them. All of this leaves many middle-class
black couples one lost paycheck away
from becoming poor.

Beyond their paychecks, most assets
in the typical middle-class black family are
tied up in their homes and automobiles.
Whites, on the other hand, more frequently also have stocks, bonds, mutual
funds, and retirement savings to fall back
on. Statistics from the Cornell study illustrate this point. Although about 74 per-

cent of whites and 62 percent of blacks
own their own homes, a typical black
household has 63 percent of its assets in
home equity. Meanwhile, because of other
investments, whites average about 43 percent of their assets in home equity.
Furthermore, black-owned homes are
often appraised for an average of $14,000
less than a white-owned homes, even
when they are the same size, design, and
appearance as white-owned homes. The
reason is that black property tends to be in
integrated urban and immediate suburban
areas outside of a city, while white property tends to be in the mostly white outer
suburbs.

Despite laws against the practice, discrimination continues in the banking and
real estate industries, making it harder for
black families to buy homes. According to
the Federal Reserve Bank, African-
American and Hispanic applicants were
denied loans two to three times more
often than whites between 1993 and 1998.
Even African Americans with equal credit

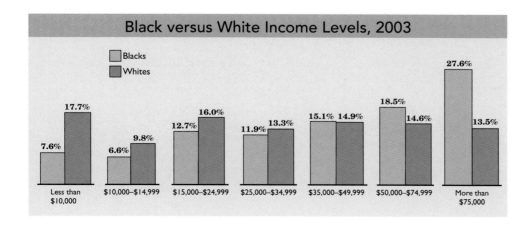

Black versus White Income Levels, 2003

ratings as whites were more frequently denied home loans.

Beyond the economic challenges, many blacks also face daily social hurdles on the job. Some successful African Americans have described a sense of living between two worlds, one in which they succeed through their own merits and another in which their race is a constant factor in how they are treated. One TV executive recalled for *Time* magazine how cab after empty cab sped by him in New York until he had his white secretary flag one down for him. "It's pretty hard to feel like you're mainstream when you're wearing $2,000 worth of clothes and you can't catch a cab at night."

While the problems of the urban black poor may seem more pressing to white observers, middle- and upper-class blacks face unique challenges. Having a steady job is one thing; worrying about whether your race will affect your promotion is another. Affirmative action has fostered workplace integration, but it has also given black workers a certain wariness that whites assume they were hired based on race rather than qualifications. Although blatant racism may have lessened, subtler forms continue. African-American workers may find themselves isolated and outnumbered in the workplace, with after-hours interra-

cial socializing very limited. Some African Americans sense that they need to be twice as good at their jobs as white workers in order to keep up.

Still, a growing number of African Americans have succeeded within the structures of the white corporate world. Kenneth Chenault, for example, received his law degree from Harvard University in 1976 and practiced law for a few years before switching to business. In 1981, Chenault was hired by American Express, and he quickly rose through the corporation, becoming president and chief operating officer (COO). In 2001, Chenault became CEO, the company's top executive. In the entertainment industry, Richard D. Parsons is CEO (since 2002) and chairman (since 2003) of Time Warner Inc., whose businesses include film entertainment, interactive services, television networks, cable systems, and publishing.

Among leaders in the financial services industry are E. Stanley O'Neal, who became executive vice president and cohead of Merrill Lynch's corporate and institutional client group in 1998, and Franklin D. Raines, who became the first African American to head a major Fortune 500 corporation when he was named chairman and CEO of Fannie Mae in 1999. One of the biggest players

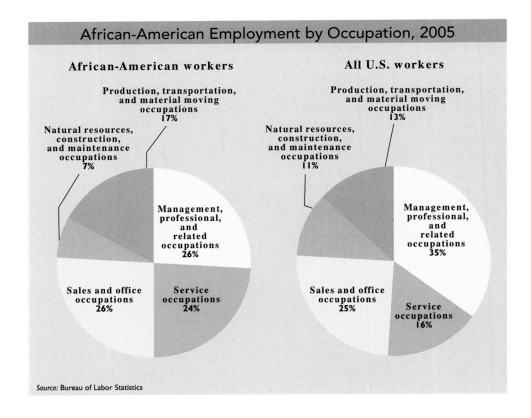

African-American Employment by Occupation, 2005

African-American workers

Production, transportation, and material moving occupations
17%

Natural resources, construction, and maintenance occupations
7%

Management, professional, and related occupations
26%

Sales and office occupations
26%

Service occupations
24%

All U.S. workers

Production, transportation, and material moving occupations
13%

Natural resources, construction, and maintenance occupations
11%

Management, professional, and related occupations
35%

Sales and office occupations
25%

Service occupations
16%

Source: Bureau of Labor Statistics

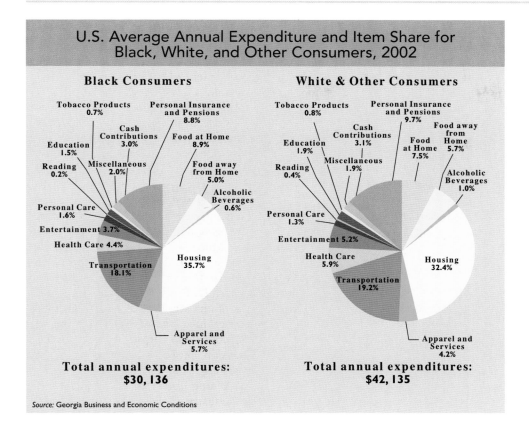

U.S. Average Annual Expenditure and Item Share for Black, White, and Other Consumers, 2002

Black Consumers

Tobacco Products 0.7%
Personal Insurance and Pensions 8.8%
Cash Contributions 3.0%
Food at Home 8.9%
Education 1.5%
Reading 0.2%
Miscellaneous 2.0%
Food away from Home 5.0%
Personal Care 1.6%
Alcoholic Beverages 0.6%
Entertainment 3.7%
Health Care 4.4%
Housing 35.7%
Transportation 18.1%
Apparel and Services 5.7%

Total annual expenditures: $30,136

White & Other Consumers

Tobacco Products 0.8%
Personal Insurance and Pensions 9.7%
Cash Contributions 3.1%
Food away from Home 5.7%
Education 1.9%
Food at Home 7.5%
Reading 0.4%
Miscellaneous 1.9%
Personal Care 1.3%
Alcoholic Beverages 1.0%
Entertainment 5.2%
Health Care 5.9%
Housing 32.4%
Transportation 19.2%
Apparel and Services 4.2%

Total annual expenditures: $42,135

Source: Georgia Business and Economic Conditions

in finance, however, was the late Reginald Lewis. In 1984 he set up the TLC Group as a vehicle to buy and sell companies. That same year TLC bought McCall Pattern Co. for $25 million and after three years restored it to such financial success that it sold for $63 million. In 1987 Lewis pulled off one of the largest leveraged buyouts of an international company when TLC bought Beatrice, a French food company, for $985 million.

Historically, however, one way that African Americans frustrated with the lack of opportunity in the white world have found success is by catering to the black community on a large scale. One of the pioneering examples of African-American business success is John H. Johnson. In 1942, Johnson founded the Johnson Publishing Company, Inc., using a $500 loan from his mother. Today, it is the home to *Ebony* and *Jet* magazines and has become the world's largest African American–owned publishing company. Other divisions of JPC include Fashion Fair Cosmetics, Supreme Beauty Products, Ebony Fashion Fair, and JPC Book Division. Johnson was publisher, chairperson, and CEO until his death in 2005. His widow, Eunice W. Johnson, is secretary and treasurer of JPC and producer-director of the Ebony Fashion Fair—one of the world's largest traveling fashion shows.

Another black entrepreneur who found success by tapping the African-American media market is media executive Robert L. Johnson. In 1979, Johnson and his wife Sheila Crump Johnson founded Black Entertainment Television (BET), the nation's first and only black-owned cable network.

For some, an initially black market grew exponentially to include large swathes of nonblack mainstream consumers. This was the case for Berry Gordy (founder of Motown Records), Russell Simmons (cofounder of the hip-hop label Def Jam), and Damon Dash (cofounder of Roc-A-Fella Records), all of whom were worth in excess of $200 million in 2006. The global rise of hip-hop music has likewise made multimillionaires of a number of black performing artists, many of whom have branched out into producing records—as well as movies, clothing, colognes, and various other products. Among them are P. Diddy (worth $346 million), Jay-Z ($340 million), Pharrell ($155 million), Dr. Dre ($150 million), Ice Cube, ($145 million), and 50 Cent ($100 million).

Not all wealthy African-American executives are men, of course. In the

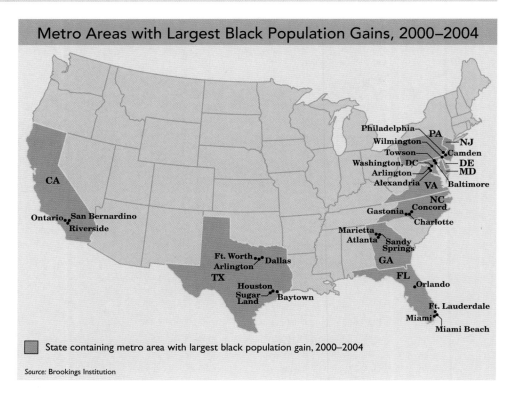

Metro Areas with Largest Black Population Gains, 2000–2004

State containing metro area with largest black population gain, 2000–2004

Source: Brookings Institution

mid-1990s, Sylvia Rhone became chairperson and CEO of Elektra Entertainment Group, a major record label that represents a multiracial roster of musicians. Eileen Norton, whose net worth is estimated at $450 million, cofounded the Norton Utilities software company; and Renetta McCann is head of U.S. and Canadian operations for Starcom MediaVest, a powerful communications agency.

Certainly the wealthiest black businesswoman on Earth is Oprah Winfrey, profiled in chapter 7. Since founding her magazine *O* in 2000 (which in 2002 *Fortune* called the industry's most successful start-up ever), Winfrey has continued to branch out into other forms of media. In 2006, for example, she signed a $55 million, three-year contract with XM Satellite Radio to establish a new radio channel. As of 2006, Winfrey was worth an estimated $1.4 billion.

In addition to her entrepreneurial success, Winfrey is well-known for philanthropy. In 1998, she launched Oprah's Angel Network, which has since raised more than $51 million for charitable organizations and projects worldwide. Because Winfrey personally pays for all of the Network's overhead costs, all funds raised go directly to charity. In 2005, she made a $10 million donation to Hurricane Katrina relief, and by 2004 she

had provided $7 million in scholarship money to put 250 black men through college. Most recently, Winfrey invested $40 million to found a school in South Africa called the Oprah Winfrey Leadership Academy for Girls, which opened in January 2007.

While Winfrey has more resources available for charitable giving than most people, many successful African Americans have also given back to support the black community. In 1989, for example, Bill Cosby donated $20 million to Spelman College, the renowned historically black college in Atlanta from which his daughter graduated. But some critics contend that wealthy African Americans have not done enough to help the black underclass. University of Chicago sociologist William Julius Wilson has argued that the seemingly intractable problem of black poverty is tied to the flight of successful blacks from the inner cities. By leaving black urban neighborhoods, Wilson suggests, middle- and upper-class blacks deprive those neighborhoods of both models of success and financial support for the social pillars of the community, such as churches, schools, and other local institutions.

This assessment is not universally accepted, however. Among the successful blacks who reject this notion is Richard Parsons, chairman of Time Warner.

"Why should I live in Harlem?" he has asked. "If given a choice between unsafe streets and poor schools on the one hand and peace and quiet and quality schools on the other, who wouldn't pick the best neighborhoods and best schools? The black underclass is not just our problem. It's all of society's problem."

AFRICAN AMERICANS IN CONTEMPORARY POLITICS

Until the Civil Rights Act of 1964 and Voting Rights Act of 1965 solidified black constitutional rights, governing power remained in the hands of white politicians, whether in small southern hamlets or large northern cities. As discussed in the previous chapter, these laws had immediate impact. African-American voter registration rates and voting rates increased rapidly. In 1966, Edward Brooke (R-Mass.) became the first black elected to the Senate since Reconstruction, and the next year, the Democratic candidate Richard Hatcher became the first black mayor of a major city, Gary, Indiana. By the early 1970s, other large cities like Detroit and Los Angeles had also elected blacks.

Besides facilitating registration and voting, one of the key provisions of the Voting Rights Act was redistricting. The act allowed blacks and other minority plaintiffs who could cite racist voting patterns to redraw local city council districts to create "majority minority" districts. A coalition of black Democrats and white Republicans likewise began redrawing congressional district lines beginning in the late 1960s to create majority black congressional districts. In short order, a growing roster of young African Americans forged by their still-fresh experiences in the Civil Rights movement entered the House of Representatives. In 1966, just six black congressmen held office in the House. In 2007, 42 African-American men and women had seats.

Prior to the 1960s, the distinct problems of the black underclass in America were rarely very high on the national political agenda. But this changed during the 1970s and 1980s, when stronger African-American representation in Congress brought greater focus on issues directly related to urban, inner-city constituents. Today, representatives like John Conyers

of Detroit or Charles Rangel of New York are long-standing voices for urban support programs and progressive politics.

The results of redistricting in the 1970s and 1980s were essentially regional and urban, however. Relatively few African Americans came to office outside of the national's northern and western cities. There were notable exceptions, like Barbara Jordan of Texas, Andrew Young of Georgia, and Harold Ford of Tennessee. But in the South, the only cities that had majority black districts during that era were Houston (represented by Jordan), Atlanta (represented by Young), Memphis (represented by Ford), and New Orleans (which did not elect its first black congressional representative until 1991). As a rule, the generation of African-American congressional representatives, mayors, and other local politicians of the 1970s and 1980s came from the North, the Midwest, and California.

Following the 1990 U.S. census, a new round of redistricting began. Many Democrats viewed redistricting efforts of the 1990s as an opportunity to give southern blacks a long-overdue voice in Washington. This time, white southern Republicans and black southern Democrats worked to cobble together oddly shaped districts that linked far-flung black neighborhoods together. In this way, new majority-black districts were created throughout the South for the first time since Reconstruction. African Americans were soon elected to Congress from urban and rural districts in Alabama, Florida, Georgia, Louisiana, North Carolina, South Carolina, and Virginia.

While redistricting in the late 20th century did increase African-American representation at the national level, the practice of creating majority minority districts has its pitfalls. Critics argue that decades of redistricting have created districts that are so racially based that the officials who represent them are virtually guaranteed re-election. According to a study by historian Stephen Erickson, published by the Cato Institute, safe electoral districts—whether for Congress, a local city council seat, or mayor's office—can lead to calcified, bureaucratic incompetence as well as outright corruption. Coalition building has always been a signature of urban politics, regardless of race, but machine-style politics almost inevitably leads toward political

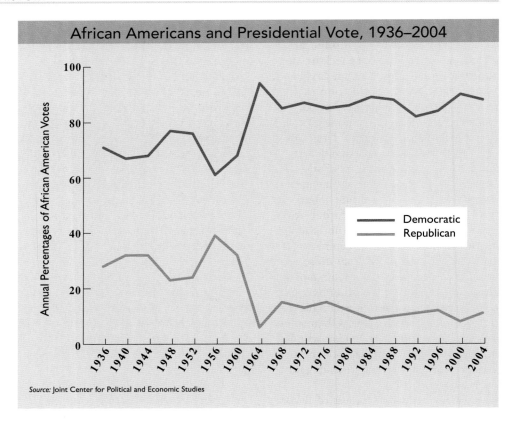

African Americans and Presidential Vote, 1936–2004

Source: Joint Center for Political and Economic Studies

temptation and away from voter oversight and accountability.

One outcome of the 1990s redistricting was the creation of more seats in Congress that black officials were likely to be elected to. Another was the creation of more safe, white majority seats. The political upshot was that an increasingly conservative Republican Party was then able to solidify its hold on Washington. In 1994, the Democratic majority that had held power for most of the post–World War II era was swept from Congress. The Republican Party seized control of the House and Senate, where they held their majority for the next dozen years.

New Democratic Voices

While African-American representation in the House increased sevenfold between 1966 and 2007, voters had far less success electing black candidates to the Senate. As discussed in chapter 7, the only black U.S. Senator elected after Edward Brooke was Democrat Carol Mosely Braun of Illinois, who served a single term in the 1990s. In 2004, however, Illinois voters again elected an African American to the Senate. When he entered the Senate the following January, Barack Obama became the fifth black U.S. Senator and only the third since Reconstruction.

Born in Hawaii in 1961, Obama served in the Illinois State Senate from 1996 to 2004 and ran for a House seat in 2000 but was defeated (by former Black Panther Bobby Rush). As a state senator, Obama was little known outside of Illinois until July 2004, when he gave the keynote address at the Democratic National Convention. In his address, he commented on the deep divisions that characterize U.S. politics in the 21st century:

The pundits like to slice and dice our country into red states and blue states, red states for Republicans, blue states for Democrats. But I've got news for them too. We worship an awesome God in the blue states, and we don't like federal agents poking around in our libraries in the red states. We coach Little League in the blue states and yes, we got some gay friends in the red states. There are patriots who opposed the war in Iraq and patriots who supported the war in Iraq. We are one people, all of us pledging allegiance to the stars and stripes, all of us defending the United States of America.

Elected to the U.S. Senate the following November, Obama immediately became one of the most listened-to voices of the Democratic Party. In January 2007, he announced his candidacy for president in the 2008 race. Public opinion polls at the time showed him trailing only Senator Hillary Rodham Clinton of New York, who also announced her candidacy that month. Obama's personal charisma has taken him to great prominence, but another strength is his cross-cultural appeal.

The child of a black father from Kenya and white mother from Kansas, Obama represents a new generation of black political leaders. Unlike those who came before him, he is not a veteran of the civil rights movement, and thus his appeal to his constituents is not based on his role in "the struggle." Rather, Obama has proven to be a careful politician who has avoided controversy, while speaking to a broader array of issues than black politicians of the past.

In many ways, the success of Barack Obama is an outgrowth of the success of the black middle class. He had what he has called a "color-blind" childhood in Hawaii, the nation's most racially diverse state, and later attended Columbia University and Harvard University, two of the country's most prestigious colleges. Although he is racially mixed, Obama is himself a product of the middle class. As a result, he has been able to articulate middle-class values that appeal to a broader cross section of voters. He has worked to implement his goals with both fellow Democrats and Republicans. For instance, in 2007, he joined with Senators Richard Lugar (R-Ind.) and Tom Harkin (D-Iowa) to promote an increase the production of ethanol, a corn-based renewable fuel that is important to farm-state voters in Illinois, Iowa, and Indiana. Likewise, he has worked extensively on immigration reform issues with Republican senator John McCain of Arizona.

While Obama is the one of most prominent of the new generation of African-American politicians, he not alone. In 2006, former Representative Harold Ford Jr., son of the longtime Memphis representative of the same

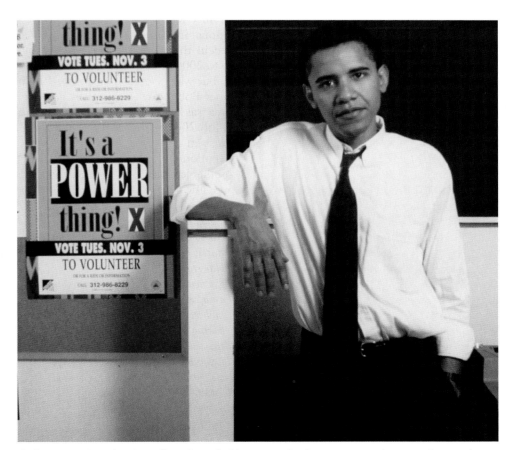

Before entering elective office, Barack Obama worked as a community organizer and as a college professor. He is seen here managing a voter registration drive in Chicago, Illinois. (courtesy of Barackobama.com)

name, narrowly missed becoming the first black senator from a southern state since 1870. Jesse L. Jackson Jr., the son of the civil rights leader Jesse Jackson, won election to the U.S. House in 2002 despite the actions of Robert Shaw, commissioner of the Cook County Board of Review. In what was widely regarded as an effort to confuse voters, Shaw had found a retired truck driver also named Jesse L. Jackson to run against Jackson. The effort failed when the trucker dropped from the race.

Another of the new breed of black politicians is Corey Booker, elected mayor of Newark, New Jersey, in 2006. Booker is also the son of civil rights activists. His parents, Cary and Carolyn Booker, were pioneers in the business world and served as two of the first black executives at IBM. Raised in a predominantly white northern New Jersey community, Booker first joined the corruption-riddled Newark City Council in 1998. Although he was often outvoted by a margin of eight to one as a councilman, his calls to promote law and order and reform City Hall won him many admirers. So too did his unorthodox actions, which included a 10-day hunger strike, a stint living in a tent in front of one of Newark's most dangerous housing projects, and another living out of a motor home for five months, which he parked on street corners known for their high levels of drug trafficking. Booker was unsuccessful when he took on Newark's longtime, controversial mayor Sharpe James in 2002. Four years later, when James decided not to seek re-election, Booker soundly defeated James's handpicked successor Ronald Rice.

The politicians discussed here represent a diversity of constituencies, from single urban districts to entire cities and states. Yet, as post–civil rights era leaders, they share a common difference from previous generations of black leaders. As evident in the careers of Obama and Ford, the politics of black identity and struggle have been less important in their respective roads to power and the importance of middle-class voters—both black and white—has grown. And, as writer Chris Thompson pointed out in a 2005 article for *Salon* magazine, middle-class voters share middle-class concerns that go beyond race: intolerance of corruption and insistence on accountability for their elected officials. These trends are likely to influence the careers of African Americans seeking elective office in the decades to come.

BLACK CONSERVATIVES

This focus on personal accountability is central to the philosophy of black conservatives as well. While the great majority of African-American politicians are members of the Democratic Party, that is not to say that all black Democrats are all of one mind politically. For example, Harold Ford Jr. ran as an anti-abortion conservative Democrat during his 2006 Senate campaign. Like Barack Obama, Ford first rose to national prominence as keynote speaker at a Democratic National Convention, in 2000. As a congressman, Ford supported a number of other favorite social conservative issues, including a ban on benefits for same-sex couples and a Federal Marriage Amendment to the U.S. Constitution, which would ban same-sex marriage throughout the United States. In addition, Ford chastised fellow Democrats for not being more supportive of the Iraq War and for attempting to filibuster the nomination of the conservative Supreme Court Justice Samuel Alito.

Not all black conservatives are Republicans, but most are. The most prominent among them is Secretary of State Condoleezza Rice, who grew up in Birmingham, Alabama, during the height of the civil rights years. "Those terrible events burned into my consciousness," she has said. "I missed many days at my segregated school because of the frequent bomb threats." In fact, one of the four young girls killed in the 1963 bombing of the Sixteenth Street Baptist Church was a playmate of Rice's:

> *I remember the bombing of that Sunday School at Sixteenth Street Baptist Church in Birmingham in 1963. I did not see it happen, but I heard it happen, and I felt it happen, just a few blocks away at my father's church. It is a sound that I will never forget, that will forever reverberate in my ears. That bomb took the lives of four young girls, including my friend and playmate Denise McNair. The crime was calculated to suck the*

*hope out of young lives, bury
their aspirations. But those fears
were not propelled forward; those
terrorists failed.*

Rather than leading her toward more
liberal politics, like so many of her contemporaries, growing up in a segregated
world inspired Rice to embrace more
conservative values. For example, she has
argued that her family would have been
put at even greater risk if gun-control
laws had required her father to register
his weapons.

For Rice, the path to equality lay
not in legislation, but individual initiative. Like many middle-class African
Americans, Rice felt compelled to
outshine both whites and blacks. As a
youth she learned French and classical
piano. After graduating Phi Beta Kappa
from the University of Denver, she pro-
ceeded to earn a master's degree from
Notre Dame and a Ph.D. from the
University of Denver, both in political
science. Her first government experience was as an intern at the State
Department in the Carter administration, but by 1982, Rice had abandoned
the Democratic Party in dissatisfaction
with President Carter's foreign policy.

After serving as a professor and sen-
ior administrator at Stanford during
most of the 1980s, Rice joined President
George H. W. Bush's administration as
Senior Director of Soviet and East
European Affairs in the National
Security Council. When his son George
W. Bush became president in 2001, he
appointed Rice National Security
Director. In 2005, following the resigna-
tion of Colin Powell, Rice succeeded
Powell as Secretary of State.

A key player in the Bush administra-
tion's foreign policy team, Rice has been
closely involved in executing the Iraq
War and the broader the U.S. War on
Terror. By the fall of 2006, U.S. policy in
Iraq faced widespread public disap-
proval. As 2007 opened, Rice found her-
self on the defensive in front of the
Senate's new Democratic-controlled
House Foreign Relations Committee.

While Rice is the highest-profile
black conservative political figure in the
early 21st century, she has important
peers. These include U.S. Supreme
Court Justice Clarence Thomas (discussed in chapter 7); Michael Steele,

Condoleezza Rice (U.S. Department of State)

former lieutenant governor of Maryland;
and Kenneth Blackwell, former secretary
of state of Ohio. What unites many
black conservatives is their emphasis on
individual personal responsibility and
achievement over government legislation in overcoming racist barriers.
Affirmative action programs, calls for
government reparations, and apologies
for the slavery of the past are anathema
to this philosophy. Conservatives are
less likely than other African Americans
to consider the ongoing impact of historical, institutional racism.

The growth of the black middle class
has spurred the rise of black conservatism,
in which mainstream "white suburban"
concerns like safe neighborhoods and
good schools take priority. Some conservative blacks, like Ward Connerly, prefer
to see themselves as part of a color-blind
society in which individual achievement,
rather than race, is what matters.

Other black conservatives do
emphasize the importance of black identity in that they condemn what they

regard as negative representations of black culture. In particular, entertainment forms such as hip-hop and rap have come under criticism as immoral and destructive in their glorification of sex, drugs, violence, and materialism. The question of how to define African-American identity was one of the key cultural debates in America at the start of the 21st century.

CONTEMPORARY CULTURE

Conservative black politicians, among others, emphasize that there is more to African-American culture than hip-hop. This is certainly true. At the same time, hip-hop has exerted a strong influence on contemporary American culture well beyond music and well beyond black listeners.

As discussed in chapter 7, hip-hop and rap music grew from a local style in the black ghettoes of the Bronx, New York, in the 1970s into one of the dominant genres in American popular music by the early 1990s. As it developed, hip-hop proved to be more than just an innovative musical form. In its broadest sense, it is an urban cultural style of artwork, dance, fashion, language, and more. And as hip-hop culture spread across genres (and across races) during the 1990s, it spawned what can only be described as a hip-hop industry.

Hip-Hop Becomes an Industry

As early hip-hop artists like DJ Kool Herc, the Sugar Hill Gang, and Grandmaster Flash helped create the sound, an acrobatic new form of dance developed alongside the music, known as break dancing or b-boying. By the early 1980s, city parks, playgrounds, and basketball courts were often jumping with breakdancers spinning on their backs, walking on their hands, and performing assorted other energetic moves for multiracial crowds of appreciative spectators.

Other aspects of early hip-hop culture met with less widespread favor. Particularly in New York and Philadelphia, graffiti became an underground art form as young people used felt markers and spray paint to write their signatures or "tags," first on the subway trains, and then on city walls. On some trains, all available space on both inside and outside of the train was covered in graffiti. Graffiti soon moved from simple tags, often representing an individual's gang or "crew," to mural-size, full-color calligraphy and illustration of great complexity.

To many observers, and certainly to local officials, the explosion of graffiti during the 1980s was nothing but an illegal eyesore. These observers identified graffiti artists with urban crime. Of course, painting graffiti on public property or the property of another person is illegal. But graffiti was also an indigenous and rebellious art form capable of respect and admiration. Recognizing this, Henry Holt & Co. published *Subway Art*, a book devoted to urban graffiti, in 1984.

In addition to graffiti, the broader hip-hop culture also embraced "street" fashion. Clothing worn by favorite hip-hop artists soon became must-have items in the inner city and—as hip-hop extended its reach—in the suburbs as well. In the early 1980s, items like oversized earrings on women and thick gold necklaces on men, Kangol brand hats, and Adidas brand sneakers with oversized shoelaces exemplified the style. As more politicized artists like Public Enemy and KRS-One emerged in the late 1980s, symbols of black pride gained a new following. More African Americans began to wear African chains and clothing in the traditional colors of Africa—red, black, and green.

During the early 1990s, the "gangsta rap" of West Coast artists like N.W.A. found a national audience. This confrontational music brought with it a certain street thug style that remains one of the most common hip-hop fashion looks even today. Baseball caps and bandanas adorned male heads. Blue jeans or other pants were baggy in the extreme, worn low on the waist (or lower), often with no belt. Some have suggested this style takes its cue from the prisons, where belts are routinely among the first items confiscated.

Later in the 1990s, clothing inspired by the mob—specifically *Scarface*, the 1983 Al Pacino film about a cocaine kingpin—came to the fore in hip-hop fashion, with the oversized New York rapper Notorious B.I.G. (also known as Biggie Smalls) personifying this style. Meanwhile, his close friend Sean "P. Diddy"

Kanye West and Jay-Z (Corbis)

Combs began popularizing his own fashion style, centered around shiny, bright-colored suits. Combs, a rapper and producer, became the first hip-hop artist to create his own clothing line, known as Sean John. By the late 1990s, other hip-hop clothing companies, such as FUBU and Baby Phat, had joined Sean John to make hip-hop fashion a multimillion-dollar segment of the clothing industry.

By the late 1990s and early 2000s, platinum and silver jewelry had replaced gold as the precious metals of choice for rap artists and fans. In 1999, the rapper Lil Wayne coined the term "bling-bling" (or simply "bling") to refer to expensive jewelry and the ostentatious lifestyle that accompanies it. In a show of such ostentation, many rappers began wearing custom-made "grills," or cosmetic metal coverings over their teeth, often made of silver, platinum, or gold inlaid with diamonds.

Hip-hop's love affair with bling is one feature that has opened the music and the broader cultural style to criticism. Critics, some black and some not, have charged that the music's focus on the luxury life plays to racist stereotypes—stereotypes suggesting that young blacks are only interested in material gain rather than moral uplift. Some of the strongest critics come from within the hip-hop community itself.

For example, rapper Missy Elliott has argued that the focus on bling encourages young black people to be irresponsible with their money. Rather than boast about their flashy jewels, she says, hip-hop artists have a responsibility as role models to teach by example.

Other hip-hop artists have chosen to highlight some of the specific consequences of the diamond trade. In 2006, rapper Kanye West was recording a song called "Diamonds" when he learned that the diamond trade in the West African nation of Sierra Leone has helped to fuel civil war, poverty, and bloodshed in that country. As a result, West remixed the song to include lyrics about the problem. That fall, former Public Enemy leader Chuck D. narrated a short film called *Bling: Consequences and Repercussions*, which also highlights the these concerns.

The argument that rap music is overly focused on materialism is just one of the criticisms leveled against it. Its purported glamorization of criminal behavior, misogynistic depictions of women, and often homophobic lyrics have all been condemned. Historically, much the same has been said about rock and roll, and like rock and roll, hip-hop has nonetheless had a profound impact on American culture.

In early 2006, the Smithsonian Institution in Washington, D.C., recognized the influence of hip-hop music and

SELECTED CONTEMPORARY LEADERS IN SCIENCE AND DISCOVERY

Name	Born	Scientific Profession	Career Highlights
Dale Emeagwali	1954	Biologist	Discoverer of an enzyme called kynurenine formamidase, Emeagwali received the National Technical Association's 1996 Scientist of the Year Award in recognition for her work in the field of cancer research.
Sylvester James Gates	1950	Physicist	Gates's research is in the mathematical laws that govern hypothetical forms of energy and matter and covers such topics as quarks, leptons, gravity, and unified field theories.
Roscoe C. Giles	1949	Computer Scientist	Named one of the "50 Most Important Blacks in Research Science" by *Science Spectrum* magazine (2004), Giles currently focuses on applications of parallel supercomputers to physics and materials problems.
Mary Styles Harris	1949	Geneticist	Once honored at the White House as one of *Glamour* magazine's Outstanding Young Women, Harris has dedicated her career to providing health care education to the minority population through her many professional roles: researcher, graduate and medical school professor, and television and radio program producer and host.
Mae Jemison	1956	Astronaut, Physician	The first black woman in space, Jemison served on the crew of the space shuttle *Endeavor* in 1992. Her scientific studies during the mission focused on the effect of weightlessness on human bones and growth tissues.
Dorothy McClendon	1924	Microbiologist	McClendon coordinates microbial research for the U.S. Army Tank Automotive Command (TACOM) in Warren, Michigan.
Isaiah M. Warner	1946	Chemist	In 1997 Warner won the Presidential Award for Excellence in Science, Mathematics, and Engineering Mentoring, awarded by the President of the United States through the National Science Foundation.
Warren M. Washington	1936	Meteorologist	Washington is senior scientist at the National Center for Atmospheric Research. In 1995, President Clinton appointed him to the National Science Board, which helps oversee the National Science Foundation and advises the Executive Branch and Congress on science-related matters.

its cultural trappings by hosting a major multi-year exhibit called "Hip-Hop Won't Stop: The Beat, the Rhymes, the Life." Pioneers like Grandmaster Flash and DJ Kool Herc were invited to the opening ceremony. As part of the initiative (which is partly funded by Russell Simmons, cofounder of the hip-hop label Def Jam), the Smithsonian is gathering objects from all aspects of hip-hop—music, graffiti, fashion, break-dancing, and language—for its permanent collection. Exhibit items to be collected include vinyl records, handwritten lyrics, boom boxes, clothing and costumes, DJ equipment, and videos and interviews.

CONTEMPORARY MUSIC

The impact of hip-hop on American popular music has been so pervasive that it has become more difficult to establish clear lines between hip-hop and other forms of contemporary African-American popular music. In the late 1980s and early 1990s, for example, a number of young hip-hop artists fused hip-hop beats to jazz rhythms to create a new fusion known as jazz rap. The group Gang Starr pioneered the combination, using sampled recordings of saxophone legend Charlie Parker. Groups like Stetsasonic, De La Soul, the Jungle Brothers, and A Tribe Called Quest extended the trend.

Contemporary rhythm and blues, or R&B, has likewise blurred the lines between its own traditions and hip-hop. While the term R&B once was originally used as a synonym for jump blues, today it is more of a catch-all term to describe modern soul and funk music. But many of today's top R&B stars, such as Beyoncé Knowles, Mary J. Blige, and Mariah Carey, are also collaborating with hip-hop artists.

During the 1990s, the R&B charts included popular singer-songwriters such as R. Kelly, Montell Jordan, and D'Angelo. D'Angelo spearheaded a 1970s soul–inspired sound, known as neo-soul, and in the late 1990s and early 2000s shared the charts with female neo-soul artists like Lauryn Hill, Erykah Badu, and India.Arie. In recent years, singers like Usher and Alicia Keys have dominated the top of the charts. They too have included hip-hop elements into their work. For instance, Usher's debut album, released in 1994, was produced by P. Diddy. Since that time, Usher has frequently interspersed raps by guest artists such as Jay-Z and Kanye West into his records. Likewise, though she is not a rapper herself, Keys has included hip-hop rhythms into some of her recordings and has worked with hip-hop producer Timbaland.

Today, the close association between contemporary R&B and hip-hop is such that the record industry publication *Billboard* combines them into one category, tracking records on a "Hot R&B/Hip-Hop Songs" chart. If anything, the overlap of genres is expanding further in the 21st century. For instance, a new generation of R&B artists, such as Erykah Badu and Jill Scott, have also infused their style with elements of jazz along with hip-hop. The influence of hip-hop is remarkably broad.

VISUAL ARTS

Artists draw inspiration from their own experience and the world around them. Consequently, the works of African-American artists often (though not exclusively) treat themes from the black experience. Among the best-known visual artists of the 20th century to do so was the legendary photographer Gordon Parks.

Parks began his career in the 1940s, shooting images for the Farm Security Administration. He later became well known for his photo essays in *Life* magazine, many of which exposed the terrible poverty, racism, and segregation that African Americans faced. He also broke new professional and artistic ground as a filmmaker in the late 1960s early 1970s.

James Hinton, an award-winning documentary filmmaker, was also noted for his photographic work. Working as an independent photojournalist in the 1960s, Hinton took thousands of photographs of the civil rights era and its major figures, including Dr. Martin Luther King Jr., Malcolm X, and Muhammad Ali.

In more recent years, the photographer Carl Robert Pope Jr. has recorded how prosperity has continued to elude some blacks. A series of his photographs in the permanent collection of the Minneapolis Museum of Art documents the black community in Carbondale, Illinois, beginning in 1982. Although the clothes people wear, their hairstyles, and their surroundings normally identify them with a specific time and place, Pope recalls a sense of a "time warp" in photographing Carbondale's ghetto, because the community was in ruins. "To me, the mark of how well a particular black community is doing is how much of that community is in present time. I ask myself when I am in some weird town and I am going into a black community, do I feel like I'm in the present moment, or do I feel like it's 1970 or 1950?"

Other black artists have used paint rather than film as the medium to express their artistic visions. As described earlier, graffiti was a prevalent and often unwelcome art form that hit the streets in the 1970s. During the 1980s, graffiti art made the move from street corners and subway trains to the walls of art galleries. Perhaps the artist who typified this trend was Jean-Michel Basquiat.

A New York City native, Basquiat first gained fame as a graffiti artist in the late 1970s. He went on to become one of the most successful neoexpressionist painters of the era. Starting in 1981, his work was championed by the major art figure Andy Warhol, and the two collaborated thereafter. Basquiat's early abstract works often included death images, including faces resembling traditional African masks. But they also incorporated icons of urban life, such as police, children's sidewalk games, and graffiti. Later works focused on his black and Haitian identity and his interest in historical African-American events and persons.

More recent African-American artists have used popular culture as source material for their work. For example, the work of painter Michael Ray Charles often examines racial stereotypes. One series of works juxtaposes advertising icons such as Aunt Jemima, late 19th- and early 20th-century images of black minstrels, and contemporary depictions of black youths, celebrities, and athletes. Profiled on the public television series *Art:21* in 2001, Charles explained, "Stereotypes have evolved. I'm trying to deal with present and past stereotypes in the context of today's society."

MULTICULTURAL AMERICA

On December 15, 2006, a 14-year-old African-American girl named Cheryl Green was on her front porch in Los Angeles, talking to friends, when a group of young Latinos unleashed a hail of gunfire, killing Green and wounding several others. The motive behind the killing was racial. The gang members were looking for a black person—any black person—to kill, and Green and her friends were the first they found. Los Angeles police believe that the gang members who killed Green were acting out of revenge for the murder of a Latino man named Arturo Mercado by blacks in the same neighborhood a week earlier.

Gang violence and interracial tension have long troubled inner-city Los Angeles. During the 1992 Los Angeles Riots, for instance, angry African Americans specifically targeted shops owned by Korean Americans, few of whom lived in black neighborhoods. By contrast, much of the current tension between blacks and Latinos in Los Angeles exists because Mexican and other Latin American immigrants have been moving into Compton, South Central, and other once solidly black neighborhoods. According to Eric Perrodin,

mayor of Compton, his city is now 60 percent Latino and 40 percent African American.

Although the deaths of Mercado and Green represent the worst-case consequences of L.A.'s interracial tensions, the hostility is evident to law-abiding citizens and violent criminals alike. Callers to black radio talk shows in Los Angeles frequently complain that Latinos are "stealing" jobs from the black community. Meanwhile some Latino shopkeepers have refused to serve black customers, arguing that black youths have targeted their businesses for theft. In 2006, the Latino immigrant community held large rallies nationwide in support of immigration rights. These high-profile demonstrations provoked anger in many U.S.-born American citizens of all races, including residents of Los Angeles, where the immigration rallies were largest.

Black and Latino community leaders in Los Angeles have been working to ease these tensions. It is ironic, observers note, that two ethnic groups that share similar socioeconomic conditions are so distrustful of each other. Rather than fight over limited resources, they suggest, blacks and Latinos would be better served by working together to revive their neighborhoods.

Some have argued that the roots of black-Latino conflict run deeper than the current competition for jobs and housing. Tanya R. Hernandez, professor of law at Rutgers University, has proposed that antiblack racism is an entrenched fact of life in Latin America and the Caribbean, where African slavery was historically more predominant than in North America: As much as 90 percent of all Africans enslaved in the Americas worked in Latin America. One legacy of Latin American slavery, Hernandez says, is the longstanding emphasis on skin color variation as a sign of social mobility. Historically, those with purely Spanish backgrounds (criollos) formed the elites in Hispanic cultures, while racially mixed mestizos (Spanish-Indian) and zambos (Spanish-African) were assigned lower social standing.

Whatever its source, the baggage of racism has carried over to the present day, in some cases to immigrant communities in the United States. In 2002, a University of Houston survey of Hispanics and blacks in that city found that the black respondents had a far more positive views of Latinos than Latinos had of African Americans. In fact, a majority of foreign-born Latinos held unfavorable views of African Americans. "I just don't trust them," said one respondent. "The men, especially, all use drugs, and they all carry guns." On a more positive note, a majority of U.S.-born Latinos had a favorable view of African Americans, suggesting that cultural and language barriers are more responsible for distrust more than race itself.

Racism is a menace anywhere, but it is a particular obstacle in the United States, where people of numerous races and cultural backgrounds come together. Interacting with people who are different from oneself is a quintessentially American experience. Moreover, America's multicultural character is only increasing as immigration, interracial marriage, and transracial adoption continue in the 21st century.

IMMIGRATION FROM AFRICA AND THE CARIBBEAN

Immigration has made black America more multicultural than ever before, with thousands of new immigrants of African

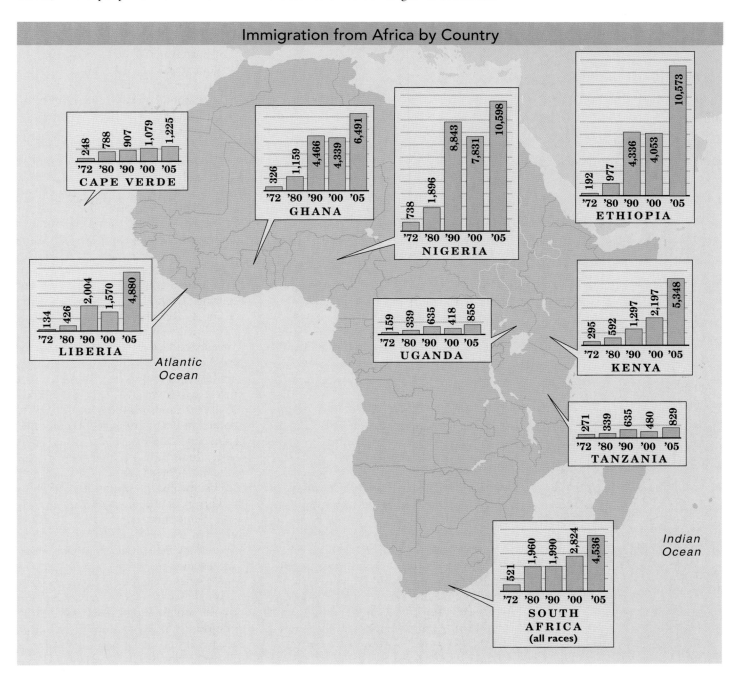

Immigration from Africa by Country

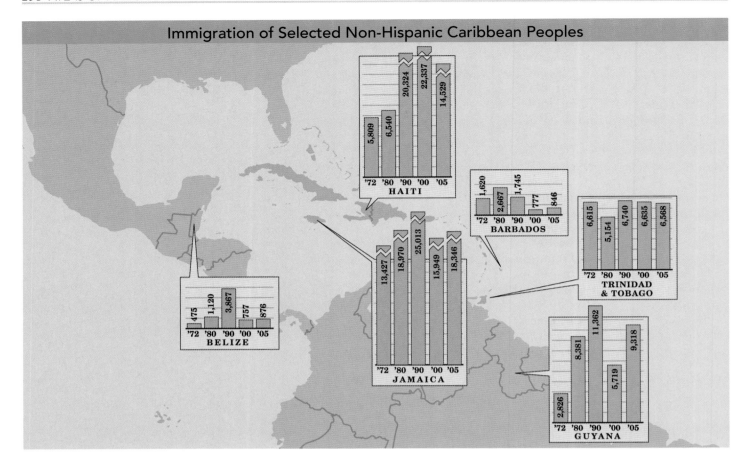

Immigration of Selected Non-Hispanic Caribbean Peoples

descent arriving each year from the Caribbean and Africa itself. A number of factors account for why so many people of African descent are moving to America. One "pull factor" is rising educational levels around the Caribbean, which have created a culture of rising expectations, a trend that the prevalence of U.S. culture in the region contributes to. In places like Jamaica, this has produced something of a brain drain, as professionals seek out better-paying positions in the United States.

But jobs are only part of the picture. Increasingly, many young people from the Caribbean—and particularly from the English-speaking islands—are flocking to U.S. institutions of higher learning. Other factors promoting immigration from the Caribbean and Africa include more convenient and faster transportation than in the past, lower ticket prices, and the communications revolution. E-mail and falling long-distance phone rates make it easier and cheaper for people to keep in touch with families and friends back home.

There are also "push factors" behind the rising tide of immigration from the Caribbean and Africa. For example, war and civil unrest have prompted thou-

sands of Haitians to take their chances of making it to the United States in unseaworthy craft. Although probably fewer than 85,000 people immigrated to the United States from Haiti during the 1960s and 1970s—a time of relative stability in that impoverished land—roughly double that number came between 1981 and 1997, a period of civil war, death-squad killings, and a U.S. military intervention. Still, poverty and a lack of job opportunities continue to be the main causes of African and Caribbean immigration to the United States. Africa, in particular, has suffered from economic stagnation since the late 1970s, when immigration from that continent began to increase.

For their part, Caribbean and African immigrants have made their mark on U.S. culture. Immigrants of African descent have added yet another piece to the ethno-cultural mosaic of many U.S. cities. The annual West Indian Day parade in Brooklyn, for instance, routinely draws more than half a million participants and viewers, and the various musical styles of immigrants' home regions have influenced popular music throughout the United States. Immigrants from the

Caribbean and Africa have made their impact felt economically, too. Like other newcomers, they have brought with them an ambition to succeed, a willingness to take financial risks, a commitment to hard work, and an entrepreneurial drive that has helped revive many urban neighborhoods.

Of course, the arrival of so many newcomers of African descent has not been without its problems. African and Caribbean immigrants often face the same racism that African Americans have experienced for centuries. Two well-publicized police killings in New York in 1999 and 2000—of West African immigrant Amadou Diallo and Haitian-American Patrick Dorismond respectively—highlight the difficulties they face.

The influx has also created tensions with the black American community. Like native-born American whites confronted with new arrivals from Eastern and Southern Europe a century ago, native-born blacks today often feel that immigrants of African descent are willing to work harder and for less, driving down wages and taking jobs. Many new arrivals feel unwelcome, sensing that black Americans look down on them as ignorant and uncultured. Cultural differences and, to a certain extent, language differences have sometimes led to misunderstandings. In fact, African Americans are feeling the impact of the new immigration more directly than whites. Concentrated in the same large metropolitan areas that attract the majority of immigrants, African Americans find themselves interacting with a diversity of new peoples.

The arrival of immigrants of African descent—along with their more numerous Hispanic and Asian counterparts—is profoundly changing the nature of race relations in the United States. As the new categories listed in recent censuses indicate, the United States can no longer look at itself as a country neatly divided between white and black. The current immigration is also shaping the culture of America's future, as immigrants—and particularly their more Americanized offspring—are being influenced by urban black culture. Whatever this cross-fertilization of world and African-American people produces, it will shape all of American culture—and through America's media empire, world culture—for much of the 21st century.

INTERRACIAL MARRIAGE AND ADOPTION

Apart from immigration, black America is becoming more multicultural in another sense as well: the growing number of multiracial marriages and interracial adoptions.

Interracial marriage remained illegal in many U.S. states until 1967, when the Supreme Court ruling in *Loving v. Virginia* struck down the last of the antimiscegenation laws. Since then, the number of interracial marriages in the United States has dramatically grown, from 321,000 in 1970 to 2.7 million in 2000. By 2000, one out of every six marriages involving an African American was a mixed-race marriage. Statistics also show that an African-American man is two and a half times more likely to marry a white woman than a black woman is to marry a white man. The 2000 census recorded 239,477 marriages between African-American males and white females, and 95,831 marriages between white males and African-American females.

Some African Americans regard these statistics as cause for concern. As more black men marry nonblacks, they say, fewer desirable black men are available for black women to marry, creating a "marriage squeeze" for African-American women. Other observers say that factors besides interracial marriage are more to blame for a shortage of marriage-age black men. Among these are higher rates of incarceration and higher death rates for black males, due to crime-related violence.

Whether or not a "marriage squeeze" truly exists, the rise in interracial marriage prior to the 2000 census was significant enough to convince the U.S. Census Bureau to introduce mixed-race categories for the first time. Today, people can identify themselves as belonging to as many as five official racial categories, and as of the 2000 census, nearly 5 percent of the American public identified themselves as multiracial.

The 2000 census was also the first to measure the percentage of all adoptions in which children were adopted by parents of a different race, known as transracial adoptions. It found that 17 percent of all adoptions are transracial. Of those, 13 percent were international adoptions.

The relevance of adoptive parents' race to the success of parenting is an emotionally laden issue. In 1972, National Association of Black Social Workers (NABSW) condemned the practice, declaring it a form of "cultural genocide." Yet advocates of transracial adoption, such as the National Council for Adoption, have long argued that because black children usually wait longer than do white children to be adopted, permanent placement should take precedence over matching adoptees with families of the same race.

Since the passage of the Multiethnic Placement Act of 1994 (MEPA) and the Interethnic Placement Act of 1996 (IEPA), federal law has banned outright consideration of race, ethnicity, or national origin in placement decisions. But the laws also emphasize, somewhat in contradiction, that states should make concerted efforts to recruit potential adoptive families from within the same cultural, racial, or national background as the child being adopted. NABSW has called for the repeal of both MEPA and IEPA. According to NABSW's official position, these laws fail to "take into consideration the cultural differences of people of African ancestry and the experiences that they daily face due to the racial divide in America." As a result, the organization says, adopted African-American children are "far too often cut off from their culture of origin."

Supporters of transracial adoption challenge the idea that children with parents of another race are less well-adjusted than other adopted children. The first academic study to address this issue was conducted by sociologist Rita Simon from 1971 to 1991. Simon's 20-year study of 300 children adopted by parents of a different race found that all of the adoptions worked well. Two thirds of them involved black or mixed black-white children.

These trends have led many Americans to ask what racial identification means. As the number of mixed-race marriages increases and more Americans identify themselves as multiracial, what does that mean for the concept of race? Likewise, if the color of a child's parents is no longer relevant, does it mean that race no longer matters?

A recurrent theme in African-American history has been the struggle for full, equal access to the opportunities of American life. In the 1950s, that meant equal access to a seat on the city bus; in the 2000s, to a seat in the corporate boardroom. As Dr. Martin Luther King put it, all Americans should be judged by the content of their character and not the color of their skin.

If the struggle for African-American equality ends with a color-blind society, does that signal the disappearance of African-American identity? Certainly not. Differences in race, culture, and heritage simply do exist. But how do we as a society maintain our pride in racial identity, regardless of race, without slipping into the mire of racist politics? Rather than ignore the differences among Americans, the challenge will be to embrace them and, in the process, continue to remove the institutionalized barriers and individual biases that block the path to opportunity for all.

Susan Martini puts her adopted daughter Erika, three, to bed for the evening. (Corbis)

SELECTED BIBLIOGRAPHY

Ahrens, Gale, ed. *Lucy Parsons: Freedom, Equality, and Solidarity—Writings and Speeches, 1878–1937.* Chicago: Charles H. Kerr, 2003.

Andrews, William L., and Henry Lewis Gates Jr. *Slave Narratives.* New York: Library of America, 2000.

Appiah, Kwame Anthony, and Henry Lewis Gates Jr. *Africana: The Encyclopedia of the African and African American Experience.* New York: Basic Civitas Books, 1999.

Asante, Molefi K., and Mark T. Mattson. *Historical and Cultural Atlas of African Americans.* New York: Macmillan, 1991.

Baulch, Vivian M., and Patricia Zacharias. "The 1943 Race Riots." *Detroit News.* Available online. URL: http://info.detnews.com/history/story/index.cfm?id=185&category=events. Updated December 19, 2002.

Bancroft, Frederic. *Slave-Trading in the Old South.* 2nd ed. Columbia: University of South Carolina Press, 1996.

Barbeau, Arthur, and Florette Henri. *The Unknown Soldiers: African American Troops in World War I.* New York: Da Capo, 1996.

Barraclough, Geoffrey, ed. *The Times Atlas of World History.* 4th ed. Maplewood, NJ: Hammond, 1993.

Beckles, Hilary, and Verene Shepherd, eds. *Caribbean Slave Society and Economy: A Student Reader.* New York: New Press, 1991.

Bennett, Lerone Jr. *Pioneers in Protest.* Chicago: Johnson Publishing, 1968.

Berlin, Ira. *Many Thousands Gone: The First Two Centuries of Slavery in North America.* Cambridge, MA: Harvard University Press, 2000.

Bernstein, Iver. *The New York City Draft Riots.* Oxford: Oxford University Press, 1990.

Black Church Burning Update. "List of Burned Black Churches." Stepshow.com. Available online. URL: http://stepshow.com/churches/list.html. Updated on June 26, 1996.

Blanchard, Peter. *Slavery and Abolition in Early Republican Peru.* Wilmington, DE: Scholarly Press, Inc., 1992.

Boley, George. *Liberia: The Rise and Fall of the First Republic.* New York: St. Martin's Press, 1983.

Bolster, Jeffrey W. *Black Jacks.* Cambridge, MA: Harvard University Press, 1997.

Bositis, David A. "The Black Vote in 2004." Joint Center for Political and Economic Studies. Available online. URL: http://www.jointcenter.org/publications1/publication-PDFs/BlackVote.pdf. Downloaded September 29, 2006.

Boyd, Herb, and Lance Tooks. *Black Panthers for Beginners.* New York: Writers and Readings Publishing, 1995.

Branch, Taylor. *Parting the Waters.* New York: Simon & Schuster, 1989.

———. *Pillar of Fire.* New York: Simon & Schuster, 1998.

Braxton, Greg, and Jim Newton. "Looting and Fires Ravage L.A." *Los Angeles Times.* Available online. URL: http://www.latimes.com/HOME/REPORTS/RIOTS/0501lede.htm. Posted on May 1, 1992.

Buhle, Paul, and Nicole Schulman, eds. *Wobblies! A Graphic History of the Industrial Workers of the World.* New York: Verso, 2005.

Bundles, A'Lelia. *On Her Own Ground: The Life and Times of Madam C. J. Walker.* New York: Scribner, 2002.

Bureau of Justice Statistics. "Jail incarceration rates by race and ethnicity, 1990–2005." U.S. Department of Justice. Available online. URL: http://www.ojp.usdoj.gov/bjs/glance/jailrair.htm. Accessed September 20, 2006.

Bureau of Labor Statistics. "Employed persons by occupation, race, Hispanic origin, and sex." Bureau of Labor Statistics. Available online. URL: http://www.bls.gov/cps/cpsaat10.pdf. Accessed September 20, 2006.

Charters, Samuel. *The Roots of the Blues: An African Search.* New York: Da Capo, 1991.

Chase, Judith Wragg. *Afro-American Art & Craft.* New York: Van Nostrand Reinhold, 1971.

Clark, Dick, and Larry Lester. *The Negro Leagues Book.* Cooperstown, NY: Society for American Baseball Research, 1994.

Conrad, Earl. *Harriet Tubman.* Washington, DC: Associated Publishers, Inc., 1990.

Conrad, Robert Edgar. *World of Sorrow: The African Slave Trade to Brazil.* Baton Rouge: Louisiana State University Press, 1986.

Courlander, Harold. *A Treasury of Afro-American Folklore.* 2nd ed. New York: Marlowe & Company, 1996.

Covington, James. *The Seminoles of Florida.* Gainesville: University Press of Florida, 1993.

Cowan, Tom, and Jack Maguire. *Timelines of African-American History: Five Hundred Years of Black Achievement.* New York: Berkley Publishing Group, 1994.

Dance, Daryl Cumber. *Shuckin' and Jivin'.* Bloomington: Indiana University Press, 1987.

de Queiros Mattoso, Katia. *To Be a Slave in Brazil*. New Brunswick, NJ: Rutgers University Press, 1987.

Diawara, Manthia. *Black American Cinema*. New York: Routledge, 1993.

DiBacco, Thomas V. *The History of the United States*. Boston: Houghton Mifflin, 1991.

Diop, Cheidh Anta. *Civilization or Barbarism: An Authentic Anthropology*. Brooklyn, NY: Lawrence Books, 1991.

DjeDje, Jacqueline Cogdell. *Turn Up the Volume!: A Celebration of African Music*. Berkeley: University of California Press, 1998.

Dodd, Donald. *Historical Statistics of the United States*. Westport, CT: Greenwood Publishing Group, Inc., 1993.

DuBois, W. E. B. *Souls of Black Folk*. New York: NAL/Dutton, 1995.

Duckett, Alfred. *Changing of the Guard: The New Breed of Black Politicians*. New York: Putnam, 1972.

Duncan, Russell. *Entrepreneur for Equality: Governor Rufus Bollack, Commerce and Race in Post–Civil War Georgia*. Athens: University of Georgia Press, 1994.

Ellis, Joseph. *American Sphinx: The Character of Thomas Jefferson*. New York: Vintage Books, 1998.

Etis, David. *Economic Growth and the Ending of the Transatlantic Slave Trade*. Oxford: Oxford University Press, 1989.

Farmer, James. *Lay Bare the Heart*. Fort Worth: Texas Christian University Press, 1998.

Finkelman, Paul. *Slavery in the Courtroom: An Annotated Bibliography of American Cases*. Washington: Lawbook Exchange, 1996.

Fogel, Robert, and Stanley Engerman. *Time on the Cross: The Economics of American Negro Slavery*. New York: W.W. Norton & Co., 1994.

Foner, Eric. *Reconstruction*. New York: HarperCollins, 1989.

Foner, Eric, and John Garraty. *The Reader's Companion to American History*. Boston: Houghton Mifflin, 1991.

Franks, Kenny A. *Stand Watie and the Agony of the Cherokee Nation*. Memphis, TN: Memphis State University Press, 1979.

Freeman-Grenville, G. S. P. *The New Atlas of African History*. New York: Simon & Schuster, 1991.

Gale Research. *The African American Almanac*. 8th ed. Detroit: Gale Research, 1998.

Garrow, David. *Bearing the Cross: Martin Luther King, Jr. and the Southern Christian Leadership Conference, 1955–1968*. New York: William Morrow, 1999.

George, Nelson. *Hip-Hop America*. New York: Penguin, 2005.

Gilje, Paul. *Rioting in America*. Bloomington: Indiana University Press, 1996.

Glatthaar, Joseph. *Forged in Battle*. New York: NAL/Dutton, 1990.

Grofman, Bernard, and Davidson, Chandler, eds. *Controversies in Minority Voting: The Voting Rights Act in Perspective*. Washington, DC: Brookings Institution, 1991.

Hamilton, Kenneth M. *Black Towns and Profit: Promotion and Development in the Trans-Appalachian West, 1877–1915*. Urbana: University of Illinois Press, 1991.

Handy, W. C., ed. *Blues: An Anthology*. New York: Da Capo, 1990.

Harding, Vincent. *We Changed the World: African Americans 1945–1970*. New York: Oxford University Press, 1997.

Harlan, Louis R., ed. *The Booker T. Washington Papers*. Vol. 14. Urbana: University of Illinois Press, 1989.

Harley, Sharon. *The Timetables of African-American History*. New York: Simon & Schuster, 1995.

Henretta, James, et al. *America's History*. New York: Worth Publishers, 1993.

Henson, Matthew. *A Negro Explorer at the North Pole*. New York: Cooper Square Press, 2001

Herold, Erich. *African Art*. London: Hamlyn, 1990.

Hirsch, James. *Riot and Remembrance: The Tulsa Race War*. Boston: Houghton Mifflin, 2003.

Holloway, Joseph, and Winifred Vass. *The African Heritage of American English*. Bloomington: Indiana University Press, 1993.

Hughes, Langston, and Arna Bontemps. *The Book of Negro Folklore*. New York: Dodd, Mead and Company, 1958.

Hughes, Langston, et al. *A Pictorial History of African Americans*. 6th ed. New York: Crown Publishing, 1995.

Humphreys, Jeffrey M. "The multicultural economy 2004: America's minority buying power." *Georgia Business and Economic Conditions* 64, no. 3 (2004): 1–8.

Jackson, Kenneth, ed. *Encyclopedia of the City of New York*. New Haven, CT: Yale University Press, 1995.

Jacobs, Donald K., ed. *Courage and Conscience: Black and White Abolitionists in Boston*. Bloomington: Indiana University Press, 1993.

James, Cyril L. R. *The Black Jacobins*. 2nd ed. New York: Vintage Books, 1989.

Jones, Evan. *American Food: The Gastronomic Story.* New York: Vintage Books, 1981.

Jones, Howard. *Mutiny on the Amistad.* Oxford: Oxford University Press, 1997.

Karasch, Mary. *Slave Life in Rio de Janeiro, 1808–1850.* Princeton, NJ: Princeton University Press, 1987.

Katz, William Loren. *A Documentary and Pictorial History of the African-American Role in the Westward Expansion of United States.* New York: Simon and Schuster, 1996.

Kelley, Robin D. G., and Earl Lewis. *To Make Ourselves Anew: A History of African Americans.* New York: Oxford University Press, 2000.

Kibbe, Jennifer, and David Hauck. *Leaving South Africa.* Washington, DC: South Africa Review Service, 1988.

Kitwana, Bakari. *The Hip Hop Generation: Young Blacks and the Crisis in African American Culture.* New York: Basic Civitas Books, 2003.

Klein, Herbert. *African Slavery in Latin America and the Caribbean.* Oxford: Oxford University Press, 1988.

Kunen, James S. "The End of Integration." *Time,* April 29, 1996. Available online. URL: http://www.time.com/time/magazine/article/0.9171.984466.00.html.

Lane, Roger, and John J. Turner, eds. *Riot, Rout and Tumult: Readings in American Social and Political Violence.* Westport, CT: Greenwood Publishing Group, 1978.

Lewis, David Levering. *W. E. B. DuBois: Biography of a Race, 1868–1919.* New York: Henry Holt and Co., 1994.

———. *W. E. B. DuBois: The Fight for Equality and the American Century, 1863–1919.* New York: Henry Holt and Co., 2000.

Lieberman, Paul, and Dean E. Murphy. "Bush Ordering Troops to L.A." *Los Angeles Times.* Available online. URL: http://www.latimes.com/HOME/REPORTS/ RIOTS/0502lede.htm. Posted on May 2, 1992.

Lindsey, Howard O. *A History of Black America.* Greenwich, CT: Brompton Books, 1994.

Littlefield, Daniel F., Jr. *Africans and Creeks: From the Colonial Period to the Civil War.* Westport, CT: Greenwood Press, 1979.

———. *Africans and Seminoles: From Removal to Emancipation.* Westport, CT: Greenwood Press, 1977.

Lloyd, Christopher. *The Navy and the Slave Trade: The Suppression of the African Slave Trade in the Nineteenth Century.* New York: Longman, 1968.

Lowe, Richard. *Republicans and Reconstruction in Virginia.* Charlottesville: University of Virginia Press, 1991.

Lowery, Charles. *Encyclopedia of African-American Civil Rights from Emancipation to the Present.* New York: Greenwood Press, 1992.

Luker, Ralph. *Historical Dictionary of the Civil Rights Movement.* Lanham, MD: Scarecrow Press, 1996.

Margo, Robert. *Race and Schooling in the South, 1880–1950: An Economic History.* Chicago: University of Chicago Press, 1991.

McKay, John, et al. *A History of World Societies.* 5th ed. Boston: Houghton Mifflin, 1999.

McLester, Cedric. *Kwanzaa: Everything You Always Wanted to Know But Didn't Know Where to Ask.* New York: Gumbs & Thomas, 1994.

McPherson, James. *Ordeal by Fire: The Civil War and Reconstruction.* New York: Knopf, 1992.

MelaNet. "What is Kwanzaa?" MelaNet's Kwanzaa Information Center. Available online. URL: http://www.melanet.com/kwanzaa.whatis.html#TOC. Downloaded October 28, 1998.

Mills, Thornton J., III. "Challenge and Response in the Montgomery Bus Boycott of 1955–1956." *Alabama Review* 33, no. 3 (1980): 153–235.

Moore, Jesse Thomas, Jr. *A Search for Equality: The National Urban League, 1910–1961.* University Park: Pennsylvania State University Press, 1989.

Morgan, Edmund. *American Slavery, American Freedom: The Ordeal of Colonia Virginia.* New York: Norton & Co., 1995.

Morgan, Philip D. *Slave Counterpoint: Black Culture in the Eighteenth Century Chesapeake.* Charlotte: University of North Carolina Press, 1998.

Morris, Robert. *Reading, 'Riting, and Reconstruction: The Education of Freedmen in the South, 1861–1870.* Chicago: University of Chicago Press, 1976.

Mosley, Walter. *Workin' on the Chain Gang: Shaking off the Dead Hand of History.* New York: Ballantine Books, 2000.

Moskos, Charles. "Success Story: Blacks in the Military." *Atlantic Monthly,* May 1986.

Neal, Mark Antho. *What the Music Said: Black Popular Music and Black Public Culture.* New York: Routledge, 1998.

NOLA.com. "Katrina: The Storm We Always Feared." NOLA.com: Everything New Orleans. Available online. URL: http://www.nola.com/katrina/. Accessed November 18, 2006.

Oates, Stephen B. *To Purge This Land with Blood: A Biography of John Brown.* Amherst: University of Massachusetts Press, 1990.

Ogbar, Jeffrey O. G. *Black Power: Radical Politics and African American Identity*. Baltimore, MD: Johns Hopkins University Press, 2004.

Packenham, Thomas. *The Scramble for Africa, 1876–1912*. New York: Random House, 1991.

Painter, Nell. *Exodusters: Black Migration to Kansas after Reconstruction*. New York: W.W. Norton & Co., 1992.

Payne, Charles M. *I've Got the Light of Freedom: The Organizing Tradition and the Mississippi Freedom Struggle*. Berkeley: University of California Press, 1999.

Peirce, Paul Skeels. *The Freedmen's Bureau: A Chapter in the History of Reconstruction*. Irvine, CA: Reprint Services Corporation, 1991.

Perry, Regenia A. *Free Within Ourselves: African-American Artists in the Collection of the National Museum of Art*. Washington, DC; San Francisco, CA: National Museum of American Art in association with Pomegranate Art Books, Inc., 1992.

Pescatello, Ann, ed. *The African in Latin America. New York: Knopf, 1975*.

Peterson, Robert W. *Only the Ball Was White*. Oxford: Oxford University Press, 1992.

Ploski, Harry, and James Williams, eds. *Encyclopedia of African-American History*. New York: Macmillan Library Reference USA, 1996.

Porter, Kenneth. *The Black Seminoles*. Gainesville: University Press of Florida, 1996.

Powledge, Fred. *Free at Last: The Civil Rights Movement and the People Who Made It*. Boston: Little, Brown, 1991.

Price, Richard, ed. *Maroon Societies*. 3rd ed. Baltimore: Johns Hopkins University Press, 1996.

Prison Policy Initiative. "U.S. incarceration rates by race." Prison Policy Initiative. Available online. URL: http://www.prisonpolicy.org/graphs/raceinc.html. Accessed October 12, 2006.

Ransom, Roger, and Richard Sutch. *One Kind of Freedom: The Economic Consequences of Emancipation*. 2nd ed. New York: Cambridge University Press, 2000.

Ripley, C. Peter, ed. *Witness for Freedom*. Chapel Hill: University of North Carolina Press, 1993.

Roberts, Bari-Ellen, and Jack E. White. *Roberts vs. Texaco: A True Story of Race and Corporate America*. New York: Avon Books, 1996.

Roebuck, Julian, and Murty Komander. *Historically Black Colleges and Universities*. Westport, CT: Greenwood Publishing Group, 1993.

Rogosin, Donn. *Invisible Men*. New York: Kodansha America, Inc., 1995.

Rummel, Jack. *Malcom X: Militant Black Leader*. New York: Chelsea House Publishers, 1991.

Salzman, Jack, et al. *Encyclopedia of African-American History*. New York: Macmillan Library Reference USA, 1996.

Saxon, Lyle, et al., eds. *Gumbo Ya-Ya*. Gretna, LA: Pelican Publishing Company, 1988.

Savitt, Todd. *Medicine and Slavery: The Diseases and Health Care of Blacks in Antebellum Virginia*. Urbana: University of Illinois Press, 1978.

Schubert, Frank. *Black Valor: Buffalo Soldiers and the Medal of Honor, 1870–1898*. Wilmington, DE: Scholarly Resources, 1997.

Serrano, Richard A., and Tracy Wilkinson. "All 4 King Beating Acquitted." *Los Angeles Times*. Available online. URL: http://www.latimes.com/HOME/NEWS/REPORTS/RIOTS/0403lede.htm. Posted on April 30, 1992.

Shick, Tom. *Behold the Promised Land: A History of Afro-American Settler Society in Nineteenth Century Liberia*. Baltimore: Johns Hopkins University Press, 1980.

Shine, Ted, and James V. Hatch. *Black Theatre USA: Plays by African Americans*. 2 vols. New York: Free Press, 1996.

Shrader, Charles Reginald, ed. *Reference Guide to United States Military History, 1919–1945*. New York: Facts On File, Inc., 1994.

Slenes, R. *Demography and Economics of Brazilian Slavery, 1850–1888*. Ann Arbor, MI: University Microfilms, 1976.

Smith, Carter, ed. *The Black Experience*. New York: Facts On File, Inc., 1990.

Smith, Jessie Carnie, and Carrell Peterson Horton, eds. *Historical Statistics of Black America*. Detroit: Gale Research, 1995.

Smith-Shomade, Beretta E. *Shaded Lives: African-American Women and Television*. Piscataway, NJ: Rutgers University Press, 2002.

Southern Poverty Law Center. "Active U.S. Hate Groups in 2005." Southern Poverty Law Center. Available online. URL: http://www.splcenter.org/intel/map/hate.jsp. Accessed on January 12, 2007.

Stanley, Jerry Hurry. *Freedom: African Americans in Gold Rush California*. New York: Crown Publishing, 2000.

Stewart, Jeffrey. *1001 Things Everyone Should Know About African American History*. New York: Gramercy Books, 2006.

Swenson, Dan, and Bob Marshall. "Flash Flood: Hurricane Katrina's Inundation of New Orleans, August 29, 2005." *Times-Picayune*, May 14, 2005. Available online. URL: http://www.nola.com/katrina/graphics/credits.swf. Accessed on November 18, 2006.

Tadman, Michael. *Speculators and Slaves: Masters, Traders, and Slaves in the Old South*. Madison: University of Wisconsin Press, 1996.

Thomas, Velma Maia. *Freedom's Children: The Passage from Emancipation to the Great Migration*. New York: Crown Publishing, 2000.

Thompson, Richard. *A History of South Africa*. New Haven, CT: Yale University Press, 1995.

Torres, Sasha. *Black, White, and in Color: Television and Black Civil Rights*. Princeton, NJ: Princeton University Press, 2003.

Trelease, Allen. *White Terror: The Ku Klux Klan Conspiracy and Southern Reconstruction*. Baton Rouge: Louisiana State University Press, 1995.

U.S. Census Bureau. *Annual Yearbook*. Washington, DC: Government Printing Office, 2005.

———. *Historical Statistics of the United States*. Washington, DC: Government Printing Office, 1975.

———. "Homeownership Rates by Race and Ethnicity of Householder." U.S. Census Bureau, Housing and Household Economic Statistics Division. Available online. URL: http:// www.census.gov/ hhes/www/housing/hvs/ annual06/ann06t20.html. Updated February 12, 2007.

———. *Reports*. Washington, DC: Government Printing Office, 1900, 1910, 1920, 1930, 1940, 1950.

———. *Statistical Abstracts*. Washington, DC: Government Printing Office, 1974, 1976.

———. "Voting and Registration in the Election of November 2004." Available online. URL: http://

www.census.gov/population/www/socdemo/voting/ cps2004.html. Accessed September 20, 2006.

U.S. Department of Education. *Historically Black Colleges and Universities*. Washington, DC: Government Printing Office, 1996.

Watts, Jill. *Hattie McDaniel: Black Ambition, White Hollywood*. New York: Amistad, 2007.

Watson, Steven. *The Harlem Renaissance: Hub of African-American Culture, 1920–1930*. New York: Pantheon Books, 1996.

Werner, Craig Hansen. *Change is Gonna Come: Music, Race, and the Soul of America*. New York: Plume, 1999.

West, Cornel, and Henry Lewis Gates Jr. *The African-American Century: How Black Americans Have Shaped Our Country*. New York: Free Press, 2000.

Williams, Juan. *Eyes on the Prize: America's Civil Rights Years, 1954–1965*. New York: Viking Penguin, 1987.

Wilson, Christine. *All Shook Up*. Jackson: Mississippi Department of Archives and History, 1995.

Wise, Stephen R. *Gate of Hell: Campaign for Charleston Harbor 1863*. Columbia: University of South Carolina Press, 1994.

Wolters, Raymond. *Negroes and the Great Depression*. Westport, CT: Greenwood Publishing Group, 1970.

Woodward, C. Vann. *The Strange Career of Jim Crow*. Oxford: Oxford University Press, 1972.

Zips, Werner. *Schwartze Rebellion*. Vienna: Promedia, 1993.

INDEX